THE ENGLISH
AND THE
NORMAN CONQUEST

Any historian, from Thucydides to Lord Macaulay, would testify that all historical narrative must of necessity incorporate a certain degree of interpretation.
Tom Holt, *Lucia in Wartime*

THE ENGLISH
AND THE
NORMAN CONQUEST

Ann Williams

THE BOYDELL PRESS

First published 1995
The Boydell Press, Woodbridge
Reprinted in paperback 2000

Transferred to digital printing

ISBN 978-0-85115-708-5

The Boydell Press is an imprint of Boydell & Brewer Ltd
PO Box 9, Woodbridge, Suffolk IP12 3DF, UK
and of Boydell & Brewer Inc.
668 Mt Hope Avenue, Rochester, NY 14620, USA
website: www.boydellandbrewer.com

A CiP catalogue record for this book is available
from the British Library

This publication is printed on acid-free paper

CONTENTS

TABLES

TO THE MEMORY OF
EVELYN CONSTANCE FAULKNER
AND
TREVOR MATTHEW WILLIAMS,
MY MOTHER AND FATHER

ERRATA

The English and the Norman Conquest

p.11, line 14: Swawold should be Saewold
p.11, line 28: 1017-18 should be 1022-23
p.55, note 44: Manning should be Mannig
p.57, note 50, line 3: note 95 should be note 45
p.99, line 5 (ie line 5 below Table 1): Herefordshire should be Hertfordshire
p.130, in note 16, line 2: Waltham should be Durham
p.218, line 3: Warwickshire should be Worcestershire
p.218, in note 170, line 1: the page numbers 331-3, 339 should be 31-3, 39

ACKNOWLEDGEMENTS

Though all errors, omissions and misconceptions in this work are mine alone, it could not have been completed without the aid of many friends and colleagues. Special thanks are due to Bill Aird, Stephen Church, David Crouch, Paul Dalton, John Gillingham, Clive Harfield, Christopher Harper-Bill, Katharine Keats-Rohan, Chris Lewis, John Moore, David Roffe, Heather Tanner, Hirokazu Tsurushima and Patrick Wormald, who contributed help, encouragement and advice; and to the members of the Wednesday seminar at the Institute of Historical Research (notably Michael Clanchy, Janet Nelson and Susan Reynolds) who listened patiently to an early draft of Chapter II and helped to refine and improve it. It will be evident from a glance at the references how much I have gained from the annual meetings of the Battle Conference on Anglo-Norman Studies, and I should like to thank those members not individually mentioned for their help and good fellowship; most especially Marjorie Chibnall, Director of the Conference from 1989 to 1993. A special acknowledgement is due to Susan Hibbert, who compiled the index, and helped to correct the text.

It is proper for an historian to acknowledge the dead as well as the living. Among the giants on whose shoulders I have perched should be named first those masters whom all of us who work on Old English and Norman history must own: F.W. Maitland, J.H. Round, F.M. Stenton, Dorothy Whitelock, Helen Cam and V.H. Galbraith. I owe a particular debt to E.A. Freeman, the pages of whose *History of the Norman Conquest* provided unfailing aid and counsel. Since I began writing this book, the world of medieval history has become poorer by the death of Cecily Clark, who put at my disposal her unrivalled knowledge of English place- and personal-names. Three of the modern masters who must be specially mentioned are my one-time supervisor R.R. Darlington, who taught me the historian's craft; John Godfrey, a dear friend and colleague, who showed me that there was more to ecclesiastical history than theological wrangling and liturgical minutiae; and above all that best of lords, R. Allen Brown, into whose *comitatus* I was accepted, and who first suggested to me that I should write this book.

Ann Williams, Wanstead, July 13, 1994

ABBREVIATIONS

Am.H.R.	*American Historical Review*
ANS	*Anglo-Norman Studies (Proceedings of the Battle Conference)*
ASE	*Anglo-Saxon England*
AS Chron	*The Anglo-Saxon Chronicle: a revised edition*, ed. Dorothy Whitelock, David C. Douglas and Susie L. Tucker (London, 1961) [cited by year]
BAR	British Archaeological Reports
Carmen	*The Carmen de Hastingi Proelio of Guy, bishop of Amiens*, ed. Catherine Morton and Hope Muntz (Oxford, 1972)
Chron Abingdon	*Chronicon Monasterii de Abingdon*, ed. Joseph Stevenson, 2 vols, Rolls Series (London, 1858)
Chron Evesham	*Chronicon Abbatiae de Evesham*, ed. W. Dunn Macray, Rolls Series (London, 1863)
Chron Ramsey	*Chronicon Abbatiae Rameseiensis*, ed. W. Dunn Macray, Rolls Series (London, 1886)
Councils and Synods	*Councils and Synods, with other documents relating to the English Church, 871–1204*, ed. D. Whitelock, M. Brett and C.N.L. Brooke, 2 vols (Oxford, 1981)
DB (with shire name)	*Domesday Book*, Phillimore (Chichester, 1975–93)
Dialogus	*Dialogus de Scaccario*, ed. Charles Johnson (Oxford, 1983)
Domesday Monachorum	*The Domesday Monachorum of Christ Church, Canterbury*, ed. David C. Douglas (London, 1944)
Douglas, Feudal Documents	D.C. Douglas, *Feudal Documents from the Abbey of Bury St Edmunds* (London, 1932)
EETS	Early English Text Society
EHD i	*English Historical Documents, c.500–1042*, ed. Dorothy Whitelock (London, 1955)
EHD ii	*English Historical Documents, 1042–1189*, ed. D.C. Douglas and George Greenaway (London, 1961)
EHR	*English Historical Review*
EPNS	English Place-Name Society

Exon	*Liber Exoniensis, Domesday Book seu Liber Censualis Willelmi Primi Regis Angliae, Additamenta* (London, 1816)
EYC	*Early Yorkshire Charters*, ed. William Farrer and C.T. Clay, Yorkshire Archaeological Society Record series, extra ser., 12 vols (Edinburgh, 1913–65)
FlW	Florence of Worcester, *Chronicon ex Chronicis*, ed. B. Thorpe, 2 vols, English Historical Society (London, 1848–9) [cited by year]
Freeman	E.A. Freeman, *The history of the Norman Conquest of England*, 6 vols (Oxford, 1870–79)
GDB	*Great Domesday: facsimile*, ed. R.W.H. Erskine, Alecto Historical Editions (London, 1986)
GEC	*Complete Peerage of England, Scotland, Ireland, Great Britain and the United Kingdom*, 13 vols in 14 (London, 1910–1959)
GP	William of Malmesbury, *De gestis pontificum Anglorum*, ed. N.E.S.A. Hamilton, Rolls Series (London, 1870)
GR	William of Malmesbury, *De gestis regum Anglorum*, ed. W. Stubbs, Rolls Series (London, 1887)
Harmer, *Writs*	F.E. Harmer, *Anglo-Saxon Writs* (Manchester, 1952)
HDE	*Historia Dunelmensis ecclesiae*, in *Symeonis . . . Opera* i, pp. 3–69 [cited by chapter]
Hemming's Cartulary	*Hemingi Chartularium Ecclesiae Wigorniensis*, ed. Thomas Hearne, 2 vols (Oxford, 1723)
HH	*Henrici archidiaconi Huntendunensi Anglorum Historia*, ed. Thomas Arnold, Rolls Series (London, 1889)
HMSO	Her Majesty's Stationery Office, London
HN	Eadmer, *Historia Novorum in Anglia*, ed. M. Rule, Rolls Series (London, 1884), translation of Books I–IV in Geoffrey Bosanquet, *Eadmer's History of Recent events in England* (London, 1964)
HR	*Historia Regum*, in *Symeonis . . . Opera* ii, pp. 3–283 [cited by year]
HRH	*The Heads of Religious Houses, England and Wales, 940–1216*, ed. David Knowles, C.N.L. Brooke and Vera C.M. London (Cambridge, 1972)
Hugh Candidus	*The Chronicle of Hugh Candidus, a monk of Peterborough*, ed. W.T. Mellows (Oxford, 1949), translation in *The Peterborough Chronicle of Hugh Candidus*, ed. W.T. Mellows (Peterborough, 1941)
Hugh the Chantor	Hugh the Chantor, *The history of the church of York, 1066–1127*, ed. Charles Johnson (London, 1961)
ICC	*Inquisitatio Comitatus Cantabrigiensis*, ed. N.E.S.A. Hamilton (London, 1876)

IE	*Inquisitio Eliensis* (The Ely Inquest), *Domesday Book seu Liber Censualis Willelmi Primi Regis Angliae, Additamenta* (London, 1816)
Inquisitio	Adolphus Ballard, 'An eleventh-century Inquisition of St Augustine's, Canterbury', *British Academy Records of the social and economic history of England and Wales* iv (1920)
LDB	Little Domesday, *Domesday Book, seu Liber Censualis Willelmi Primi Regis Angliae*, ed. Abraham Farley, vol II (London, 1783)
Lestorie des Engles	*Lestorie des Engles solum la translacion Maistre Geffrei Gaimar*, ed. Thomas Duffus Hardy and Charles Trice Martin, Rolls Series (London, 1888)
Letters of Lanfranc	*The letters of Lanfranc, Archbishop of Canterbury*, ed. Helen Clover and Margaret Gibson (Oxford, 1979)
LHP	*Leges Henrici Primi*, ed. L. J. Downer (Oxford, 1972)
Liber Eliensis	*Liber Eliensis*, ed. E.O. Blake, Camden Society 3rd series 92 (1962)
Liebermann	F. Liebermann, *Die Gesetze der Angelsachsen*, 3 vols (Halle, 1903–16)
Mem. St Dunstan	*Memorials of Saint Dunstan, archbishop of Canterbury*, ed. William Stubbs, Rolls Series (London, 1874)
Mem. St Edmunds	*Memorials of St Edmund's Abbey, Bury*, ed. Thomas Arnold, Rolls Series (London, 1890–96)
Monasticon	William Dugdale, *Monasticon Anglicanum*, ed. J. Caley, H. Ellis and B. Bandinel, 6 vols in 8 (London, 1817–30)
OE	Old English
ON	Old Norse
OV	*The ecclesiastical history of Orderic Vitalis*, ed. Marjorie Chibnall, 6 vols (Oxford, 1969–80)
P&P	*Past and Present*
Pelteret, *Vernacular documents*	David A.E. Pelteret, *Catalogue of English post-Conquest vernacular documents* (Woodbridge, 1990)
Regesta	*Regesta Regum Anglo-Normannorum*, i, ed. H.W.C. Davis, ii, ed. C. Johnson and H.A. Cronne, iii, ed. H.A. Cronne and R.H.C. Davis (Oxford, 1913–1968)
Robertson, Charters	A.J. Robertson, *Anglo-Saxon Charters* (Cambridge, 1956)
S.	P. H. Sawyer, *Anglo-Saxon Charters: an annotated list and bibliography*, Royal Historical Society (London, 1968)
SCH	Studies in Church History

Stenton, ASE	F.M. Stenton, *Anglo-Saxon England*, 3rd edn (Oxford, 1971)
Symeonis . . . Collectanea	*Symeonis Dunelmensis Opera et Collectanea* i, ed. Hodgson Hinde, Surtees Society 51 (1868)
Symeonis . . . Opera	*Symeonis monachi Opera omnia*, ed. Thomas Arnold, 2 vols, Rolls Series (London, 1882–5)
Textus Roffensis	*Textus Roffensis*, ed. P.H. Sawyer, 2 vols, Early English Manuscripts in facsimile 7, 11 (Copenhagen, 1957–62).
TRE	*Tempore Regis Edwardi*
TRHS	*Transactions of the Royal Historical Society*
VA	*The life of St Anselm, archbishop of Canterbury, by Eadmer*, ed. Sir Richard Southern (Oxford, 1962)
Van Caeneghem	R.C. van Caeneghem, *English lawsuits from William I to Richard I*, 2 vols, Selden Society 106–7 (1990–91)
VCH	*Victoria History of the Counties of England*
Vita Edwardi	*The life of King Edward who lies at Westminster*, ed. F. Barlow (London, 1962); 2nd rev. edn (Oxford, 1992)
Vita Wulfstani	*The Vita Wulfstani of William of Malmesbury*, ed. R.R. Darlington, Camden Society 3rd series 40 (1928)
WmJ	William of Jumieges, *Gesta Normannorum Ducum*, ed. J. Marx, Societe de l'histoire de Normandie, 1914 [cited by chapter]
WmP	William of Poitiers, *Gesta Guillielmi*, ed. R. Foreville (Paris, 1952)

GENEALOGICAL TABLE 1a. KINGS OF ENGLAND: THE WEST SAXON LINE

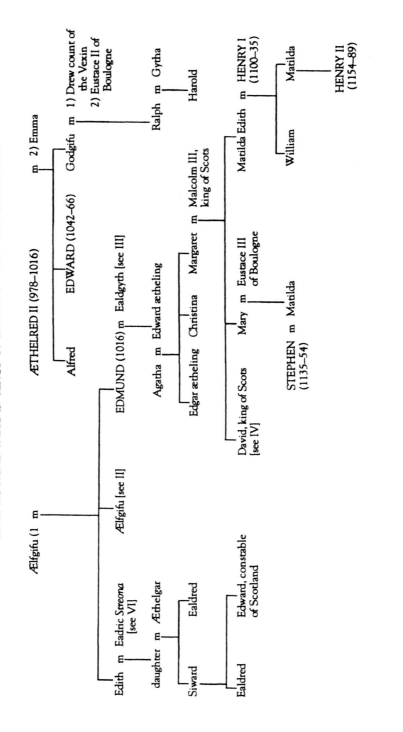

GENEALOGICAL TABLE Ib. KINGS OF ENGLAND: THE DANISH KINGS

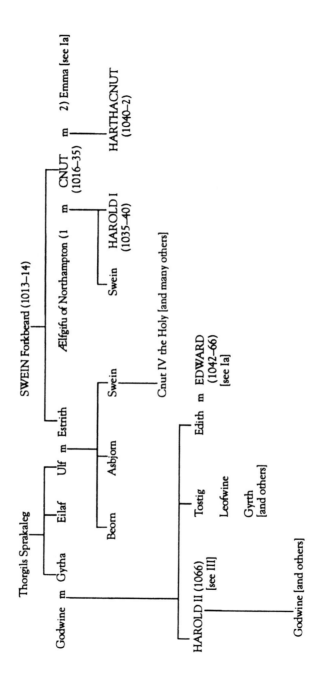

INTRODUCTION

> Then came the Normans with their evil power
> . . . they harmed this nation.
>
> Layamon, *Brut*, lines 3547–48

THE NORMAN CONQUEST was a traumatic event and a vein of bitterness against the conquerors can be discerned throughout the twelfth century in the works of English writers; it is exemplified in the quotation above, written at the turn of the twelfth and thirteenth centuries. This alone may be sufficient justification for yet another book on the topic; but this study differs from many others in being concerned with the conquered rather than the conquerors. The subject may seem perverse, but it touches closely upon the question of English national identity, a matter which is still of some moment. At a time when the submergence of England in Europe is once more a subject for impassioned debate, to 'surmise about the present from the past, the future from the present' may not be entirely irrelevant.[1]

In the final volume of his *History of the Norman Conquest of England*, Edward Augustus Freeman devoted an appendix to an attack on the view then current about the relations between 'Saxons' and 'Normans' in the century and a half after 1066, a view summed up in Sir Walter Scott's *Ivanhoe*. Freeman characterized it as 'the notion that, for many generations, there was a broadly marked line, recognized on both sides, between "Normans" and "Saxons".' Freeman maintained that to describe the English before 1066 as Saxons was in itself misconceived; it was only their enemies, the Scots and the Welsh, who used this term for the people who always called themselves 'English'.[2] Freeman's words have rarely been heeded; nowadays the practice is to call them 'Anglo-Saxons', a term used in contemporary texts only in specific circumstances.[3] The point may seem academic, but names matter; calling the pre-Conquest inhabitants of

---

[1] For the quotation, see the heading to Chapter VII below.

[2] Freeman, v, p. 825; see also ibid., p. 510: 'I have to protest . . . against the unhappy custom of speaking of all Englishmen who lived before the coming of William [the Conqueror] by some other name than that by which Englishmen have ever called themselves'.

[3] Susan Reynolds, 'What do we mean by "Anglo-Saxon" and "Anglo-Saxons"?' *Journal of British Studies* 24 (1985), pp. 395–414 and see note 18 below. Alfred used the royal title *rex Angol Saxonum* and variants in the 880s; 'probably in conjunction with the submission to Alfred in 886 of "all the English people that were not under subjection to the Danes" ' (Simon Keynes and Michael Lapidge, *Alfred the Great*, Penguin Classics (Harmondsworth, 1983), p. 227).

England by a different name from their post-Conquest successors encourages the assumption that 'English' history begins in 1066, an assumption satirized by the immortal Sellars and Yeatman: 'the Norman Conquest was a GOOD THING, as from this time onward England stopped being conquered and was thus able to become top nation'.

This was certainly not the opinion of the twelfth-century historians. They were very conscious that the history of the English nation went back to the settlement of Britain in the fifth and sixth centuries, and that the Norman Conquest was an event in English history.[4] By this time, Freeman maintained, 'the plain facts of the case are that the lowest class would . . . be almost wholly of Old-English descent, that the highest class would be almost wholly of Norman descent, while in the intermediate classes, among the smaller land-owners and the inhabitants of the towns, the two were so mixed together that at last, towards the end of the [twelfth] century, it was . . . impossible to tell one from the other'.[5]

It is this process of intermixture which is the subject of this book. It is not concerned with the events leading up to Duke William's victory on 14 October 1066, but with the response of the conquered to that victory. The first chapters deal with the actions of those English magnates who were not directly involved in the battle of Hastings. History has not dealt kindly with them. Those who co-operated with the invaders have been regarded as quislings and traitors; those who resisted as foolish and incompetent. Thus the 'D' chronicler, writing towards the end of the eleventh century, says of the English magnates' submission to Duke William at Berkhampstead in December, 1066, that 'it was a great piece of folly that they had not done it earlier'.[6] The same criticism appears, implicitly or explicitly, in modern accounts of William's reign. Such judgements are based on that besetting sin of historians, hindsight. The English magnates of the late 1060s could not read Domesday Book and did not know that by the end of William's reign England would have not just a foreign king and a foreign royal kindred, but a foreign aristocracy and a foreign church hierarchy as well; and if we are to understand the true significance of their actions, we must set aside any idea that the situation in 1086 was the inevitable result of William's victory twenty years earlier. It was in part the result of the English resistance to Norman pressure, and for this reason alone, that resistance demands serious study.[7]

The Conquest and the upheavals which followed swept away the great magnates of pre-Conquest England, earls and king's thegns, bishops and abbots. It left *in situ* the lowest groups in society, dependent villagers and smallholders, ploughmen and dairymaids, and all those inhabitants of the towns who were not burgesses, but had to make their living as small craftsmen, or as servants and employees of the urban elite. If I have said little of them, it is not because they were unimportant. A king, said Alfred, 'must have his land fully manned: he

4 See Chapter VII below.
5 Freeman, loc. cit. (note 2 above).
6 *AS Chron*, 'D', 1066.
7 See Chapters I, II and III below.

must have praying men, fighting men and working men'.[8] Ælfric of Cerne, a century later, expanded this theme: '*laboratores* are those who labour to feed us, husbandmen (*yrðlingas*) and bondsmen (*æhtemen*) dedicated to that end alone'.[9] But though the 'praying men' (*oratores*) have left plentiful evidence of their feelings and thoughts, and those of the 'fighting men' (*bellatores*) can be deduced (in some wise) from their recorded deeds, the views of the *laboratores* cannot even be guessed at. They are not invisible in the surviving sources. A Kentish document of the ninth century is attested by the *gemettan* of Canterbury: 'sharers of food' or perhaps 'those who receive meals', like the 2,000 poor men (*pauperes*) to whom bread and cheese (or dripping) and a penny were to be distributed on the anniversary of Archbishop Wulfred (who died in 832).[10] Their rural counterparts, the *geburas*, are listed, sometimes by name, in estate records, like the Kentish *æhtemen* (bondsmen, serfs) who settled at Wouldham in the early eleventh century.[11] Their successors appear in Domesday Book and in the estate surveys of the twelfth century, which reveal much about their services, economic condition, social status and so on; but nothing about their opinions. Normandy and England were in 1066 at the same stage of economic and technical development; the Conquest introduced no new systems of agricultural exploitation or estate management. The new lords may have been harsher landlords than the old, but the evidence on this subject is slight and much depends on its interpretation; and in any case, we have no way of knowing what those on the receiving end thought about the matter.[12]

Previous studies of the Norman settlement have been concerned (and rightly so) with the great lords who shared out the spoils of conquest, but such men (Montgomery, Warenne, Clare, Lacy and their ilk) are only the most visible of the invaders. In their wake came vassals, knights, men-at-arms, sergeants and servants; and non-noble free men, who settled in the countryside as well as the towns. It is with such people and above all with their English counterparts, the tenants and commended men (and women) of the displaced magnates – with Freeman's 'intermediate classes', in fact – that this book is concerned. Only if such people are ignored can the old picture of Norman barons and English peasants be preserved. Many more English families of modest rank survived and even prospered than has previously been thought.[13] Their survival has important consequences. One of the questions to be asked in the post-Conquest period is

---

[8] Keynes and Lapidge, *Alfred the Great*, p. 132; Georges Duby, *The Three Orders: Feudal Society imagined* (London, 1980), pp. 99–109.

[9] Cited and discussed in D.A.E. Pelteret, 'Two Old English lists of serfs', *Medieval Studies* 48 (1986), p. 498.

[10] Nicholas Brooks, *The early history of the Church of Canterbury* (Leicester, 1984), pp. 28–30.

[11] Pelteret, 'Two Old English lists of serfs', pp. 492–504.

[12] See, for example, William E. Kapelle, *The Norman Conquest of the North* (London, 1979), pp. 158–90, for the impact of the Norman settlement on the rural economy of northern England.

[13] See Chapters IV and V below.

when did the Norman settlers begin to think of themselves as 'English'? In one sense, of course, the answer is 'at once'. William the Conqueror was 'king of the English', not of the English and the Normans and certainly not of the Anglo-Normans, an historian's device for which there is even less warrant than for 'Anglo-Saxon'.[14] The fact that those Normans and Frenchmen who settled in England before 1066 were regarded as *anglici* may have a bearing on the attitudes of their peers who arrived after the Conquest.[15] Intermarriage between the less exalted of the incomers and English families of middling rank, whether land-holders, free men or burgesses, was probably much more common than the surviving sources allow us to see, and may well have produced an 'English' identity at this level of society by – at the latest – the second generation.[16]

When the twelfth century writers speak of 'the English', it is not always clear that they mean only the 'Old English' and their lineal descendants. In his description of the siege of Sainte-Suzanne, written in the early 1130s, Orderic Vitalis describes the capture of *multotiens opulenti Normannorum et Anglorum proceres*, who were held to ransom.[17] Who are these 'rich English magnates', if not Normans settled in England, as opposed to Normans of Normandy? They may be the people whom the author of the Chronicle of Hyde, writing in the latter part of Henry I's reign, perhaps in Normandy, calls *Normangli* or *Normanangli*; Normans of England, as opposed to Normans of Normandy. In just such a way were 'Anglo-Saxon' and variants thereof occasionally used on the continent of Europe to distinguish the English (the Saxons of Britain) from their kinsmen the Saxons of Saxony.[18] When in the mid twelfth century the scribe of the *Liber Eliensis* wrote of the Normans who conquered England a century earlier, he felt obliged to define whom he meant by Normans: 'I mean those whose parents are both Norman, and who were reared (*educati sunt*) in Normandy'.[19] Presumably by that time there were other 'Normans', who came of mixed parentage and were reared in England.

There are likely to have been differences of perception between those who retained strong ties with Normandy, and those whose fortunes were more closely bound up with their English possessions. It has recently been argued that when the twelfth-century writers spoke of 'Normans' and 'English', they meant not merely the inhabitants of Normandy as opposed to those of England, but different

[14] The so-called Hyde Chronicle (which has no connection with the abbey of Hyde, Winchester) uses the terms *Normangli* and variants for the inhabitants of late eleventh century England; see David Bates, 'Normandy and England after 1066', EHR 104 (1989), pp. 877–80 and see below.
[15] For the use of *anglici* in this sense, see Chapter 1, pp. 10–11 below.
[16] See Chapter VIII below.
[17] OV iv, 48–9.
[18] Reynolds, 'What do we mean by "Anglo-Saxon"?', pp. 395–8. For the suggestion that the Hyde Chronicle was written in Normandy, see the article of John Gillingham cited in note 20 below.
[19] *Liber Eliensis*, p. 171.

groups – even different court factions – within England itself.[20] In this reading, the 'Normans' are the great nobles, with cross-Channel estates; people like the Beaumont twins, Waleran count of Meulan and Robert earl of Leicester. In his account of the rebellion of 1124, Orderic Vitalis describes how Waleran's supporters mocked at the troops sent against them by the king (whom they call 'the English') as *pagenses et gregarios*, 'rustics and mercenaries'.[21] As with Orderic's account of the events at the siege of Sainte-Suzanne, 'English' may mean those men of lesser rank, with little or no property in Normandy, who had made their homes in England.

Speaking of Count Waleran's father, Robert of Meulan, Eadmer says that 'he had no love for the English and could not bear that any one of them should be preferred to any position of dignity in the Church'.[22] Eadmer complains elsewhere about the preferment of foreigners over Englishmen in appointments to bishoprics and abbeys, but his attitude to Count Robert is shaped by the latter's hostility towards Archbishop Anselm. The 'English' ecclesiastics whom Robert did not wish to see promoted might have included 'men born of Norman parents in England' as well as 'men of pure English descent.'[23] Churchmen had powerful incentives to identify with the traditions of their communities.[24] In the 1070s Archbishop Lanfranc could speak of himself as a *novus Anglicus*, and twenty years later Reginald of Canterbury, a French monk of St Augustine's, wrote of the English as 'our nation' (*gens Anglica nostra*). In Stephen's reign, the court faction opposed to that of the Beaumonts was headed by Roger, bishop of Salisbury and his kinsmen; and though Roger himself was Norman, his nephews, Nigel of Ely and Alexander of Lincoln, may have been of mixed descent.[25]

In a series of recent papers, John Gillingham has argued that the 1130s were the crucial decade in the union of English and Norman. The English identity was defined, at least in part, by a consciousness of difference from the other inhabitants of Britain, the Welsh, Scots and Irish. From the second quarter of the twelfth century, and especially in the works of William of Malmesbury, Gillingham detects 'a new and contemptuous attitude to Celtic peoples'.[26] This attitude he connects with a shift in English perceptions about the ethics of war, brought to England by the Conqueror, 'in which a key element was the attempt to limit the brutality of conflict by treating prisoners, at any rate when they were

[20] John Gillingham, 'Henry of Huntingdon and the twelfth-century revival of the English nation', forthcoming. I am very grateful to Mr Gillingham for allowing me to read this paper in advance of publication.
[21] OV vi, pp. 350–1. In the event it was the 'rustics and mercenaries' who prevailed over Waleran and his friends at the battle of Bourgtheroulde.
[22] HN, p. 205.
[23] Freeman v, pp. 827–9.
[24] See Chapter VI below.
[25] See Chapter VII below.
[26] John Gillingham, 'Conquering the barbarians: war and chivalry in twelfth-century Britain', *Haskins Society Journal* 4 (1992), pp. 67–84; the quotation appears on p. 69.

men of "gentle" birth, in a relatively humane fashion'.[27] The Celts, whether Welsh, Scots or Irish, adhered to older standards rejected by the Normans and, under their influence, the English. It is in the context of the resistance to David I, king of Scots, uncle of the Empress Matilda, that the first references to a united nation of English and Normans appear.[28]

This is not to say that the descendants of the Conqueror's men lost their Norman identity in becoming English. It was perfectly possible for them to feel pride both in their continental origins and in the traditions of their adoptive nation. Thus Ailred of Rievaulx and Henry of Huntingdon, the one certainly, the other probably of English descent, can extol the glories of the Norman *gens*, and call upon its sons to emulate the deeds of their ancestors.[29] By the time they wrote, intermarriage had ensured that most families, save the very greatest and the very least, were both Norman and English.

Freeman disapproved of the misleading picture painted by Sir Walter Scott's *Ivanhoe*. He might have been more kindly disposed to the scenario envisaged by Rudyard Kipling. In *Puck of Pook's Hill*, the young Norman settler, Richard Dalyngridge, married to an Englishwoman, describes his problems with his manorial court: 'I let the Saxons go their stubborn way, but when my own men-at-arms, Normans not six months in England, stood up and told me what was the custom of the country, *then* I was angry'. This imaginative picture may not be so far from the truth.

---

[27] John Gillingham, '1066 and the introduction of chivalry into England', *Law and government in medieval England and Normandy: essays in honour of Sir James Holt*, ed. George Garnett and John Hudson (Cambridge, 1994), pp. 31–55. See also Matthew Strickland, 'Slaughter, slavery and ransom: the impact of the Conquest on conduct in warfare', *England in the eleventh century*, ed. Carola Hicks (Stamford, 1992), pp. 41–59.
[28] Mr Gillingham has argued ('Henry of Huntingdon and the twelfth-century revival of the English nation') that in the 1120s, both William of Malmesbury and Henry of Huntingdon saw 'England's population as divided into two distinct groups: Norman rulers and English subjects', but that in their later works, they came to perceive the English as a united *gens*. See also Chapter VII below.
[29] See below, Chapter VII.

Chapter I

THE NORMAN SETTLEMENT

> Then on Christmas Day, Archbishop Ealdred
> consecrated him king at Westminster. And he
> promised Ealdred on Christ's book, and swore
> moreover (before Ealdred would put the crown
> on his head) that he would rule all this people
> as well as the best of the kings before him, if
> they would be loyal to him.
>
> *Anglo-Saxon Chronicle*, 'D', 1066

AT THE OUTSET OF his reign, William I was faced with a conflict of interests: how to reconcile his coronation oath with the need to reward his Norman and continental followers. Cnut had confronted a similar problem in 1016. William's initial response was milder than that of his Danish predecessor. There were no massacres like that of Christmas 1017, nor were the surviving members of the West Saxon royal house pursued to exile or death.[1] Edgar ætheling was treated as a kinsman and 'endowed with wide lands', which he lost only when he rebelled against the king.[2] To all those Englishmen who 'submitted to him and sought his peace' the king confirmed land and office.[3]

The royal progress which William undertook in the early months of 1067 was intended to reconcile the English nobles to Norman rule. Only one general submission, that at Barking in January 1067, is described in detail. It was attended by the leading thegns of Mercia, who made formal submission, led by their earl,

---

[1] At Christmas 1017 Cnut had Eadric *Streona*, ealdorman of Mercia, and several other high-ranking nobles murdered (*AS Chron*, 1017). The ætheling Eadwig was exiled and perhaps killed (see H.P.R. Finberg, *Tavistock Abbey* (Cambridge, 1951), pp. 3, 226) and the sons of Edmund Ironside were smuggled abroad to escape Cnut's assassins (see Nicholas Hooper, 'Edgar ætheling, Anglo-Saxon prince, rebel and crusader', *ASE* 14 (1985), pp. 197–214; Gabriel Ronay, *The lost king of England* (Woodbridge, 1989). More nobles were exiled in 1020.

[2] By 1086 Edgar held only two manors in Hertfordshire and his pre-Conquest lands in Huntingdonshire (Upton and Coppingford) had passed to Earl Hugh of Chester (C.P. Lewis, 'The formation of the Honour of Chester, 1066–1100', *Journal of the Chester Archaeological Society* 71 (1991), pp. 45, 47). See also below, Chapter V.

[3] *WmP*, pp. 238–9. In 917 Edward the Elder confirmed the lands of the Danes who submitted to him and confiscated the estates of those who did not (*Liber Eliensis*, pp. 98–9).

Edwin, and his brother Morcar, earl of Northumbria. Those specifically named are the Shropshire magnates Siward son of Æthelgar and his brother Ealdred, their cousin Eadric the Wild, and Thorkell of *Limis*, who may be the Warwickshire landholder Thorkell of Arden. Also present was the Yorkshire thegn Copsi, an adherent of Earl Tostig, who had shared his lord's exile.[4] Another such meeting took place at Pevensey in March, when the king was preparing to return to Normandy. No names are mentioned, but those present probably included the Gloucestershire thegn Beorhtric of Leckhampton.[5] Lesser men did their homage via the royal agents rather than to the king himself.

Some obtained written confirmation of their lands and rights. William I's writ for the citizens of London, which confirms the laws of King Edward and safeguards the rights of heirs, probably dates from soon after his coronation.[6] Most surviving writs and charters are in favour of the church but written grants to laymen are mentioned even if they are no longer extant.[7] Azur, King Edward's steward, produced the king's writ, issued at Windsor, in respect of his Berkshire holding.[8] In the same shire, Ælfric of Thatcham testified that he had seen the king's writ granting Hendred to the widow of Godric the sheriff, though he was the only one who had.[9] In Bedfordshire, Augi was confirmed in his land by King William, who also 'commended him through his writ to Ralph Taillebois (the sheriff), so that he should protect him as long as he lived'.[10] In the same shire two burgesses of Bedford had writs for lands once held by their fathers.[11] None of these writs can be precisely dated, but they illustrate the kinds of transactions which were proceeding in 1067.[12]

King William did not, of course, perform these favours for nothing. According

---

4 WmP, pp. 236–7; OV ii, pp. 194–5. The *Anglo-Saxon Chronicle* places the submission of Edwin and Morcar at Berkhampstead, before the king's coronation, but if, as suggested here, the Barking meeting constituted the formal submission of the Mercians, Edwin would have been present on both occasions. John of Worcester denies that Eadric the Wild submitted to the king in 1067 (*FlW*, 1067). For Eadric, Siward and Thorkell of Warwick, see also Chapter V below.
5 OV ii, pp. 196–7; GDB, fol. 170v; Ann Williams, 'An introduction to the Gloucestershire Domesday', *The Gloucestershire Domesday*, ed. Ann Williams and R.W.H. Erskine (London, 1989), p. 34.
6 *Regesta* i, no. 15; David Bates, *William the Conqueror* (London, 1989), p. 73.
7 For the ecclesiastical grants see *Regesta* i, nos. 3, 8, 12, 14, 17 (cf. 16, 18), 19, for the archbishop of York, the abbots of Peterborough, Bury St Edmunds, St Augustine's, Canterbury, Chertsey and Westminster, and the priest (and chancellor) Regenbald.
8 GDB, fol. 62. Azur *dapifer regis* attests charters of King Edward in 1059 and 1062 (S.1038, 1032, Simon Keynes, 'Regenbald the chancellor (*sic*)', ANS 10 (1988), pp. 206–7). He still held the land in 1086, but as the tenant of Robert d'Oilly. See also Frank Barlow, *Edward the Confessor* (London, 1970), p. 164.
9 GDB, fol. 57v.
10 GDB, fol. 211v. When Ralph died, Augi commended himself to William de Warenne.
11 GDB, fol. 218.
12 A writ issued after 1081 confirmed the manor of Tewin, Herts, to Halfdane and his mother, for the soul of Richard the king's son, killed in a hunting-accident in the New Forest (GDB, fol. 41; see below, Chapter IV).

to the *Anglo-Saxon Chronicle* the English 'bought their lands' of the king, and the sums involved could be high.[13] The payments imposed on the greater nobles may be judged by the 40 gold marks (£240) delivered by Abbot Brand of Peterborough to redeem the lands which he and his brothers had given the abbey.[14] Such payments throw light on the sources of the treasure distributed by the king in Normandy in the course of 1067.[15] The amounts paid by lesser thegns for more modest tenements were also substantial. In Suffolk, Baldwin, abbot of Bury St Edmunds, held Stoneham in pledge for a loan of two gold marks (£12) from 'the time when the English redeemed their lands', having presumably lent the money to the pre-Conquest holder, Wulfweard. At the same time, he had also redeemed the land of an unnamed free man at Ixworth Thorpe for 100s (£5).[16] Other undated transactions which may relate to the same process are found in Norfolk, Hampshire and Hertfordshire. In Norfolk, Eadric of Saxlingham had pledged his land to the abbot of St Benet's, Holme, for a gold mark and £7 (£13 in all) 'to redeem himself from arrest by the king's officer, Waleran'.[17] In Hampshire, the monks of the Old Minster had a pledge of £12 on Enham Alamein, 'which a certain man who is now dead demised to them'. The manor was held before 1066 by a woman called Wulfgifu and in 1086 by Alsige the chamberlain, who had also pledged his own manor of Hatch Warren, Hants, to Oda of Winchester, for £10.[18] In Hertfordshire an unnamed sokeman had paid nine ounces of gold (£6.15s) for his tenement in Tiscott, perhaps advanced to him by Wigot of Wallingford, to whom he had commended himself for protection after the Conquest.[19] If these references all relate to the immediate post-Conquest period (which cannot be proven) the redemption affected mainly Wessex and East Anglia, the areas under tightest royal control in 1067. If the loans were not repaid, the lands given in pledge would revert to the lender, and there are signs that this happened on a wide scale. King William's writ to Bury confirmed to Abbot Baldwin all the lands of the abbey, 'whether redeemed from his neighbours with his own money or acquired by their own free and voluntary

---

[13] *AS Chron*, 'E', 1066.
[14] *Regesta* i, no. 8; *AS Chron*, 'E', 1066; Hugh Candidus, p. 77. Peterborough's military quota was extraordinarily high (Edmund King, *Peterborough Abbey, 1086–1310* (Cambridge, 1973), p. 14 and see Chapter III below).
[15] C.R. Dodwell, *Anglo-Saxon Art* (Manchester, 1982), p. 217.
[16] *LDB*, fols 360v, 367v; Douglas, *Feudal documents*, p. xcviii. The transactions took place before the king's barons, William bishop of London, Earl Ralph the staller and Engelric, a royal priest (see below).
[17] *LDB*, fol. 217. Waleran was dead by 1076 and in 1086 Saxlingham was held of St Benet's by his nephew, John; his son, also called John, was also holding land in 1086 (C.R. Hart, *Early charters of Essex*, 2nd edn (Leicester, 1971), p. 37, no. 86). Dr Fleming regards the payment as a ransom paid by Eadric to Waleran (Robin Fleming, *Kings and lords in Conquest England* (Cambridge, 1991), p. 201).
[18] *GDB*, fols 49, 50. For Alsige the chamberlain (*burcniht*) see below, Chapter V.
[19] *GDB*, fol. 137v.

gifts'; and at the other side of the kingdom, Abbot Æthelwig of Evesham acquired 36 estates 'by paying the appropriate price'.[20]

Much land, of course, was not restored, but given to the king's continental followers. Before his departure to Normandy in 1067, William distributed 'rich fiefs' to such of his men as chose to take up land in England, though we are assured that 'to no Frenchman was given anything unjustly taken from an Englishman'.[21] The main source of this largesse was presumably the confiscated estates of the Godwineson family. Queen Edith was confirmed in her lands, and similar provision may have been made for her mother Gytha, but the manors of the dead king, Harold II, and his brothers Gyrth and Leofwine provided an ample reservoir of royal benefactions. Harold's earldom of Wessex was divided between William fitzOsbern, who received the central shires and the Western Provinces, and Odo of Bayeux who got Kent and the south-east. William fitzOsbern also received Harold's earldom of Hereford, and Odo that of Leofwine in the east midlands.[22] The castle at Winchester was entrusted to Hugh de Grandmesnil and in the south-east castleries were established for Humphrey de Tilleul at Hastings, Hugh de Montfort at Dover and William de Warenne at Lewes.[23]

William of Poitiers claimed that Englishmen as well as Frenchmen profited from the king's liberality. When it is remembered that the Normans established in England in Edward the Confessor's day counted as 'English', his assertion may well be true.[24] Humphrey de Tilleul, who held Hastings castle from the moment of its building, might almost be numbered among them, for he had been in King Edward's service, and his son, Robert of Rhuddlan, is said to have 'received the belt of knighthood' from the Confessor's hands.[25] Ralph the staller, who was given the earldom of Gyrth in East Anglia, is a more representative specimen of the pre-Conquest settlers.[26] Robert fitzWymarc, who was part-Breton, and whose castle at Clavering dates from 1052 at the latest, was made sheriff of Essex.[27] In

[20] Regesta i, no. 12; Mem. St Edmunds i, p. 344; Douglas, Feudal documents, p. xcviii; Chron Evesham, pp. 96–7; Hemming's Cartulary i, pp. 269–73.

[21] WmP, pp. 238–9.

[22] C.P. Lewis, 'The early earls of Norman England', ANS 13 (1991), pp. 216–18; David Bates, 'Odo of Bayeux', Speculum 50 (1975), p. 10. For Leofwine's earldom, see Ann Williams, 'The king's nephew: the family, career and connections of Ralph, earl of Hereford', Studies in medieval history presented to R. Allen Brown, ed. Christopher Harper-Bill, Christopher Holdsworth and Janet L. Nelson (Woodbridge, 1989), pp. 338–40.

[23] OV ii, pp. 194–7, 220–1.

[24] WmP, pp. 238–9; George Garnett, ' "Franci et Angli": the legal distinctions between peoples after the Conquest', ANS 8 (1986), p. 118.

[25] OV iv, pp. 138–9.

[26] AS Chron, 1075 and see below, Chapter III.

[27] Judith Green, English sheriffs to 1154 (London, 1990), p. 39. For Clavering, see AS Chron, 1052 (Robert's Castle) and R. Allen Brown, Castles from the Air (Cambridge, 1989), pp. 90–1.

the west Alvred of Marlborough received a number of estates once the property of King Harold to add to his single pre-Conquest manor in Herefordshire.[28]

Native-born Englishmen were retained and, in some cases, advanced. We do not know how William Leofric managed to hold on to at least a portion of his father Asgot's lands in Gloucestershire, Berkshire and Essex, but a speedy submission seems to be the clue; Beorhtric of Leckhampton, who probably did homage to the king at Pevensey in 1067, was almost certainly a kinsman, probably an uncle.[29] Most of the survivors were connected with the royal administration, like Azur, King Edward's steward, whom we have already mentioned. The early writs and charters of the Conqueror supply other names: Eadnoth the staller, a West country magnate; the midland thegns, Bondi the staller and Ulf son of Tope; Thorkell of Arden, who may have been sheriff of Warwickshire in the 1070s; Eadric, sheriff of Wiltshire and Tovi sheriff of Somerset; Swawold, sheriff of Oxfordshire and Northmann of Suffolk; Mærle-Sveinn, sheriff of Lincolnshire and Gamall son of Osbert of Yorkshire.[30] Few of these men lasted long, but their co-operation was essential in the early years of the Conqueror's reign for the effective running of royal government, at least until its intricacies were mastered by the newcomers.

By March 1067 the dual processes of rewarding Frenchmen and conciliating Englishmen had produced sufficient stability for William to undertake a triumphal tour of Normandy. He took many of the leading magnates with him: the ætheling, Edgar; the earls, Edwin of Mercia, Morcar of Northumbria and Waltheof of the north midlands; the Kentish magnate Æthelnoth 'the Kentishman' of Canterbury; Archbishop Stigand and Æthelnoth, abbot of Glastonbury.[31] William of Poitiers says that the king was suspicious of their loyalty but he was writing after the events of 1068–70 and influenced by hindsight.[32] There was nothing necessarily sinister in the king's action; Cnut had taken Earl Godwine with him to Denmark in 1017–18, to test his abilities.[33]

In the king's absence the government of England was left to William fitzOsbern and Odo of Bayeux.[34] Opinion naturally varies on how well they performed their duties. William of Poitiers maintains that 'they laudably performed their respective stewardships', while the Anglo-Saxon Chronicle complains that they 'built

---

[28] GDB, fol. 186; C.P. Lewis, 'The Norman settlement of Herefordshire under William I', ANS 7 (1985), p. 203.

[29] Williams, 'An introduction to the Gloucestershire Domesday', pp. 24–5, 34 and see footnote 5 above.

[30] For Eadnoth, see Regesta i, no. 7, AS Chron, 1068; Bondi, Regesta i, nos. 18, 23; Ulf Tope's son, Regesta i, no. 18; Thorkell, Regesta i, no. 25 and below, Chapter V; Eadric, Regesta i, no. 9; Tovi, Regesta i, nos. 7, 23 and below, p. 22; Swawold, Regesta i, no. 18; Mærle-Sveinn, Regesta i, no. 8 and below, p. 22; Gamel, EYC i, p. 186.

[31] AS Chron, 1066; FlW, 1066; OV ii, pp. 196–7.

[32] WmP, pp. 244–5.

[33] Vita Edwardi, pp. 5–6.

[34] For the activities of Odo and William (not all necessarily in this period), see David Bates, 'The origins of the justiarship', ANS 4 (1982), pp. 2–5.

castles far and wide throughout this kingdom and distressed the wretched folk'.[35] Orderic Vitalis castigates the 'petty lords' (*prefecti minores*) who oppressed both nobles and commoners with 'unjust exactions', while fitzOsbern and Odo, 'swollen with pride', ignored all complaints against their underlings.[36] In the absence of strictly contemporary evidence it is difficult to evaluate these judgements but two causes of friction are possible. The first is hinted at in William of Poitiers' statement that Frenchmen were forbidden to engage in illicit relationships with English women. An obvious way to secure land was to marry an heiress. The Breton, Geoffrey de la Guerche, apparently acquired the lands of Leofwine and his son, Leofric *cild*, in Warwickshire, Leicestershire and Lincolnshire by marriage with his daughter Ælfgifu, and Richard *iuvenis*, a pre-Conquest settler, held only a small manor in Worcestershire until the king gave him the widow and land of Alwine, sheriff of Gloucestershire.[37] Since Richard's lands were held in 1086 by William Goizenboded, who was probably his son, the marriage presumably took place early in William's reign.[38] Such unions might be perfectly satisfactory to both parties; the impeccably English bishop, Wulfstan of Worcester, gave the daughter and land of his thegn, Sigref of Croome, to one of his knights, so that he could support Sigref's widow and perform the service due from the estate.[39] Other matches may have been achieved less amicably and the fact that Englishwomen are known to have taken refuge in nunneries 'not for love of the religious life but from fear of the French' suggests that exploitation was not uncommon. The enforced marriage of widows had been a source of complaint in the period of Danish settlement after the conquest of Cnut.[40]

Another cause for complaint may have been the geld levied in 1067. It is described as 'very severe' by the 'D' chronicler, which may not mean much, but its temporary suspension in 1051 had been prompted by its excessive demands.[41] Particularly objectionable was the fact that those unable to pay it might lose their land to those who did. In the time of Cnut both Danes and Englishmen had acquired the lands of impoverished thegns by paying the outstanding geld.[42]

---

[35] *WmP*, pp. 262–3; *AS Chron*, 'D', 1066.

[36] *OV* ii, pp. 202–3.

[37] For Geoffrey and Leofwine, see D.E. Greenway, *Charters of the Honour of Mowbray, 1107–1191* (Oxford, 1972), pp. xx–xxi. It is not only in Warwickshire and Leicestershire that Geoffrey succeeded Leofwine; one of his nine Lincolnshire manors had also belonged to Leofric *cild* (*GDB*, fol. 369). For Richard *iuvenis*, see next note.

[38] *GDB*, fols 167, 177v; Williams, 'An introduction to the Gloucestershire Domesday', p. 35.

[39] *GDB*, fol. 173. The tenant of Croome in 1086, Siward, might be the son of this marriage.

[40] *Letters of Lanfranc*, pp. 166–7 and see *OV* ii, pp. 268–9: 'noble maidens were exposed to the insults of low-born soldiers and lamented their dishonouring by the scum of the earth'. For the enforced marriage of widows in Cnut's time, see Cnut's Proclamation of 1020, caps 16–17, and II Cnut 73–4.

[41] *AS Chron*, 'D', 1051.

[42] II Cnut, cap. 79; *Hemming's Cartulary* i, p. 278. See Ann Williams, ' "Cockles

There are signs of the same practice after 1066: Peter de Valognes, one-time sheriff of Hertfordshire, confiscated the land of a sokeman at Libury for non-payment of geld and Ralph Taillebois, sheriff of Bedfordshire, paid the tribute (*gafol*) on Tovi the houscarl's manor at Sharnbrook and gave it to one of his knights.[43] In the case of Libury the shire and hundred courts maintained that the land was exempt from geld and the confiscation thus illegal. Numerous complaints of extortion on the part of royal officers surfaced during the Domesday enquiry, though it is rarely possible to date the incidents with any precision.

William fitzOsbern died at the Battle of Cassel in February 1071 and any activities in which he was involved must therefore date from between 1067 and that year. He evidently continued to supervise the submission of the English nobles and the restoration of lands. A writ, which must date from before the summer of 1068, is issued in the name of fitzOsbern as well as the king and confirms the manor of Charlcombe, Somerset, to the abbot of Bath; it had been held of the church by an unnamed thegn.[44] In Hampshire, Ælfric of Hartley Westfall paid two gold marks (£12) to Earl William for his manor and it was from the earl that Cola of Basing redeemed the land of his kinsmen at *Sudeberie*.[45] Tovi of Meon had had his debt remitted, for he held half his manor of the king 'for money' and the remainder 'by the gift of Earl William'.[46] Conversely the earl or his men may have been responsible for the illegal seizure of Ealdred's estate at Compton 'after King William had crossed the sea'.[47] In Herefordshire, where fitzOsbern had succeeded to Harold's rank and responsibilities, the castle-building of which the chronicler complained is very evident; fitzOsbern established castles at Chepstow, Clifford, Monmouth and Wigmore and built or re-built Ewias Harold.[48] He and his men are accused of despoiling the church of Worcester and its tenants; indeed the Worcester monk Hemming, who compiled a list of the church's losses, complains of Normans 'usurping the inheritances of Englishmen'.[49] In East Anglia, where the process of redemption was overseen by Earl Ralph the staller, William, bishop of London, and the royal priest Engelric, there is considerable evidence of sharp practice, which tends to support Orderic Vitalis' strictures on the activities of 'petty lords'.[50]

---

amongst the wheat": Danes and English in the west midlands in the first half of the eleventh century', *Midland History* 11 (1985), p. 13.
[43] GDB, fol. 141 (*pro forisfactura de gildo regis se non reddidisse*); fol. 216 (*gablum dedit et pro forisfacto ipsam terram supersit*). See also R. Welldon Finn, *Domesday Book: the eastern counties* (London, 1967), p. 11.
[44] *Regesta* i, no. 7; see Lewis, 'The early earls of Norman England', p. 217.
[45] GDB, fol. 50.
[46] GDB, fol. 40v.
[47] GDB, fol. 48v.
[48] Ewias Harold was once thought to have been built before the Conquest, but the land seems not to have been in English hands before 1066 (Lewis, 'The Norman settlement of Herefordshire under William the Conqueror', p. 211; GDB, fol. 186).
[49] Hemming's Cartulary i, p. 269.
[50] See, for example, LDB, fols 360v, 367v. For Engelric, see Keynes, 'Regenbald the chancellor (*sic*)', pp. 218–19.

Odo of Bayeux survived in power until 1082 and his activities are harder to date. The bulk of his fief lay in Kent and in the shires to the north of London, where a great part of his land had belonged to Earl Leofwine and to Æthelnoth 'the Kentishman' of Canterbury, all of whose property, except for his Sussex estates (held in 1086 by Battle Abbey) had passed to Odo.[51] After 1072 Odo's comital powers seem to have been confined to Kent, which suggests that his activities elsewhere may be earlier.[52] His confirmation of Leofwine's sale of Nuneham Courtenay, Oxon, to Abingdon Abbey may indeed have taken place in 1067, for it was done 'while the king was abroad and Odo governed England'.[53] His seizure of Langton, Lincs, from Ramsey Abbey is said to have occurred 'during the overturning of the kingdom' (*in permutatione regni*), which seems likely to refer to the Conquest and its aftermath. It must also have been while he exercised comital authority in Hertfordshire that he confiscated half a hide from King Edward's reeve Leofsige because it had been appropriated *super regem*.[54] Odo's reputation has suffered because of his disgrace in 1082 and his subsequent rebellion against William Rufus in 1088, but he may well have been sympathetic to some aspects of English culture. It was he who commissioned the Bayeux Tapestry from an atelier in Kent (probably in Canterbury) and he was on good terms with St Augustine's, Canterbury, a house with strong indigenous traditions.[55]

The attitudes of later writers to fitzOsbern and Odo may be coloured by the disturbances of 1067, which have been interpreted as the opening shots in a general uprising of the English nation against Norman rule. This view is erroneous. Neither the disturbances in Herefordshire, in fitzOsbern's jurisdiction, nor those in Kent, in Odo's *scir*, have the character of national rebellions. They resemble the many local disputes which frequently resulted in violence throughout the tenth and eleventh centuries (and later).[56] The events in Herefordshire are described briefly in the *Anglo-Saxon Chronicle* and elaborated by John of Worcester. Eadric *cild*, also known as 'the Wild' (*se wilde, silvaticus, salvage*), in alliance with the Welsh prince Bleddyn of Gwynedd, attacked the garrison at Hereford and laid waste the shire 'up to the bridge over the River Lugg'.[57] John of Worcester claims that Eadric had never accepted King William's rule (though

---

51 For Æthelnoth 'the Kentishman' of Canterbury, who may have been portreeve, see Ann Williams, 'From kingdom to shire: Kent c.800–1066', forthcoming.

52 Lewis, 'The early earls of Norman England', pp. 218–19.

53 *Chron Abingdon* ii, p. 9 (see also below, Chapter V). There were other years when Odo was ruling in the king's absence, but, since the transaction involves an Englishman, 1067 is as likely as any.

54 *Chron Ramsey*, pp. 153–4 (see also below, Chapter V); GDB, fol. 139.

55 Bates, 'Odo of Bayeux', p. 10; N.P. Brooks and the late H.E. Walker, 'The authority and interpretation of the Bayeux Tapestry', ANS 1 (1978), pp. 6–10.

56 For examples, see AS Chron, 1002, 1021, 1023, 1041 and note 67 below.

57 AS Chron, 'D', 1067; FlW, 1067. The Chronicle's description of Eadric as *cild* has been taken as an error for *se wilde* but a man of Eadric's rank might well be called *cild* (see Chapter IV below).

Orderic Vitalis says that he submitted in January 1067) and that as a result his lands were frequently ravaged by the *castellani* of Hereford and by Richard fitzScrob of Richard's Castle, one of the Confessor's Norman settlers. Though Orderic says that Eadric was later involved in the rebellion of 1069, it would be unwise to read back his motives on that occasion to explain his actions in 1067. If he had in fact made formal submission in January 1067, he may simply have been reacting to some local provocation on the part of Richard fitzScrob and the Hereford garrison. No action against him is recorded after the king's return in December. Indeed it may have been his opponents who felt the royal displeasure. Not all Richard fitzScrob's pre-Conquest holdings were allowed to pass to his son Osbern, and the family was not treated with noticeable generosity.[58]

The events in Kent are recorded only by the Norman chroniclers William of Jumieges and William of Poitiers (followed by Orderic).[59] No English source covers them, not even the 'E' Chronicle which was being compiled at St Augustine's, Canterbury, in the mid eleventh century.[60] Despite the partiality of the Norman writers, the chief mover in the Kentish disturbance was clearly Eustace of Boulogne. His interests in England go back to his marriage with King Edward's sister Gode (Godgifu), after the death of her first husband in 1035. She was dead by 1049, but the friendship between Eustace and King Edward continued.[61] In 1051 Eustace visited England, and it seems that the king intended to install him at Dover, perhaps as castellan of a projected castle.[62] The resistance of the men of Dover provoked a fight which left twenty of the townsmen and nineteen of Eustace's retainers dead. Eustace next appears in England as one of King William's commanders at the battle of Hastings. There are conflicting reports of his conduct, some flattering, some not, but he received land and perhaps some official position in England in 1067.[63] By the summer of 1067 he

---

[58] GDB, fol. 185 (*DB Herefordshire*, no. 11,14 and note); Lewis, 'The Norman settlement of Herefordshire under William the Conqueror', p. 202. Richard fitzScrob's father (ON Skrupi) may have been English, see Hooper, 'Edgar ætheling', p. 174.

[59] *WmJ*, chap. 18; *WmP*, pp. 264–9; OV ii, pp. 204–7.

[60] AS Chron, p. xvi. It is 'E' which gives the fullest account of Eustace of Boulogne's brush with the men of Dover in 1051.

[61] David Bates, 'Lord Sudeley's ancestors: the family of the counts of Amiens, Valois and the Vexin in France and England during the eleventh century', *The Sudeleys, lords of Toddington*, The Manorial Society (London, 1987), pp. 38–9.

[62] Williams, 'From kingdom to shire: Kent c.800–1066', forthcoming. The 'D' Chronicle appears to refer to a castle at Dover in 1051 and was interpreted in this way by John of Worcester (compare AS Chron, 'D', 1051 and FlW, 1051). William of Poitiers says that Harold, in 1064, promised to yield up to Duke William the castle of Dover (*WmP*, pp. 104–5). Dover lay close to the heartland of Earl Godwine's power and a castle there would have intruded on his authority, as that at Hereford did on the authority of his son Swein (see AS Chron, 'E', 1051). The castle at Clavering, Essex, ('Robert's castle') lay in Harold's earldom of East Anglia (AS Chron, 'E', 1052, and see above, p. 10).

[63] Shirley Ann Brown, 'The Bayeux Tapestry: why Eustace, Odo and William?', ANS 12 (1989), pp. 7–28; *Regesta* i, nos. 9, 45. William of Poitiers says that he lost his land, presumably in England, after the Dover raid. Eustace's career is discussed by Heather

15

had quarrelled with the king and returned to Boulogne. The coolness between Eustace and William may have concerned the castlery of Dover, which was entrusted to Hugh de Montfort. Perhaps Eustace thought it should have been given to him. Other men had regained property which they or their families had once held but had forfeited through the influence of Earl Godwine; Alvred of Marlborough had been reinstated in the manors of Burghill and Brinsop, Herefordshire, lost by his uncle Osbern Pentecost.[64] Eustace's attack on Dover may have been an attempt to seize by force what he considered should have been his by right. He chose a moment when both the castellan, Hugh de Montfort, and Odo of Bayeux were absent north of the Thames but the spirited defence of the garrison frustrated him and he received little or no local support. His forces were scattered and destroyed and he himself 'cravenly fled by ship'.[65] His subsequent reconciliation with the king may have led William of Poitiers to throw the blame for the assault on the thegns of Kent, who are said to have offered Eustace not only the castle of Dover but the kingship itself. Such claims are well-nigh incredible and William of Poitiers himself was moved to remark that Eustace had formerly been the bitterest enemy of the Kentish people.[66] Eustace's actions look very like an attempt by a disgruntled man to seize what he thought his due. The Dover raid of 1067 is in the tradition of similar expeditions by exiled or dispossessed lords attempting to regain their rights and has nothing to do with a national English uprising.[67]

Only one of the disturbances in 1067 was truly ominous. In February the king had appointed Copsi as earl of Northumbria beyond the Tyne. William of Poitiers describes him as 'a man of great courage and integrity' and perhaps he was but there could scarcely have been a worse choice for the northern earldom.[68] Copsi had been an adherent of Earl Tostig, whose government of the north had provoked rebellion in 1065. When the earl was exiled Copsi shared his lord's fate and may even have been with the Norwegian host at the battle of Stamfordbridge.[69] His appearance at Barking in 1067 was an opportunistic attempt to obtain from King William what he had lost under King Harold. His unsuitability for the lordship of Bamburgh was compounded by the fact that he was a

---

Tanner, 'The expansion of the power and influence of the counts of Boulogne under Eustace II', ANS 14 (1992), pp. 251–86.
64 GDB, fol. 186.
65 WmJ, chap. 18.
66 WmP, pp. 266–7.
67 For comparable events, see AS Chron, 1009, 1046, 1052, 1055, 1063 and see footnote 56 above.
68 WmP, pp. 268–71.
69 HDE, chapter 49, which lists Copsi's donations to the church of Durham, and describes him as having 'charge of the whole earldom under Tostig', defines his authority as 'the province of the men of Northumbria, that is, of those who reside on the north of the River Tyne'; for his presence at Stamfordbridge, see Lestorie des Engles i, p. 219, where he is described as a man from Orkney.

Yorkshireman.[70] Bamburgh had its own line of earls, who had ruled northern Northumbria since the time of King Alfred (and probably before), and was resistant to control from York.[71] Earl Osulf, the current representative of the Bamburgh line, had been installed by Earl Morcar after Tostig's expulsion. He was unlikely to welcome one of Tostig's men, for the earl had been party to the murder of his kinsman Gospatric in 1064.[72] It comes as no surprise that Copsi was murdered by Osulf almost as soon as he set foot north of the Tyne. On 12 March 'in the fifth week after he received the earldom' Copsi was feasting at Newburn (now a suburb of Newcastle) when the house was attacked by Earl Osulf and his men. Copsi took refuge in the nearby church, which was set on fire, and as he tried to escape from the burning building, Osulf himself cut off his head.[73] Copsi's murder was no index of anti-Norman feeling. It was rule from the south, whether West Saxon or Norman, which was resented, as King William was about to discover.

The king returned to England on 6 December 1067. His arrival coincided with the burning-down of the archiepiscopal church at Canterbury, an inauspicious conjunction. In the next few months William continued to balance French and English interests. In the far north Earl Osulf had been killed in the autumn of 1067, 'rushing headlong against the spear of a robber' and William allowed his cousin, Gospatric son of Maldred, to buy the earldom of Bamburgh.[74] Other appointments went to foreigners. The bishop of Dorchester-on-Thames, Wulfwig, had died in the king's absence and William gave the vacant see to Remigius, a Fecamp monk. He made his profession to Archbishop Stigand, which was to cause him some embarrassment in the future.[75] Godric, abbot of Winchcombe had been deposed for unspecified reasons but for three years his abbey was administered by another Englishman, Æthelwig, abbot of Evesham, and it was not until 1069 that he was replaced by Galandus, a monk from Cerisy-la-Foret.[76]

---

[70] For his lands see GDB, fols 298v, 310, 327.
[71] W. Kapelle, The Norman Conquest of the North (London, 1979), pp. 106–7.
[72] See below, Chapter II.
[73] HR, 1070; De primo adventu Saxonum, Symeonis . . . Collectanea, p. 213.
[74] HR, 1072 (see Chapter II).
[75] AS Chron, 1067; Frank Barlow, The English Church 1000–1066 (London, 1963), pp. 302–4, 309–12. Remigius' appointment was by way of a reward for his assistance in King William's successful bid for the English crown (HN, p. 11; GP, p. 312).
[76] HRH, p. 79; Chron Evesham, p. 90. Godric is said to have been imprisoned at Gloucester, but was soon moved into Æthelwig's custody at Evesham (Emma Mason, St Wulfstan of Worcester (Oxford, 1990), p. 198). He was the son of Godman, one of the Confessor's clerks, perhaps identical with Godman the priest, whose land in Devon was held in 1086 by Baldwin de Meulles (GDB, fols 106v, 107v, 108v, Exon fols 296, 307v; Barlow, The English Church 1000–1066, pp. 118, 157). When Galandus died in 1075, it was again to Æthelwig that the abbey of Winchcombe was entrusted, and the next abbot, Ralph, was appointed only when Æthelwig himself died in 1077.

Another Fecamp monk, Turold, was installed at Malmesbury, though the English abbot, Beorhtric, was not deposed but simply moved to Burton.[77]

One of those who accompanied the king to England in 1067 was Roger de Montgomery. He was installed at Arundel, alongside Humphrey de Tilleul at Hastings and William de Warenne at Lewes, and it was about the same time that Robert of Mortain received Pevensey. These four castles dominated the Sussex rapes named after them; the fifth rape, Bramber, held by William de Braose, was in existence by 1084.[78] Whatever their origins, the rapes of Sussex were effectively castleries on the continental model, superseding former administrative units, and their introduction led to much disruption. Between 1068 and 1070 the bishopric of Selsey lost two manors to Robert de Eu, Humphrey de Tilleul's successor at Hastings, and outlying berewicks were cut off from their parent manors. The reorganization also affected the hundredal structure.[79] Something similar may have been planned for Kent. Domesday several times mentions the *divisiones* of Odo of Bayeux and Hugh de Montfort and uses the same word for the rapes of Sussex.[80] One clearly new unit in Kent is the lowy (*leuga*) of Tonbridge, a castlery created (perhaps in 1068) for Richard son of Count Gilbert de Brionne.[81]

Such developments may underlie the *Anglo-Saxon Chronicle's* complaint that when King William returned from Normandy he 'gave away every man's land'. Since the king had been concerned to restore land to the English who accepted his rule, this statement needs examination. The explanation lies in what happened in Normandy in 1067. At Easter (8 April) the Penitential Ordinance, laying down penances due from William's men who had participated in the Conquest, was first promulgated.[82] It distinguished three phases of the campaign: the battle of Hastings itself; the period between the battle and the king's coronation; and the post-coronation period. The first two constituted states of 'public war' and the penalties for homicide and injury were correspondingly lessened, whereas the same acts committed after the coronation carried the full penance, unless the victims were still resisting the king. The inference is that

---

[77] HRH, pp. 31, 55; David Knowles, *The Monastic Order in England, 940–1216*, 2nd edn (Cambridge, 1963), p. 105 (see also Chapter III below).

[78] Roger may have been made Earl of Shrewsbury in 1068, see Chapter II below. For Robert of Mortain at Pevensey, see Brian Golding, 'Robert of Mortain', *ANS* 13 (1991), p. 125.

[79] Frank Thorn, 'Hundreds and wapentakes', *The Sussex Domesday*, ed. Ann Williams and R.W.H. Erskine (London, 1990), pp. 299–33.

[80] *GDB*, fols 9v, 10v, 11, 11v, 13, 13v (Hugh's *divisio*); 10v (Odo's *divisio*). For the *divisio* (rape) of the count of Eu, see *GDB*, fol. 10v (*DB Sussex*, no. 5,175, Bilsington).

[81] For Richard fitzGilbert and Tonbridge, see Richard Mortimer, 'The beginnings of the Honour of Clare', *ANS* 3 (1981), pp. 119–41.

[82] *Councils and Synods* I ii, pp. 81–4: see George Garnett, 'Coronation and propaganda: some implications of the Norman claim to the throne of England in 1066', *TRHS* 36 (1986), pp. 96–9; H.E.J. Cowdrey, 'The Anglo-Norman *Laudes Regiae*', *Viator* 12 (1981), p. 59 and note 68.

the English were in rebellion against the king even before he was consecrated and this forms the ideological basis for the dispossession of those who died in resisting the Norman invasion. Only those who survived to submit could redeem their lands. An undated but arguably early writ to the abbot of Bury St Edmunds articulates this position; it orders the surrender of 'all the lands which those men held who stood against me in battle and were killed there, who belonged to St Edmund's soke'.[83] The monks of Abingdon claimed that they had been despoiled of land held of them by Godric the sheriff and Thorkell because both men had been killed in the battle of Hastings.[84]

If there was a general dispossession in 1068 it probably bore most heavily on the men of eastern Wessex, the east midlands and East Anglia, who took the major part in the battle of Hastings. These are also the areas in which King Harold and his brothers, Gyrth and Leofwine, were most powerful. There are some traces of such a dispossession in Domesday Book. In Buckinghamshire, Alric *bolest* forfeited his land at Soulbury 'through King William's arrival' (*propter adventum Regis Willelmi*).[85] In Hampshire the tenure of Alwig son of Thorbeorht at West Tytherley was challenged because he could not produce evidence of the title of his predecessors, two of whom were killed at the battle of Hastings.[86] In Essex Beorhtsige of Foulton and Brune of Tolleshunt lost their manors 'after the king came into this land'; Beorhtsige was also exiled.[87] In the same shire, the tenure of Kelvedon Hatch by Westminster Abbey was challenged because the donor, Æthelric, 'went away to a naval battle against King William' (*abiit in navale proelium contra Willelmi regis*), presumably the battle mentioned in the 'E' Chronicle for 1066.[88] Ælfwold, abbot of St Benet's, Holme in Norfolk, whom King Harold had set to defend the east coast in 1066, was outlawed for a time in the early years of William's reign and at least two of his men shared his exile and lost their lands: Eadric the steersman, captain of St Benet's ship, and Ringulf of Oby.[89]

It seems that by the spring of 1068 some Englishmen were becoming alarmed by the seizure of English estates and the advancement of foreigners; the great geld of 1068, described as 'insupportable' by John of Worcester, may have exacerbated such feelings. This might be the explanation for the events at Exeter

---

[83] *Regesta* i, no. 40. The writ is in English which may imply a date before 1070.
[84] *Chron Abingdon* i, pp. 484–5, 491. GDB, fol. 60v implies that Godric survived the battle, but the principle may be sound even if the facts are wrong.
[85] GDB, fol. 153.
[86] GDB, fol. 50.
[87] LDB, fols 48, 48v (*DB Essex*, nos. 24,65–6).
[88] LDB, fol. 14v (*DB Essex*, no. 6,9); AS *Chron*, 'E', 1066; Harmer, *Writs*, p. 302. Alternatively he may have been with the 700 ships sent by King Harold to blockade William's fleet at Pevensey (*WmP*, pp. 180–1) but the timing would be fairly tight.
[89] LDB, fol. 200 (*DB Essex*, nos 10,76–7); Ann Williams, 'Land and power in the eleventh century: the estates of Harold Godwineson', ANS 3 (1981), pp. 197–80; LDB, fols 174v, 267 (*DB Essex*, nos 9,14;27: 50,8); F.M Stenton, 'St Benet of Holme and the Norman Conquest', EHR 33 (1922), pp. 227, 233.

whose citizens responded to a formal demand for submission with an ill-judged attempt to bargain with the king.[90] Their intransigence may have had something to do with the presence in the city of Gytha, widow of Earl Godwine and mother of the dead king. After her attempt to buy the body of her son from William, she seems to have retired, with or without his leave, to her western estates. She had considerable weight in the area. She had given Tavistock Abbey an estate at Werrington, Devon, certainly after the Confessor's death and perhaps after that of Harold.[91] Indeed all her known benefactions lie in the west. She was a patron of St Olave's, Exeter, which stood close to the residence of *Irlesbyri* ('the earl's *burh*'), probably the hall of the Godwine family in the city.[92] Gytha gave two Somerset manors to the Old Minster, Winchester, and had some connection with the church of Berkeley in Gloucestershire, of which her brother Eilaf had been earl in Cnut's reign.[93] It was in Somerset too that the only known lands of her grandson, Godwine son of Harold, lay.[94] A memory of Gytha's standing in the west may be preserved in the Abingdon tradition that it was her breach with King William that encouraged Abbot Ealdred to withdraw his allegiance.[95]

The king's response to Exeter's stand was to besiege the city. It surrendered after eighteen days and was treated by William with remarkable clemency. Perhaps Queen Edith had intervened; she had always supported William's cause, and Exeter was part of the queen's dower.[96] It is also clear that many in the west favoured submission to the new king. The Chronicle says that the citizens had to surrender 'because the thegns had betrayed them'.[97] Gytha and her companions escaped from the city before its fall. She took refuge on the island of Flatholme in the Severn estuary 'and many distinguished men's wives with her'.

---

90 *OV* ii, pp. 210–11.
91 For Gytha's offer of its weight in gold for Harold's body (*WmP*, pp. 204–5) see also Chapter VII below; for her gift of Werrington to Tavistock, see Exon, fol. 178v, *DB Devon*, no. 1,50 and note. Since Tavistock did not hold the estate 'on the day when King Edward was alive and dead', its possession of Werrington was still being challenged in William II's reign (van Caeneghem i, no. 144, pp. 117–18; H.P.R. Finberg, 'The making of a boundary', *Lucerna* (Leicester, 1964), pp. 171–8; idem, *Tavistock Abbey*, pp. 6–12).
92 S.1236; *The Chronicle of Battle Abbey*, ed. Eleanor Searle (Oxford, 1980), pp. 80, 82; *GDB*, fol. 100v; *Regesta* i, no. 58. For *Irlesbyri* see Jeremy Haslam, 'Saxon Exeter', *Anglo-Saxon towns in southern England*, ed. Jeremy Haslam (Chichester, 1984), pp. 402–4. There was an *Earlesburgh* in York (in the area later called Marygate), close to another St Olave's, this one built by Earl Siward of Northumbria (see Alfred P. Smyth, *Scandinavian York and Dublin* (Dublin, 1979), ii, p. 235; *AS Chron*, 1055).
93 C.R. Hart, *Early charters of Wessex* (Leicester, 1964), p. 150 (no. 532); *GDB*, fol. 164.
94 *GDB*, fol. 86v.
95 *Chron Abingdon* ii, p. 283. Ealdred had been appointed in the time of Harold II (*Chron Abingdon* i, p. 482) and the house was patronized by the West Saxon earls (Williams, 'Land and power in the eleventh century', pp. 183–4).
96 It was Edith who arranged the surrender of Winchester after the battle of Hastings (*Carmen*, p. 40). Her reeve in Exeter, Colwine, was still in receipt of the queen's share of its revenues in 1086, and he held land in Devon, including (as reeve) some of Edith's former estates (*GDB*, fols 100, 100v (Exon, fol. 93), 106, 106v, 116, 118).
97 *AS Chron*, 'D', 1067.

Their husbands may have taken flight to Ireland, whither the sons of King Harold had gone to seek the aid of their father's old ally, King Diarmid of Leinster.[98] Diarmid obliged with ships and men but when Godwine Haroldson and his brothers descended on the Bristol Avon in the summer of 1068, they met with little or no support. An attack on Bristol was beaten off by its citizens and when Godwine's fleet moved into Somerset, it was met by the English levies commanded by Eadnoth the staller. A battle ensued at Bleadon (one of the manors given by Gytha to the Old Minster) and though Eadnoth was killed, the raiders were driven off. It was probably after this that Gytha left England for good.[99]

The fall of Exeter was followed by fresh Norman settlement in western Wessex. The castle of Rougemont, built at Exeter, was entrusted to Baldwin de Meulles, brother of Richard fitzGilbert of Tonbridge; he was sheriff of Devon by 1070, and in 1086 was the greatest landowner in the shire.[100] Judhael of Totnes, who was perhaps castellan of Totnes castle, and held, by 1086, lands which formed the later honour of Totnes, may have arrived at the same time.[101] Brian of Brittany held some kind of command in the west for it was he who, with William Gualdi, beat off the second attack of the sons of Harold in 1069.[102] In Somerset, Robert of Mortain received the manor of Bishopstone where he had built his castle of Montacute by 1069.[103] Geoffrey de Mowbray, bishop of Coutances, was probably made port-reeve of Bristol, for he was defending Somerset in 1069, and was in receipt of the third penny of Bristol's revenues in 1086, as well as holding a large fief in the shire.[104]

King William's other dispositions in the west are suggested by the witness-list of a charter issued on 11 May 1068. It restores to Giso, bishop of Wells, the manor of Banwell, Somerset, taken from him by King (sic) Harold.[105] Several of those

---

[98] AS Chron, 'D', 1067; FIW, 1067. For Diarmid and Harold, see Ben Hudson, 'The family of Harold Godwineson and the Irish Sea province', Journal of the Royal Society of Antiquaries of Ireland 109 (1979), pp. 92–100.
[99] John of Worcester places Gytha's departure after the fall of Exeter (FIW, 1068). Orderic Vitalis records her flight, with 'a great store of treasure', after the second raid of her grandsons in 1069, but is vague about the actual date (OV ii, pp. 224–5). She went first to Flanders and thence to Denmark, taking with her her daughter Gunhild and Harold's daughter Gytha.
[100] Regesta i, nos. 58, 59; GDB, fols 100v, 101, 105v–108v (Exon, fols 93–4, 96–97v). Orderic Vitalis reports that on the 1 January 1091 Baldwin and his brother Richard were seen riding in the Wild Hunt with other condemned souls (OV iv, pp. 242–3).
[101] For Judhael's career, see John Williams, 'Judhael of Totnes', ANS 16 (1994), pp. 271–89.
[102] OV ii, pp. 190–1; R. Allen Brown, The Normans and the Norman Conquest, 2nd edn (Woodbridge, 1985), p. 181 note 28. William Gualdi may be William de Vauville, who preceded Baldwin de Meulles as sheriff of Devon (Green, English sheriffs to 1154, p. 35).
[103] It was attacked by the men of Dorset and Somerset in 1069, see below, Chapter II.
[104] GDB, fols 163, 188; G.A. Loud, 'An introduction to the Somerset Domesday', The Somerset Domesday, ed. Ann Williams and R.W.H. Erskine (London, 1988), p. 18; OV ii, pp. 228–9.
[105] Regesta i, no. 23. George Garnett ('Coronation and propaganda', pp. 98–100) has

who attest can be identified as Somerset landholders. They include Tovi, sheriff of Somerset; Dunna, who had lands in Gloucestershire as well as Somerset; Wulfweard White, an official in the queen's service; Harding son of Eadnoth the staller; Azur, perhaps Azur son of Thorth who sold land at Combe St Nicholas to Bishop Giso in 1072; and Beorhtsige, who was a landholder in Gloucestershire and Dorset as well as Somerset.[106] Beside these English names appear those of Serlo de Burcy, Roger Arundel and William de Courseulles, who were about to become prominent landowners in Somerset and the neighbouring shires. By 1086 Serlo de Burcy held land in both Somerset and Dorset and much of his land in the former shire came from two thegns, Almaer and Everwacer.[107] At the same date Roger Arundel held land in Somerset and Dorset which later became the honour of Powerstock; the bulk of it came from two thegns, Æthelfrith and Almaer.[108] William de Courseulles was dead by 1086 and his land was held by his son Roger. The family was associated with Odo of Bayeux, which may explain why Roger held the third largest fief in Somerset after the count of Mortain and the bishop of Coutances. He also had a single manor in Dorset, another in Wiltshire and land in Shropshire.[109] These men need not have received all their land in 1068, but their appearance as witnesses to Bishop Giso's charter suggests that their enrichment was already in train and that the dispossession of the English thegns of Somerset had begun.[110]

One Somerset landholder who had already fled before the issue of Bishop Giso's charter was Mærle-Sveinn. He went to Scotland in the company of the ætheling, before the coronation of Queen Matilda (11 May 1068).[111] Mærle-Sveinn's land in the south was a small part of his total wealth. He was primarily a northerner, with land in Yorkshire and Lincolnshire, of which he was sheriff in the reign of King Harold, and he was left in charge of the north after the battle

shown the significance of the royal title accorded to Harold in the early writs of William's reign.

[106] Tovi, see *Regesta* i, no. 7, GDB, fols 98v, 99; Dunna, see GDB, fols 92v, 166v; Wulfweard White and Harding son of Eadnoth, see below Chapter V; Azur, see Pelteret, *Vernacular documents*, p. 83 (no. 56), GDB, fol. 89 (Exon, fol. 156); Beorhtsige, see VCH *Wilts* ii, p. 66, VCH *Dorset* iii, pp. 32–3, 34, GDB, fols 69v, 83, 94, 96, 98v, 167.

[107] GDB, fols 81, 97v–98; Loud, ' An introduction to the Somerset Domesday', p. 25; VCH *Dorset* iii, p. 48.

[108] GDB, fols 82v, 94; Loud 'An introduction to the Somerset Domesday', p. 24; VCH *Dorset* iii, p. 47.

[109] GDB, fols 72v, 80, 93–94v, 256; Loud, 'An introduction to the Somerset Domesday', pp. 18, 23–4; Judith Green, 'The sheriffs of William the Conqueror', ANS 5 (1983), p. 137.

[110] The continuing importance of Englishmen at the local level is shown by the English witnesses to Azur son of Thorth's sale of Combe St Nicholas to Bishop Giso (see note 106 above) and to the declaration of the customs of Taunton (1066 x 1085), Robertson, *Charters*, pp. 236–9.

[111] AS *Chron*, 'D', 1067; FIW, 1068; Brown, *The Normans and the Norman Conquest*, p. 167.

of Stamfordbridge.[112] He was confirmed in his land and office by King William and his departure in the spring of 1068 suggests that he may have been involved in the Exeter affair; he held a scatter of lands in Gloucestershire, Somerset, Devon and Cornwall, possibly as a result of his connection with Harold.[113]

The siege of Exeter and its aftermath marks a change in the relations between English and Normans. The enrichment of Normans produced distrust and, as a result, defiance in the English; this led in turn to a growing suspicion of the English in the king's mind and produced further displacement in favour of Normans. As the balance altered, attitudes hardened on both sides and any chance of a genuine Anglo-Norman society, comparable to the Anglo-Danish society of Cnut's reign, slipped away. Paradoxically it may have been William's early mildness that produced this result. Cnut's initial conquest was far more brutal but no revolts resulted and those English magnates not killed in the course of the Danish takeover retained their wealth and power.

The flight of the ætheling who had (according to William of Poitiers) been showered with honours by the new king, reflects a growing unease among the English magnates. Yet most of the leaders were still in office when King William brought his wife Matilda to England for her coronation on 11 May 1068.[114] The witness-lists of two charters issued on that occasion reflect the composition of the royal court at the time.[115] Beside the Norman magnates appear the names of Edwin, earl of Mercia, his brother Morcar of Northumbria, Waltheof, earl of the east midlands and many lesser thegns. This fragile balance was not to last. The king was about to discover how hard it was for a ruler based in Winchester to control the men of the north.

[112] *Lestorie des Engles* i, p. 222 (line 5255). For Mærle-Sveinn's land in the north, see GDB, fols 289v, 298, 313, 325, 336, 337v, 362v–363; David Roffe, 'From thegnage to barony: sake and soke, title and tenants-in-chief', ANS 12 (1990), p. 166. For his office in Lincolnshire, see GDB, fol. 376, where he held the land of a convicted thegn 'in the year in which King Edward died', a circumlocution for the reign of Harold; *Regesta* i, no. 8 (dated 1067); Green, *English sheriffs to 1154*, p. 54.

[113] For Mærle-Sveinn's lands in the west see GDB, fols 95, 96v, 113v; 121v; 122, 122v, 124v; 168.

[114] AS Chron, 'D', 1067; FIW, 1068.

[115] *Regesta* i, no 22 (for which see W.H. Stevenson, 'An Old-English charter of William the Conqueror in favour of St. Martin's-le-Grand, London, A.D.1068', EHR 11 (1896), pp. 731–44); no. 23 (Bishop Giso's charter, discussed above). See also Keynes, 'Regenbald the chancellor (*sic*)', pp. 219–20.

Chapter II

THE ENGLISH REVOLT, 1068–1070

> Then the king was informed that the men of
> the north were gathered together and meant to
> make a stand against him if he came.
>
> *Anglo-Saxon Chronicle*, 'D', 1068

SOON AFTER THE CORONATION OF Queen Matilda on 11 May 1068, Edwin of
Mercia and his brother, Morcar of Northumbria, turned against the king. Orderic
Vitalis, who had some sympathy for Edwin, claimed that he had been promised
one of the king's daughters in marriage, but that William, 'listening to the
dishonest counsels of his envious and greedy Norman followers, withheld the
maiden from the noble youth'. Edwin therefore became suspicious of the king's
intentions and sought the aid of King Bleddyn of Gwynedd.[1] Orderic is the sole
source for this projected marriage and for the defiance of the Mercian brothers
in 1068 but he was drawing on the lost conclusion to the *Gesta Guillielmi* of
William of Poitiers and it is quite likely that Edwin might have felt threatened
by developments in 1068. It was probably in that year that the king gave judicial
authority throughout the shires of Mercia (with the significant exception of
Cheshire, where the bulk of Edwin's power lay) to Æthelwig, abbot of Evesham.[2]
Evesham was a house favoured by the Mercian earls and perhaps Æthelwig's
advancement did not, in itself, greatly threaten Edwin's position. A writ of 1068
relating to Staffordshire, addressed to Bishop Leofwine of Lichfield and Earl
Edwin, simply names Æthelwig as one of the king's officers.[3] A more serious
development was the appearance of Roger of Montgomery as earl of Shrewsbury
and his construction of a castle there.[4] There were pre-Conquest precedents for
the creation of smaller earldoms within the *sciras* of greater earls. Cnut had carved

---

[1] OV ii, pp. 214–15. For earlier relations between the Welsh and the earls of Mercia,
see note 8 below.
[2] R.R. Darlington, 'Aethelwig, abbot of Evesham', *EHR* 48 (1933), pp. 1–22, 177–98.
[3] *Regesta* i, no. 25. For the benefactions of the Mercian earls to Evesham, see S.1052,
1223, 1238, 1398. Not all of these charters are of unimpeachable authority but they
preserve a tradition of Evesham's relationship with the family.
[4] Roger of Montgomery attests *Regesta* i, no. 22, issued at Whitsun (11 May) 1068, as
comes and the title is applied in the same text to William fitzOsbern, Robert count of
Eu, Edwin, Morcar and Waltheof. In *Regesta* i, no. 23, issued on the same occasion, Roger
of Montgomery attests as *princeps* and fitzOsbern, Edwin and Waltheof as *duces*. The
significance of these titles is discussed by Lewis 'The early earls of Norman England',

earldoms based on Hereford, Gloucester and Worcester out of the *scir* of Mercia in the time of Edwine's great-grandfather Leofwine.[5] Nevertheless the arrival of Roger of Montgomery on Edwin's doorstep cannot have been very welcome.

Orderic presents Edwin's alliance with Bleddyn of Gwynedd as the signal for a general insurrection against Norman rule:

> After large numbers of the leading men of England and Wales had met together, a general outcry arose against the injustice and tyranny which the Normans and their allies had inflicted on the English. They sent envoys into every corner of Albion, to incite men to recover their former liberty and bind themselves by weighty oaths against the Normans.

He adds the famous comment that 'many men lived in tents, disdaining to sleep in houses lest they should become soft, so that the Normans called them *silvatici*' (wild men, men of the woods).[6]

Orderic's words find an echo in the *Gesta* of William of Jumièges, who also describes a general conspiracy but not in 1068.[7] It is hard, however, to accept Edwin as the mover. The *Anglo-Saxon Chronicle* ignores his part in events and describes what happened in 1068–70 as a purely Northumbrian matter. Even Orderic's account does not give Edwin a leading role for his speedy submission has no effect on the outcome. It makes more sense to see the disturbances of 1068 as King William's first brush with the Northerners and Edwin's pique as incidental. His actions are little different from the sporadic acts of defiance committed by disaffected nobles in the Confessor's reign (notably by his father Ælfgar, who also allied with the Welsh), none of which amounted to actual rebellion.[8] Orderic's picture of the *silvatici* itself is rendered suspect by the fact that the most famous *silvaticus*, Eadric the Wild, took no part in the events of 1068.[9]

The root of the trouble may have lain in a formal demand for the submission of the Northumbrian magnates, perhaps conveyed by Ealdred, archbishop of York, whose successor as bishop of Worcester, St Wulfstan, was sent on a similar but more successful errand by King Harold in 1066.[10] The response of the

---

pp. 219–20, who argues that Roger was earl of Shrewsbury by 1068. There was a castle at Shrewsbury by 1069 (OV ii, pp. 228–9 and see below).

[5] Williams, 'Cockles amongst the wheat', pp. 2, 6–8.

[6] OV ii, pp. 214, note 3; 216–19.

[7] *WmJ*, chap. 19 and see below.

[8] *AS Chron*, 1046, 1049, 1055, 1058; for Ælfgar see Kari Maund, 'The Welsh alliances of Earl Ælfgar of Mercia and his family in the mid-eleventh century', ANS 11 (1989), pp. 181–90.

[9] For Eadric's career see below, Chapter IV.

[10] Such a demand is mentioned by Gaimar (*Lestorie des Engles* i, p. 228, lines 5379–5404) but he places it after the king's occupation of Nottingham (see below). See also OV ii, pp. 216–17: 'the city of York ... showed no respect for the holy office of the archbishop when he tried to appease it'. For Wulfstan's mission to the Northumbrians in 1066, see *Vita Wulfstani*, p. 22 and Mason, *St Wulfstan of Worcester*, pp. 102–3.

magnates of York fell short of revolt. They tried, like the men of Exeter before them, to bargain with the king. His response was the same, to march upon them in force, scattering castles broadcast as he came. The first was Warwick, presumably intended to bring Edwin to heel; this was certainly the outcome, for he and his brother immediately submitted and took no part in what followed.[11] Warwick castle was entrusted to Henry de Beaumont, whose brother, Robert of Meulan was one of the chief landowners in the shire by 1086.[12] Though one of the Warwickshire manors of Coventry Abbey, a house founded and endowed by the Mercian earls, was described in 1086 as 'waste on account of the king's army', there is no reason to suppose that William met with much resistance in Warwickshire.[13] The Englishman Thorkell of Arden was still a tenant-in-chief there in 1086 and a number of Englishmen were holding their own or their fathers' lands as his tenants. Indeed unusual numbers of Englishmen appear as tenants of Robert of Meulan in Warwickshire.[14]

From Warwick the king moved to Nottingham, where a second castle was built and entrusted to William Peverel. Nottingham had lain in the *scir* of Earl Tostig, whose office and land had reverted to the king when he rebelled in 1065. Comital lands probably formed the basis of the fief held by William Peverel in 1086, for the description of his fief in Domesday reveals a number of estates and manors held by successive pre-Conquest earls and their kindred.[15] The building of Nottingham castle seems to have thrown the thegns of York into a panic. They sent the king the keys of York and gave hostages, including Gospatric son of Arnkell, whose father is described by Orderic as 'the most powerful of the Northumbrians'.[16] The king entered York unopposed and built the first castle, on the site of the later Clifford's Tower.[17] Robert fitzRichard was its castellan and William Malet was made sheriff of Yorkshire.[18] This demonstration of power led most of the northern thegns to make peace. Æthelwine, bishop of Durham 'returned to the king's favour' and was sent to negotiate terms with Malcolm

---

11 Both Edwin and Morcar attest *Regesta* i, no. 28, dated 1069 and Edwin attests *Regesta* i, no. 39, dated 1070.

12 GDB, fols 239v–240v.

13 GDB, fol. 239. Harbury, valued at 10s in King Edward's day and 2s in 1086, was assessed at 5 virgates, with land for one plough and 20 acres of meadow; no peasant population is recorded. This is the only place in Domesday where 'waste' is attributed to military activity (see also note 112 below).

14 GDB, fols 240–241v. For Thorkell, see Chapter V below.

15 GDB, fols 287–288; Roffe, 'From thegnage to barony', pp. 173–4. William Peverel held the estates of 'Countess' Gytha, wife of Ralph, earl of the east Midlands from 1050 to 1057 (Williams, 'The king's nephew: the family and career of Ralph, earl of Hereford', pp. 336–7).

16 OV ii, pp. 218–19.

17 Allen Brown, *The Normans and the Norman conquest*, p. 167.

18 OV ii, pp. 222–3.

Canmore, king of Scots.[19] Some magnates, however, took flight, including Earl
Gospatric of Bamburgh, who found refuge in Scotland.[20]

The king then moved from York to Lincoln, where the castle was built; it may
have been entrusted to Turold of Lincoln, who was sheriff by the 1070s.[21]
Hostages were taken from Lincoln as well as York, including Thorgod lagr, one
of the 'hostages for all Lindsey' held in the castle.[22] Two more castles were raised
as the king returned to the south, at Huntingdon and at Cambridge, the first
certainly and the second probably within the scir of Earl Waltheof.[23] By autumn
1068 the king felt secure enough to dismiss his stipendiary knights and some
Normans also returned home, abandoning their English lands.[24] The king himself
went to Normandy before the end of the year, having appointed a Norman,
Robert de Commines, to the earldom of Bamburgh abandoned by Gospatric.[25]

The earldom north of the Tyne had already claimed the lives of two earls since
1067 and Robert took a substantial force with him to his new command.[26] He is
described by Simeon of Durham as 'one of those persons who paid the wages of
their followers by licensing their ravages and murders' and on his arrival in the
north in December 1068, allowed his men to plunder unchecked.[27] Not even the
lands of St Cuthbert were spared. Nevertheless Robert was received with 'all
courtesy and honour' by Bishop Æthelwine, who even warned him that the
Northumbrians were planning to attack him. And so it fell out; at the end of
January 1069 the Northumbrians broke into the city of Durham, killed all the
Normans they found in the streets and laid siege to the bishop's house, where
the earl was lodged. Unable to take it by storm, they set it on fire, and Robert,
like Earl Copsi before him, was killed as he tried to escape from the burning
building.[28]

It seems to have been at Durham, in the aftermath of this slaughter, that the
killers of Earl Robert planned the English revolt. The earliest account is that of

[19] OV ii, pp. 218–19.
[20] AS Chron, 'D', 1067. John of Worcester places Gospatric's flight earlier in the year,
in company with the ætheling and thus before the queen's coronation on 11 May (FlW,
1068).
[21] Green, English sheriffs to 1154, p. 54; idem, 'The sheriffs of William the Conqueror',
p. 132.
[22] HR, 1079. Thorgod (Turgot) later became a monk of Durham and (briefly) bishop of
St Andrews, see Chapter VI below.
[23] OV ii, pp. 218–19; for the castles see GDB, fols 189, 203.
[24] OV ii, pp. 218–19. Among those who returned to Normandy were Hugh de Grandmesnil, castellan of Winchester, and his brother-in-law Humphrey de Tilleul, castellan
of Hastings; Hugh subsequently came back to England and received a large fief in the
midlands.
[25] Bates, William the Conqueror, p. 77.
[26] The number of men varies: 900 (AS Chron, 'D', 1068), 700 (HDE, chap. 50), or 500
(OV ii, pp. 220–1).
[27] HDE, chap. 50.
[28] The date of Robert's murder is given as 31 January by Simeon of Durham (HDE,
chap. 50) and as 28 January in HR, 1069.

GENEALOGICAL TABLE II. THE LORDS OF BAMBURGH

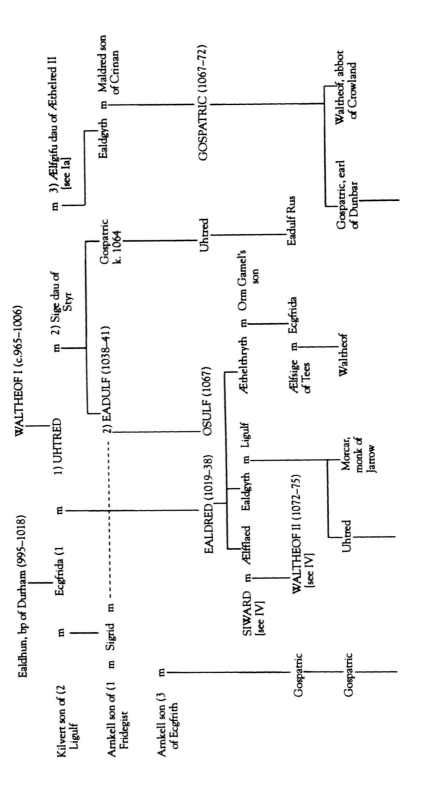

William of Jumièges, writing *circa* 1070–71. His chronology is not always clear (he seems to move straight from 1067 to 1069, ignoring 1068) but his words have a certain coherence:

> In a certain place in one county, rendered inaccessible both by water and by forest, they built a castle with a most powerful rampart, which they called in their own language Durham. From there they made various attacks and then returned home to await the arrival of Swein, king of the Danes, to whom they had sent messengers requesting aid. They also sent to enlist the people of York to their cause . . . Once united with them, they furnished the city with an abundance of arms and money, prepared themselves for a strong resistance, and chose as their king a certain boy, nobly descended from the stock of King Edward.[29]

This account of the genesis of the English rebellion is close to the version of the *Anglo-Saxon Chronicle*, which records the arrival of Edgar ætheling and the Northumbrians at York immediately after the murder of Robert de Commines.[30] Apart from the ætheling, William of Jumièges does not name the leaders of the revolt, but one of them was certainly Earl Gospatric.[31] Orderic supplies a list of those who attacked the castle of York in the spring of 1069: Mærle-Sveinn, Earl Gospatric, Arnkell and the four sons of Karli.[32] The backgrounds of these men reveal the threat posed by the revolt to Norman rule.

With the exception of Mærle-Sveinn, all the leaders were linked in some way with the house of Bamburgh, which had ruled in the north since the ninth century.[33] Its senior member in 1069 was Earl Gospatric, a kinsman of the ætheling ; his mother Ealdgyth was a daughter of Earl Uhtred of Bamburgh (1006–16) by his third wife Ælfgifu, Æthelred II's daughter and thus the ætheling's great-aunt.[34] As a young man he served in the household of Earl Tostig and accompanied him to Rome in 1060. When the party was attacked by bandits, Gospatric, who was richly-dressed as befitted his rank, pretended to be the earl, allowing his lord to escape; the robbers, impressed by his devotion to duty,

---

[29] *WmJ*, chap. 19. I am very grateful to Dr Graham Loud for allowing me to use his unpublished translation.

[30] *AS Chron*, 'D', 'E', 1068.

[31] *HR*, 1072; for Bishop Æthelwine and the Durham community, see below, p. 39.

[32] *OV* ii, pp. 222–3.

[33] Dorothy Whitelock, 'The dealings of the kings of England with Northumbria in the tenth and eleventh centuries', *The Anglo-Saxons; studies . . . presented to Bruce Dickins*, ed. Peter Clemoes (London, 1959), pp. 76–84.

[34] *HR*, 1072; *De obsessione Dunelmi, Symeonis . . . Opera* i, pp. 215–20 (translated in Christopher J. Morris, *Marriage and murder in eleventh-century Northumbria*, Borthwick Papers 82 (York, 1992), pp. 1–5). Gospatric's father, Maldred son of Crinan the thegn, has been identified as the younger brother of Duncan, king of Scots from 1034 to 1040 (William Skene, *Celtic Scotland* (Edinburgh, 1886), i, pp. 394, 408, 419) but there seems to be no basis for this suggestion (William Aird, personal communication).

allowed him to depart unharmed.[35] Gospatric was perhaps lucky to survive in Tostig's household for his uncle and namesake was murdered in 1064 on the orders of Tostig's sister, Queen Edith.[36] It was partly as a result of the murder of the elder Gospatric that Tostig was driven from Northumbria in 1065, in favour of Earl Morcar, who gave the earldom of Bamburgh to the dead man's nephew, Osulf.[37]

Arnkell son of Ecgfrith was connected to the house of Bamburgh by marriage. His wife Sigrid was half-sister to Ealdred of Bamburgh (1019–38) and had previously been married to Earl Eadulf (1038–41) by whom she was Earl Osulf's mother; she was thus the aunt of Gospatric son of Maldred.[38] Arnkell's own family were Yorkshire thegns; he and his son, Gospatric, held some 285 carucates of land in the shire, to which must be added the estates of the bishopric of Durham claimed by Sigrid in right of her mother, the daughter of Bishop Ealdhun of Durham (995–?1018).[39]

The four sons of Karli were connected with the house of Bamburgh neither by blood nor marriage, but by a long-standing feud, as much political as personal. It went back to 1016, when Karli's father, Thorbrand the hold, killed Earl Uhtred of Bamburgh. Thorbrand himself was killed by Uhtred's son Ealdred in or before 1024, and Ealdred in turn fell victim to Karli Thorbrandson, who in 1038 invited him to his hall in the forest of Risewood (Yorks. ER) and murdered him in an ambush.[40] There the matter rested for some time. Karli himself was probably dead by 1069, when his four sons appear among the rebel leaders. Orderic does not give their names, but two of the younger brothers were called Cnut and Sumarlithr and the eldest had a hall at Settrington (Yorks. NR).[41] He is presumably the Thorbrand whose land at Settrington and elsewhere, 63 carucates in all, passed to Berengar de Tosny. The fourth brother was perhaps Berengar's only other named predecessor, Gamall, who held another 61 carucates, since one manor, 8 carucates at Duggleby, was held jointly by Thorbrand and Gamall.[42] Thorbrand's father Karli and his brothers Cnut and Sumarlithr held, at the least, another

---

[35] *Vita Edwardi*, pp. 35–6.

[36] *FlW*, 1065.

[37] HR, 1072; *De primo adventu Saxonum, Symeonis . . . Collectanea*, p. 213. For Osulf's tenure of the earldom and its purchase by Gospatric son of Maldred, see Chapter I above.

[38] *De Obsessione Dunelmi, Symeonis . . . Opera* i, p. 220; Morris, *Marriage and murder in eleventh-century Northumbria*, p. 5.

[39] GDB, fols 302v, 310v–312v, 330. For the Durham lands, see previous note.

[40] The story of the feud is narrated in *De Obsessione Dunelmi* (see note 34 above) and discussed by William E. Kapelle, *The Norman Conquest of the north: the region and its transformation, 1000–1135* (London 1979), pp. 19–26; Morris, *Marriage and murder in eleventh-century Northumbria*, pp. 20–3.

[41] Cnut and Sumarlithr (the youngest) are named in *De Obsessione Dunelmi*.

[42] GDB, fols 314, 314v; *DB Yorkshire* ii, Appendix 3. It is probably this Thorbrand whose house in York is recorded in the 'Rights and Laws' of Archbishop Thomas (F. Liebermann, 'An English document of about 1080', *Yorkshire Archaeological Journal* 18 (1905), pp. 412–15); it may date from 1086 (D.M. Palliser, *Domesday York*, Borthwick Paper 78 (York, 1990), pp. 7–8, 25).

63½ carucates; the lands of Cnut lay in Holderness and included a manor at Rise.[43] The name 'Holderness' means 'the promontory of the *hold*' and it is perhaps permissible to speculate that lands there had once belonged to Cnut's grand-father, Thorbrand the hold.[44]

The presence of both Gospatric and the sons of Karli in the same host is an indication of the scale of the northern revolt.[45] Their feud, though dormant, was capable of being revived and in fact was in 1074. Some fairly powerful motive was required for entrenched enmities to be abandoned. Presumably the Norman presence in the north was the key. The castle at York may have been a source of grievance, if the reaction to the construction of a castle at Hereford in 1051 was typical; it was claimed that its castellans 'inflicted every possible insult and injury on the king's men living in those parts'.[46] A writ of 1069 addressed to 'all the thegns, French and English, of Yorkshire' shows that the Norman settlement of the north had begun.[47] William de Percy and Gilbert de Ghent had been established in Yorkshire by 1069 at the latest and it may be significant that the latter's only manor in the shire was Hunmanby, once the possession of Karli Thorbrandson.[48] William Malet held three estates in Holderness which had belonged to Cnut Karlison, and in 1086 the jurors of Holderness testified concerning these and other lands that 'they had not seen the king's writ or seal for them'.[49] This suggestion of illegality on Malet's part does not stand alone. The jurors of Ainsty Wapentake testified concerning land in Scagglethorpe and Poppleton that 'they saw William Malet in possession . . . but they do not know in what manner he held it'.[50] The community of York Minster later believed that Malet had seized the goods, if not the land, of the church.[51] If William Malet's

---

[43] Sumarlithr's name appears only once in the Yorkshire folios, in the entry for Crambe (*GDB*, fol. 300v); there are other references in Devon, Hunts. and Suffolk (*GDB*, fols 117v, 206v, 208, *LDB*, fol. 300v) but the references most likely to apply to Karli's son are those in Lincs. (*GDB*, fols 340v, 341v, 351v, 356v, 371, 375). Sumarlithr's name is uncommon; it means 'Midsummer', cf. Vetrlithr, 'Midwinter'. For Karli's manor of Hunmanby, see note 48 below, and for Cnut, see next note.

[44] GDB, fol. 374. For the name Holderness, see A.H. Smith, *The place-names of the East Riding of Yorkshire*, EPNS (Cambridge, 1937), p. 15. The term *hold* is of Scandinavian origin and indicates a member of the upper aristocracy in northern England (*EHD* i, p. 433, no. 191 note 9)

[45] Kapelle, *The Norman Conquest of the north*, pp. 112–13.

[46] AS Chron, 'E', 1051.

[47] Regesta i, no. 31; GDB, fols 373v, 374.

[48] GDB, fols 321v, 374 (Bolton Percy); 326 (Hunmanby); *DB Yorkshire* ii, Appendix 3; VCH Yorks. ii, p. 175.

[49] GDB, fols 374, 374v. William Malet died at Ely in 1071 and his tenure must date from before this.

[50] GDB, fol. 374.

[51] See the *Anonymous Chronicle of the Church of York, Historians of the Church of York*, ed. J. Raine, Rolls Series (London, 1879), ii, pp. 340ff; van Caeneghem i, pp. 1–2; *Regesta* i, no. 33 (dated 1066 x 9); Hugh Thomas, 'An alleged confrontation between Bishop Ealdred and William the Conqueror', *The Anglo-Norman Anonymous* 8 no. 2 (May 1990), pp. 2–3.

remit included collection of the geld levied in 1068, his actions may well have aroused hostility. William of Malmesbury mentions a quarrel between Archbishop Ealdred and the king over an 'unsupportable tax' levied on the diocese, presumably in 1068.[52]

The root cause of Northumbrian dissatisfaction was the unwillingness of the northerners, both the Anglo-Danes of York and the English of Bamburgh, to accept direct rule from the south. The legal particularism of the Danelaw (York and the 'Five Boroughs') had been recognized by King Edgar, and was jealously guarded. The rebellion of 1065 was in part occasioned by Earl Tostig's attempts to introduce West Saxon customs (especially in matters of taxation) and it was only ended by King Edward's promise to renew 'the laws of King Cnut'. As for the lords of Bamburgh (north of the Tyne) they had been as likely to acknowledge the authority of Scottish kings as that of the West Saxons.[53] The men of the north slaughtered Norman knights in 1069 in the same spirit in which they had massacred Earl Tostig's housecarls in 1065. In only one respect did they go further. In 1065 they chose themselves a new earl of Northumbria; in 1069 they elected a rival king.

This was an eventuality the West Saxon kings had long feared, ever since the days of the Danish kingdom of York, when the archbishop of the northern province could support a Scandinavian ruler against the king in Winchester. In 1013 Uhtred of Bamburgh, earl of Northumbria, and the northern magnates had been the first to acknowledge Swein Forkbeard of Denmark as king of the English.[54] Now they had an ætheling of the West Saxon line, whom in 1066 Archbishop Ealdred of York had been willing to consecrate after the death of Harold II; though if Edgar hoped that Ealdred would crown him in 1069 he was disappointed, for the archbishop staunchly supported King William.[55] Nevertheless the threat which Edgar posed to the Conqueror was real; indeed his rights were still being articulated by twelfth century writers.[56] King William's

---

[52] GP, p. 252; Kapelle, The Norman Conquest of the north, pp. 107–11; see also the article of Thomas cited in the previous note.

[53] AS Chron, 'D', 'E', 1065; IV Edgar 2i, 12, 15; II Cnut 15, 48, 62 and esp 71, where 'the Danes' are distinguished from the West Saxons, Mercians and East Anglians; see also note 96 below. For the relations of the lords of Bamburgh, see A.P. Smyth, Warlords and Holy Men: Scotland AD 80–1000 (London, 1984), p. 237; Skene, Celtic Scotland i, p. 419.

[54] AS Chron, 'D', 947, 948; 'C', 'D', 'E', 1013. The danger was still remembered in the twelfth century, when Hugh the Chantor attributed Lanfranc's determination to enforce the primacy of Canterbury over York to the fear that 'some one of the Danes, Norwegians or Scots, who used to sail up to York in their attacks on the realm, might be made king by the archbishop of York and the fickle and treacherous Yorkshiremen' (Hugh the Chantor, p. 3).

[55] AS Chron, 'D', 1066. For Ealdred's stance in 1069 see note 87 below.

[56] OV ii, pp. 276–7, and see Henry of Huntingdon's account of William's death in 1087 when 'there was now no prince of the ancient royal race living in England', Edgar having left for Scotland in 1086 (HH, p. 208). See also the Anglo-Saxon Chronicle's description of Queen Edith/Matilda as 'of the rightful kingly line' (AS Chron, 1100) and William

appreciation of the danger is shown by the crown-wearing in York at Christmas 1069 after the revolt was crushed; there was to be no doubt who was the true king of the English.[57]

The murder of Robert de Commines was the first act in the English revolt. Soon afterwards 'the ætheling Edgar came to York with all the Northumbrians and the citizens made peace with him'. Robert fitzRichard and his men were caught away from their castle and slaughtered, and the remaining Normans, under Malet's command, shut themselves up in the castle and sent to the king for aid. William returned from Normandy and moved north with a speed rivalling that of Harold's march to York in 1066.[58] Like Harold before him he 'came upon them by surprise from the south with an overwhelming army, and routed them, and killed those who could not escape, which was many hundreds of men'.[59] The king remained a week in the city and built the second castle at York, on the Old Baile site.[60] Gilbert de Ghent was its castellan. An expedition of Flemish troops was sent against Durham, but was foiled by the intervention of St Cuthbert who enveloped the invaders in a black mist.[61]

The king returned to Winchester, leaving William fitzOsbern to mop up; by Easter (12 April) the earl joined the king for the festival.[62] Despite his apparent success, King William took the precaution of sending his queen back to Normandy.[63] He had reason to be wary for the leaders of the revolt were still at large. William of Jumièges says that they escaped by way of the Humber, presumably by ship, and the ætheling at least returned to Scotland.[64] During the summer of 1069 fresh recruits joined the cause. The most eminent was Earl Waltheof, son of Earl Siward by his second wife, Earl Ealdred's daughter, and thus cousin to Earl Gospatric.[65] Waltheof had twice been passed over as earl of Northumbria, once in 1055, in favour of Tostig Godwineson, and once in 1065, in favour of Morcar. In 1065 he had been compensated with an earldom which included Northamptonshire and Huntingdonshire and perhaps the shires of Cambridge and Bedford as well.[66] He had evidently been confirmed in this office by the Conqueror and

of Malmesbury (GR ii, pp. 495–6). Hugh the Chantor's reference to the 'Scots' whom the archbishop of York might crown (see note 54 above) may relate to the descent of the Scots kings from the West Saxon royal house (Walter Daniel's Life of Ailred, abbot of Rievaulx, ed. F.M. Powicke (London, 1950, repr. 1963), p. xlii).
[57] See note 96 below.
[58] For William's march, see Allen Brown, The Normans and the Norman conquest, p. 167.
[59] AS Chron, 'D', 1068; OV ii, pp. 222–3.
[60] Allen Brown, The Normans and the Norman Conquest, p. 168, note 265.
[61] HDE, chap. 50. Gaimar (Lestorie des Engles i, pp. 229–30, lines 5423–5430) omits the miracle. St Cuthbert performed a similar feat on 30 April 1942, when Durham was threatened by the Luftwaffe (Edwin Webb and John Duncan, Blitz over Britain (Tunbridge Wells, 1990), p. 163).
[62] Regesta i, no. 26 (dated Easter 1069) is attested by fitzOsbern.
[63] OV ii, pp. 222–3.
[64] WmJ, chap. 19; AS Chron, 'D', 'E', 1068.
[65] AS Chron, 'D', 'E', 1069; OV ii, pp. 226–7.
[66] Stenton, ASE, p. 599; Barlow, Edward the Confessor, p. 194, note 3. It was the northern

it is a mystery why he joined the revolt in 1069. Possibly he felt his authority threatened by the castles at Huntingdon and Cambridge built in the previous year.

Another new face was that of Siward Barn.[67] He held a single manor in Yorkshire but most of his land lay in Nottinghamshire and Derbyshire (36 carucates) and Warwickshire (31½ hides).[68] He is listed among those lords with sake and soke in Nottinghamshire and in Lincolnshire and some of the lesser thegns of the north-east may have been his dependants.[69] It has been claimed that Siward Barn was yet another member of the house of Bamburgh; he has been identified with Siward son of Æthelgar, great-nephew of the Confessor, supposed to descend from Uhtred of Bamburgh and Æthelred II's daughter Ælfgifu.[70] Siward Barn cannot, however, be the same man as Siward son of Æthelgar, for the latter was holding land in Shropshire in 1086, when Siward Barn was either in prison in Normandy (according to John of Worcester) or leading the English emigrants in Byzantium.[71] Whoever Siward Barn was and whatever his eventual fate, he had been a rich and powerful thegn, with lands assessed at over 109 hides in seven shires.[72]

The defection of Waltheof may have drawn lesser men from the east midlands and East Anglia in his wake. Skalpi, who died 'at York in outlawry', held a small estate in Essex, Norfolk and Suffolk of just over seven hides.[73] He was no great lord but a median thegn, a housecarl of Earl Harold, and such men are unlikely to be noticed in contemporary chronicles, yet they must have formed the rank and file in the English revolt.[74] That an East Anglian contingent was involved

section of the earldom of the east midlands, the southern part of which was held by Earl Leofwine, see Williams, 'The king's nephew: the family and career of Ralph, earl of Hereford', pp. 338–40.

[67] OV ii, pp. 227–8; HR, 1070.

[68] GDB, fols 242; 274, 275, 275v, 291v; 326. For the most recent discussion of Siward Barn's lands, most of which passed to Henry de Ferrers, see C.R. Hart, 'Hereward "the Wake" and his companions', Hart, The Danelaw (London, 1992), pp. 640–4.

[69] GDB, fols 280v, 337. Amcotts (Lincs.) belonged to Siward Barn, but was sokeland of Crowle, whose pre-Conquest tenant is named Alwine; he may have been holding under Siward.

[70] Freeman iv, pp. 21, 428; DB Yorkshire ii, Appendix 3 (Sigvarthr).

[71] FlW, 1087. For Earl 'Sigurd' and the English in Byzantium, see John Godfrey, 'The defeated Anglo-Saxons take service with the Byzantine Emperor', ANS 1 (1978), p. 69; Christine Fell, 'The Icelandic saga of Edward the Confessor: its version of the Anglo-Saxon emigration to Byzantium', ASE 3 (1973), p. 194. For Siward son of Æthelgar, who is more likely to have been a grandson of Eadric Streona than of Uhtred of Bamburgh, see Chapter IV below.

[72] The remainder of Siward Barn's land (see note 68 above) lay in Glos., Lincs. and Norfolk (GDB, fols 169, 353v, 369, 376v; LDB, fol. 223, cf. 128). He may have had land in Berks. (GDB, fol. 60v) and Essex (LDB, fol. 56v, Stebbing), but it is difficult to distinguish him from Siward of Maldon (see Chapter III below).

[73] LDB, fols 59, 67v, 68, 240, 262, 377, 420, 420v. The date of his death is not recorded but the years 1069–70 seem the likeliest. See also next note.

[74] For Skalpi see Williams. 'Land and power in the eleventh century', pp. 178–80.

in the York rising is suggested by some of the exiles harboured by Swein of Denmark. These included Ælfwold, abbot of St Benet's, Holme, whom King Harold had charged to defend the east coast in 1066, and at least two of his men, Eadric the steersman and Ringulf of Oby; and Æthelsige, abbot of St Augustine's, Canterbury, who had been administering the Fenland abbey of Ramsey. The Lincolnshire thegn Hereward 'the Wake', who had strong Fenland connections, may also have taken part in the 1069 rising.[75]

Whether the northerners were also in touch with the west of England is doubtful. The raid on Devon by the sons of King Harold in the summer of 1069 has been seen as a botched attempt to liaise with the northern revolt.[76] It is more likely to have been coincidental. The sons of Harold sailed (as before) from Ireland and landed in Devon, in the mouth of the Tavy, on the south coast.[77] The nine manors in Stanborough Hundred (south Devon) said by Exon Domesday to have been devastated by the Irish were probably damaged at this time.[78] Their raid met with little support and was driven off by Count Brian and William Gualdi.[79]

The sons of Harold were long gone when the Danes arrived. Their role in the English revolt is stressed in all accounts but their objectives are ambiguous. The fullest account of King Swein Estrithson's motives is given by Orderic Vitalis, who presents him as 'moved by the death and disaster which had overtaken *his men* (my italics) in Harold's war'.[80] This raises some unanswerable questions. Who were these 'men' of Swein? A Danish contingent fighting for Harold Godwineson at Hastings?[81] Or does Orderic mean to imply that the Anglo-

---

[75] For Ælfwold and his men, see Stenton, 'St Benet of Holme and the Norman Conquest', pp. 227, 263; for Æthelsige, see HRH, pp. 35–6, 62 and GDB, fols 62v, 208; for Hereward, see Chapter III below.

[76] Freeman iv, pp. 184, 224–7. It is unlikely that Swein was in alliance with the sons of Harold; by the 1060s, the whole kindred was being blamed for the murder, in 1049, of Swein's brother Beorn, earl of the east midlands, though in fact it was the responsibility of Earl Swein Godwineson alone (Adam of Bremen, *History of the archbishops of Hamburg-Bremen*, ed. F.J. Tschan (New York, 1959), pp. 124–5; Eric Christiansen, *Saxo Grammaticus, Books X–XVI*, BAR International series 84 (Oxford, 1980), i, p. 210, note 163; AS Chron, 1049). Swein was, however, harbouring his aunt Gytha and her namesake, Harold's daughter, whom he gave in marriage to Vladimir Monomakh, prince of Smolensk and later of Kiev (Christiansen, *Saxo Grammaticus* i, pp. 58, 228, note 20).

[77] The *Anglo-Saxon Chronicle* places the raid in the Taw estuary, on the north coast, but the correct location is given by John of Worcester (AS Chron, 1069; FlW, 1069). See also WmJ, chap. 20.

[78] Exon, fol. 322. The nine manors belonged to Judhael of Totnes (GDB, fol. 109) who was perhaps castellan of Totnes (Williams, 'Judhael of Totnes', pp. 274–5) and the sons of Harold may have been attempting to immobilize an important local official.

[79] OV ii, pp. 224–5. William *Gualdi* may be William de Vauville, who held some official position in Devon early in the Conqueror's reign (GDB, fols 100v, 102v and see Chapter I, p. 21).

[80] OV ii, pp. 226–7.

[81] A Danish contingent at Hastings is mentioned by William of Poitiers (WmP, pp. 186–7).

Danish magnates of York were in some sense under Swein's protection? Whatever he meant there is the additional problem of how far his interpretation of events which took place before he was born relates to the actual situation at the time. His second explanation of Swein's intervention carries more weight (or at least is easier to believe): 'his desire for the kingdom, to which, as a nephew of King Edward (sic) and son of Harthacnut (sic) he had a claim of inheritance'. Swein, of course, was neither the Confessor's nephew nor Harthacnut's son. He was the son of Ulf by Estrith, Cnut's sister, and thus cousin to Harthacnut, and to the Confessor's wife, Edith. It was, however, as Harthacnut's successor that he derived any claim he had to the English kingship. It was just about the time of the English revolt that Swein told Adam of Bremen that Edward the Confessor, when he succeeded to the English kingdom on Harthacnut's death, had promised that Swein should be his legitimate heir.[82] Needless to say this is highly unlikely, and it is difficult to decide how seriously Swein took the claim, but his son, Cnut the Holy, seems to have believed in it, and subsequent Danish kings revived it from time to time until 1193, when Cnut VI made over his rights in the English crown to Philip Augustus.[83] Despite this, it is far from clear that the fleet which was sent to the Humber in 1069 had come to claim the kingship for Cnut the Great's successor, nor how such a claim would sit with the election by the northerners of Edgar ætheling.

The motives of the Danes may be obscure but their actions are not. King Swein was taking no chances; he did not lead his fleet in person, but appointed his brother Asbjorn, two of his (many) sons, Harold and Cnut, and Christian, bishop of Aarhus, as commanders.[84] They followed the old Viking route, striking first at Dover and Sandwich, and then moving north along the east coast, harrying Ipswich and Norwich, until they reached the Humber. Their aim was to damage the main bases of the English shipfyrd and it succeeded; King William had no ships with him when he attacked Northumbria in the autumn of 1069.[85] They

[82] Adam of Bremen, ed. Tschan, p. 108; Christiansen, Saxo Grammaticus i, p. 210, note 163 (cf. p. 208, note 157). The alleged pact between Magnus of Norway (1035–47) and Harthacnut (1035–42), that whichever of them lived longest should inherit the whole empire of Cnut the Great, appears for the first time in the Roskilde Chronicle, written between 1139 and 1143 (Christiansen, loc. cit., p. 209, note 158).

[83] Christiansen, Saxo Grammaticus i, p. 229, note 20. The occasion was the ill-fated marriage of the French king to Ingibjorg of Denmark. Edward the Confessor seems to have been unsympathetic to Swein; Gunnhildr, Cnut's niece and Swein's cousin, was expelled from England in 1044, and Swein's requests for English aid against, successively, Magnus and Harold Hardrada, were refused, despite the support of Earl Godwine for his nephew (AS Chron, 1044, 1047, 1048; FlW, 1047) and despite the fact that Swein had done some kind of homage to Edward (Vita Edwardi, p. 11 and notes).

[84] AS Chron, 'D', 1069, 'E', 1069, 1070; FlW, 1969. The 'D' Chronicle and John of Worcester give the size of the Danish fleet as 240 ships; 'E' gives 300 ships.

[85] The route is given by Orderic (OV ii, pp. 226–7) and should be compared with those of Olafr Tryggvason (AS Chron, 991, 993) and Swein Forkbeard (AS Chron, 1013). The lack of an English fleet in 1069 should be compared with the attack on Ely in 1071 and the campaign in Scotland in 1072, both undertaken by land and sea.

arrived in the Humber 'between the two feasts of St Mary', the Assumption on 15 August and the Nativity on 8 September, and were met by the ætheling, the earls Gospatric and Waltheof, Mærle-Sveinn, Siward Barn, Arnkell and the sons of Karli 'with all the Northumbrians and all the people, riding and marching with an immense army, rejoicing exceedingly'.[86] The only dissenting voice was that of Ealdred, archbishop of York, who died on 11 September.[87]

King William was hunting in the Forest of Dean when news reached him of the approach of the Danes. He sent to York to warn his castellans, who replied that they could hold out for a year if need be. Their confidence was misplaced. On 19 September, the houses around the two castles were set on fire, lest the enemy should use their fabric to fill up the ditches to aid an assault. The flames spread, engulfing the whole city, including St Peter's minster. Two days later, on Monday 21 September, the combined host of English and Danes fell on the city. They stormed both castles, slaughtering the garrisons and preserving only the castellans, Gilbert de Ghent and William Malet, with his family, as captives. Waltheof's part in the slaughter was celebrated by his Icelandic skald, Thorkell Skallason, and remembered much later by William of Malmesbury: 'he singly killed many of the Normans in the battle of York, cutting off their heads one by one as they entered the gate'.[88]

The advent of the Danes set off a series of disturbances in the south and west. Exeter was attacked by men from Devon and Cornwall, and the men of Dorset and Somerset besieged Robert of Mortain's new castle at Montacute. There are no grounds for supposing that this was part of a nation-wide uprising for it is clear that most of the south-west remained loyal to William. The siege of Montacute was raised by Geoffrey de Mowbray, bishop of Coutances, who was probably port-reeve of Bristol, and a force of 'the men of Winchester, London and Salisbury'; perhaps the castle-garrisons of these cities. Exeter was defended by its own citizens as well as the castle-garrison, who drove the attackers into the arms of the Norman force sent to relieve them; this was commanded by William fitzOsbern and Brian of Brittany.[89] More serious was the attack on Shrewsbury, launched by Eadric the Wild and the men of Chester, in alliance (once more) with Bleddyn of Gwynedd. They succeeded in burning down the town, but could not take the castle and moved on to Stafford.[90]

The king's first objective was to prevent the Danes from establishing a secure

---

[86] AS Chron, 'D', 1069; OV iii, 226–9. Orderic also names Elnocinus, possibly Dunstan son of Æthelnoth, whom John of Worcester describes as one of the leaders of the 1065 revolt (FIW, 1065).
[87] AS Chron, 'D', 1059; FIW, 1069.
[88] AS Chron, 'E', 1069; FIW, 1069; HR, 1069; OV ii, pp. 226–7. For Waltheof's exploits, see GR ii, p. 311 and for Thorkell Skallason's verses, see Alistair Campbell, *Skaldic verse and Anglo-Saxon history*, The Dorothea Coke Memorial Lecture (London 1970), p. 16.
[89] OV ii, pp. 228–9.
[90] The castle of Stafford had been destroyed by 1086 (GDB, fol. 248v). Eadric's participation is only in Orderic (see previous note); John of Worcester mentions neither the Mercian rising, nor the participation of Eadric the Wild, but does record Eadric's

base on the southern bank of the Humber, where they were sheltering in the Isle of Axholme.[91] The garrison of Lincoln castle had already repelled a foraging raid led by the aetheling and a larger band was destroyed by the king's army. William then left Robert of Mortain and his namesake, the count of Eu 'to prevent the Danes from breaking out', while he himself moved against the Mercians, who with their Welsh allies had advanced to Stafford. While the king was repulsing this force, the Danes, in Orderic's words, 'came out of the marshes to share the feasts of the country folk which are colloquially known as "feorms" '.[92] It is difficult to see Orderic's meaning; the *feorm* was not a feast but a rent in kind, often commuted for money, and the word suggests a foraging-expedition rather than a dinner-party. Perhaps all that Orderic means is that the Danes received aid and provisions from the people of Lindsey. They were in any case driven off by the counts of Mortain and Eu, who, lacking a fleet, could not prevent the Danes retreating across the Humber. Meanwhile the king, having repulsed the Mercians from Stafford, moved to Nottingham. Thence he marched towards York but was held up for three weeks at the River Aire, until a ford was found by Lisois de Moutiers.[93] When he reached York the Danes had withdrawn their fleet into the Humber, where, as the Chronicle says 'he could not get at them', because he had no ships.[94] William resorted to bribery (the word 'Danegeld' is avoided), offering Earl Asbjorn money and a free hand to pillage in return for a promise to depart in the following spring. The Danes 'took a large amount of treasure on board, and kept the chief men (the captives from York) in bonds, and lay between the Ouse and the Trent all that winter'.[95]

York itself lay open to the king, for the English had withdrawn at his approach. William ordered the repair of the two castles and set out to deal with the rebels by the normal methods of medieval warfare, the destruction of the countryside where his enemies might find food and shelter. As Christmas approached, he returned to York and, having had all his insignia and plate fetched from Winchester, wore his crown in the ceremony customary at great feasts. Orderic specifically states that the king interrupted his campaign for this demonstration of regality, whose symbolic importance in the context of Edgar ætheling's election has already been discussed. No-one was to have any doubt who was king of the English.[96] With Christmas past he set out again, dislodging the rebel leaders

reconciliation with the king in 1070 and his presence in the royal host that campaigned in Scotland in 1072 (*FIW*, 1070, 1072, and see Chapter III below).

[91] OV ii, pp. 228–9; Stenton, *ASE*, p. 603.
[92] OV ii, pp. 230–1.
[93] OV ii, pp. 228–31. Lisois was dead by the time of Domesday but had held lands in Cambridgeshire, Bedfordshire, Norfolk, Suffolk and Essex which later passed to Eudo *dapifer* (*GDB*, fols 197v, 212v; *LDB*, fols 49v, 239v, 240, 279v, 403).
[94] AS *Chron*, 'D', 1069.
[95] AS *Chron*, 'E', 1069. William's bribery of Asbjorn is recorded by John of Worcester (*FIW*, 1069).
[96] OV ii, pp. 232–3 see pp. 32–33 above. According to the twelfth-century *Leges Edwardi Confessoris*, it was in 1069–70 (the fourth year of his reign) that William confirmed the

from their refuge in Holderness.[97] He pursued them overland as far as the Tees, where Waltheof submitted in person and Gospatric by proxy; both (surprisingly) were pardoned and restored to their earldoms. The ætheling and his family, with Mærle-Sveinn and Siward Barn, moved on to Wearmouth, where they remained until the summer of 1070. Though William's men harried as far as the Tyne and burnt down the church of Jarrow, they somehow missed the ætheling's party.[98] Gospatric's earldom beyond the Tyne was left, for the moment, undisturbed.

Bishop Æthelwine and the Durham community had already fled, 'fearing lest the king's sword should include equally the innocent and the guilty in indiscriminate slaughter'. Carrying with them the body of St Cuthbert and all the portable treasure of their church, they sought safety in their ancient home at Lindisfarne.[99] Æthelwine's flight should not be taken to imply complicity in the revolt. Despite much that has been asserted to the contrary, there is little indication of any community of interest between the church of Durham and the lords of Bamburgh; indeed the reverse is more likely. Earl Tostig, the enemy of the Bamburgh earls, was a benefactor of Durham, and it may be significant that his gift, the great crucifix, was deliberately slighted in Gospatric's raid on Durham. In 1069 Æthelwine had warned Robert de Commines of impending attack, and had sheltered the doomed earl in his own house, which was burnt by the rebels. Caught between two centres of rebellion, York and Bamburgh, Æthelwine was in an invidious position, mistrusted both by the king, and by the insurgent leaders.[100]

Towards the end of January 1070, the king, having garrisoned the York castles, set out to quell the Mercians. In the snows of February he led his armies across the Pennines, a fearful journey which provoked a near-mutiny among his non-Norman troops, who complained that 'they could not obey a lord . . . who commanded them to do the impossible'. The Normans themselves did not, of course, succumb to such timidity.[101] The king's exploit achieved its purpose, for his unexpected arrival before Chester, whither the Mercian insurgents had retired, brought the western rising to an end without a blow struck. William built

laws of King Edward (Liebermann, i, p. 627 and see Chapter VII below); if this is a true tradition it recalls King Edward's confirmation of Cnut's laws after the rebellion of 1065 (see note 53 above).

[97]   OV ii, pp. 232–3. An alternative site for the refuge is Tod Point, in the Tees, but see the arguments for Holderness in Kapelle, *The Norman Conquest of the north*, pp. 118, 263 note 87.

[98]   HR, 1069, 1070. Among the ætheling's party was Alwine son of Northmann, perhaps the Yorkshire thegn whose lands passed to Gilbert Tison and whose son Uhtred attested Gilbert's grant to Selby Abbey (GDB, fol. 326v, DB Yorkshire ii, Appendix 3 (Alwine) and note 109 below).

[99]   HDE, chap. 50; HR, 1079.

[100] William Aird, 'St Cuthbert, the Scots and the Normans', ANS 16 (1994), pp. 1–20, especially pp. 10–13, and see Chapter III below. Copsi, another victim of the Bamburgh earls, was also a benefactor of Durham (HDE, chap. 49; Aird, loc. cit., p. 9).

[101] OV ii, pp. 234–5.

castles at Chester and at Stafford, and visited on the shires of northern Mercia the same retribution he had inflicted on Yorkshire and the lands of Durham. Refugees fled as far south as Evesham, in Worcestershire, where they were given aid by Abbot Æthelwig, of whom (it was said) even the French were afraid.[102]

The Harrying of the North is perhaps the best-known incident of William I's reign after the battle of Hastings itself. It received almost universal condemnation, at the time and later, but its actual effects are difficult to gauge. Obviously (one would suppose) the destruction of the native aristocracy of the north paved the way for the Norman settlement, and it seems to have been in the aftermath of the revolt that compact lordships were created for the defence of York and conferred upon William de Percy and Hugh fitzBaldric.[103] Yet few of the leaders of the revolt who survived the fighting were immediately dispossessed. It is true that Mærle-Sveinn seems never to have returned from Scotland and Siward Barn's later career (for which see below, Chapter III) suggests that he lost his lands. Yet Edgar ætheling, who submitted in 1074, was received at William's court and granted unspecified honours, which he eventually found insufficient.[104] Waltheof and Gospatric retained their earldoms, though in neither case for long. The sons of Karli were still holding at least some of their land in 1074 and it was not the Normans, but their traditional foe, Earl Waltheof, who caused their downfall.[105] Eadric the Wild made his peace with the Conqueror and was among the host that invaded Scotland in 1072 and he and his family may have retained at least some of their Shropshire estates.[106] Arnkell was indeed exiled, but his son Gospatric, the hostage of 1068, was still holding much of his own and his father's land in 1086, both as a tenant-in-chief and of Count Alan.[107] Indeed he may have been holding of other lords as well, for the list of mesne-tenants in Domesday is far from comprehensive and the number of English families holding their own or other Englishmen's lands in 1086 and on into the twelfth century has been under-estimated.[108] Alwine son of Northmann fled to Scotland with

---

[102] Darlington, 'Aethelwig, abbot of Evesham', pp. 177–98. For Aethelwig's reputation, see Hemming's Cartulary i, p. 270.

[103] I am very grateful to Dr Paul Dalton for help and advice on the chronology of the Norman settlement of the north, which is illuminated by his book, Conquest, Anarchy and Lordship, 1066–1154 (Cambridge, 1994).

[104] AS Chron, 1075; Hooper, 'Edgar ætheling', p. 205; see also Chapter V, p. 99 below.

[105] See below, Chapter III, p. 59.

[106] For Eadric the Wild, see Chapter IV below.

[107] GDB, fols 330, 309v–313; his descendants retained much of his land and his grandson Uhtred was a benefactor of Whitby Priory (VCH Yorks. ii, pp. 183–5; DB Yorkshire ii, Appendix 3). Another possibility is that Gospatric's heirs (like Bernard the scribe, see Chapter V below) rebuilt their ancestor's estate.

[108] D.S.H. Michelmore, 'Township and tenure', West Yorkshire: an archaeological study to AD 1500, ed. M.L. Faull and S.A Moorhouse (Wakefield, 1981), i, pp. 247, 251–60. Gospatric's land at Bingley was held by Erneis de Burun in 1086, but is later found in the possession of his grandson, Simon de Mohaut (son of Gospatric son of Gospatric son of Arnkell) which suggests that Gospatric son of Arnkell may have been holding in 1086 as Erneis de Burun's tenant.

the ætheling and his lands are found in the hands of Gilbert Tison, but when Gilbert granted lands which Alwine had once held to Selby Abbey, his charter was attested by Uhtred son of Alwine, and members of the same family were still holding some of Alwine's land of the Tison fee at the end of the twelfth century.[109] As Stenton observed long ago, 'most of the great families of which the English descent is beyond question . . . belong to Northumbria or to the northern parts of Mercia which the Conqueror laid waste'.[110] Some Yorkshire thegns even profited from the opportunities offered by the re-organization of lands and fiefs after 1070.[111]

As for the devastation of Yorkshire and the lands of Durham, its long-term effects are hard to assess. The entries for 'waste' in the Yorkshire folios of Domesday Book have been taken as evidence of lasting destruction but it is far from clear that this interpretation is correct. 'Waste' can denote simply land for which information is lacking, and the explanation for the missing data may have more to do with the compilation of the Yorkshire folios than the actions of King William's army.[112] It is interesting to compare the treatment of the Harrying of the North by the various commentators, none of whom are strictly contemporary. The *Anglo-Saxon Chronicle*, both versions of which were originally written in the late eleventh century, is fairly restrained. The king 'went into the shire (of York) and ravaged it completely ('E'); he 'utterly ravaged and laid waste that shire' ('D'). This is stronger language than that used in 1041 when Harthacnut 'had all Worcestershire ravaged', or in 986 when Æthelred II 'laid waste the diocese of Rochester', but is much milder than the description of the ravages of the Danish army in 1006:

Then so great a terror of the Danish army arose that no-one could think or conceive how to drive them from the country, or to defend this country from them, for they had cruelly left their mark on every shire of Wessex with their burning and their harrying.

John of Worcester, writing in the second decade of the twelfth century, embroi-

109 HR, 1070; EYC xii, no. 15, pp. 47–50. Northmann son of Uhtred and his son Adam were knight-tenants of the Percy fee (EYC xi, pp. 85, 243–6). One Yorkshireman who may have been displaced in the aftermath of the revolt was Ligulf, uncle by marriage of Earl Waltheof (see Chapter III below) but his son Morcar was still a lawman of York in the early twelfth century (see Chapter VII below).
110 F.M. Stenton, 'English families and the Norman Conquest', *Preparatory to Anglo-Saxon England*, ed. D.M. Stenton (Oxford, 1970), p. 333, citing Greystoke, Stanley, Audley, Neville of Raby, FitzWilliam of Sprotborough, FitzWilliam of Hinderskelfe.
111 Hugh Thomas, 'A Yorkshire thegn and his descendants after the Conquest', *Medieval Prosopography* 8 (1987), pp. 1–22; S.A. Moorhouse, 'Castles and administrative centres', *West Yorkshire: an archaeological survey to AD 1500*, ed. Faull and Moorhouse, iii, p. 736.
112 D.M. Palliser, 'Domesday Book and the "Harrying of the North"', *Northern History* 29 (1993), pp. 1–23; David Roffe, 'Domesday Book and northern society: a reassessment', *EHR* 105 (1990), pp. 310–36, esp. 323. See also note 13 above.

ders the Chronicle account. He describes how the king, 'hastening with an angry heart into Northumbria, ceased not, during the whole winter, to lay waste the land, to murder the inhabitants and to inflict numerous injuries'.[113] A few years later, Hugh the Chantor claims that the city of York 'and the whole district round it' was 'destroyed by the French with the sword, famine and flames' and goes on to describe how Archbishop Thomas I found only three of the seven canons remaining in a 'burnt city and a ruined church'.[114] The author of the *Historia Regum*, presumably a northerner, who used John's Chronicle, goes far beyond his exemplar, recording that so many died that there was no-one left to bury them; he is also responsible for the allegation that 'there was no village inhabited between York and Durham' and the land remained uncultivated for nine years.[115] It is instructive, however, to compare the *Historia Regum* with Simeon's *Historia Dunelmensis ecclesiae*, written in the first decade of the twelfth century. In the *Historia Regum*, those fleeing the king's army take refuge in the church of Durham, where they are found by Bishop Æthelwine on his return from Lindisfarne during Lent (17 February to 28 March) 1070. In the earlier version, the bishop finds his church plundered and the great crucifix, the gift of Earl Tostig and his wife Judith, 'thrown down upon the ground and stripped of the ornaments with which it had been clothed'. It is not, however, the Normans, but Earl Gospatric who is accused of this outrage.[116] Simeon's fulminations against the 'bandits' who harrassed the community of Durham find an echo in the Evesham Chronicle, which attributes the harrying of northern Mercia, to the king's wish to extirpate the 'outlaws and thieves (*exules et latrones*)' who infested the woods in those parts.[117]

It is Orderic Vitalis, who also read John of Worcester's account, who voices the harshest and most specific criticism of the king's actions:

> My narrative has frequently had occasion to praise William but for this act which condemned the innocent and the guilty alike to die by slow starvation, I cannot commend him . . . I would rather lament the griefs and sufferings of the wretched people than make a vain attempt to flatter the perpetrators of such infamy.

Orderic's editor has said that in this passage 'it is certainly Orderic and not William of Poitiers (his source) who speaks' and his words should be given due

---

[113] *FlW*, 1069, 1070. John also records a famine in 1069–70 which compelled people to eat horses, dogs, cats and each other.

[114] Hugh the Chantor, pp. 1, 11; see however the remarks of Palliser, *Domesday York*, pp. 4–6.

[115] *HR*, 1069, 1070. The text of the *Historia Regum* as we have it dates from the later twelfth century (Peter Hunter Blair, 'Some observations on the *Historia Regum* attributed to Symeon of Durham', *Celt and Saxon*, ed. Nora K. Chadwick and others (Cambridge, 1964), pp. 77–118).

[116] *HR*, 1070; *HDE*, chaps 50, 51.

[117] *Chron Evesham*, p. 90. The passage occurs in the section based on the early *Vita* of Æthelwig (Darlington, 'Aethelwig, abbot of Evesham', pp. 177–98).

weight.[118] He was born in Shropshire in 1075 and spent the first ten years of his life there, while memories of the Harrying of the North, and of Mercia, were still fresh. Orderic may well have heard tales from those who suffered from it. Perhaps all one can say of the Harrying of the North is that, even by contemporary standards, it was unusually severe.

In the midst of all the carnage, a monk from Burgundy was innocently engaged in founding a religious house at Selby, which, lying on the River Ouse, was very much in the thick of things. Though the account of his adventures was only written down a century later, it is worth relating for the light it throws on what was remembered of this dreadful time.[119] Benedict, sacrist of Saint-German of Auxerre, was commanded by his patron in a vision to found a cell of the house at Selby, on the banks of the Ouse, not far from York. He duly travelled to England and, misled by the similarity of name, arrived at Salisbury. As he sought vainly for the river Ouse, he was befriended by a citizen of the town, Edward the Rich (dives) and a chaplain called Theobald. They explained to him that he was not, in fact, in Yorkshire but in Wiltshire, and put him on a merchant-ship plying between Lyme Regis and York. Thus he finally reached Selby and, in the fourth year of King William (Christmas 1069 to Christmas 1070), made himself a temporary dwelling beneath a great tree called Stricca's Oak. Here he was found by the sheriff of York, Hugh fitzBaldric, who was travelling along the Ouse by ship for safety, since the local inhabitants were at war with the French. Hugh took Benedict under his wing (clearly some-one had to) and persuaded the king to grant him land. Benedict soon collected the nucleus of a community, though he was troubled by the activities of a band of outlaws in the neighbouring wood, led by one Swein son of Sicga. By 1086, the abbot of Selby (presumably Benedict) held seven carucates at Sherburn-in-Elmet, Yorks., of the bishop of York and six carucates at Crowle, Lincs., of Geoffrey de la Guerche.[120]

A source such as this should not be pressed too far, but it may preserve something of the condition of Yorkshire in 1069. It correctly identifies the sheriff, Hugh fitzBaldric, who replaced William Malet after the latter's capture. Edward the Rich of Salisbury is clearly Edward of Salisbury, sheriff of Wiltshire, who not only attests Selby Abbey's spurious foundation charter (which is not remarkable) but also really did have some connection with the northern shires; he presided over a court at Lincoln late in the reign of Edward the Confessor.[121] The outlaw Swein son of Sicga is an interesting figure. William of Jumièges says that the defeated rebels took to raiding and amassing wealth by 'piratical theft' and the Historia Regum adds that the deserted villages 'became lurking-places for wild

[118] OV ii, pp. 232–3.
[119] The Coucher Book of Selby Abbey, ed. J.T. Fowler, Yorks. Arch. Soc. x (1891), pp. 3–16; Freeman iv, pp. 794–8; EYC i, pp. 359–63. For the date, see Antonia Gransden, Historical Writing in England from c. 550 to 1300 (London, 1974), p. 295.
[120] GDB, fols 302v, 369v.
[121] For Hugh fitzBaldric, see Green, English sheriffs to 1154, p. 89. For Edward of Salisbury, see below, Chapter V.

beasts and robbers and were a great dread to travellers'.[122] Benedict's problems with Swein son of Sicga recall the experiences of the Durham community who, as they fled to Lindisfarne, were harried by a bandit named Gillemichel, who operated north of the Tyne and 'inflicted many injuries upon the fugitives'. Gillemichel's fate was revealed to one of the clerks in a vision; he dreamt that he stood in the church at Durham and beheld two men, one dressed in episcopal robes and the other wearing red (the colour of martyrdom). It was scarcely necessary for them to introduce themselves as SS Cuthbert and Oswald. They showed the clerk 'a deep valley filled with the souls of men', including that of Gillemichel, impaled upon a hay-scythe.[123] Such stories suggest that the chief result of the Harrying of the North was an increase in the banditry to which the region had long been prone; Earl Osulf, it will be recalled, was killed in 1067 while 'rushing headlong against the spear of a robber'.[124]

After the revolt of 1069–70 there were no more general risings of the English nobles and William's campaign, however distasteful, was a success, though it did not dispose, either immediately or in the long run, of the Danes. The most important consequence of the English revolt was its effect on the king's attitude. If William had ever intended to create a genuine Anglo-Norman realm, like the Anglo-Danish synthesis achieved by Cnut before him, the revolt put paid to the idea. From this time onwards he took every opportunity to replace the English magnates, lay and ecclesiastical, with Normans and others on whom he felt he could rely. It is this wholesale replacement of Englishmen at the highest levels of society and government that gives the Norman Conquest its special character. The English revolt had, in a way, been too successful. Had the magnates not posed such a threat to William's power, it would not have been necessary to remove them and they might have survived to absorb William's Normans as their grandfathers had absorbed Cnut's Danes.

---

122 WmJ, chap. 19; HR, 1069.
123 HDE, chaps 50, 51.
124 HR, 1072 and see Chapter I above. See also Kapelle (The Norman Conquest of the North, pp. 127–33) on Northumbrian banditry, and (for the Mercian situation) note 117 above.

Chapter III

THE FALL OF THE EARLS

> He had earls in his fetters who acted against his
> will. He expelled bishops from their sees and
> abbots from their abbeys and put thegns in
> prison.
>
> *Anglo-Saxon Chronicle*, 'E', 1087

THE EPILOGUE TO the English revolt was played out at Ely. Though often
regarded as a side-show, the Fenland defiance had important consequences, not
least as the genesis of a celebrated legend which acted as a focus for English
sentiment into the twelfth century and beyond. It involved the ruin of many
English magnates, including Earl Morcar of Northumbria and Æthelwine, bishop
of Durham. When Ely fell in 1071, another step had been taken towards the
Normanization of England.

It was during the Lenten season of 1070 (Ash Wednesday fell on 17 February)
that King William, on the advice of William fitzOsbern, 'had all the monasteries
that were in England plundered' in order to seize 'the money which the richer
English had deposited in them'.[1] The monks of Abingdon claimed that the king's
officers carried off not only the property of laymen, but the church's treasures as
well.[2] Worse was to follow. At a synod held at Easter (4 April) at Winchester,
Archbishop Stigand was deposed. With him fell his brother Æthelmaer, bishop
of East Anglia, and several abbots, among whom should probably be numbered
Ecgfrith of St Albans.[3] A second meeting at Whitsun (23 May) deposed
Æthelric, bishop of Selsey. The other Æthelric, Bishop Æthelwine's brother and
predecessor as bishop of Durham, who was living in retirement at Peterborough,
was arrested and imprisoned at Westminster.[4] The vacant sees were filled by

---

[1] *AS Chron*, 1070; *FlW*, 1070.

[2] *Chron Abingdon* i, p. 486. Some-one at Worcester made a list of the church's treasures
redeemed from the king, 'apart from the geld on every hide which no-one but God can
reckon'; it is undated and A.J. Robertson connected it with the 6s geld of 1084
(Robertson, *Charters*, pp. 242–3, 493) but it could relate to the 'plunder' of 1070, for the
sums paid for each item are 'amazingly high'.

[3] *Liber Eliensis*, pp. 176–7; *HRH*, pp. 65–6. Leofwine, bishop of Lichfield, who (like
Æthelmaer) was a married man, surrendered his see and retired to Coventry Abbey; his
diocese was administered by Wulfstan of Worcester until the appointment of Peter in
1072 (Barlow, *The English Church, 1000–1066*, p. 218).

[4] *FlW*, 1070; *OV* ii, pp. 236–7; *Letters of Lanfranc*, pp. 34–5; *HRH*, pp. 65–6. Why

foreigners. Winchester (held by Stigand in plurality) went to Walkeline, a canon of Rouen, East Anglia to Herfast, and Selsey to (another) Stigand. All three were royal clerks, and Herfast was the king's chancellor. Canterbury was for the moment left vacant, but the archbishopric of York, empty since the death of Ealdred in 1069, was given to Thomas, a canon of Bayeux.[5]

This was not the first time that English churchmen had been replaced or even ousted by foreigners, but the scale was unprecedented.[6] Though canon law was invoked to justify them, the depositions were clearly political. John of Worcester complained that men 'whom neither the ecclesiastical councils nor the civil laws could convict of any open crime' were nevertheless deprived and imprisoned simply through the king's mistrust of their allegiance.[7] Æthelmaer of East Anglia was indeed a married man but so was Herfast, his successor, whose sons (and a niece called Heloise) were holding property in Norfolk in 1086.[8] Æthelric of Selsey, a Canterbury monk, had been consecrated by Stigand but so had Remigius of Dorchester-on-Thames, who had to seek papal forgiveness for this lapse.[9] Æthelric's deposition was in fact regarded as uncanonical, although he never regained his see.[10]

The timing of these depositions, immediately after the pacification of the north, must be significant. It has been suggested that men from East Anglia and the east midlands had participated in the English revolt, and it is possible that the king was about to take measures to secure the area. It was precisely in this region that Stigand's land and connections lay. His family probably came from Norwich, where his sister had held property, and the church of SS Simon and Jude in the same city had belonged to his brother Æthelmaer *de patrimonio*. Æthelmaer's wife had brought him the nearby manor of Blofield.[11] Stigand himself held extensive lands not only in East Anglia itself but also in Cambridgeshire,

Æthelric of Durham was arrested is unclear. He had resigned his see to his brother Æthelwine in 1056 and returned to Peterborough, where they had both been monks. It is possible that his imprisonment reflects the king's distrust of Bishop Æthelwine, though there is no indication that he had been involved in the English revolt. Æthelwine's flight to Scotland (for which see below) seems to have been the result of his brother's arrest, not the cause.

[5] Frank Barlow, *The English Church, 1066–1154* (London, 1979), p. 62.
[6] Godric of Winchcombe had been deposed and replaced by Galandus in 1067 and Beorhtric of Malmesbury had been transferred to Burton (see Chapter 1 above). Saewold, abbot of Bath, had resigned his office and gone to Saint-Vaast, Arras (HRH, p. 28).
[7] FlW, 1070; see also OV ii, pp. 270–1.
[8] LDB, fols 118v, 200 (DB Norfolk, nos. 69,10;81).
[9] Barlow, *The English Church, 1000–1066*, pp. 222, 303–4.
[10] *Letters of Lanfranc*, pp. 62–3.
[11] LDB, fols 116, 117v, 194v–195 (DB Norfolk, nos. 61,10;28). For the most recent survey of Stigand's estates, see Mary Frances Smith, 'Archbishop Stigand and the eye of the needle', ANS 16 (1994), pp. 199–219.

Bedfordshire and Huntingdonshire.[12] He was a patron of Ely and had deposited his personal treasure there in the spring of 1070.

Some royal action was certainly needed for the situation in the Fenland was deteriorating in the early months of 1070.[13] Despite the agreement which King William had made with Earl Asbjorn, the Danish fleet did not leave England in the spring of 1070. Instead it was reinforced by a second fleet, commanded by King Swein Estrithson himself. Though he was welcomed by the local people on his arrival, it must have been obvious that there was no fight left in the Northumbrians. The performance of the Danes in 1069 had itself been lacklustre and Swein's displeasure was soon to manifest itself in the outlawry of his brother Asbjorn for taking King William's bribes.[14] It was probably to save some face that the Danish force divided, one group remaining with Swein in the Humber and the other, under Asbjorn, Bishop Christian and (probably) Cnut moving into the Fens. Here they were welcomed by all the people, who 'expected that they were going to conquer all the country'.

Even before this, the king had had some reason to suspect the loyalties of the east midlands. The last pre-Conquest abbot of Peterborough, Leofric, had been the nephew of Earl Leofric of Mercia; he was with King Harold in the Hastings campaign, and when he died soon afterwards, his successor Brand sought confirmation of his election from Edgar ætheling. Thurstan, abbot of Ely, had been appointed by Harold II and was a friend of the disgraced archbishop, Stigand, whose personal treasure was in his safe-keeping. He was also harbouring Ecgfrith, the deposed abbot of St Albans.[15] One can well believe that Thurstan feared he was about to be deposed in favour of a Norman.[16]

It is against this background that the appointment of Turold as abbot of Peterborough should be seen. He was the Fécamp monk appointed to Malmesbury in 1067, but he had fallen out with his community. William of Malmesbury preserves the alleged remark of King William that, since Turold behaved more like a knight than an abbot, he might as well go where there was someone to fight, and Hugh Candidus claimed that when the monks of Ramsey attempted to retain some of Peterborough's relics of St Oswald, Turold threatened to burn down their church unless they were returned.[17] The origins of his reputation for

---

[12] Barlow suggests that 'if they [Stigand's kindred] came from Norse trading stock, their business acumen is understandable' (*The English Church 1000–1066*, pp. 76–81).

[13] *AS Chron*, 'D', 'E', 1070. The details in 'E' come from the *Peterborough Chronicle*, copied, with additions, at Peterborough in 1121 from an earlier version of the Chronicle (Cecily Clark, *The Peterborough Chronicle, 1070–1154* (Oxford 1955), pp. xi, xii–xvii).

[14] *FlW*, 1070.

[15] *HRH*, pp. 65–6; *Liber Eliensis*, pp. xxxvii–viii, 176–7. There may have been some previous trouble at Ely, perhaps as a result of the castles constructed at Cambridge and Huntingdon in 1068 (*Liber Eliensis*, p. lvi).

[16] *Gesta Herewardi, Lestorie des Engles* i, p. 374.

[17] *GP*, p. 420; Hugh Candidus, p. 83. Turold also fell out with Baldwin, abbot of Bury St Edmunds, and was ordered to allow him to take and transport stone for his church and 'cause him no more hindrance . . . than you did previously' (*Regesta* i, no. 369; van

belligerence must lie in the circumstances of his arrival at Peterborough, with a force of 160 fully-armed knights. Military entourages for bishops and abbots were not novel, but clearly trouble was expected; Turold's appointment was military as well as ecclesiastical.[18]

The need for Turold's appointment soon became clear. The 'D' Chronicler records that the monastery of Peterborough was plundered 'namely by those men that Bishop Æthelric [formerly of Durham] had excommunicated because they had taken there all that he had'. Further details are provided by the Peterborough Chronicler, writing in 1121. While Turold and his knights were still at Stamford, the monks of Peterborough 'heard it said that their own men meant to plunder the abbey – that was Hereward and his *genge*'.[19] The sacristan Ivarr (*Iware*) collected all the moveable wealth that he could carry and set off to meet the new abbot. On 2 June, Hereward and his *genge* arrived, fired the town, sacked the abbey and carried its treasure off to Ely. They also carried off many of the monks, including the prior, Æthelwine, and the remainder scattered, except for Leofwine the Tall, who was lying sick in the infirmary. Turold arrived to find 'everything burnt, inside and out, except the church' and when ex-bishop Æthelric heard the news, he excommunicated the perpetrators from his prison at Westminster.

The rebels themselves were to claim that they had merely taken Peterborough's valuables into safe-keeping to preserve them from Abbot Turold and his Normans, but they were acting in alliance with the Danes, not the men to leave anything portable behind them. Soon after the sack of Peterborough, Swein and William negotiated a truce, and both fleets left England on 24 June, carrying with them the Peterborough treasure. It was believed at Peterborough that Asbjorn's fleet was lost in a great storm and the Peterborough treasure with it, except for some which got to Denmark but was destroyed in a fire, and the relics of St Oswald, which Prior Æthelwine had managed to remove and send to Ramsey for safe-keeping. Some relics of St Oswald and of St Alban did reach Denmark at some point, and were installed in the church of Odense by Cnut the Holy, one of the Danish leaders in 1069.[20]

Caeneghem i, p. 112). Turold was not the only ecclesiastic to be castigated for his worldly tastes: Orderic Vitalis describes Geoffrey de Mowbray, bishop of Coutances as 'a man of noble birth, devoted more to knightly than to clerical activities, and so better able to instruct knights in hauberks to fight than clerks in vestments to sing psalms' (OV iii, pp. 278–9).
[18] Hugh Candidus mentions the castle, 'Mount Thurold', which Turold built next to the church at Peterborough (Hugh Candidus, pp. 84–5). The exceptionally heavy quota (60 knights) of knight-service was imposed on Peterborough in Turold's time (King, *Peterborough Abbey, 1066–1320*, pp. 13–17; Hart, 'Hereward "the Wake" and his companions', p. 647).
[19] AS Chron, 'E', 1070. The significance of the word *genge*, 'outlaws', is shown by comparison with AS Chron, 'C', 1055, where the men of the exiled Earl Ælfgar are called a *micel genge*.
[20] See below, p. 70.

The story of Hereward is entangled in so much romantic embroidery that the facts are hard to establish. The monks of Peterborough might see him as an excommunicate outlaw but at Ely and Crowland and in his native Lincolnshire, he was remembered as a hero.[21] The fullest account of his early life is in the *Gesta Herewardi*, composed at Ely in the twelfth century.[22] His father, Leofric of Bourne, is said to have been the nephew of Ralph the staller and his mother Eadgifu is described as *trinepta* (great-grand-niece) of Oslac, earl of Northumbria from 966 to 975.[23] Heroes need illustrious ancestors and these claims may merely reflect the Ely tradition that Hereward was involved in the rebellion of Ralph the staller's son in 1075, but Ralph the staller did have English kinsmen, as will appear. Hereward's outlawry is attributed to a quarrel with his father, who persuaded King Edward (in 1062, according to the Crowland version) to banish his turbulent son. Hereward went to Flanders, where he married, and returned to England after the Conquest to find his father dead, his brother murdered and Bourne in the hands of the Normans. Hereward killed the Norman lord of Bourne, gathered a band of forty companions, was knighted by Brand of Peterborough (his paternal uncle in the Crowland version) and, after fetching his wife and nephews from Flanders, was summoned to Ely by Abbot Thurstan to undertake the defence of the Isle.

Hereward's leading role in the defence of Ely is borne out by the 'D' Chronicle, which records the surrender of all the leaders in 1071 'except Hereward alone

[21] The Ely tradition, which places the sack of Peterborough after the fall of Ely in 1071, is enshrined in the *Gesta Herewardi*, probably composed by Richard, a monk of Ely, during the episcopate of Bishop Hervey (1109–1131). The *Gesta* is allegedly based on a vernacular text written by Hereward's priest, Leofric the deacon, and on the reminiscences of Hereward's followers. Richard's early draft was used by the compiler of the *Liber Eliensis* as the basis of an account of the Ely campaign in chapters 104–7 of Book II; two other accounts of Hereward's deeds (one written from a Norman standpoint) underlie chapters 102 and 109–11 (*Liber Eliensis*, pp. xxxiv–vi, lv–lvii). Crowland's traditions are included the *Historia Croylandensis* (the 'Pseudo-Ingulf') once thought to be the work of Abbot Ingulf (1085/6–1109) but actually much later, though based on earlier material (see also below, Chapter VI). Hereward's reputation in Lincolnshire may be judged by the representation of his deeds in Gaimar's *Lestorie des Engles*, composed for the wife of the Lincolnshire landowner, Ralph fitzGilbert (see below, Chapter VII). The Peterborough tradition is in the *Peterborough Chronicle* (see note 13 above) and the Chronicle of Hugh Candidus, the sub-prior, written 1155 x 1175. See the discussions in John Hayward, 'Hereward the outlaw', *Journal of Medieval History* 14 (1988), pp. 293–304; Hart, 'Hereward "the Wake" and his companions', pp. 626–36; David Roffe, 'Hereward "the Wake" and the barony of Bourne': a reassessment of a Fenland legend, *Lincolnshire History and Archaeology* 29 (1994), pp. 7–10.

[22] The text is printed in *Lestorie des Engles* i, pp. 339–404 and there is a modern translation in Michael Swanton, *Three Lives of the last Englishmen*, Garland Library of Medieval Literature, series B, vol. 10 (New York and London, 1984).

[23] The Pseudo-Ingulf makes Leofric a nephew of Ralph, earl of 'Hertford' (i.e., King Edward's nephew, earl of Hereford and the east Midlands) though the fact that Ralph is said to be married to his own mother does not inspire belief (Joseph Stevenson, *The Church historians of England* (London, 1854), ii part 2, p. 662).

and those who could escape with him, and he led them out valiantly'. Some estimate of his standing can be derived from Domesday Book. He appears as the pre-Conquest tenant of three manors in Lincolnshire. One was at Laughton, which he held in conjunction with with one Toli, in whom the eye of faith might perceive the younger brother murdered by the Normans. He held a second manor at Rippingale from Crowland Abbey, for an annual rent to be agreed between himself and the abbot, and at Witham he was a tenant of Peterborough.[24] The Wapentake said that Hereward had not been in possession of Witham 'on the day when he fled (aufugit)' and that Abbot Ulfkell of Crowland (1061/2–1085/6) had repossessed Rippingale before Hereward 'fled the country (de patria fugeret)'. These statements confirm his outlawry, but do not date it. Since his men appear to have been outlaws when they attacked Peterborough in 1070, it is possible that Hereward had been involved in the English revolt of 1069.

Witham was held by Peterborough in 1086, but Hereward's other lands belonged to Ogier the Breton, who also held two manors at Bourne, one of which had been held by Earl Morcar and the other by Leofwine. It is possible that Morcar, as earl of Northumbria, was holding Bourne because of Hereward's outlawry, as Mærle-Sveinn the sheriff had held the land forfeited by Grimkell in Lincolnshire, and as Earl Waltheof was to hold lands confiscated from the Ely rebels. Ogier also held land at Morton which had belonged to Leofric, who has the same name as Hereward's father.[25] At first sight the Domesday evidence seems to confirm the description of Hereward in the Peterborough Chronicle as one of the abbey's tenants but the terms of his tenure of Crowland's manor of Rippingale suggest that he was rather more than a median thegn. A mutually-agreed annual rent is indicative of the relationship between an abbey and one of its lay protectors, and it is likely that Hereward was a king's thegn. The succession of Ogier both to Hereward's manor of Laughton and to that at Rippingale suggests that Hereward was Ogier's antecessor in Lincolnshire; indeed he may be the Ogier named in the Gesta Herewardi as one of Hereward's chief enemies.[26]

After the departure of the Danes, Ely seems to have become the rallying-point for outlawed, disinherited and disaffected men. Few of the companions of Hereward can be identified, but some were substantial landowners, who had either been or feared to be dispossessed. One such was Thorkell (Turchil) of Harringworth, whom the Liber Eliensis describes as a procer and illuster vir.[27] His

---

[24] GDB, fols 346, 364v, 376v, 377–377v.

[25] GDB, fols 364–364v, 377; for Grimkell's land, see GDB, fols 362v, 376 and for Waltheof's tenure of forfeited lands, see below, p. 51.

[26] Roffe, 'Hereward "the Wake" and the barony of Bourne': a reassessment of a Fenland legend, Lincolnshire History and Archaeology 29 (1994), pp. 7–10. Ogier's lands descended to the Wake family, who regarded Hereward as an ancestor, and though this descent was challenged by J.H. Round (Feudal England (London, 1964), pp. 132–6) it may well be true.

[27] Liber Eliensis, p. 179; the Gesta Herewardi calls him puer (OE cild) and describes him and Hereward sitting in the place of honour beside Abbot Thurstan (Lestorie des Engles i, pp. 379, 381).

lands, in Northamptonshire, Huntingdonshire and Lincolnshire, included Leighton Bromswold, named from the forest of *Bruneswald* to which Hereward and his men retired when they were expelled from Ely. Thorkell and his wife Thorgund (who was dead by 1070) were commemorated in the *Liber Vitae* of Thorney Abbey and Thorkell was remembered there as a man of Danish stock, who after the Conquest joined the Danes who were his kinsmen; as a result his lands were confiscated and given to Earl Waltheof.[28] It seems likely that Thorkell was one of those who welcomed Earl Asbjorn in the spring of 1070. If he is to be identified with the thegn Toki whose lands in Cambridgeshire and Norfolk were held by Frederick, brother-in-law of William de Warenne, his property had been confiscated by 1070 at the latest, for Frederick was killed, by Hereward, in that year; however Thorkell and Toki are completely separate names.[29] Another thegn who joined the Danes at this time might be Wulfwine *cild*, whose manor at Little Catford, Hunts, was claimed by Countess Judith because 'the king gave the land to Earl Waltheof'.[30] Siward of Maldon, a benefactor of Ely, and a landholder in Cambridgeshire, Suffolk and Essex, is described as a companion of Hereward (*socius Aerewardi*) in the *Liber Eliensis*.[31]

It was the arrival of Earl Morcar which transformed Ely from a refuge for outlaws into a centre of potential rebellion. Neither he nor his brother Edwin had participated in the revolt of 1069 but their men must have been involved in the Mercian uprising that accompanied it. The Mercian rebels had retired to Chester after being driven from Stafford, and Cheshire was to the lords of Mercia what Sussex was to the Godwinesons, the centre of their power in land and men; it was there and in neighbouring Shropshire that the greatest concentration of Edwin's land lay. His domination of Cheshire was the greater in that there was, by 1066, no royal demesne in the shire and many, perhaps most, of the landholders were probably his men.[32] It was to Chester that he sent his sister Ealdgyth,

---

[28] Dorothy Whitelock, 'Scandinavian personal names in the *Liber Vitae* of Thorney Abbey', *Saga-Book of the Viking Society for Northern Research* 12 (1949), p. 140; C.R. Hart, *Early charters of Eastern England* (Leicester, 1966), pp. 236–8. Earl Waltheof gave Leighton Bromswold to Remigius, bishop of Lincoln (formerly Dorchester); the pre-Conquest holder is described as Thorkell *danus*. Other lands once held by Thorkell, at Conington and Sawtry, Hunts, and at Harringworth, Fotheringay, East Farndon and Lilford, Northants, belonged to Waltheof's widow, Countess Judith, in 1086 (*GDB*, fols 203v, 206v, 228, 228v).

[29] For the lands of Thorkell of Harringworth and his son Godwine, see Hart, 'Hereward "the Wake" and his companions', pp. 636–40. The identification of Thorkell and Toki is by no means proven; the names are distinct and Toki may well be another of the Ely rebels.

[30] *GDB*, fols 205v, 208. Wulfwine's land at Little Catworth was held in 1086 by William de Warenne as belonging to Earl Harold's manor of Kimbolton, but the jurors deposed that this was not the case. Wulfwine also held a manor at Hail Weston, which had passed to Robert son of Fafiton (*GDB*, fols 207, 208).

[31] *Liber Eliensis*, p. 173, note 291. For his lands, most of which passed to Rannulf Peverel, see Hart, 'Hereward "the Wake" and his companions', pp. 644–7.

[32] The Domesday account of Edwin's land gives him 380 hides and 220 carucates; the

GENEALOGICAL TABLE III. THE EARLS OF MERCIA

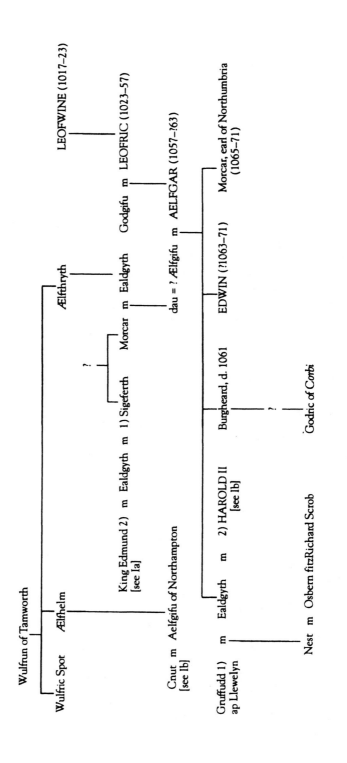

King Harold's widow, after the battle of Hastings.[33] Given Edwin's position in north Mercia, he cannot have been unaffected by the Harrying of the North. Many of those who fled to Evesham and elsewhere must have been his men and their families, and no lord who wished to keep the fidelity of his retainers could view such a catastrophe with indifference. Nor had the king's dispositions within Mercia been encouraging. Edwin's alliance with Bleddyn of Gwynedd in 1068 had not lost him his earldom, but it may have made a dent in the king's confidence in him. It was probably in 1069 that William appointed Gherbod the Fleming as earl of Chester and though Gherbod returned to Flanders in 1070, he was immediately replaced by Hugh d'Avranches.[34]

It is not therefore surprising that in the spring of 1071 'Earl Edwin and Earl Morcar fled away and travelled aimlessly in woods and moors'. The precise chronology of their final, fatal adventures is unclear. The 'E' Chronicle says that Morcar 'went to Ely in a ship and Earl Edwin was killed treacherously by his own men', while 'D' reverses these events and sends Morcar to Ely only after Edwin's death.[35] Orderic Vitalis gives an original and highly-coloured account of the brothers' fates, which places the death of Edwin after the fall of Ely and the capture and imprisonment of his brother. In this version, Edwin was betrayed by three brothers 'who were his most intimate servants' and, trapped on the banks of a river by the rising tide, was killed with twenty of his *equites*, 'all fighting desperately to the last'. The source for this sounds like an epic poem on the fall of the earls.[36] Orderic's sympathetic treatment of the Mercian brothers presumably reflects their reputation in Shropshire, where Orderic was born and reared.

main concentrations were in Yorkshire (210 carucates excluding dependencies), Shropshire (over 100 hides) and Cheshire (99 and a half hides). He was probably also holding the estates in Staffordshire (over 100 hides) entered in the name of his father, Earl Ælfgar. For Cheshire in particular, see C.P. Lewis, 'An introduction to the Cheshire Domesday', *The Cheshire Domesday*, ed. Ann Williams and R.W.H. Erskine (London, 1989), pp. 13–16.

[33] *FtW*, 1066. Ealdgyth's eventual fate is obscure. She may have retired to the Auvergne, where the monks of La-Chaise-Dieu commemorated an English Queen 'Edith' who paid for the building of their dormitory (George Beech, 'England and Aquitaine in the century before the Norman Conquest', *ASE* 19 (1991), pp. 94–5). The names Edith (Eadgyth) and Ealdgyth were often confused. Ealdgyth's son by Harold, Ulf, was kept in custody during the Conqueror's reign but released by William Rufus (*FtW*, 1087) and Nest, her daughter by her first husband, Gruffudd ap Llewelyn, married Osbern son of Richard Scrob.

[34] Lewis, 'The formation of the honour of Chester, 1066–1100', pp. 38–41. Gherbod was the brother of Gundrada, William de Warenne's wife, and of Frederick, who was killed in a skirmish with Hereward in 1070.

[35] *AS Chron*, 'D', 'E', 1071; John of Worcester follows 'D'. The *Liber Eliensis* even has Edwin present during the siege of Ely, though this is clearly wrong.

[36] *OV* ii, pp. 258–9. The account of Edwin's death has certain elements in common with that of Byrhtnoth of Essex in *The Battle of Maldon*: the site, a river-bank with a rising tide; the faithful retainers fighting to the last; and the three treacherous brothers, who, in Byrhtnoth's case, steal their lord's horse when fleeing the field.

On his way to Ely, Earl Morcar joined forces with Siward Barn and Æthelwine, bishop of Durham. Both were returning from Scotland, whither Siward had fled in company with the ætheling in 1070, and Æthelwine a little later, after the arrest of his brother Æthelric.[37] For all concerned, the stand at Ely was very much a last throw by men with nothing left to lose. Siward Barn's land had probably already been confiscated and Æthelwine's bishopric had been given to the Lotharingian Walcher, who took up his office in March 1071.[38] The motive for his return to the Fenland may have been little more than the desire to go home.[39] Morcar, who was still a young man, may have hoped for something more positive. His family, though they had been earls in Mercia since the late tenth century, may have come from the east midlands, for his paternal kinsman, Saxi, was holding land in Woodwalton (Hunts.) and Westmill (Herts.) in King Edward's reign.[40] The lands of Morcar's mother Ælfgifu also lay in the east midlands and East Anglia.[41]

These connections lend some colour to the *Gesta Herewardi*'s inclusion of three kinsmen of Earl Morcar among its hero's following: Godric of *Corbi* (perhaps Corby, Northants) Tostig of *Davenesse* (possibly Daventry, Northants)

[37] HR, 1070. The flight of the ætheling is placed before King Malcolm's invasion of Northumbria in 1070 and both (implicitly) before Easter (4 April) of that year. Æthelwine's arrival in Scotland is placed at about the same time. However, both the *Historia Regum* (*sub anno* 1069) and the *Historia Dunelmensis Ecclesiae* (chapter 50) have Æthelwine replacing St Cuthbert in his shrine at Durham (after the sojourn on Lindisfarne) on 25 March 1070. Both sources agree that when Æthelwine abandoned his see he intended to go to Cologne, but was driven to Scotland by adverse weather (HR, 1070, HDE, chap. 52). HDE places the bishop's flight in the sixteenth year of his episcopate, which should be 1071 rather than 1070; but his successor Walcher became bishop in March 1071 (see next note).
[38] *Letters of Lanfranc*, p. 140; Barlow, *The English church, 1066–1154*, p. 62.
[39] The early chronicle produced by the pre-1083 community at Durham describes how Æthelwine's brother, Bishop Æthelric, 'seeing that there was no help to be had, nor hope of resisting the violence of evil men who infested and infringed the liberty of the church, and preferring to relinquish his bishopric rather than that, because of his weakness, the liberty and peace of the church should be impaired, returned to his own monastery and ended his life without the episcopal office'; some similar motive may lie behind Æthelwine's departure (E. Craster, 'The Red Book of Durham', EHR 40 (1925), p. 528. I owe this reference to William Aird).
[40] Hart, *Early charters of Eastern England*, pp. 35–6; GDB, fols 138, 205v. Woodwalton in 1086 was held by Hugh de Bolbec of 'Earl' William, possibly William de Warenne (see C.P. Lewis, 'The earldom of Surrey and the date of Domesday Book', *Historical Research* 63 (1990), pp. 329–30).
[41] She held land in Herts., Northants, Lincs. and Suffolk (GDB, fols 134v, 222, 231v, LDB, fols 286v, 287, 374). It is possible that Ælfgifu herself was related to one of the powerful local kindreds, for her father may have been Morcar, who married Ealdgyth, Wulfric Spot's niece and a cousin of Ælfgifu of Northampton, first wife of King Cnut; the widow of Morcar's brother Sigehelm married King Edmund Ironside and was the ætheling's grandmother (P.H. Sawyer, *Charters of Burton Abbey*, Royal Historical Society (London, 1979), pp. xli–iii and see Genealogical Table III).

and *Turbertinus*. Godric is described as the *nepos* of the earl of Warwick, a title applied elsewhere to Earl Morcar.[42] If this statement is to be taken at face-value, Godric must have been a son of Morcar's brother Burgheard, who died in 1061 while returning from a visit to Rome, and was buried at Rheims.[43] Tostig of *Davenesse* is said to have been the earl of Warwick's (i.e. Morcar's) kinsman and to have received the same name at baptism; if so he had two names, which was not uncommon in the eleventh century.[44] *Turbertinus* (?Thorbeorht) is said to have been Earl Edwin's *pronepos* (great-nephew), which cannot be true. Whether these men really were related to Earl Morcar and if so, how, is uncertain, but not impossible.

The rebels may have had supporters further afield, for the monks of Abingdon remembered that the abbey's men had at some point gone in arms 'to join a gathering of the enemies of the realm' but had been intercepted and captured.[45] The incident is not dated but Ealdred of Abingdon, like Thurstan of Ely, was elected in King Harold's time and may have feared that he was to be replaced by a Norman; that his men did attempt to aid the rebels in Ely is suggested by his deposition and imprisonment in 1071.[46] Ironically it was at Abingdon, under Ealdred's successor Adelelm (a monk of Jumièges), that Bishop Æthelwine was imprisoned; Ealdred himself was sent first to Wallingford Castle and thence to the custody of Bishop Walkeline at Winchester.[47]

The heroic defence of the Isle against a combined land and water-borne attack led by the king in person is narrated in the Gesta Herewardi. The earliest account, in the 'D' Chronicle, merely records the siege and the surrender of all the

---

[42] Gesta Herewardi, Lestorie des Engles i, pp. 372–3, 376.
[43] Earl Ælfgar gave the manor of Lapley (Staffs., but entered in the Northants folios in Domesday Book) to Saint-Remi of Rheims on the occasion of his son's death and burial (S.1237, GDB, fol. 222v, VCH Staffs. iv, p. 28). Saint-Remi also held Meaford and Hamstall Ridware (Staffs.) by the gift of Earl Ælfgar, and a tenement in Shropshire, probably Sillington, which belonged to Lapley Priory in the thirteenth century (GDB, fols 247v, 252, DB Shropshire, no. 3a,1 and note). If a son of Burgheard was of fighting age in 1071, then he himself cannot have been born much after 1030, which would put the marriage of Earl Ælfgar and Ælfgifu (assuming she was Burgheard's mother) in the later 1020s. This is chronologically possible; if Ælfgifu was the daughter of Wulfric Spot's niece (note 41 above) she was born before his death in 1002, since she is mentioned (though not named) in his will.
[44] Manning, abbot of Evesham (1044–58) was also called Wulfmaer, Odda of Deerhurst was also known as Aethelwine or Edwin and Ealdred, abbot of Abingdon, was also called Beorhtwine (HRH, p. 47; Robertson, Charters, p. 457; Chron Abingdon i, p. 486). One of the leaders in the Liber Eliensis is called Tostig, presumably the same man (Liber Eliensis, p. 179). If Davenesse is Daventry, Northants, it may be significant that land there was held in 1086 by Judith, widow of Earl Waltheof, to whom other lands forfeited by the Ely rebels had been given (GDB, fol. 228v and see notes 28, 30 above).
[45] Chron Abingdon i, pp. 485–6. The incident is related in the context of the imprisonment at Abingdon of Bishop Æthelwine of Durham, i.e. after the fall of the Isle in 1071.
[46] HRH, p. 24, FlW, 1071.
[47] Chron Abingdon i, p. 486.

GENEALOGICAL TABLE IV. THE FAMILY OF EARL WALTHEOF

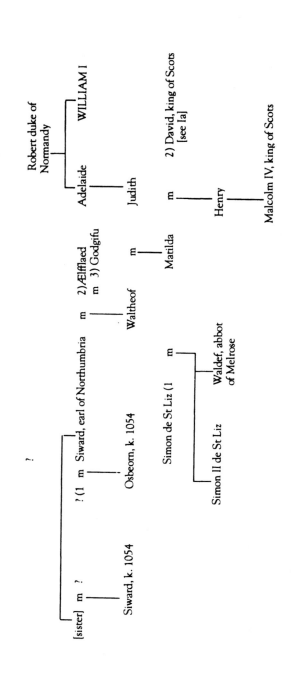

defenders 'except Hereward alone and those who could escape with him, and he led them out valiantly'. Abbot Thurstan bought the king's forgiveness with £1,000 of silver and died, still abbot, in 1072 or 1073.[48] Siward Barn is included among a list of prisoners whom William freed on his deathbed.[49] Morcar was placed in the custody of Roger de Beaumont. He too was freed by the Conqueror *in articulo mortis* but was imprisoned again by William Rufus, and spent the rest of his life in captivity.[50]

The fall of Ely allowed King William to turn his attention to Scotland, where other English dissidents were being sheltered by Malcolm Canmore. What practical help he was prepared to give is another matter. In 1070 the Scots raided into Teesdale and Holderness, but it is a moot point whether this was intended to aid the English or merely to acquire plunder. The raid was countered by Earl Gospatric, who attacked Cumbria and thereby drew a punitive Scottish force into Bernicia; it invested Durham and burnt down the church of Wearmouth.[51] It was at this point (according to the Chronicle of Melrose) that Malcolm married the ætheling's sister Margaret.[52] It was perhaps because of this marriage that King William decided to assert English overlordship over Scotland. To this end he led a combined land and sea-force (whose leaders included Eadric the Wild) to Scotland in 1072.[53] The Normans crossed the Firth of Forth but 'found nothing there that they were any the better for'. Malcolm preferred negotiation to battle and the kings met at Abernethy, where Malcolm did homage to William and gave hostages, including his eldest son Duncan.[54] One consequence of the Abernethy agreement was the temporary withdrawal of the ætheling to Flanders. Another was the fall of Earl Gospatric. With an understanding with the Scots in place, William no longer needed him and he was deprived of his office on the grounds that he had given aid and counsel to those involved in the murder of Robert de Commines and 'had been on the side of the enemy when the Normans were slain at York'. Like his ally the ætheling, Gospatric fled to Flanders.[55] He was replaced, not by a Norman, but by his kinsman Waltheof.

---

[48] *Liber Eliensis*, pp. 429–30; HRH, p. 45.

[49] FlW, 1087. He has also been identified as Sigurd Jarl, who, in the Icelandic tradition, led the English exiles to Byzantium, apparently in the 1070s (see Fell, 'The Icelandic saga of Edward the Confessor', pp. 183–6).

[50] OV ii, pp. 258–9. Orderic presents the capture and imprisonment of Morcar as an act of treachery on the king's part. Morcar *comes* attests a charter of Roger de Beaumont (Lewis, 'The early earls of Norman England', p. 215 note 95).

[51] HR, 1070; Kapelle, *The Norman conquest of the North*, pp. 123–4.

[52] A.O. Anderson, *Early sources of Scottish history, A.D. 500–1286* (Stamford, 1990), ii, pp. 23–30.

[53] FlW, 1072; Anderson, *Early sources of Scottish history* ii, p. 21, citing Benoit of Saint-Maure's *Chroniques des ducs de Normandie*.

[54] AS Chron, 1072, 1093; Anderson, *Early sources of Scottish history* ii, p. 34.

[55] For the ætheling, see Hooper, 'Edgar ætheling', p. 205; for Gospatric see HR, 1072. Both had returned to Scotland by 1074, when the ætheling made his peace with King William and Gospatric was installed as earl of Dunbar.

Waltheof was the obvious choice for the earldom of Bamburgh. His father, Siward, had been made earl of Northumbria by Cnut, in or before 1033, and had exercised direct control of Bamburgh after 1041, when he murdered Earl Eadulf. It was probably then that Siward married (as his second wife) the earl's niece Ælfflaed, who was Waltheof's mother.[56] Since Waltheof was too young to succeed when Siward died in 1055, he was probably born no earlier than 1042. Even after the failed revolt of 1069, Waltheof's maternal kindred were a power to be reckoned with in the north and as late as 1080 his uncle by marriage, Ligulf, was one of the closest advisors of Bishop Walcher of Durham. He was one of the few remaining men whose connections gave him a chance of success in the difficult territory north of the Tyne. The king clearly wanted his services, for he not only pardoned his part in the revolt but married him to his own niece Judith.[57] Waltheof retained his earldom in the east midlands, and (as described above) received lands there forfeited by the men who took part in the rebellion at Ely. His estates passed to his widow and appear in her name in 1086. The bulk of his fief lay in Northamptonshire, Huntingdonshire and Leicestershire, but extended into Lincolnshire, Cambridgeshire and Bedfordshire, with smaller holdings in Yorkshire, Middlesex and Essex.[58]

Over the next few years Waltheof was active both in the midlands and in Bamburgh. At some date between 1072 and 1075, he was among the commissioners who enquired into encroachments on the lands of Ely Abbey, one of the houses which preserved his memory.[59] He also restored to Crowland the manors which Thorkell of Harringworth had held of the house, and both he and his wife Judith were commemorated in the Liber Vitae of Thorney. He gave Thorkell's manor at Leighton Bromswold to the bishopric of Lincoln and Judith founded a nunnery at Elstow, Beds.[60] Only at Peterborough is conflict recorded, for

---

56 AS Chron, 1041; HR, 1072.
57 Judith was the daughter of Adelaide, countess of Aumale, who in 1086 was holding land in Essex and Suffolk (LDB, fols 91v–92, 430v–431). Adelaide married, firstly, Enguerrand count of Ponthieu, lord of Aumale (died 1054); secondly, Lambert, count of Lens (died 1055), brother of Eustace II of Boulogne; and thirdly, Eudo of Champagne, who became (after 1086) lord of Holderness. The Vita Waldevi makes Judith Lambert's daughter, but she may have been the child of Enguerrand of Ponthieu (see Carmen, p. 12).
58 GDB, fols 130v; 202–202v; 206v–207v, 208; 217, 217v, 219; 228–228v; 233, 236–236v; 320, 336, 336v; 362, 366v–367; LDB fol. 92. See also G.W.S. Barrow, The kingdom of the Scots (London, 1973), pp. 9–10, 19–21.
59 Van Caeneghem i, no. 18A (pp. 43–4); Edward Miller, 'The Ely land pleas in the reign of William I', EHR 62 (1947), p. 43; F. Scott, 'Earl Waltheof of Northumbria', Archaeologia Aeliana, fourth ser, 30 (1952), p. 202. Waltheof's obit is entered in the Ely calendar, but on the wrong day, 31 July for 31 May.
60 Whitelock, 'Scandinavian names in the Liber Vitae of Thorney Abbey', pp. 132, 140–1; Cecily Clark, 'British Library Additional MS. 40,000, ff. 1v–12r', ANS 7 (1985), pp. 52, 53, 57–8; for Elstow, see GDB, fols 203v, 217. For Leighton Bromswold, see above, and for Waltheof and Crowland, see below.

Waltheof was involved in a dispute with the church over land bequeathed to it by his stepmother Godgifu.[61]

In the north Waltheof was remembered as a friend and supporter of Walcher, bishop of Durham.[62] In a less positive way, Waltheof's identification with his mother's kindred surfaced in a revival of the old feud with the sons of Karli. In 1074 a force from Bamburgh surprised the three eldest sons at Thorbrand's hall of Settrington. Thorbrand himself and one of his brothers (presumably Gamall) were killed, but Cnut was spared 'because of his innate goodness' and Sumarlithr, the youngest, was away from home. The incident shows that a family prominent in the English revolt was still holding at least some of its land as late as 1074, and it may be that Waltheof was not so much prosecuting an ancient feud as clearing the ground of some of the king's enemies.[63]

In 1074 Waltheof's position seemed unassailable. Two years later he was dead, executed for treason, the only English magnate to suffer such a fate. His downfall was the result of his participation in the revolt of the Three Earls, hatched at the wedding-feast of Emma, sister of Roger de Breteuil, earl of Hereford and Ralph Guader, earl of East Anglia. The 'bride-ale that was many men's bale' is located by the Anglo-Saxon Chronicle at Norwich, but John of Worcester puts it at Exning (now in Suffolk but then in Cambridgeshire), a manor which probably belonged to Earl Ralph.[64] Though Waltheof was among the wedding-guests, the Norman Earl Roger (son of William fitzOsbern) and the Anglo-Breton Earl Ralph (son of Ralph the staller) are presented as the initiators and ringleaders of the conspiracy. The 'D' Chronicle says that 'they plotted to drive their royal lord out of his kingdom' (hi woldon heora kynehlaford of his cynerice adrifan), highly pejorative language which recalls Wulfstan II of York's strictures on the expulsion of Æthelred II in 1013.[65]

---

61 Hart, Early charters of Eastern England, pp. 107–8; David Roffe, 'Lady Godiva, the Book and Washingborough', forthcoming.
62 HR, 1070 and see below.
63 HR, 1074; De Obsessione Dunelmi, Morris, Marriage and murder in eleventh-century Northumbria, pp. 3–4; Kapelle, The Norman Conquest of the north, pp. 134–5. De Obsessione Dunelmi represents Waltheof as avenging his grandfather but Ealdred died in 1038, before Waltheof was born.
64 AS Chron, 1075; FlW, 1075. Exning was in the king's hand in 1086 and was managed by Godric, presumably Godric the steward (for whom see Chapter V below) who administered Earl Ralph's former estates in Essex, Norfolk and Suffolk (GDB, fol. 189; ICC, p. 4; R. Lennard, Rural England, 1066–1135 (Oxford, 1959), p. 147, note 3). It had belonged to Eadgifu the Fair, many of whose lands passed through Earl Ralph's hands, and a second tenement in the vill was held in 1086 by Count Alan, who had succeeded to lands once held by Earl Ralph in Suffolk (GDB, fol. l95v, LDB, fol. 290).
65 Ful micel hlafordswice eac biðon worolde þæt man his hlaford of life forræde oððan of lande lifiendne drife (a full great treachery it is in the world that a man deprive his lord of life, or drive him in his lifetime from the land); see Dorothy Bethurum, The Homilies of Wulfstan (Oxford, 1957), p. 270. The language of the 'E' Chronicle is less strong: hi woldon þone cyng gesettan ut of Englelandes cynedome (they plotted to expel the king from the realm of England).

The behaviour of the three earls in 1075 has always aroused puzzlement. John of Worcester explained it by the king's refusal of his consent to the marriage of Ralph and Emma, but the *Anglo-Saxon Chronicle* explicitly records the king's permission. Orderic includes in his account a long list of complaints against the king's government; these may well 'embody criticisms of King William that must have been widely circulated' but are no more than guesses at the actual motives of the conspirators of 1075.[66] The grievances of Roger de Breteuil have been most fully investigated. He was the younger son of William fitzOsbern, the Conqueror's most trusted friend, who was killed at the battle of Cassel, in Flanders, on 22 February 1071. FitzOsbern's Norman estates went to his elder son and namesake, and the English honours, including the earldom of Hereford, to Roger. Roger did not receive his father's share of the earldom of Wessex, nor was he so high in the king's counsels. Some sense of belittlement can be glimpsed in one of the admonitory letters sent him by Archbishop Lanfranc, which refers to a dispute between the earl and the royal sheriffs in his earldom, the settlement of which the king had reserved to himself when next he should be in England. It may be significant that one of Roger's supporters in 1075 was Ralph de Bernay, who had been his father's sheriff in Herefordshire.[67] Roger may have felt aggrieved that he had not the power his father had enjoyed, a complaint which the other conspirators might have shared. Waltheof's father Siward had been earl of all Northumbria, not merely Bamburgh, and Waltheof, who had been passed over twice in the succession to Northumbria, perhaps felt that he should have been lucky on the third occasion. As for Ralph Guader, his earldom seems to have been confined to Norfolk and Suffolk, but the old earldom of East Anglia had also included the shires of the east midlands and Essex.[68]

Archbishop Lanfranc, who was entrusted with the governance of England in the king's absence, saw Roger as a youth led astray by the counsel of 'evil men'. There is no doubt whom the archbishop had in mind. In a letter to the king in Normandy, he announces that he is proceeding against 'Ralph the Traitor' and

66 OV ii, pp. 310–13, 312 note 2.
67 *Letters of Lanfranc,* p. 31; Lewis, 'The Norman settlement of Herefordshire under William I', pp. 207–8; Hemming's Cartulary i, p. 250. By no means all of his father's men supported Roger; apart from Ralph de Bernay only five are known, Eon the Breton (whose nationality may be significant), Turstin the Fleming and three men who held only in the vicinity of Monmouth. Roger's support, such as it was, lay in west Herefordshire and when he attempted to cross the Severn, he was prevented by a force commanded by Wulfstan, bishop of Worcester, Abbot Æthelwig of Evesham, Walter de Lacy and Urse d'Abetot, sheriff of Worcester (FIW, 1075).
68 Dr Lewis ('The early earls of Norman England', pp. 221–2) draws attention to Orderic's statement that the rebels proposed to divide the kingdom into three, one portion held by one of their number as king, and the remaining portions by the others as *duces,* a term which Dr Lewis associates with the older, pre-Conquest and immediately post-Conquest earldoms, rather than the more restricted commands (whose holders are termed *comites*) of the Conqueror's later years. Waltheof was passed over for the earldom of Northumbria by Earl Tostig in 1055 and Earl Morcar in 1065.

GENEALOGICAL TABLE V. RALPH THE STALLER

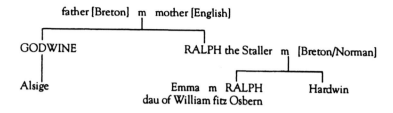

his army of 'oath-breakers' and a subsequent missive refers to the 'Breton dung' of which the kingdom has been purged.[69] Ralph Guader was the son of Ralph the staller, one of King Edward's household officers. The *Anglo-Saxon Chronicle* describes Ralph the staller as an Englishman, born in Norfolk. The Normans and other Frenchmen who entered King Edward's service were counted as *Anglici* in King William's time, but Ralph the staller was already known as Ralph *anglicus* when he attested a charter of Alan, duke of Brittany, which cannot be later than 1034.[70] Ralph must thus have been born not long after 1010 at the latest and his father, a Breton of the Montfort-Gael line, may have come to England in the entourage of Emma of Normandy, when she married Æthelred II in 1002.[71] Ralph's mother, to judge from his English kindred recorded in Domesday, was an Englishwoman. Godwine, who held manors at Sall and Burnham Thorpe and sokeland at Field Dalling (all in Norfolk) and was alive in 1069, was probably his brother.[72] Godwine may have been the father of Alsige, described in the

[69] *Letters of Lanfranc*, pp. 33, 34, 35; William of Malmesbury describes Ralph as 'a man of disposition foreign to anything good' (GR ii, p. 313).
[70] K.S.B. Keats-Rohan, 'The Breton contingent in the non-Norman conquest', ANS 13 (1991), p. 167, note 140. Ralph the staller and his son Ralph Guader are both called *anglicus* in Breton ducal charters. Helen Cam ('The English lands of the abbey of St Riquier', EHR 31 (1916), pp. 443–7) suggested that Ralph was Flemish and acquired the barony of Gael, Brittany in right of a Breton wife, but the chronicler Hariulf, who records his gifts to St Riquier, calls Ralph the staller a Breton, as does William of Malmesbury (GR ii, p. 313). For the lands given to St Riquier by Ralph, see *LDB*, fols 119v (Sporle), 144 (Swaffham); the only land held by St Riquier in 1086 was a carucate in Palgrave, held *de feudo Friderici* of William de Warenne (*LDB*, fol. 167v). I am grateful to Dr Keats-Rohan for help on the origins of the two Ralphs.
[71] Emma certainly brought men from north France with her, like the 'French *ceorl* Hugh' whom the Æthelredian chronicler blames for the Danish sack of Exeter in 1003 (AS Chron, 1003). Since Exeter was part of the queen's dower, Hugh was presumably Emma's reeve (for Queen Edith's reeve Colwine, see Chapter I above). Though the bulk of Ralph the staller's recorded land was in the east, he did hold one manor in Cornwall (GDB, fol. 121v), perhaps given to him or his father by Emma.
[72] *LDB*, fols 131, 262 and see fol. 127v for his seizure of Quidenham 'three years after King William came'. In two of these entries Godwine is described as *avunculus* of Earl Ralph, with no indication of whether the father or the son is meant, but the Ralph of

Suffolk folios as Earl Ralph's nephew. This Alsige had held (with his wife) a two-life *læn* on a manor at Gislingham from Abbot Leofstan of Bury St Edmunds and had free men commended to him in Old Newton. He may also be the Alsige who held Cantley of Ralph the staller and the king's thegn who held Fersfield, later in the hands of the younger Ralph.[73] In Norfolk an Alsige had held land in Field Dalling, where Godwine, Ralph Guader's uncle, had sokeland. The names God and Robert are interlined above that of Alsige, perhaps indicating later tenants of the land; if God is an abbreviation of 'Godwine', Alsige may have predeceased him.[74] Alsige and Godwine are common names but it is worth noticing two kinsmen bearing them in Cambridgeshire. Alsige of *Langwathe* and his wife Leofa gave the reversion of their estate at Burwell to Ramsey Abbey and after Alsige's death, Abbot Ælfwine (1043–1079/80) leased it to their kinsman, Godwine; but it was seized after the Conquest by Ralph Guader.[75]

His half-English origin may have made Ralph the staller an obvious choice for the earldom of East Anglia, vacant after the death of Earl Gyrth at the battle of Hastings. A series of Bury writs, all from the early years of King William's reign, are addressed to Ralph as earl, and he appears in company with William, bishop of London, and Engelric the priest supervising the redemption of their lands by the English.[76] He was alive in 1068 but died before the deposition of Bishop Æthelmaer in 1070.[77] He left two sons, Ralph Guader and Hardwin, whose lands in Essex, Norfolk and Suffolk were forfeited, presumably for his part in his brother's rebellion.[78]

the Burnham Thorpe entry is certainly Ralph Guader, for he was holding 'when he forfeited'. Godwine was thus either his paternal or maternal uncle, and since Ralph Guader's mother is said by the *Anglo-Saxon Chronicle* to have been a Breton (though she is just as likely to have been Norman), probably the former. It is intrinsically unlikely that Godwine, who was living in 1069, was the uncle of Ralph the staller, who died in 1069 or 1070.

[73] For Gislingham, see *LDB*, fols 444v (cf. 312, 324); Old Newton, 350v, 374; Cantley, 122v–123; Fersfield, 130–130v (cf. 275v, 276v). For the lease of Gislingham and an earlier lease to Wulfgeat and his wife, see Hart, *Early Charters of Eastern England*, pp. 70–1.

[74] *LDB*, fol. 178v; *DB Norfolk*, no. 9,86 and note. The 'Robert' might be Robert de Verly, the 1086 holder of Godwine's lands at Burnham Thorpe and Field Dalling, Norfolk. Robert de Verly's only Suffolk manor, Market Weston, had been held by a man called Alsige, who may therefore be Ralph the staller's nephew (*LDB*, fol. 437).

[75] *Chron Ramsey*, pp. 174–5 and see Hart, *Early Charters of eastern England*, pp. 239–40. If *Langwathe* represents Landwade, Cambs, east of Exning, then Alsige of *Langwathe* may be the Alsige who held land at Exning, the site of the fatal 'bride-ale' (*GDB*, fol. 195v and see above). Landwade does not appear by name in Domesday, but Leofwine *sac* of Exning and Wulfwine of Landwade (*Landwathe*) were jurors of the Cambridgeshire shire-court in the period 1077 x 1082 (*Textus Roffensis*, ff. 175–175v and see Chapter IV below).

[76] *Regesta* i, nos. 40–43; *LDB*, fol. 360v.

[77] *LDB*, fol. 194; Robertson, *Charters*, p. 464.

[78] Ralph Guader appears as 'Ralph, son of Ralph the Englishman' in a charter dated 1056 x 1060, and was probably born before 1040 (*GEC* x, p. 572) For Hardwin, see *LDB*,

Sir Frank Stenton saw both Waltheof and Ralph Guader as 'survivors from the Old English order' but it is Ralph's Breton connections which are emphasized both by Archbishop Lanfranc and the *Anglo-Saxon Chronicle*.[79] Indeed Ralph Guader seems to have been in Brittany, in his lordship of Gael, in King Edward's time, and may only have come to England after 1066. Part of the animus displayed against him and his men must be due to the fact that he had supported Conan of Brittany against Duke William in 1064.[80] It is difficult to say how many Bretons were established in East Anglia in Ralph Guader's time for those of his men who were not killed in 1076 fled with him to Brittany and, apart from Walter of Dol, have left little trace in English sources.[81] The only Breton (if that was indeed his *natio*) known to have held land in East Anglia before the Conquest is Robert fitzWymarc, of Clavering, Essex, and he seems to have had no connection with Earl Ralph and took no part in the rebellion.[82] As in Hereford-shire, the insurgents of East Anglia seem to have been the earl's immediate following and the *Anglo-Saxon Chronicle* records that they were opposed by the *castelmen* (the castle-garrisons) and the local levies. The army sent by Lanfranc against Ralph was led by Geoffrey de Mowbray, bishop of Coutances, William de Warenne and Robert Malet.[83] They met the rebels at Ralph Guader's manor of Fawdon, in Whaddon, where Ralph's force was routed.[84] He escaped to Norwich, whence he took ship to Brittany, leaving his wife Emma to hold Norwich castle. It was she who arranged safe conduct for herself and her men and, yielding up the castle to the king's officers, joined her husband in Brittany.[85]

But for the part played by Earl Waltheof, the revolt of the Three Earls would have little place in a work devoted to the English experience of the Norman

---

fols 90–90v and *VCH Essex* i, p. 553; *LDB*, fols 223v, 224, 225–225v, 245, 291v, 353–353v, 338, 382v–383, 389. All his lands were held in William's reign and none before 1066, which indicates that he was the brother of Ralph Guader not Ralph the staller. Since Ralph Guader was in Brittany before 1066 (see below) it may be that he was intended to hold his father's Breton lands and Hardwin the English estates.

[79] Stenton, ASE, p. 610.

[80] Keats-Rohan, 'The Breton contingent in the non-Norman Conquest', p. 167. Ralph Guader may only have come to England after his father's death, in 1069 or 1070.

[81] For Walter of Dol, see Keats-Rohan, 'The Breton contingent in the non-Norman Conquest', pp. 167–8. His lands, all of which were forfeited, lay in Suffolk (*LDB*, fols 299v, 321v, 322, 377, 407v).

[82] Robert fitzWymarc had a Breton mother but was perhaps more Norman than Breton (Barlow, *Edward the Confessor*, p. 191) He was sheriff of Essex in the early years of William's reign, and was succeeded by his son Swein, holding in 1086 (Green, *English sheriffs to 1154*, p. 39).

[83] AS Chron, 1075; *Letters of Lanfranc*, p. 35. John of Worcester names Geoffrey de Mowbray and Odo of Bayeux as the leaders and Orderic includes William de Warenne and Richard fitzGilbert of Tonbridge (FIW, 1075, OV ii, 316–17).

[84] OV ii, pp. 316–17; GDB, fol. 196v. For the identification, see Bruce Dickins, 'Fagaduna in Orderic (A.D.1075)', *Otium et negotium, studies presented to Olof von Feilitzen*, ed. Folke Sandgren (Stockholm, 1973), pp. 44–5.

[85] *Letters of Lanfranc*, p.35; AS Chron, 1075.

Conquest. Waltheof's role is difficult to assess, since those who record it were influenced by the cult which grew up around his tomb at Crowland. Thus John of Worcester asserts his firm belief that the earl 'is now rejoicing with the saints in heaven' and Orderic incorporates the laudatory epitaph for Waltheof which he himself composed at the request of the Crowland monks.[86] William of Malmesbury was more sceptical:

> some assert that he joined the league of treachery more through necessity than inclination. This is the excuse the English make for him and those of the greater credit, for the Normans assert to the contrary, to whose decision the Divinity itself appears to assent, showing many and great miracles at his tomb.[87]

Waltheof's cult developed rapidly. In 1092 his body was translated from the chapter-house into the church of Crowland and miracles began to occur soon afterwards. A second focus of veneration at the nunnery of Romsey, near the place of his execution at Winchester, was scotched by Archbishop Anselm.[88]

The effects of the developing cult of Waltheof can be seen in the sources for the rebellion of 1075. The 'E' Chronicle merely records his presence at the bride-ale, his arrest and his execution (the monks of Peterborough, whither the Chronicle moved in the twelfth century, did not remember Waltheof with favour). The 'D' Chronicle adds that after the flight of Earl Ralph, Waltheof sought out the king in Normandy and 'accused himself and asked for pardon and offered treasure'. It then records his execution in 1076, giving the date, 31 May, which 'E' omits, and his burial at Crowland. John of Worcester embellishes the Chronicle account, describing how the conspirators compelled Waltheof, 'whom they had insidiously surprised', to join them; how he then went to Lanfranc to be absolved of his forced oath of secrecy and how Lanfranc despatched him to the king; how Waltheof imparted the details of the plot to William and threw himself on the king's mercy; and how Lanfranc after Waltheof's unjust execution not only declared him innocent of any crime but said 'that he should esteem himself happy could he enjoy, after his own departure, the blessed repose of the earl'. Once again William of Malmesbury is more circumspect: one of the conspirators 'said to have been Waltheof' went, on Lanfranc's advice, to the king in Normandy and told him of the plot, 'concealing merely his own share of the business'.[89]

Orderic's account is the most elaborate and draws upon the traditions of

---

[86] FlW, 1075; OV ii pp. 350–1.
[87] GR ii, p. 312.
[88] OV ii, pp. 346–9; D.H. Farmer, The Oxford dictionary of Saints (Oxford, 1978), p. 396. Archbishop Anselm forbade the nuns of Romsey to pay honour to Waltheof as if to a saint, and ordered the expulsion from their midst of an otherwise unknown son of the earl (F.S. Schmitt, Sancti Anselmi Opera Omnia (Edinburgh, 1949), iii, p. 144).
[89] FlW, 1075; GR ii, pp. 313–14.

Crowland, which he visited about 1119. It is he who describes how the earl was executed as he was reciting the Lord's Prayer and had reached the sentence 'And lead us not into temptation' when he was beheaded; 'then the severed head was heard by all present to say in a clear voice, "But deliver us from evil. Amen".'[90] Though it has little, if any bearing, on the development of Waltheof's cult, the lament of his skald, Thorkell Skallason, should be included for completeness and because it, too, regards the earl's arrest and execution as an act of treachery on King William's part:

William, who reddened steel and cut through the icy sea from the south, has indeed betrayed the doughty Waltheof under a truce. Truly the slaying of men will be long ceasing in England, but no more glorious lord than was my gallant chief shall die.[91]

Given these hagiographical embellishments, Waltheof's motives and actions are impossible to establish.[92] Only in one letter does Lanfranc, the only contemporary source, mention the north and he does not refer to Waltheof. He merely tells Walcher of Durham of his relief that the north is at peace 'which in our alarm at the many reports reaching us from many quarters we believed to be far from you'. Lanfranc warns Walcher, however, that 'the Danes are indeed coming, as the king told us' and bids the bishop fortify his castle.[93] The Danes in question were a fleet of two hundred ships, commanded by Cnut the Holy, which arrived in the autumn of 1075, too late to help the earls. It contented itself with an attack on York and retired to Flanders.[94]

Waltheof, we may well believe, submitted to the king, as he had done before. William's temper, however, was shortening. Both Waltheof and Roger de Breteuil (who also threw himself on the king's mercy) were arrested. Roger was condemned to perpetual imprisonment but Waltheof, an Englishman subject to English law, was sentenced to death and executed, at Winchester, on 31 May 1076. He was the last of his line to rule in Northumbria. The king appointed no successor and Bamburgh was left in the hands of Walcher, bishop of Durham.

---

[90] OV ii, pp. 320–1.

[91] Campbell, *Skaldic verse and Anglo-Saxon history*, p. 16.

[92] It has been suggested that Waltheof was experiencing problems in the north which predisposed him to give ear to the conspiracy, but whether the signs of an unsuccessful attempt to levy tribute north of the Tyne in 1073 or 1074 really indicates a breakdown of royal authority in the area is debateable (see Kapelle, *The Norman conquest of the north*, pp. 134–6).

[93] *Letters of Lanfranc*, p. 36. It is probably significant that the letter, written after the expulsion of Earl Ralph, is addressed to the bishop and not to the earl. The castle at Durham was built in 1072 (see HR, 1072). The role of the Danes is also mentioned by the *Anglo-Saxon Chronicle*, and Orderic (OV ii, pp. 316–17) sends Earl Ralph from Norwich to Brittany via Denmark.

[94] The raid is most interesting for the light it throws on the ambitions of Cnut the Holy (see below).

Walcher was neither an Englishman nor a Norman, but a Lotharingian from Liege, a secular clerk well-suited to preside over the priests of St Cuthbert. He was remembered at Durham as a saintly, learned and able man, who obtained from King William 'that valuable property called Waltham, along with its noble church, celebrated for its body of canons'.[95] Waltham Holy Cross, worth £100 in 1086, must have made a significant contribution to Durham's finances.[96] The basis of Walcher's reputation, however, was his patronage of Aldwine, prior of Winchcombe, and his companions. They had come to the north in the wake of the English revolt, inspired by their reading of Bede's *Historia Ecclesiastica* to visit the sites of the ancient monasteries which he described, and, if possible, to revive the monastic life there. Hugh fitzBaldric, sheriff of Yorkshire, had sent them to Newcastle but Walcher moved them to Jarrow, Bede's own home, and gave them the episcopal manor of Tynemouth.[97]

Aldwine's party was very much Anglo-Norman, for his chief companion was Reinfred, a knight once in the service of William de Percy, who had decided to adopt the religious life on a visit to the deserted monastery at Whitby.[98] The same synthesis is to be found in Bishop Walcher's entourage. The king had taken some care to introduce him into his see in the right company. In 1071 he was escorted as far as York by Eilaf the housecarl whom the king 'held in especial honour'.[99] At York he was met by Earl Gospatric, who conducted him to Durham. After the Scottish campaign of 1072 and the expulsion of Gospatric, the king stayed at Durham, where he had a castle built for the bishop. It was probably at this time that King William confirmed the privileges of St Cuthbert and restored the manor of Billingham, lost since the tenth century. The king's scepticism about the incorruption of St Cuthbert's body was allegedly punished by a

[95] HDE, chap. 58. Waltham passed out of Durham's control in Henry I's reign, into the hands of Queen Matilda II (H.S. Offler, *Durham Episcopal Charters, 1071–1152*, Surtees Society 179 (1968), p. 23; Rosalind Ransford, *The early charters of Waltham Abbey, 1062–1230* (Woodbridge, 1989), pp. 1–2. The 'noble church' was that built by Harold Godwineson; its school was headed by Master Adelard, another clerk who had come from Liege, this time at Harold's invitation (see Chapter VI below).
[96] The grant included other manors which had been held by the church of Waltham, see GDB, fols 58, 133, 210v, LDB, fol. 15v. The manor of Waltham is discussed by Barrow, *The kingdom of the Scots*, p. 10.
[97] The charter recording the gift of Tynemouth is in the name of Earl Waltheof but since it is attested, *inter alia*, by his grandfather Ealdred (died 1038), it is unlikely to be genuine. Waltheof's cousin, Morcar, was a monk at Jarrow, and his entry into the community is the ostensible reason for the donation: see Offler, *Durham Episcopal Charters*, no. 2c, 5, pp. 4–6, 39–45.
[98] R.H.C. Davis, 'Bede after Bede', *Studies in medieval history presented to R.Allen Brown*, ed. Harper-Bill, Holdsworth and Nelson, pp. 106–9. Whitby was held in 1086 by William de Percy of Earl Hugh of Chester (GDB, fol. 305). See further below, Chapter VI.
[99] HR, 1071; HDE, chap. 53. Eilaf's name occurs four times in the Yorkshire folios but whether all or any of these references are to Eilaf the housecarl it is impossible to say. The most likely is the Eilaf who had a *hospitium* (lodging) in York itself, which had passed by 1086 to Odo the crossbowman (GDB, fols 298v, 300v, 301, 324v).

visitation of 'extreme heat' which caused him to break short his visit and make a swift departure.[100]

The castle was garrisoned by Frenchmen and Flemings but there were Englishmen in the bishop's household, including Leofwine the dean and a scribe able to write Standard Old English.[101] Walcher himself made efforts to conciliate the local magnates. He was on good terms with Earl Waltheof and, after the earl's disgrace, his chief advisor was Ligulf, who had married Ealdgyth, daughter of Ealdred and thus Waltheof's maternal aunt. Ligulf is said to have possessed wide estates throughout England but 'inasmuch as the Normans continually gave scope to their ferocity in every quarter, he betook himself with his family to Durham'.[102] From this it might be concluded that Ligulf had either been involved in the revolt of 1069–70, or had been displaced in the upheavals which followed. His name is not uncommon. A Ligulf appears among the lawmen of York who gave evidence on the archbishop's liberty about 1080 and Waltheof's kinsman might also be the Ligulf whose land in Yorkshire passed to Robert count of Mortain. These estates were divided between the count's tenants, Nigel Fossard (58 carucates and 6 bovates) and Richard de Sourdeval (24 carucates and 2 bovates), and Richard also held the only manor in Yorkshire assigned to Ealdgyth, who may be identical with Ligulf's wife.[103] A lady named Ealdgyth was granted land at Thornley and Wingate, co Durham, by Bishop Walcher, but it is not certain that she was Ligulf's wife; she might be Earl Gospatric's mother.[104] Ligulf and his wife had two sons, Uhtred (presumably the elder) and Morcar, who became a monk at Jarrow. Uhtred may be the king's thegn who succeeded a Ligulf at Rudston, Yorks (8 carucates).[105] Morcar is presumably the Morcar son

---

[100] HDE, chaps 54–5; see Aird, 'St Cuthbert, the Scots and the Normans', pp. 16–18. For the loss of Billingham, see C.R. Hart, *Early charters of northern England and the North Midlands* (Leicester 1975), pp. 138, 141–2.

[101] See the lease in favour of Ealdgyth, note 104 below.

[102] HR, 1080.

[103] If the declaration on the 'Rights and Laws' of Archbishop Thomas dates from the time of the Domesday Inquest (Palliser, *Domesday York*, pp. 7–8, 25), then the Ligulf mentioned in it clearly cannot be Waltheof's kinsman (see also note 106 below). For Ligulf's lands, see GDB, fols 298, 306, 306v, 307, 307v (apart from these estates, Richard and Nigel held of the count another 12½ carucates for which no previous tenant is named). Ealdgyth's manor, 3 carucates and 5 bovates at Middleton on the Wolds, had not belonged to the count of Mortain's *antecessor* and 'was not delivered to Count Robert' (*non fuit deliberata Roberto comite*), see GDB, fols 306v, 373. For another Yorkshire lady whose property was held independently of her husband see Asa wife of Beornwulf (or Bjornulfr), GDB, fol. 373.

[104] Offler, *Durham Episcopal Charters*, no. 1, pp. 1–3; Robertson, *Charters*, pp. 230–1. The lease is written in Standard Old English, the literary form developed at Winchester in the tenth century.

[105] GDB, fol. 331: DB Yorkshire, no. 29,E14. Rudstone was given by William Peverel to St Mary's, York (VCH Yorks. ii, p. 185).

of Ligulf who appears as a lawman of York in 1106.[106] Ealdgyth's kindred were still holding land in the north in the twelfth century.[107]

Bishop Walcher was criticised on three grounds: he did not exercise sufficient control over his followers; his dean (Leofwine) appropriated the revenues and treasure of the church for his own friends and kinsmen; and his knights plundered and even killed the local people without being curbed or punished.[108] Walcher's inability to deal with the Scottish raid of 1079 may have added to his unpopularity. It was, however, a more personal quarrel which brought about his downfall. Leobwin, the bishop's chaplain, had conceived a violent jealousy of Ligulf and in 1080, with the connivance of Gilbert, Walcher's kinsman and household officer, murdered him in his own house, thus committing the capital offence of *hamsocn*. The whole affair is narrated in detail by John of Worcester and it is instructive to compare the account with the ordinance on the regulation of the blood-feud, promulgated by Edmund.[109] Walcher took immediate steps to open negotiations with the aggrieved kindred, by sending go-betweens who negotiated a meeting at Gateshead (II Edmund 7).[110] At Gateshead he took refuge in the church, along with his clergy and knights, including Leobwin and Gilbert; thus, when the negotiations broke down, he himself incurred the feud (II Edmund 1 requires the kin to abandon the slayer if they wish to escape the feud). Ligulf's kinsmen attacked the church, and killed first Gilbert and his knights, then the Englishman Leofwine the dean, then Walcher himself, and finally Leobwin. The kindred themselves were in breach of II Edmund 2, which imposes outlawry and

106 HR, 1080; van Caeneghem, i, p. 139 and see note 97 above. If the lawman of 1106 was identical with the monk of Jarrow, he may have succeeded to his father's position (see note 103 above).
107 Ealdgyth's sister Æthelthryth married Orm Gamel's son of Yorkshire and their daughter Ecgfrida was the wife of Ælfsige of Tees. Waltheof their son was still disputing ownership of Barmpton and Skirmingham (granted to his daughter by Bishop Ealdhun) with Gospatric, son of Gospatric son of Arnkell (*De Obsessione Dunelmi*, Morris, *Marriage and murder in eleventh-century Northumbria*, 1–5). Waltheof of Tees was successful in retaining the estates, which were restored to Durham by his lord, Nigel d'Aubigny, in the reign of Henry I (1109 x 1114), see Diana Greenway, *Charters of the Honour of Mowbray* (London, 1972), no. 2, pp. 6–7. Uhtred son of Dolfin, a grandson of Gospatric son of Arnkell, was also a Mowbray tenant (Greenway, *Charters of the Honour of Mowbray*, nos. 392–6, pp. 250–3.
108 HDE, chap. 58; FlW, 1080. John of Worcester carefully distinguishes between Leofwine the dean and Leobwin the bishop's chaplain, for whom see below. Kapelle (*The Norman Conquest of the North*, pp. 183ff) argues that Walcher had 'manorialized' some of the Durham estates by increasing demesne cultivation and imposing week-work.
109 FlW, 1080; II Edmund.
110 There was probably a residence of the earls of Bamburgh at Gateshead in the area now known as *Bottle Bank* (OE *botl*, 'dwelling, house, palace', see Eilert Ekwall, *The concise Oxford dictionary of English place-names* (Oxford, 1960), p. 54). Bishop Walcher may, therefore, have been called to a traditional trysting place on the boundary between the *Haliwerfolc* and the earldom of Northumbria (William Aird, personal communication).

forfeiture on whoever violates the sanctuary of a church in pursuit of the feud. John of Worcester does not name the leader of the killers, but the *Historia Regum* identifies him as Eadulf Rus, son or grandson of the Gospatric killed in 1064.[111]

The murder of Bishop Walcher may be seen as the last act of native resistance to King William. In the autumn of 1080, two armies were sent north: one, under Odo of Bayeux, ravaged Northumbria and the other, led by Robert Curthose, advanced into Scotland. No engagement took place, but on his return southwards, Robert built the 'new castle' on the Tyne, opposite Gateshead. Newcastle was a harbinger of the future settlement of the North.

One final threat to King William's security remained. In 1080, Cnut the Holy succeeded to the Danish kingdom.[112] He was an energetic, not to say ruthless, king, with ambitions to restore the empire of his great-uncle and namesake. His previous expeditions to England had been, to say the least, inconclusive. The blame for the first, in 1069–70, could be laid at the door of his uncle, Asbjorn, but Cnut himself had commanded the host of 1075, which (according to the *Anglo-Saxon Chronicle*) 'dared not fight with King William'. Once king of Denmark, Cnut prepared an altogether more formidable challenge. He allied himself with Count Robert the Frisian of Flanders, an enemy of King William, by marrying his daughter Adela, probably in 1080, though the alliance may go back to 1075, when, according to the 'E' Chronicle, Cnut went to Flanders after his withdrawal from England.[113] When they assembled their fleets in 1085, there was no ambiguity about Cnut's objectives; 'people said and declared for a fact that Cnut, king of Denmark, son of King Swein, was setting out in this direction and meant to conquer the country'.[114] In the event, problems at home prevented Cnut from proceeding, and his oppressive collection of fines and dues had provoked resistance.[115] When he attempted to regroup his forces next year, he

---

[111] HR, 1072; *De primo Saxonum adventu, Symeonis . . . Collectanea*, p. 213. Simeon of Durham (*HDE*, chap. 58) calls him Waltheof, possibly Waltheof son of Earl Gospatric, who became a monk at Crowland, and abbot from c.1126–38 (D.W. Rollason, 'Simeon of Durham and the community of Durham in the eleventh century', *England in the eleventh century*, ed. Carola Hicks (Stamford 1992), p. 196; OV ii, pp. 350–1; HRH, p. 42).

[112] He was one of the numerous sons of Swein Estrithson, who died on 28 April, probably in 1076; his immediate successor was his eldest surviving son, Harold *Hein* (Christiansen, *Saxo Grammaticus* i, p. 236, note 34).

[113] Robert the Frisian had usurped the county from his nephew Arnulf, and in the ensuing battle, at Cassel, in 1071, William fitzOsbern had been killed. More recently, in 1079, Robert had allied with King William's rebellious son, Robert Curthose. For the date of the marriage of Cnut and Adela, see Galbert of Bruges, *The murder of Charles the Good, count of Flanders*, ed. James Bruce Ross (New York, 1967), p. 13. Adela subsequently married Roger Borsa, count of Apulia. Her son by Cnut, Charles the Good, was brought up in Flanders and became count in 1119; he met the same fate as his father, being murdered as he prayed.

[114] *AS Chron*, 1085.

[115] Christiansen, *Saxo Grammaticus* i, pp. 249–50, note 66; Niels Lund, 'The armies of Swein Forkbeard and Cnut: "*leding*" or "*lið*"?', ASE 15 (1986), p. 107.

was murdered on 10 July 1086, as he prayed in his church at Odense, before the relics of St Alban and St Oswald which he had brought, probably in 1070, from England. The *Anglo-Saxon Chronicle* records his slaying as 'the greatest disloyalty and the greatest treachery that could ever happen' and its circumstances led to his canonization, in which English ecclesiastics played a leading role. The author of his epitaph, which describes his death and names the faithful men killed with him, was perhaps an Englishman; this account, inscribed on a metal tablet, was placed in the king's tomb when his remains were translated in 1095. By this time his brother Eric 'Evergood' was king and he, with the permission of William Rufus, imported English monks from Evesham to colonize Odense.[116] One of them may have been the author of the first *Passio* for he tells us that he was present at the translation of the relics. In 1101 King Eric persuaded the pope to issue a bull of canonization and Cnut's remains were moved into the cathedral of Odense, whose bishop, Hubald, was supposedly an Englishman, and whose chapter was monastic, an arrangement highly unusual outside England. The second *Passio* was written by Æthelnoth of Canterbury in the reign of Nicholas (1104–34).[117] Both the author of the *Passio* and Æthelnoth claim that Cnut's projected invasion in 1085 was prompted by the wish to free the English from Norman rule, and that he had been implored to intervene by the English magnates. Be that as it may, the threat was taken very seriously by King William, who not only brought to England 'a larger force of mounted men and infantry from France and Brittany than had ever come to this country' but also 'had the land near the sea laid waste, so that if his enemies landed, they should have nothing to seize on'.[118] The upheavals connected with the provisioning of this force may have been a contributory factor in the king's decision, at Gloucester, 1085, to have a *descriptio* made of his kingdom. The resultant survey produced the text which more than anything else reveals the nature of the Norman settlement and the fate of the English inhabitants: Domesday Book.

---

116 *Chron Evesham*, p. 325 (Dominic of Evesham's Life of St Wistan).
117 Peter King, 'English influence on the church of Odense in the early middle ages', *Journal of Ecclesiastical History* 13 (1962), pp. 145–55; for the sources for Cnut, see Christiansen, *Saxo Grammaticus* i, pp. 219, 255 note 77, 258 note 80.
118AS *Chron*, 1086. The Abingdon Chronicle also records these 'stipendiary knights' (*quos solidarios vocant*) who were raised and supported for nearly a year by everyone, 'including bishoprics and abbeys', before being sent home (*Chron Abingdon* ii, p. 11). The obstreporous behaviour of the stipendiaries quartered on the bishop of Worcester's household are noticed in the *Vita Wulfstani*, pp. 55–6.

Chapter IV

SURVIVORS

In the twenty-first year of the reign of King
William . . . there was now no prince of the
ancient royal race living in England, and all
the English were brought to a reluctant submission, so that it was a disgrace to be called an
Englishman.

Henry of Huntingdon , *Historia Anglorum*, chap. vi

IT IS IMPOSSIBLE TO understand the effect of the Norman settlement on English
landholding without some discussion of pre-Conquest land-tenure. Many post-
Conquest fiefs (the Sussex rapes are an obvious example) were new creations,
compact blocks of territory which cut across previous patterns of tenure. Other
fiefs, however, were constructed by granting to each Norman or French magnate
the lands of one or more named *antecessores*; such grants conveyed both demesne
(manors and berewicks), whether retained by the *antecessor* or granted as *lænland*,
and rights over sokeland owing service to the demesne manors. There has been
considerable dispute over the relative frequency of these two methods of re-
distribution. The prevalence of antecessorial grants has been argued by Professor
Sawyer and Dr Roffe, whereas Dr Fleming has emphasised the widespread
disruption caused by the creation of new, territorial fiefs.[1] Dr Fleming has also
shown that antecessorial grants are in the main earlier than territorial grants.[2]

It was pre-Conquest tenure which determined rights of ownership in 1086;
just as the king ruled as the successor to the Confessor, so his men were to hold
with all the rights, and all the obligations, of the Confessor's thegns. Thus
antecessorial grants did not include lands held by men linked to the *antecessor*

---

[1] P.H. Sawyer, '1066–1086: a tenurial revolution?', *Domesday Book: a reassessment*, ed.
P.H. Sawyer (London, 1985), pp. 71–85; Roffe, 'From thegnage to barony', pp. 157–76;
idem, 'An introduction to the Nottinghamshire Domesday', *The Nottinghamshire Domes-
day*, ed. Ann Williams and R.W.H. Erskine (London, 1990), pp. 10–17; Robin Fleming,
'The tenurial revolution of 1066', *ANS* 9 (1987), pp. 87–102; idem, *Kings and Lords in
Conquest England*, pp.107–44. The controversy turns largely on the nature of pre-
Conquest overlordship; compare the contrasting treatment of the Peverel fief in Roffe,
'From thegnage to barony', pp. 173–4, and Fleming, *Kings and lords in Conquest England*,
pp. 148–9. For the sake of clarity I should say that I have followed Dr Roffe's interpre-
tation.
[2] Fleming, *Kings and lords in Conquest England*, pp. 160–82.

by commendation alone, though such lands were often appropriated (as were *lænlands* held of other pre-Conquest lords by the *antecessor*) by Norman successors. Indeed many of the disputes recorded in Domesday arise from the seizure by one Norman of land whose holder was commended to his own *antecessor*, but whose soke belonged to the *antecessor* of another Norman landholder. It was difficult for men used to the continental practice, in which land and personal homage were much more closely linked, to appreciate the distinction between personal lordship and lordship over land. Since the distinction has also been hard for modern historians to grasp, a brief account may clarify the situation.

Old English society was highly stratified. To the basic distinction between slave and free was added the division into noblemen (thegns) and non-nobles (ceorls) and each group was further differentiated. The laws of Cnut reveal a threefold gradation among the thegns, into earls, king's thegns and median thegns; 'among the Danes' (in the earldom of Northumbria) the king's thegns were further sub-divided into he 'who has his soke' and he who 'has a closer relationship with the king'.[3] By 1066 the highest rank, that of earl, was restricted in effect to four great families, those of Godwine, Leofric, Siward and the house of Bamburgh. Other families, whose members had once been earls and ealdormen, had died out, or dwindled in rank, or were represented by minors.[4]

The king's thegns constituted a larger group. Some, including the stallers, who were members of the royal household, were rich landholders with estates in several shires. Others were men of more local importance, with small amounts of land but nevertheless dignified by being in the king's service. Their numbers are difficult to estimate. For Kent and the northern shires, Domesday Book provides lists of the major landholders and when the earls are excluded, the figures for each county are 23 (Kent) 9 (Nottinghamshire with Derbyshire) 7 (Yorkshire) and 26 (Lincolnshire).[5] There is some overlap between the three northern lists and some of the men named in the Kentish list held land in other shires. It is likely that the king's thegns of the pre-Conquest period should be

---

[3] II Cnut 71; N.P. Brooks, 'Arms, status and warfare in Late-Saxon England', *Ethelred the Unready: papers from the Millenary Conference*, ed. David Hill, BAR British series 59 (1978), pp. 81–103. See also *Norðleoda laga*, where the wergeld of the hold and the high-reeve is double that of the king's thegn (Liebermann i, p. 460, *EHD* i, no. 52(b), pp. 432–30). In the tenth century men of the upper rank were sometimes called *pedisequus* or *sequipedus* (*Liber Eliensis*, pp. xiii, 102). As for the *ceorlisc menn*, the basic distinction was between the free men (including *geneatas*, *liberi homines*, sokemen, radmen and radcnihts) and the dependent peasants, who appear in pre-Conquest texts as *geburas*, *kotsetlan* and *æhtemen* and in Domesday as *villani*, bordars, cotsets, cotmen and cottars. The slaves, as the property of their owners, lay outside the wergild classification.
[4] Odda of Deerhurst, earl first of the Western Shires and then of Worcester, died without issue in 1056 and his brother predeceased him (Williams, 'An introduction to the Gloucestershire Domesday', pp. 28–9). For the descendants of Eadric *Streona*, earl of Mercia (1007–17) and of Ralph, earl of the east midlands and of Hereford (1050–7), see below, pp. 91–96 and Chapter V.
[5] *GDB*, fols 1, 1v; 280v; 298v; 337.

numbered in hundreds rather than thousands, and the very richest among them (described as *proceres* or *optimates*) at not more than a hundred at most.[6]

Many more men and women than this are recorded in Domesday Book as holding land on the eve of the Conquest; the usual estimate is between 4,000 and 5,000.[7] It is likely that many of them fell into the third category, the median thegns. Their status was defined not just by birth and wealth but by service; they were men of some-one other than the king.[8] The ranks of the median thegns shaded off into those of the non-noble free men, who performed similar services.[9] There was a certain amount of movement between the ranks of thegns and ceorls; as Archbishop Wulfstan II put it, 'it often happens that a miserable slave earns freedom by a ceorl's gift, and a ceorl becomes worthy of a thegn's rights by an earl's gift, and a thegn, through a king's gift, becomes worthy of an earldom'.[10] Relationships between free men and median thegns on the one hand, and the greater magnates (king's thegns, abbots, bishops and earls) on the other were governed partly by ties of personal loyalty (commendation) and partly by customary obligation (sake and soke). In the first case, service was due from the man, regardless of whether or not he held land of his lord; in the second, it was due from the land, irrespective of who held it, or to whom he was commended. The law-codes distinguished between these two kinds of lordship. The *hlaford* held the personal homage of his men, the *landrica* or *landhlaford* was entitled to dues and services from the land, regardless of whether the holder was commended to him.[11] The rights of the *landrica* (at least in the south) derived from his tenure of bookland, land held by a royal charter or *landboc*, which freed the estate concerned from most royal demands, military service and the more important judicial rights excepted. The bookholder could thus divert all the exempted dues and services for his own benefit. A *landboc* did not grant land alone, but rights

---

6 Fleming (*Kings and Lords in Conquest England*, p. 65, note 47) calculates that there were 70 thegns holding land worth £60 or more a year. Compare Peter A. Clarke's estimate (*The English nobility under Edward the Confessor* (Oxford, 1994), pp. 32–3) of 90 thegns below the rank of earl with estates valued at £40 or more. Clarke's £40 limit is based on the 40 hides said by the *Liber Eliensis* to qualify a thegn for the rank of *procer* (*Liber Eliensis*, pp. 167, 424–5).
7 H.R. Loyn, *Anglo-Saxon England and the Norman Conquest*, 2nd edn (London, 1991), p. 331.
8 See the will of Ketel (S. 1519) whose heriot, that of a median thegn, was rendered to his lord, Archbishop Stigand; and *Geþyncðo* (the 'Promotion Law'), chap. 3, for the thegn who has another thegn who serves him (Liebermann i, p. 456: EHD i, p. 432).
9 Ann Williams, 'An introduction to the Worcestershire Domesday', *The Worcestershire Domesday*, ed. Ann Williams and R.W.H. Erskine (London, 1988), pp. 6–7; Barrow, *The kingdom of the Scots*, pp. 16–19.
10 F.M. Stenton, 'The thriving of the Anglo-Saxon ceorl', *Preparatory to Anglo-Saxon England*, ed. D.M. Stenton, p. 388.
11 III Æthelred II, 4 (The Wantage Code); I Cnut, 8,2. The distinction is developed by David Roffe in an unpublished paper, 'Brought to book: lordship and land in Anglo-Saxon England'. I am most grateful to Dr Roffe for allowing me to read and cite this paper.

over the men who dwelt on that land, whether they were thegns or free men. The service which they had once performed for the king, at a royal vill, was now due to the hall of the bookholder and their lands were appurtenant to the central vill (or *caput*) where that hall lay. Such estates were held with 'sake and soke' (*saca and soca*). Jurisdiction was one of the mediatized dues, but sake and soke also involved services and renders in cash and kind, described in Domesday as *consuetudines*, customary dues. The identity of the two is shown by comparing the Domesday account of the tenures at Canterbury with that in the *Inquisitio* of St Augustine's. In the first, the king has sake and soke throughout the city, except over the lands of specified religious bodies and secular landholders; in the latter, these same people have their *consuetudines* over their men.[12] The tributary holdings were called sokeland, to distinguish them from the demesne land which belonged to the lord.[13]

The *landrica* did not own the sokeland appurtenant to his manor; it belonged to its holders, who remained free (in Domesday's phrase) 'to give and sell' it, though the service had still to be performed to the *landrica*. Nor did the *landrica* automatically hold the personal commendation of the holders of this dependent sokeland. They might commend themselves to him, but they were free (to quote Domesday again) 'to go' or more specifically 'to commend themselves (*se vertere*) to whatever lord they would'.[14] There are numerous variants of these formulae but the import is the same. Sometimes, where disputes are being recorded, the

---

12 *Per totam civitatem Cantuarie habet rex sacam et socam excepta terra aecclesie Sancte Trinitatis et Sancti Augustini et Eddeuae reginae et Alnod cild et Esber biga et Siret de Cilleham* (GDB, fol. 2); *Regina E et Alnoth cild et Osbernn* (sic) *bigga et Sired de Chileham isti habuerunt in civitate consuetudines suas de suis homines* (Inquisitio, p. 9). For the rights inherent in sake and soke, see Roffe, 'From thegnage to barony', pp. 164–6.

13 Such estates are better-evidenced in the northern and eastern shires, for which pre-Conquest charters (*landbec*) are few. This may be because such charters were preserved in the archives of Benedictine abbeys, few of which had been re-founded in the north and north-east before 1066. There is no reason to suppose that charters were not as prevalent in this area as in the south and west. When Edward the Elder reconquered the Danish earldoms of the east midlands, he confirmed those who submitted to him in possession of their lands, whereas those who did not submit forfeited their estates (*Liber Eliensis*, pp. xi, 98–9). Given the importance of the event, it is unlikely that charters were not issued.

14 *Vertere* (to turn, turn round, put to flight, flee) translates OE *bugan* (to bow (down), stoop, bend, swerve, turn, go, flee from, avoid, go over to, submit), which was used to express the submission of the man to his lord. Thus in the abbacy of Wulfric (989–1006), Ealdred son of Lyfing *gebeh . . . mid lande* to St Augustine's, Canterbury and fifty years later, Ælfric Modercope received King Edward's permission to *bugan* to the abbots of Bury St Edmunds and Ely (S.1455, Robertson, *Charters*, pp. 128–9, 371–2; S.1081, Harmer, *Writs*, pp. 149–50, 162–3, 459–50). Since Ealdred's land seems to have been in dispute and that of Ælfric was bequeathed (*inter alia*) to Bury and Ely, there may have been special reason to record these acts of commendation. The ceremony is described in a tract of c.920, which gives the words of the hold-oath (*hold*, faithful) to be sworn by the man to his lord, *ða ic to him gebeah* (William Stubbs, *Select charters and other illustrations of English constitutional history*, ninth edition (Oxford, 1921), pp. 73–4).

meaning is spelt out. Land at Alveston, Warks, had been held by Beorhtwine, but Archbishop Ealdred had 'sake and soke and toll and team and churchscot and all other forfeitures except the four which the king has throughout the whole kingdom'. The sons of Beorhtwine, who held the land in 1086, did not dispute Ealdred's rights, but said that 'they did not know from whom Beorhtwine held the land, whether from the church (of Worcester) or from Earl Leofric, whom he served'. They themselves, however, held from Earl Leofric and 'could commend themselves (se vertere) where they would with the land'.[15] The sons of Beorhtwine were prepared to render service to the church of Worcester, but regarded the land as their own, though the fact that it is enrolled in the church's breve suggests that they had not made good their claim. There is a similar case in Kent, where half a sulung of land at Stokenbury had been incorporated into the manor of East Peckham, belonging to the monks of Christ Church, although it did not belong there, 'except for rent (scot) because it was free land (libera terra)' and the scot had been paid by the pre-Conquest tenant, Eadric, 'voluntarily' (spontanee). Eadric was not commended to the abbot, but was the king's man.[16]

The distinction between sokeland and thegnland lies precisely in whether or not the holders had freedom to commend themselves and to alienate their land. Holders of sokeland could do both; holders of thegnland neither.[17] Sokeland belonged to its holder but owed services to a landrica; thegnland belonged to a hlaford who bestowed it, in return for service, upon his man.[18] If the service was not performed, the land was forfeit and returned to the lord's demesne.[19] Just as

---

Compare the account of the ceremony of homage at Salisbury in 1086: ealle hi bugon to him and weron his menn and him hold aðas sweron (AS Chron, 1086).

[15] GDB, 238v.

[16] GDB, fol. 4v; Domesday Monachorum, p. 94. See Ballard, 'An eleventh-century Inquisition from St Augustine's, Canterbury', p. xxi: 'a man who held free land had liberty of commendation and was said to hold of the king'. Compare the half-sulung of free land held by Sired of Alfred bigga, which was appurtenant to Alfred's manor of Wickhambreux (GDB, fols 9–9v); and the land at Feckenham, Worcs, (GDB, fol. 180v) which five thegns had held of Earl Edwin: 'they could go where they would with the land, and had under them four milites as free as themselves'. The milites and the thegns owed service, but had freedom of commendation. See also the case of Badlesmere, Kent, p. 83 below.

[17] Edward Miller, The Abbey and Bishopric of Ely (Cambridge, 1969), pp. 50–1.

[18] The sons of Ælfgeard held Lyford, Berks, of Abingdon Abbey and could not go elsewhere without the abbot's permission. 'Nevertheless' (et tamen) after the Conquest they commended themselves, without the abbot's leave, to Walter Giffard. But the land belonged to Abingdon, and Walter was therefore the abbey's tenant in 1086 (GDB, fol. 59).

[19] Thegnland is clearly a dependent tenure; it was often held by joint-tenants who made special arrangements to discharge the service. Thus Durnford, Wilts, was held by three Englishmen, two of whom paid 5s while the third serviebat sicut tainus (GDB, fol. 67; VCH Dorset iii, p. 39). If the service was not performed, the land reverted to the demesne (see the case of Isham, Northants, held by Eustace, sheriff of Huntingdon, of Ramsey Abbey, van Caeneghem i, p. 89).

the personal tie between *hlaford* and man could be reinforced by a grant of thegnland (or *lænland*), so the tenurial relationship between *landrica* and tenant could be reinforced by commendation. Some, however, chose not to commend themselves to the *landrica*, but to some other *hlaford*. In some shires and some circuits, Domesday records the names of the *hlafordas* to whom the holders of sokeland were commended, presumably to avoid claims on their lands by the Normans who succeeded to the property of those *hlafordas*, for it was sake and soke, not commendation which conferred title to land.[20]

Lænland resembled thegnland in that it belonged to the lord. It was demesne, usually (and perhaps invariably) bookland, which was granted for a fixed term (a life or three lives are the most common) in return for service. Three-life grants were usually made to husband, widow and one heir, but within the term of a such a lease there was obviously some freedom of disposition. Wulfwine had bought the manor of Selly Oak, Worcs., from the church of Lichfield for three lives, but his deathbed will returned it to the church.[21] Such land could be difficult to recover at the end of the term if the heirs proved obstructive; there are cases of priests and monks being bribed to hand over the landbooks relating to such estates, so that the tenants could claim outright ownership.[22] It was not even unknown for the *lænland* of a miscreant to be confiscated along with his own land, though in such cases the *lænland* should have reverted to the original grantor.[23] Like thegnland, *lænland* is best recorded on ecclesiastical estates, but this is a function of the survival of evidence and there is no reason to believe that lay lords did not make similar arrangements.[24] It is these tenurial and personal ties that helped determine the nature of the Norman usurpation.

Many aspects of the Norman settlement are contentious but the extent to which the land was redistributed is not one of them. A glance at the lists of tenants-in-chief in Domesday Book reveals the dominance of foreigners and the same is true of the mesne-tenants. Men with English names are few and those who do appear hold less land than their foreign counterparts; they have been described in a memorable phrase as 'the flotsam and jetsam of an aristocracy wrecked in the storms of the Conquest'.[25] The greater lords, the earls and king's

---

[20] A free man who had held a hide at Vange, Essex, TRE 'was made the man of Rannulf Peverel's *antecessor* but did not give his land to him; nevertheless when the king gave the land of the *antecessor* to Rannulf, he took possession of this along with the rest' (*LDB*, fol. 71v). See Richard Abels, 'An introduction to the Hertforshire Domesday', *The Hertfordshire Domesday*, ed. Ann Williams and G.H. Martin (London, 1991), pp. 24, 32; Roffe, 'From thegnage to barony', pp. 167–8.

[21] *GDB*, fol. 177. There were special circumstances; Wulfwine's son, Leofwine, was bishop of Lichfield (1053–71).

[22] See, for example, Robertson, *Charters*, pp. 122–3.

[23] II Cnut 77; Hemming's Cartulary i, p. 254; but see *GDB*, fol. 172v: *DB Worcestershire*, no. 2,14.

[24] Lennard, *Rural England*, p. 166.

[25] Lennard, *Rural England*, p. 67. Some will object to the use in this and the following chapter of the expressions 'tenant-in-chief' and 'mesne-tenant'. I fully accept the

thegns, had foundered completely, and it was the lesser men who had managed to salvage something from the wreckage. They were too useful to be dispossessed entirely, for not only were they required as estate-managers but also in the running of local administration.[26] A hundred years later their survival was rationalized by Richard fitzNigel, treasurer to Henry II:

> there was a general complaint by the native English, which came to the king's ears, that since they were hated by everyone and robbed by everyone, *they would be forced to take service abroad* (my italics). At last, after discussion in council, it was decreed that they should be given an inviolate title to whatever they had acquired from their lords by their own deserts and by a lawful bargain. But they did not succeed in establishing a title to pre-Conquest property.[27]

This is not, of course, history, but the link between English tenures and service may be significant.[28] At the very least it shows a need, in the late twelfth century, to account for the tenure of land by English families, and to synchronize their title (like that of the Normans) with the Conquest.

It would not be practicable here to attempt a survey of all the Englishmen and women holding land in 1086. Those who held of the king, whether as tenants-in-chief or *taini regis*, will be discussed in Chapter V. Those who held as mesne-tenants are an even larger group, and four shires have been taken as exemplars. They have not been chosen quite at random, for each is particularly well-documented. For Dorset we have, besides Domesday itself, the partial account of the shire in Exon Domesday, the Dorset Geld Rolls (contemporary with Domesday) and the twelfth-century surveys from Shaftesbury Abbey.[29] Kent

conclusions of Susan Reynolds ('Bookland, folkland and fiefs', ANS 14 (1992), pp. 225–7) that these words give a misleading impression of a 'hierarchy of property', which there is no reason to suppose existed in 1086 (and still less in 1066). I have nevertheless retained them 'without prejudice' for convenience, to avoid cumbersome circumlocutions for those said to hold of the king (*de rege*) and those who held of (*de*) or under (*sub*) someone else.

[26] They did not hold the more honourable and lucrative offices, which went to French and Norman adherents of the great nobles (J.F.A. Mason, 'Barons and their officials in the later eleventh century', ANS 13 (1991), pp. 256–7; D.C. Crouch, *The Beaumont Twins* (Cambridge, 1986), pp. 136–76). James Campbell discusses the role of local thegns in the operation of government ('Some agents and agencies of the late Anglo-Saxon state', *Domesday Studies*, ed. J.C. Holt (Woodbridge, 1987), pp. 215–17).

[27] *Dialogus*, p. 54.

[28] At Amport, Hants, Ralph de Mortimer established a brother of the pre-Conquest tenant on five hides of land 'so long as he behaved well towards him'; if the Englishman wished to dispose of the land, he had to give or sell it to Ralph (*GDB*, fol. 48v). Ralph himself was holding Amport of Hugh de Port.

[29] For the Dorset sections of Exon and the Geld Rolls, see *VCH Dorset* iii. The Shaftesbury Abbey cartulary, though compiled in the fifteenth century, contains a mass of documentation from the early twelfth century onwards, including lists of tenants and

is covered by the *Domesday Monachorum* of Christchurch, Canterbury and the *Inquisitio* of St Augustine's, both of which contain materials associated with or derived from the Domesday survey, and the *Textus Roffensis*, the cartulary of Rochester Cathedral Priory. The Domesday account of Cambridgeshire is supplemented by the Ely Inquest (IE) and the *Inquisitatio Comitatus Cantabrigiensis* (ICC), which derive from the survey and preserve much additional material. In Shropshire, the tenurial structure of the county makes its record of mesne-tenants particularly revealing.

DORSET

Dorset lay outside the areas directly affected by the fighting in 1066 but its thegns had probably contributed to the host which fought at Hastings. Most of its major landowners were also prominent in Somerset and thus affected by the Norman penetration of the west after the siege of Exeter in 1068, and men from both Dorset and Somerset besieged the castle of Montacute in 1069. On the other hand, one magnate with land in Dorset, Eadnoth the staller, fell fighting for the king against the sons of Harold in 1068. There is some cause to believe that the townsmen of the Dorset boroughs had been in conflict with the Norman sheriff, Hugh fitzGrip.[30]

By 1086, the leading landowners of King Edward's day had vanished from the scene. Among the mesne-tenants Domesday records only thirteen with English names, plus ten anonymous thegns, two 'free Englishmen' and four women, two of whom were widows. This is not, however, a complete record, as comparison with Exon and the Geld Rolls shows. Exon reveals the tenure of Bolle the priest (who also appears as a *tainus regis* and a tenant in alms) at Shilvinghampton and shows that the nine thegns who held Rollington before 1066 continued to hold it as tenants of Roger de Tilly. Since Roger de Tilly himself was holding of Roger Arundel, Exon here affords a glimpse of a third level of tenure rarely revealed in the main Domesday text.[31] The Geld Rolls show that one of the two thegns who held Winterbourne Belet in 1066 continued to hold it at farm of William Belet. Likewise Harding (who is perhaps the queen's *pincerna*) continued to hold his manor at Little Bredy at farm of Berengar Giffard and the unnamed thegn who held Tatton of Cerne Abbey continued to hold it as the tenant of Aiulf the chamberlain.[32]

Most of the Dorset survivors held of religious houses and some clearly had

three (incomplete) surveys of the abbey's land, dating c.1130, c.1170 and c.1200 (BL Harleian Ms 61, fols 37–89; see Ann Williams, 'The knights of Shaftesbury Abbey', *ANS* 8 (1986), pp. 214–15).
[30] For the sieges of Exeter and Montacute, and the death of Eadnoth, see Chapters I and II above; for Hugh fitzGrip, see *VCH Dorset* iii, p. 27; Laurence Keen, 'An introduction to the Dorset Domesday', *The Dorset Domesday*, ed. Ann Williams and R.W.H. Erskine (London, 1990), pp. 18–20.
[31] GDB, fol. 78v, Exon, fol. 39v (*DB Dorset*, no. 13,5); GDB, fol. 82v, Exon, fol. 51v (*DB Dorset*, no. 47,10)
[32] *VCH Dorset* iii, p. 36. For Harding, see Chapter V below.

ministerial tenures. Beorhtwine held four hides of thegnland of Cerne Abbey, for which he paid 30s a year as well as (or perhaps instead of) service.[33] The three thegns who held three hides at Cranbourne of the king (and before 1066 of Beorhtric son of Ælfgar) paid £3 'as well as service' (*excepto servitio*).[34] One suspects that the three *milites* who held Bowood (6 hides) of the bishop of Salisbury were identical with the three thegns who held in 1066, for two of them (Osmaer and Ælfric) have English names, but Exon does not now include the Dorset lands of the bishop of Salisbury.[35]

Some English mesne-tenants held at farm (*ad firmam*), that is, they paid a fixed annual rent in return for the profits of the estate. The *Anglo-Saxon Chronicle* has some bitter words on the king's abuse of this system:

> The king sold his land on very hard terms – as hard as he could. Then came somebody else and offered more than the other had given, and the king let it go to the man who had offered him more. Then came the third, and offered still more, and the king gave it into the hands of the man who offered him most of all, and did not care how sinfully the reeves got it from poor men, nor how many unlawful things they did.[36]

That the king's men had as few scruples as their royal lord is suggested by the case of Æthelric, who continued to hold his manor at Marsh Gibbon, Bucks, at farm of William fitzAnsculf, 'in heaviness and misery'.[37] In Essex too, Richard fitzGilbert leased Thaxted to an unnamed Englishman for £60 rent (*ad censum*), £10 more than its value, and each year the renders 'are deficient in at least £10'.[38] Of course not only the English were farming land, but 'names of native origin form a remarkably high proportion' of those who did.[39]

Against these suggestions of exploitation may be set some signs of good will. Eadgifu held one and half hides in Edmondsham at farm of Humphrey the chamberlain. The Geld Rolls describe her as a widow, and reveal that the land had been freed of geld by Queen Matilda in memory of her son Richard, killed in a hunting-accident in the New Forest in 1081.[40] Why Matilda chose Eadgifu

---

[33] GDB, fol. 77v, Exon, fol. 36 (*DB Dorset*, no. 11,1 and note).
[34] GDB, fol. 75v, Exon, fol. 29 (*DB Dorset*, no. 1,16). It is Exon which reveals that the three thegns held TRE.
[35] GDB, fol. 77 (*DB Dorset*, no. 3,17). The third knight, Godfrey, may be French; a *miles francigenus* held two hides of thegnland at Nettlecombe of Cerne Abbey (GDB, fol. 78, Exon, fol. 38, *DB Dorset*, no. 11,13 and note).
[36] *AS Chron*, 1087.
[37] GDB, fol. 148v. William fitzAnsculf's father, Ansculf de Picquigny, had been sheriff of Bucks (Green, *English sheriffs to 1154*, p. 28).
[38] LDB, fol. 38v.
[39] Lennard, *Rural England*, p. 154.
[40] GDB, fol. 83; VCH *Dorset* iii, p. 47. Humphrey the chamberlain seems to have been in Queen Matilda's service.

for this pious benefaction is unknown. King William made a similar grant in Richard's memory when he gave Tewin, Herts to Halfdane and his mother.[41]

In addition to those actually holding land some were attempting to regain expropriated property. *Toxus* (Toki) was claiming a parcel of land at Swyre, given him by King Edward, against William de Eu and the son of Oda the chamberlain claimed three hides at West Chelborough against William de Moyon. The outcome is not recorded in Toki's case, but the king had ordered that Oda's son should have right in respect of the land (*rex iussit ut inde rectum habeat*). Toki's appeal to pre-Conquest conditions has a parallel in the claim of the Berkshire thegn Ordgar that he ought to hold Berrick Salome and Gangsdown, not of Miles Crispin, but of the king, because 'he and his father and uncle held freely TRE'.[42]

Domesday's information on English subtenants can be supplemented from the surveys in the cartulary of Shaftesbury Abbey.[43] These reveal layers of society not visible in Domesday, particularly free men, and give additional information on the abbey's mesne-tenants. They show that the two free Englishmen (*anglici liberi*) recorded at Sixpenny Handley probably lived at Gussage St Michael, one of the manorial berewicks not separately recorded in Domesday. Two hides at Gussage were given to the abbey as the dowry of a woman with the English name Ailveva (OE Æthelgifu). She may have been a relative of the unnamed *anglici*, in which case they were almost certainly of thegnly status. They may have been related to a family of knightly tenants, for in the early twelfth century Ailveva's dower was in the hands of Turstin fitzReinfred, who held a fee of the abbey at Hazledon; one of his sons bore the name Alvred, which could represent OE Alfred.[44]

KENT

One would not expect to find many English survivors in Kent, a shire which, with Sussex, had borne the brunt of the Norman invasion, and suffered further upheavals from the activities of Eustace of Boulogne. Domesday names most of the 'better men' of the shire on the eve of the Conquest but none appear in 1086.[45] Æthelnoth of Canterbury, the most prominent, is not heard of after 1067, when he was taken as a hostage to Normandy, and by 1078 his estates were in

---

[41] *GDB*, fols 141–141v. It is possible, though perhaps unlikely, that Halfdane was Eadgifu's son. Her husband may have been Dodda, who held two estates at Edmondsham, one of which was held in 1086 by Schelin of the king (and before that, of the queen) and the other by Humphrey the chamberlain (*GDB*, fols 75v (Exon, fol. 29v), 83). On the other hand, Dodda may be the unnamed thegn who held of Humphrey at farm in 1086 (*VCH Dorset* iii, p. 128).

[42] *GDB*, fols 80, 81v, 159v.

[43] See note 29 above.

[44] Williams, 'The knights of Shaftesbury Abbey', pp. 218–20, 225, 228. She is probably the Aileva recorded among the nuns of Shaftesbury c.1113 (Kathleen Cooke, 'Donors and daughters: Shaftesbury Abbey's benefactors, endowments and nuns', *ANS* 12 (1990), pp. 31–2, 34 note 21).

[45] *GDB*, fols 1, 1v (*DB Kent*, nos. D11, 17,25).

other hands.[46] By 1086, only eleven or twelve named Englishmen appear as tenants. A few more can be added from the *Domesday Monachorum* and St. Augustine's *Inquisitio*, of whom the only man of substance appears to be Deormann of London.[47] The old order seems to have been completely swept away and in the early twelfth century, an exiled Kentishman living in Denmark was lamenting the fate of *Anglorum gens nobilissima*, slain or scattered or reduced to 'public servitude'.[48]

There are, however, indications that this is not the whole story. In the first year of King John's reign (1199–1200), Richard of Garrington, Kent, claimed a carucate in Yalding in right of Ailred, grandfather of his mother Ailveva. Theobald of Twitham (in Wingham) contested this, claiming that the land was his *hereditas* from his father Hamon, through Hawise, second wife of the same Ailred who was Richard's maternal great-grandfather.[49] That two Kentish families at the turn of the twelfth and thirteenth centuries should claim through an Englishman is in itself striking, regardless of the possibility that the genealogical details may have been misremembered or indeed invented. At the very least, Richard is unlikely to have got the name of his mother Ailveva (OE Æthelgifu) wrong. The interest does not, however, end there for the Ailred (Æthelred) from whom both Richard and Theobald claimed must be Æthelred of Yalding, the pre-Conquest tenant of Yalding and one of those who had sake and soke over their lands in West Kent.[50] That he is said, in 1199–1200, to have been holding on the day King Henry I died (in 1135) is not significant, for appeals to pre-Conquest tenure were not allowable – which in itself suggests that they were sometimes made. Since both Richard and Theobald claimed in right of their descent from Æthelred (it was what happened afterwards that was in dispute)

---

[46] See the memorandum of 1078–9 printed in D.C. Douglas, 'Odo, Lanfranc and the Domesday survey', *Historical Essays in honour of James Tait*, ed. J.G. Edwards, V.H. Galbraith and E.F. Jacob (Manchester, 1933), pp. 47–57; translated in F.R.H. du Boulay, *The Lordship of Canterbury* (London, 1966), pp. 38–9.

[47] There is some doubt about the nationality of Christchurch's tenant at Seasalter, whose name is rendered *Blize*; it might be 'a garbled Anglo-Norman attempt at the rare OE personal name Blithhere' or perhaps continental Germanic Blithgaer (*GDB*, fol. 5, *DB Kent*, no. 3,10 and note). For Deormann of London, see Chapter VIII below.

[48] Ælnoth of Canterbury, in *Scriptores Rerum Danicarum*, ed. Jacob Langebek (Copenhagen 1774), iii, pp. 346–7. For Ælnoth (Æthelnoth) see Chapter III above.

[49] *Curia Regis Rolls, Richard I–2 John*, HMSO (London, 1922) pp. 158, 220. The jurors found for Theobald. For the place-names, see J.K. Wallenberg, *The place-names of Kent* (Uppsala, 1934), pp. 523, 539.

[50] Æthelred's name appears as *Aldret* (Ealdred) in the entry for Yalding (*GDB*, fol. 14) but as *Alret de Ellinges* in the list of landholders (*GDB*, fol. 1v). The correct form of his name, *Adalredus* (Æthelred) appears in the memorandum of 1078–9 cited in note 46 above (see also Olof von Feilitzen, *The pre-Conquest personal names of Domesday Book* (Uppsala, 1937), p. 186 and note 5). As well as Yalding, Æthelred held lands in Pimp's Court and Kennington in Chart, which do not appear in Domesday Book.

they could collude in the fiction that their ancestor had held in 1135 – the limit of legal memory at the time.[51]

It is possible that Æthelred was holding Yalding, and his other manor at East Barming, as a tenant of Richard fitzGilbert in 1086, having survived the Norman settlement in reduced circumstances. He might not have been alone. Godric of Brabourne was one of the sokeholders (*alodiarii*) in East Kent, holding, apart from Brabourne itself and its berewick of Aldglose, manors at Little Delce and Offham, the last of which he had bought from his sister Eadgifu in the late 1040s. Godric may have been a descendant of Brihtmaer of Bourne, holder of Brabourne in the tenth century.[52] All his land was in other hands by 1086. Brabourne was held by Hugh de Montfort, Offham by Hugh de Port of the bishop of Bayeux and Aldglose and Little Delce of the same bishop by William de Thaon's son (unnamed).[53] By 1100 Little Delce had passed to one Geoffrey of Delce, a vassal of Walter Tirel, who gave its tithes to Rochester Cathedral in return for membership of the church's fraternity. At about the same time, one Godric of Delce gave the tithe of his grain-rent (*annona*) for the same privilege.[54] It is most unlikely that the donor of c.1100 is the same as the pre-Conquest holder of Little Delce, who was active in the 1040s, but he might be a kinsman, perhaps a grandson. There may be another such case at Monks Horton; the Alnoth who

---

[51] It was from the time of Henry II that *anglici* (and seemingly only *anglici*) were prohibited from making claims through ancestors holding before the time of Henry I (R.C. van Caeneghem, *Royal writs in England from the Conquest to Glanville*, Selden Society 77 (London, 1959), pp. 217–18; nos. 165, 169, 172, 175). Nevertheless in the thirteenth century one William son of Albert of Ramsey claimed land at *Uppenhale* (probably Upwood, Hunts.) in right of his ancestor Aylwin, who held in the time of King Æthelred II – perhaps Æthelwine, ealdorman of East Anglia, who 'had his hall and held his court' at Upwood (Public Record Office, Common Pleas, 40/14 m. 19, see VCH Hunts. ii, p. 239, *Chron Ramsey*, p. 52 and Paul Brand, 'Time out of mind: the knowledge and use of the eleventh- and twelfth-century past in thirteenth-century litigation', ANS 16 (1994), pp. 37–9. I have to thank Dr Brand for this reference and for discussing the case of Yalding, though he is not responsible for the opinions expressed here).

[52] GDB, fols 1, 7, 8v, 10, 13v; S. 1473; Robertson, *Charters*, pp. 192–3, 372, 439 He witnesses charters of Archbishop Eadsige in 1045 and 1048–9 (S. 1400, 1471; Robertson, *Charters*, pp. 188–9, 200–5. For some reason he is called Godric of Bishopsbourne in DB Kent, nos. D17, 9, 42, but Bishopsbourne is distinguished from *Godricesburne* (Brabourne) in *Domesday Monachorum*, p. 80.

[53] Hugh de Montfort may have received Brabourne immediately after the Conquest, for his charter granting its tithes to Saint-Ymer-en-Auge is witnessed by Mauritius, bishop of Rouen, who died on 9 April 1067, but the charter 'cannot be considered as authentic in its present form' (*Domesday Monachorum*, p. 67, note 1).

[54] *Textus Roffensis*, fols 190, 195; Hirokazu Tsurushima, 'The Fraternity of Rochester Cathedral Priory c.1100', ANS 14 (1992), p. 319). Geoffrey also gave 30 acres at Prestfield when his son became a monk at Rochester (*Textus Roffensis*, fol. 194v). My notes on Kentish survivors are heavily dependent on the work of Mr Tsurushima, who has also discussed the topic with me and made many personal contributions to my findings.

held it of Hugh de Montfort in 1086 may be the heir of the pre-Conquest tenant Leofwine.[55]

As in Dorset, Domesday Book does not name all the men holding land in Kent in 1086. The manor of Badlesmere was held by Ansfrid of Odo of Bayeux but claimed by St Augustine's. The hundred-court supported the abbey, and the shire-court testified that the pre-Conquest abbot had sake and soke over the holder of Badlesmere but against this 'the man's son' says (present tense) that his father could commend himself (*se vertere*) where he would.[56] Domesday Book does not name the pre-Conquest holder, but the corresponding entry in St Augustine's *Inquisitio* calls him Godric Wisce.[57] The dispute illustrates the distinction between rights over land (sake and soke) and rights over men (commendation) and it is significant that the shire and hundred courts found in favour of the sokeholder, though Ansfrid was still in possession of the land. Moreover it is clear that Godric's son was still holding Badlesmere in 1086, presumably as Ansfrid's tenant. It seems likely that he (or perhaps his father) had commended himself to Ansfrid, who then appropriated the estate. As Galbraith said, commenting on this case, 'we can easily exaggerate the severity of the tenurial upheaval . . . behind Norman subtenants, in short, there may have been a great many unrecorded Saxons who continued actually to farm the land'.[58]

'Farming' in the medieval sense was, as we have seen, common. The *Textus Roffensis* reveals the English origin of one major 'farmer' in Kent, Robert Latimer, who held seven manors at farm of the bishop of Bayeux and more modest tenements of the archbishop of Canterbury and St Augustine's.[59] None of this had belonged to Robert before the Conquest. His largest manors, Lessness, Chatham and Boxley, had been held by Azur of Lessness, Earl Godwine and Æthelnoth *cild* of Canterbury respectively; the smaller estates were held by men commended to, or holding under, the earl, Æthelnoth *cild* and Edward of Stone.[60]

[55] Leofwine son of Godwine of Horton witnessed a Kentish marriage-agreement between 1016 and 1020 (S.1461; Robertson, *Charters*, pp. 150–1, 399).

[56] GDB, fols 10, 12v: DB Kent, nos. 5,149: 7,30. The dispute is exactly parallel to that between the sons of Beorhtwine and the church of Worcester, see note 15 above.

[57] *Inquisitio*, pp. 4–5. Godric's by-name may be a toponymic, OE *wisc*, 'a damp meadow or marsh' (ME *atte wisce*), see G. Tengvik, *Old English by-names* (Uppsala, 1938), p. 126; P.H. Reaney, *A dictionary of British surnames*, 2nd edn (London, 1976), p. 387 (Wish).

[58] V.H. Galbraith, *The Making of Domesday Book* (Oxford, 1961), p. 155. A similar case is that of Luddington, Hunts, held by Drew de Hastings of Ramsey Abbey *in feudo* and of Drew by Leofwine *ad censum* (*Cartularium Monasterii de Rameseia*, ed. W.H. Hart and P.A. Lyons, Rolls Series (London, 1884–93), i, p. 131). This Leofwine's brother, Colgrim of Grantham, was a tenant-in-chief in 1086 (see Chapter V note 53 below).

[59] GDB, fols 3, 6v, 8, 8v, 11v, 12 and see *Domesday Monachorum*, p. 87; Lennard, *Rural England*, p. 114 and note 4.

[60] According to Domesday the manor of Teston was held of King Edward by Edward, and also by three brothers as three manors (GDB, fol. 8v). Such multiple manor entries can indicate dependent tenures (Roffe, 'From thegnage to barony', pp. 162–3) and the brothers probably held under Edward, the comparative rarity of whose name allows us to identify him with Edward of Stone, a sokeholder in West Kent (GDB, fol. 1v).

Three of Robert's manors were paying farms in excess of their value: Chatham, worth £15, paid £35; Boxley, worth £30, paid £55; Harbilton, worth £3, paid £4. Clearly Robert was a man of some substance (he was paying over £114 per annum for his estates) but the sources of his wealth are not immediately obvious. Some perhaps came from 'sub-letting'; Lessness was worth £22 but 'he who holds it' paid £30 and there is no indication that the payer was Robert himself.[61]

The clue to Robert's affluence lies in his origins. He was the son of Æthelric, priest of Chatham and canon of Rochester, and Godgifu his wife, and his brother Ælfwine was reeve of Chatham. Æthelric had property in Rochester and Ælfwine held land in the Isle of Grain; Robert Latimer's wife (her name is unknown) left land at Homden in Frindsbury to Rochester.[62] It was not on land, however, that the family's prosperity depended. A charter issued soon after Domesday describes Robert and his brother, Ælfwine the reeve, as officers (ministri) of the sheriff. They belonged to the ministerial thegnage, who looked to the greater lords for patronage and support in return for service. After the Conquest they had managed to attach themselves to the new aristocracy and Robert Latimer had gone so far as to adopt a Norman name.[63] His by-name Latimer (latinarius) shows the service he performed, for it means 'interpreter' (he is called Robert interpres in the Domesday Monachorum).[64] Public service could be very lucrative and goes far to explain Robert's prosperity.[65] He had a daughter

[61] Lennard, Rural England, pp. 150–1; DB Kent, no. 5,19. For the significance of 'he who holds', see the entries for Hoo (GDB, fol. 8v) and Chelsfield (GDB, fol. 6v; Tsurushima, 'The fraternity of Rochester Cathedral Priory circa 1100', pp. 324–5).
[62] Textus Roffensis, fols 182v–183, 190v–191, 200v–201 and see Tsurushima, 'The fraternity of Rochester Cathedral Priory circa 1100', pp. 329–31.
[63] As had another Robert, son of Ailwin (Æthelwine) the priest, who leased land in Essex of St Paul's, London (Lennard, Rural England, p. 179). Robert Latimer's original name may have been Leofgeat, if he is identical with the Robert Liuegit (Leofgeat) who held half a fee of the archbishop in 1093/6; this fee passed, like Robert Latimer's lands, to the Crevequers (Domesday Monachorum, p. 105; du Boulay, Lordship of Canterbury, p. 387). Another Kentishman who was known by a continental as well as an English name is Eadsige Gerald, son of Edward, whose memorial stone, possibly of the late tenth or eleventh century, was found in the ruins of St Augustine's, Canterbury (Elisabeth Okasha, 'A supplement to Handlist of Anglo-Saxon non-runic inscriptions', ASE 11 (1983), pp. 88–9).
[64] Domesday Monachorum, pp. 87, 101. A Godric Latimer held Buckland, Kent, of St Martin's, Dover, in succession to Oswig Wild the priest (GDB, fol. 1v, DB Kent, no. M24 and note) and in Herefordshire Leofwine Latimer held land at Leominster and Yarpole (GDB, fols 180, 180v). Robert and Godric were sons of priests (like Robert son of Ailwin in Essex, see previous note) and perhaps in a good position to receive an education.
[65] For the opportunities, legal and illegal, available to reeves, see Campbell, 'Some agents and agencies of the late Anglo-Saxon state', pp. 207–8; see also Eadmer's opinion of the reeves on the manors of Christ Church, Canterbury: 'if he (Archbishop Anselm) had never been present on his manors to hear their complaints, his reeves would have oppressed them in many ways (as often happened) until, as the oppression got worse and worse, they were utterly destroyed' (VA, p. 71).

who married Brod the priest, but, since his land descended to the Crevequer family, presumably no male heirs.

Men like Robert were essential both to the Norman magnates who received confiscated estates and to the royal officers who took over the running of local government. Their expertise was needed by the newcomers, and they in turn needed the patronage and protection of the new lords. Nothing is more likely than that many median thegns and free men remained *in situ*, though appearing but rarely in the surviving sources. The Rochester charters and memoranda are especially valuable in preserving the names not only of great lords who enriched the church but also of the smaller benefactions of those lords' men.[66] When a lord entered the fraternity of the church, his men often entered with him. Between 1100 and 1108, William d'Aubigny, *pincerna* (butler) of Henry I, gave to Rochester the tithes of his manor at Elham, with a carucate in Exted and a wood called *Acholte* ('oakwood'). Eleven of his men (*homines*) made donations and entered the fraternity with him. Four have continental (French) names: Ralph of *Chieresburh*, William's *dapifer* (steward); Roger of Elham, a *miles* (knight); Rainald of Boykewood; Herbert of *Gatindene*. The rest have insular names (names used in England before the Conquest): Leofwine of Exted; Leofwine *Scone* of Beerforstall (Farm); Ealdwulf of Shuttlesfield; Blaeccmann of Bladbean; Wulfric the trader (*se mangere*); and Edward and Baldwin of *Oferland*. All the identifiable toponymics relate to places in the neighbourhood of Elham.[67] The existence of these tenants could not be guessed from the Domesday account of Elham, which records only the dependent peasants: 41 villans, 8 bordars and 8 slaves. It seems that here, as elsewhere, the Domesday commissioners simply left out a whole stratum of free men, whose descendants appear in the *Textus Roffensis*.[68] Their predecessors presumably held under the pre-Conquest lord of Elham, Eadric. Though his name does not appear among the *alodiarii* of East Kent, the list is not complete, and his lands suggest that he was an important local magnate. Besides Elham he held Temple Ewell and Tickenhurst, and witnessed a grant to Rochester by Archbishop Eadsige in 1048/50.[69] It is possible that, like Æthelred of Yalding, Eadric or his heir was still holding Elham at farm in 1086, for the manor, though worth £40 nevertheless (*tamen*) renders £50. It might even be that Roger *miles* of Elham was Eadric's heir and the family one of those who were 'given an inviolable title to whatever they had acquired from their lords by their own deserts and a lawful bargain'.

---

[66] Tsurushima, 'The fraternity of Rochester Cathedral Priory, c.1100', pp. 319–22.
[67] *Textus Roffensis*, fols 187v–189v. Similar groups of English and Norman tenants, some 'knightly', some not, are found on the estates of Shaftesbury Abbey at a similar date (Williams, 'The knights of Shaftesbury Abbey', pp. 230–2).
[68] GDB, fol. 9v; DB Kent, no. 5,129. For other 'missing' free men, see VCH *Dorset* iii, pp. 14–5; David Roffe, 'Domesday Book and northern society' EHR 105 (1991), p. 332.
[69] GDB, fols 11, 11v (DB Kent, nos. 5,185:210); S.1400 (Robertson, *Charters*, pp. 204–5, 451). Only eight *alodiarii* are mentioned by name and Eadric of Elham is probably one of those *qui habent sacam et socam* (GDB, fol. 1, DB Kent, no. D17, and see D11).

CAMBRIDGESHIRE

Cambridgeshire lay in the territory of the East Anglian earldom, in the area whose inhabitants were known in the tenth century as 'the East Mercians'. From the 1030s the east midlands constituted an earldom, subordinate to the earl of East Anglia, and held in turn by Thuri *comes Mediterraneorum* (1038–1044), Beorn Estrithson (1044–49) and Ralph of Hereford (1050–57); after Ralph's death, it was divided, the southern shires passing to Earl Leofwine and the northern shires, probably including Cambridgeshire, to Earl Tostig and, after 1065, to Earl Waltheof.[70] It is possible that some Cambridgeshire thegns went to the battles of Stamfordbridge and Hastings in 1066 but its worst moments were in 1075, when the shire bore the brunt of the fighting in the rebellion of the Three Earls.

By 1086, seventeen named Englishmen appear among the mesne-tenants, plus a number of unnamed *anglici* and sokemen. To these must be added the English hundredal jurors recorded in the ICC and the Ely Inquest. For each hundred eight names are recorded, four French, four English.[71] Some can be identified among the mesne-tenants in Domesday but most of the English, and many of the French jurors, do not appear at all. Robert the Englishman (*anglicus*) of Fordham was one of the jurors of Staploe hundred but does not appear in the entry for Fordham, which was held of Count Alan by his steward, Wymarc.[72] Wulfmaer, Wighen's man, was a juror in Cheveley hundred, but though Wighen Delamere held Woodditton of Count Alan, Wulfmaer is not mentioned.[73] Some of the jurors are clearly the pre-Conquest tenants, still *in situ*. Thorbjorn of Orwell, a juror in Wetherley hundred, held three and a quarter virgates and five acres in Orwell under Eadgifu the Fair in 1066, and Huscarl of Swaffham, a juror in Staine hundred, held three virgates in Swaffham as King Edward's man; neither is entered as holding in 1086.[74] Altogether the lists of jurors add about 60 names to our tally of 'survivors' in Cambridgeshire.

Most of these men were of modest standing and some held ministerial tenures. Alwine *Hamelcoc*, who held half a virgate at Abington Pigotts (and had held before 1066 also), was a royal beadle.[75] A more eminent royal servant was Godric the steward, who held the king's manor of Exning at farm and also had charge

---

[70] Williams, 'The king's nephew: the family and career of Ralph, earl of Hereford', pp. 327–43.

[71] C.P. Lewis, 'The Domesday Jurors', *Haskins Soc. J.* 5 (1993), pp. 17–44. The English jurors are listed on pp. 41–4; see also *DB Cambridgeshire*, Appendices A-P. The same principle (equal numbers of French and English jurors) appears in the account of the Ely pleas of the 1070s, heard by 'Hardwin, Guy, Wimer, Wihumer, Godric, Northmann, Colswein, Godwine and many other *milites probati Francigene et Angli*' from the four shires of Essex, Hertford, Huntingdon and Bedford (*Liber Eliensis*, pp. 198–9; van Caeneghem i, p. 43).

[72] GDB, fol. 195v, *DB Cambridgeshire*, no. 14,71 and note; Appendix A.

[73] GDB, fol. 195, *DB Cambridgeshire*, no. 14,61 and note; Appendix B.

[74] GDB, fols 194v, 195; *DB Cambridgeshire*, nos. 14,41:64; Appendices K and C.

[75] GDB, fol. 190; *DB Cambridgeshire*, no. 1,20 and note.

of royal manors in Essex, Norfolk and Suffolk.[76] Sigar, who held Thriplow, Foxton, Shepreth and Orwell of Geoffrey de Mandeville, had held the same manors under Geoffrey's *antecessor*, Esger the staller and was Esger's steward; he is still called Sigar the steward when he appears among the jurors of Thriplow hundred.[77] His survival is probably due to his ministerial abilities, though there is nothing to suggest that he was Geoffrey de Mandeville's steward. He is more likely to have served as a reeve; Ælfric, Eudo fitzHubert's reeve, was a juror in Longstowe hundred.[78] Though it has been suggested that the English jurors as a group were of lower status than their French counterparts, the most recent work on the jurors' lists suggests that they were socially on a par.[79] Only one held land as a tenant-in-chief, and his holding was very small. Most jurors were either mesne-tenants of modest standing, or unrecorded sub-tenants of the mesne-tenants themselves, or farmers and lessees. It was on men of this type, resident (unlike their baronial masters) in the shires and hundreds, that the local business of administration, both public and private, must often have devolved.

Ordmaer of Badlingham, a juror of Staploe hundred, does appear in Domesday, holding Badlingham of Count Alan; he had been a tenant of the count's *antecessor*, Eadgifu the Fair.[80] He was among the jurors of a shire-court who, between 1077 and 1082, were fined for giving a false judgement. The case, recorded in the *Textus Roffensis*, gives a rare glimpse of local conditions in William the Conqueror's reign. The parties in the suit were Gundulf, bishop of Rochester, and Picot, sheriff of Cambridgeshire, and the dispute concerned the ownership of Isleham, Cambs, a berewick of Freckenham, Suffolk.[81] The bishop claimed that it had been seized by Ulfkell (*Olchete[l]*), a royal *serviens* and, by his name, an Englishman. He had acted with Picot's connivance and the shire-court, 'for fear of the sheriff' (*timore vicecomitis*) found against the bishop. Odo of Bayeux, who was presiding, ordered the shire to choose twelve of their number to confirm the decision on oath. The six who are named were all English:

[76] For Godric the steward, see Chapter V below. Like the East Anglian manors, Exning had belonged to Eadgifu the Fair and (probably) to Earl Ralph Guader (see Chapter III above).

[77] GDB, fol. 197: DB *Cambridgeshire*, no. 22,2 (and note): 3–4: 9–10 and Appendix H. Sigar had also held Sawston and Haslingfield of Esger, but in 1086 they belonged to one Roger as Geoffey de Mandeville's tenant.

[78] DB *Cambridgeshire*, Appendix L.

[79] Lewis, 'The Domesday jurors', pp. 23–5. I am very grateful to Dr Lewis for allowing me to read his paper before publication, and for his helpful comments on the identification of the Cambridgeshire jurors and their lands.

[80] GDB, fol. 195v: DB *Cambridgeshire*, no. 14,67 and Appendix A. He had also held land at Swaffham (no. 14,65).

[81] *Textus Roffensis*, fols 175–175v; van Caeneghem i, no. 19, pp. 50–1. It is important to remember that what we have is Rochester's view of the case; Picot may have had more right on his side than the account implies. The tenurial history of the estate is fairly complicated, see Robin Fleming, 'Testimony, the Domesday Inquest and Domesday Book', ANS 17 (1995), forthcoming; idem, *Kings and lords in Conquest England*, p. 86, note 139.

Ordmaer himself, Edward of Chippenham, Harold and Leofwine *sac* of Exning, Wulfwine of Landwade, near Exning, and Eadric of Isleham. News of the false verdict came to the ears of a former reeve of Freckenham, Grim the priest, who had received its *servitia et costumas* and had had one of the jurors (presumably Eadric of Isleham) 'in the manor under him'. Grim went to Gundulf of Rochester and accused the jurors of perjury. Gundulf complained to Bishop Odo and the twelve were summoned to London, where before an assembly of 'most of the better barons of all England' (*multos ex melioribus totius Angliae barones*) they were found guilty. Rochester got its land, and the false jurors, with the rest of the shire-court, were fined £300.[82] One hopes that Picot helped them pay it, but his reputation – 'a hungry lion, a ravening wolf, a cunning fox, a dirty pig, an impudent dog', as the monks of Ely put it – is not encouraging.[83] What is most interesting in the present context is that the jurors and minor officials recorded were all English.

One of the more substantial jurors (at least before 1066) was Almaer *cild* of Bourn, a juror of Longstowe hundred.[84] He was Count Alan's tenant at East Hatley and Croydon, both in Armingford hundred, and at Kingston, Bourn, Caldecote, Longstowe and Hatley St George, all in Longstowe hundred. Most of this land (apart from Croydon and Kingston) had been held by Almaer of Eadgifu the Fair, to whom he was commended.[85] Almaer's name is common and it is difficult to identify him further, but since he is called Almaer of Bourn in the ICC, he is probably Almaer, King Edward's thegn, who had held a hide and three virgates at Bourn. The tenement was held in 1086 by Peter de Valognes, sheriff of Essex, and of him by Picot of Cambridgeshire, which suggests that Almaer must also be the unnamed thegn who preceded Picot the sheriff at the manor of Bourn in the same vill.[86] The manor was assessed at 13 hides, three of which were in demesne; 20 men, commended to various lords, held nine hides, and one hide, belonging to the church of Bourn, was held by two priests commended to the unnamed thegn. All could give and sell their lands, but the priests' holding could not be withdrawn from the church of Bourn.[87]

Since Almaer held land in Armingford hundred, as well as in Longstowe, he

---

[82] In 1086 the bishop of Rochester held one and a half hides and 20 acres in Isleham under Archbishop Lanfranc; according to the Suffolk Domesday, it was Lanfranc who had judged Freckenham to belong to the bishopric of Rochester (GDB, fol. 190v; LDB, fol. 381).

[83] *Liber Eliensis*, p. 211.

[84] DB *Cambridgeshire*, Appendices J, L.

[85] GDB, fols 194, 194v, 195: DB *Cambridgeshire*, nos. 14,23–4:47:49–52 and notes.

[86] In all Domesday records 4 tenements in Bourn: (i) the 13-hide manor held by the unnamed thegn (GDB, fols 200v–201); (ii) a hide and three virgates held by Almaer, King Edward's thegn (GDB, fol. 201v); (iii) 4¼ hides held by Almaer of Eadgifu the Fair and subsequently of Count Alan (GDB, fol. 195); (iv) 1 hide held by Ramsey Abbey as a berewick of Longstowe (GDB, fol. 192v). It seems that Bourn was originally a 20-hide vill, of which Almaer, in 1066, held 19 hides in one way or another.

[87] They were probably the priests of Bourn itself and Caldecote, for Picot gave Bourn

may be identical with Almaer or Æthelmaer son of Colswein, who was a juror in Armingford, as was his father.[88] Colswein, like Almaer, was a tenant of Count Alan, with land at Whaddon, Meldreth and Melbourn, all in Armingford hundred; he had held the same land under Eadgifu the Fair.[89] Before the Conquest Almaer may have held about 22 hides of land in Cambridgeshire. He subsequently lost most of Bourn, but kept the land (2 hides, 3½ virgates) which he had held of Eadgifu the Fair, probably by commending himself to her ultimate successor, Count Alan, and acquired tenements in Croydon and Kingston (3½ virgates) which had belonged to others before 1066. Thus he survived, though reduced both in status and wealth.

SHROPSHIRE

Shropshire, like its neighbour Cheshire and for the same reasons, had no royal demesne in 1086. Virtually the whole shire, with the exception of a few lay and ecclesiastical estates, was in the hands of its earl, Roger de Montgomery, who also held the rape of Arundel, Sussex.[90] As a result, the Domesday scribe subdivided his huge fief into sections for each of his mesne-tenants, and went on to name their tenants as well. The Shropshire Domesday thus reveals the third level of tenure, glimpsed only rarely elsewhere. Though many of these tenants are French, some are English, which reinforces the impression that Englishmen were not so much dispossessed as depressed in tenurial status.

Pre-Conquest Shropshire had been dominated by the king, who retained administrative and judicial control, and by the Mercian earls, who were the major landholders. Next come the richer thegns, the most important of whom were Eadric (the Wild) and Siward (son of Æthelgar), with perhaps 100 hides and 80 hides respectively. They in turn are followed by a group of less wealthy but still prominent local thegns: Leofwine cild, Almund, Ealdred (Siward's brother), Earnwig, Godwine, Hunning, Swein and Thorth.[91]

It is noticeable that several of these men continued to hold land in 1086, though reduced both in wealth and status. Earnwig retained his manors at Pontesbury and Onslow (7 hides) as the tenant of Roger and Robert fitzCorbet, who also held Earnwig's former manors at Westbury and Oaks (4 hides).[92]

church and the chapel at Caldecote to St Giles, Cambridge (later Barnwell Priory) before 1092 (VCH Cambs. v, pp. 13, 23–4). I owe this reference to Dr C.P. Lewis.
[88] GDB, fols 200v–201, 201v; DB Cambridgeshire, nos. 32,23; 33,1.
[89] GDB, fol. 194v; DB Cambridgeshire, nos. 14,28:32–3 and notes.
[90] For the earldoms of Shrewsbury and Chester, see Lewis, 'The early earls of Norman England', pp. 219–20. Earl Hugh d'Avranches held the same position in Cheshire as did Roger de Montgomery in Shropshire.
[91] C.P. Lewis, 'An introduction to the Shropshire Domesday', The Shropshire Domesday, ed. Ann Williams and R.W.H. Erskine (London, 1990), pp. 1–2, 7, 20–1. The same pattern of tenure – one or two great men and a larger number of more modest, but still prosperous landholders – is found in Gloucestershire (see Williams, 'An introduction to the Gloucestershire Domesday', p. 18).
[92] GDB, fols 255v, 256: DB Shropshire, nos. 4,4,12:15; 4,5,3:7. He may be the Earnwine

Hunning's name is not found outside Shropshire and all the references are thus likely to be to one individual, who held close on 19 hides, in association with his brother Wulfgeat.[93] The brothers had retained only four hides, at Lawley, Moreton Corbett, Preston Brockhurst and Willey, which they held of Turold de Verley; they may also be the two unnamed *milites* who held 4 hides of the same Turold at Longford.[94] These manors later passed to the fitzTorets, and from them to the fitzCorbets.

The fitzTorets were presumably the descendants of Thorth (whose name is rendered as *Toret* or *Thored* in Domesday). In 1066 he held nearly 13 hides in Shropshire and 24½ hides in Cheshire.[95] How and why he acquired Hunning's land is unknown but soon after 1108 he witnessed a charter of Robert, son of Hunning's lord, Turold de Verley.[96] Thorth's own land is not, for some reason, found in the hands of his descendants, although he retained about nine hides as the tenant of Reginald de Bailleul, to whom the remainder of his land passed.[97] The rarity of his name suggests that he is the Thorth who held half a hide at Langley of Earl Roger. This tenement appears in the section which, in another shire, would probably have covered the lands of the *taini regis* and was later held by the service of carrying a goshawk each year from Shrewsbury Castle to Stepney, Middlesex.[98]

Almund and his son Alweard also appear among the earl's tenants, holding between them five manors assessed at a total of eight and a half hides; one of these was held of Alweard by another Englishman, called Ordmaer. All had belonged to Almund before 1066.[99] There were at least two men of this name in pre-Conquest Shropshire, but the one whose land (15 hides in all) had passed to Reginald de Bailleul is presumably Alweard's father, since an Alweard also appears among Reginald's predecessors.[100] Almund also preceded Reginald de Bailleul in Staffordshire, where he held two hides, and in Warwickshire, ten and a quarter hides. In 1066 he held just over 32 hides of land in three shires, but by 1086 had lost most of it, and retained the rest as tenant of a Norman.

who held Farley (1 hide) of Roger fitzCorbet (and had held it TRE), since the names Earnwig and Earnwine are easily confused (GDB, fol. 255v: DB Shropshire, no. 4,4,13).
93 GDB, fols 255, 255v, 258, 259, 259v, 260: DB Shropshire, nos. 4,3,56; 4,4,1–2; 4,19,6:9–11; 4,20,15–16; 4,26,4; 4,27,8:27; 6,7. No TRE tenant is recorded at Lawley, which Hunning held of Turold de Verley in 1086 (see next note).
94 GDB, fols 257v, 258: DB Shropshire, nos. 4,19,1:6:9–11; VCH Shropshire i, p. 299, note 131.
95 C.P. Lewis, 'An introduction to the Cheshire Domesday', The Cheshire Domesday, ed. Ann Williams and R.W.H. Erskine (London, 1990), p. 15.
96 Una Rees, The Shrewsbury Cartulary (Aberystwyth, 1975), i, p. 34; R.W. Eyton, Antiquities of Shropshire, ii (London, 1855), p. 49; x (London, 1860), pp. 181–5.
97 GDB, fols 254v, 255; DB Shropshire, nos. 4,3,14:20:26:30–1:69.
98 GDB, fol. 259v; DB Shropshire, no. 4,27,10 and note.
99 GDB, fol. 259v: DB Shropshire, nos. 4,27,17–21.
100 GDB, fol. 255: DB Shropshire, nos. 4,3,45:47–8:61:63–4:67–8:70. For the second Almund, see GDB, fol. 258; DB Shropshire, no. 4,20,3.

GENEALOGICAL TABLE VI. EADRIC STREONA

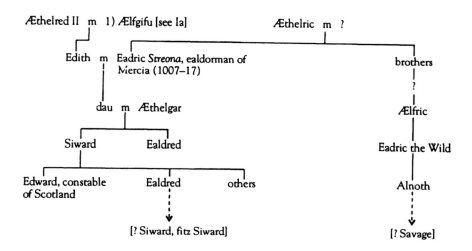

Not all the Englishmen holding land in 1086 appear among the pre-Conquest tenants. Ealhhere (*Alcher*) is presumably English, though his name is commoner in 1086 than before the Conquest.[101] He held four manors from Reginald de Bailleul and one from Earl Roger, and can presumably be identifed with the Ealhhere who held Mundham, Sussex, of the earl.[102] Ealhhere and his son Robert *fitzAerii* were benefactors of Shrewsbury Abbey and ancestors of the Ayer family.[103]

The richest thegns in pre-Conquest Shropshire were Eadric the Wild and his cousin, Siward son of Æthelgar. They belonged to the family of Eadric *Streona*, ealdorman of Mercia (1007–17).[104] John of Worcester, who took a particular interest in Eadric the Wild's career, made him the son of Eadric *Streona's* brother, Ælfric. John is the only source for a brother of Eadric *Streona* called Ælfric, and although his names for the other five brothers, and their father, Æthelric, appear in the witness-lists of Æthelred II's charters at appropriate dates, no Ælfric attests

---

[101] Feilitzen, *Pre-conquest personal names of Domesday Book*, p. 242, has 3 references, all in Devon. In 1086, an Ealhhere held a manor in Staffs. and 4 in Derby., all of Henry de Ferrers and another Ealhhere appears in Essex, holding a manor of Hugh de Montfort (GDB, fols 248v, 274v, 275; LDB, fol. 53v.

[102] GDB, fols 24, 254, 255, 255v; *DB Sussex*, no. 11,41; *DB Shropshire*, nos. 4,3,4:60:65:71; 4,27,35.

[103] Rees, *Shrewsbury Cartulary* i, p. xix (*Alherius*); ii, no. 346, p. 312; Reaney, *Dictionary of British surnames*, p. 17.

[104] For Eadric *Streona*, see Williams, 'Cockles amongst the wheat', pp. 3–6; for Eadric the Wild, see Susan Reynolds, 'Eadric *silvaticus* and the English resistance' *Bulletin of the Institute of Historical Research* 54 (1981), pp. 102–5.

after 990.[105] Perhaps he was the nephew, rather than the brother, of Ealdorman Eadric, which would put Eadric the Wild in the same generation as Siward son of Æthelgar, the ealdorman's grandson.

Eadric's name is one of the commonest and only when he appears with his distinctive by-name, se wilde, silvaticus, salvage, can he be identified with certainty. He held about 12 hides in Herefordshire, which passed to Ralph de Mortimer but most of his land was in Shropshire.[106] Five of his estates (eight hides) had passed, like the Herefordshire land, to Ralph de Mortimer, and another 28½ hides of land can reasonably be assigned to him; his full estate may have been something in the region of 100 hides.[107] He may have submitted to King William in January 1067 (see Chapter I above) but by the summer of that year he was in revolt, and he took part in the rebellion of 1069–70. In 1070 he was reconciled with the king, and is last heard of in the royal host which invaded Scotland in 1072.[108] He might be expected to hold land in 1086, and an Eadric son of Ælfric appears as the tenant of Much Wenlock Priory, holding land at Bourton and an unidentified tenement, probably Hughley.[109] Bourton was assessed at just under three hides and had a mill 'which serves the court', implying the presence of a manor-house. Eadric son of Ælfric is presumably to be identified with Eadric of Wenlock, who witnessed two charters, one issued by the bishop of Hereford and one by Earl Roger of Shrewsbury, both almost contemporary with Domesday.[110]

Though the identity of Eadric son of Ælfric of Wenlock and Eadric the Wild cannot be proven, the latter was almost certainly holding land in 1086. Three of the manors which he held before 1066 (Eudon George (formerly Eudon Savage), Walton (formerly Walton Savage) and Overton) were later held by William le Savage of the Mortimers and the surname suggests that William was a descendant of Eadric the Wild (salvage).[111] Walter Map, writing in the reign of Henry II, tells the famous story of Eadric's fairy bride, itself a variant of a wide-spread folktale, particularly popular in Wales, and records a son of Eadric,

105 Simon Keynes, The diplomas of Æthelred II "the Unready" (Cambridge, 1980), p. 212.
106 GDB, fol. 183v; C.P. Lewis, 'An introduction to the Herefordshire Domesday', The Herefordshire Domesday, ed. Ann Williams and R.W.H. Erskine (London, 1988), p. 9.
107 GDB, fols 253v, 254, 256, 256v, 258v, 260; Lewis, 'An introduction to the Shropshire Domesday', p. 20.
108 FlW, 1070, 1072.
109 GDB, fol. 252v: DB Shropshire, nos. 3c,8:14 and notes.
110 V.H. Galbraith, 'An episcopal land-grant of 1085', EHR 44 (1929), pp. 353–72; J.F.A. Mason, 'Eadric of Bayston', Transactions of the Shropshire Archaeological Society 55 (1954), pp. 112–18.
111 GDB, fol. 257; DB Shropshire, nos. 4,11,5:12:16 and notes; Eyton, Antiquities of Shropshire, iii (London, 1856), pp. 48–51. The Savage family also held Neen Savage, The Sheet and Letton, in succession to Ingelrann, who (in 1086) also held Eadric's manors in Walton (Savage) and Overton. The pre-Conquest holder of The Sheet and Letton was Siward, perhaps Eadric's cousin (GDB, fol. 260; DB Shropshire, nos. 6,7:10:18 and notes).

Alnoth, who was cured of paralysis at the shrine of St Æthelberht, Hereford, and in gratitude gave to the church his father's manor of Lydbury North.[112] Lydbury North was a huge multiple estate with several berewicks, which, according to Domesday, had been held by the bishops of Hereford before the Conquest; no tenants are recorded in 1086, but Eadric might have held part of the manor, especially if he is identical with Eadric of Wenlock, who witnessed one of the bishop's charters.

Two men called Eadric attest Bishop Robert's charter of 1085; Eadric of Wenlock and Eadric *dapifer*, the bishop's steward. The second Eadric is probably the man who had held Bayston, Shrops, of the bishop on a life-lease. By 1086 Bayston had been appropriated by William Pantulf, and Eadric of Bayston may have died in 1085.[113] It is tempting to identify Eadric of Bayston with Eadric of Hindlip, Worcs. Before 1066, Eadric of Hindlip had been the steersman of the bishop of Worcester's ship and leader of the contingent of men which fought and sailed it, and at some time between 1077 and 1086, he appeared for the bishop in a lawsuit against Walter, abbot of Evesham. At that time, he 'was the man of Robert, bishop of Hereford . . . and held nothing of Bishop Wulfstan (of Worcester)'. If, however, Eadric of Bayston died in 1085, he cannot be Eadric of Hindlip, for the latter witnesses the final settlement of the dispute between Worcester and Evesham before the Domesday commissioners in 1086.[114]

Eadric the Wild, if he has been correctly identified, had lost much of his land by 1086, but continued to hold as a tenant of Much Wenlock and (perhaps) of Ralph de Mortimer and the bishop of Hereford. A similar fate had befallen his cousins Siward and Ealdred, sons of Æthelgar. The details of Siward's career are provided by Orderic Vitalis, whose interest stems from the fact that Siward was the original patron of St Peter's, Shrewsbury, the minster which Earl Roger gave to Orderic's father, Odelerius of Orleans. Orderic, whose mother was English, was educated by Siward, a 'noble priest' of St Peter's and perhaps a kinsman of

[112] Walter Map, *De Nugis Curialium*, ed. T. Wright, Camden Society 50 (1850), pp. 79–82; trans. M.R. James, *Walter Map's "De Nugis Curialium"*, ed. E. Sidney Hartland, *Cymmrodorion Record Series* 9 (1923), pp. 82–5.
[113] GDB, fol. 257; *DB Shropshire* 4,14,12. A marginal 'k' indicates a claim (*kalumpnia*) regarding the land. For Eadric of Bayston, see Galbraith, 'An episcopal land-grant of 1085', p. 364; Mason, 'Eadric of Bayston', pp. 112–18.
[114] GDB, fol. 173v: *DB Worcestershire*, no. 2,52 and Appendix V; Hemming's Cartulary i, pp. 75–6, 80–3, 296–7. Dr Mason would identify Eadric of Hindlip with Eadric the Wild and it is true that Eadric the Wild's priest, Earnwine (or Earnwig) was a tenant of Worcester (GDB, fol. 172v), and that Eadric the Wild's cousin, Siward, appeared for the bishop at the same suit as Eadric of Hindlip (Mason, *St Wulfstan of Worcester, c.1008–1095*, pp. 145–6). If Eadric the Wild had been connected with the bishopric of Worcester, this would explain the interest taken by John of Worcester in his career, but the name is very common. The identity of Eadric the Wild and Eadric of Wenlock is probable; a further identification with Eadric of Hindlip is more speculative. What is certain is that neither Eadric (the Wild?) of Wenlock nor Eadric of Hindlip are to be identified with Eadric of Bayston (*dapifer* of Bishop Robert), who seems to have died in 1085–6.

Siward son of Æthelgar, and may have known the family as a child in Shrews-bury.[115] Orderic makes Siward and his brother Ealdred the great-nephews of Edward the Confessor. They were probably the grand-children of Edward's half-sister Edith and her husband, Eadric Streona, ealdorman of Mercia.[116]

Siward's pre-Conquest holdings can be reconstructed with reasonable cer-tainty. He must be Siward 'thegn and kinsman of King Edward' who held three hides at Hollow Court, Worcs, to which were attached four salt-houses in Droitwich and a messuage in Worcester; this manor had been seized by Willliam fitzOsbern, who died in February 1071. In Shropshire he held Cheyney Lon-gueville, Frodesley and Overs (three hides in all), which he continued to hold in 1086 as tenant of the earl.[117] Since he was patron of St Peter's, the fate of the church's endowment offers a clue to that of Siward. Of its pre-Conquest lands, St Peter's retained only Boreton. Upton Magna, whose tithes had belonged to St Peter's, had passed to Reginald de Bailleul. The pre-Conquest tenant is named as Siward, who must be the son of Æthelgar; the manor was assessed at five hides and had a number of unnamed berewicks. Twelve more of Reginald's manors (40 hides in all) had been held by Siward and one (assessed at two hides) by Ealdred. St Peter's only other land, at Lowe, had passed to Ralph de Mortimer, who also held two manors (three and a half hides) which had belonged to Siward and one (one and a half hides) which had belonged to Ealdred.

All the manors which Roger de Lacy held of the king in Shropshire had been held either by Siward (29½ hides) or by Ealdred (7 hides).[118] Two of these manors, at Cleobury North and Hopton Wafers were claimed, with Maerbroc, by the church of Worcester, as having been seized by Swein Godwineson, earl of the west midlands from 1043 to 1051.[119] Maerbroc is the manor of Testhill with Marlbrook (one hide) held in 1086 by Osbern fitzRichard Scrob. His predecessor was Sawardus, perhaps an error for Siward, who held the neighbouring manor at Neen Sollars as Osbern's tenant in 1086, and had held it before the Conquest.[120] Neen Sollars had never been hidated and did not pay geld but its berewick at Milson was assessed at three and a half hides. It seems possible that all four estates (Cleobury North, Hopton Wafers, Testhill with Marlbrook and Neen Sollars) had been comital manors, once held by Siward's grandfather, Ealdorman Eadric. At all events Siward held just over 85 hides in Shropshire and three hides in Worcestershire and Ealdred a further 10 hides. Not much remained by 1086. Siward held Cheney Longueville, Frodesley and Overs (three hides) of Earl Roger, Neen Sollars (unhidated) and Milson (three hides) of Osbern fitzRichard

115 OV iii, pp. 6–7 and note. Orderic was born at Atcham on 16 February 1075 and baptized by the priest Ordric, after whom he was named.
116 OV ii, pp. 194–5; iii, pp. 142–3. For the confusion between Siward son of Æthelgar and Siward Barn, see Chapter III above.
117 GDB, fols 178, 180v, 259v.
118 GDB, fols 252v, 254v, 255 (see also DB Shropshire, no. 4,3,24 note), 260, 260v.
119 Hemming's Cartulary i, p. 276.
120 GDB, fol. 260: DB Shropshire, no. 5,2 and note.

and three hides at Waters Upton of Roger de Lacy; Ealdred held Acton Scott (three hides) of the earl and Aldon (unassessed) of Roger de Lacy. Yet Siward was still described as a rich man (*dives*) when he attended the bishop of Worcester's suit against the abbot of Evesham in the period between 1077 and 1086.

Siward evidently had some connection with St Wulfstan of Worcester, possibly stemming from his property in the episcopal city. St Wulfstan's biographer describes how the bishop, when visiting Shrewsbury in 1071, chose to pray in St Peter's, although it was 'the least of churches' and prophesied that it would become 'the most glorious place in all Shrewsbury and the joy of the entire region'.[121] By the time his prediction was fulfilled, Siward had been replaced as patron by Earl Roger and his chaplain Odelerius of Orleans, and the minster had been transformed into a Benedictine abbey. The new church was dedicated on 25 February 1083, but work on the conventual buildings was still in progress in 1086.[122] The monks of Shrewsbury later claimed that Earl Roger had given Cheney Longueville to Siward in return for the site of the monastery, but Domesday does not support this contention. It was Siward who gave Cheney Longueville to the church but the donation was disputed and Abbot Fulchered (1087–1119) had to pay £15 to secure the land to Siward's son Ealdred and his brothers, one of whom was called Edward. Some of the men who later bore the surname Seward may have been descendants of Siward son of Æthelgar, King Æthelred II's great-grandson.[123]

Clearly Siward's family survived in reduced circumstances, which may have caused the younger sons to seek their fortunes elsewhere. In 1130 a rebellion against King David of Scotland was put down by the royal constable, Edward son of Siward. Orderic describes him as King David's *consobrinus* and says that his father was a *tribunus Merciorum*.[124] The literal meaning of *consobrinus* is 'cousin on the mother's side', but it can also mean 'second, or third cousin' or simply 'cousin' *tout court*. Since Edward son of Siward is the earliest recorded royal constable of Scotland, his origins have received some attention. It has been suggested that he was the grandson (not son) of the Siward, nephew and namesake of Earl Siward of Northumbria, killed in 1054. This involves supposing that the wife of King Duncan (King David's grandfather) was a sister, or sister-in-law of Earl Siward; or that it was King David's wife (Earl Siward's grand-daughter) who was Edward son of Siward's cousin, rather than the king himself.[125] There is a simpler solution. If Siward *tribunus Merciorum* were Siward

[121] *Vita Wulfstani*, pp. 27–8; Mason, *St Wulfstan of Worcester*, p. 109.

[122] OV iii, pp. 142ff; GDB, fols 252, 252v; *DB Shropshire*, nos. C14; 3,6,1.

[123] Rees, *The Shrewsbury Cartulary* i, pp. x–xii, and nos. 1 (pp. 1–5); ii, no. 256. Reaney (*A dictionary of British surnames*, p. 314) lists a Richard Seward in the Shropshire area in 1275.

[124] OV iv, pp. 276–7.

[125] *Regesta Regum Scottorum I: The acts of Malcolm IV, king of Scots, 1153–1165*, ed. G.W.S. Barrow (Edinburgh, 1960), p. 34; Anderson, *Early sources of Scottish History* i,

son of Æthelgar, who is known to have had a son called Edward, the relationship *consobrinus*, (second) cousin on the mother's side, to King David is a simple statement of the facts (see Genealogical Table Ia). If this identification is correct, Edward son of Siward was one of the many impoverished Englishmen who sought employment at the Scots court, with more reason than most to do so, since he was related to the king.[126]

It would be both presumptuous and premature to suggest that these four shires are typical of the whole of England, but recent research on Yorkshire has reached conclusions very similar to those advanced here.[127] Some common elements – and some significant differences – emerge from this survey. The English who appear as mesne-tenants in 1086 are not the great thegns whose estates were spread over several shires, but either men whose wealth and influence were localized or dependents of greater lords. They have been reduced in wealth and in social standing, and have survived by commending themselves to the incoming continental magnates, by undertaking ministerial duties, and by taking land at farm, sometimes on onerous terms. In comparison with continental mesne-tenants, their numbers are few (though greater than Domesday would lead us to believe) and they are less wealthy. Moreover they have had to adapt to new circumstances. The sweeping-away of the pre-Conquest earls and the great thegns constituted a unprecedented social upheaval, well-described by Dr Fleming.[128] When the lesser men came to commend themselves to the victors, they had to accept new customs (a closer link, perhaps, between landholding and lordship) and new social *mores* (symbolized by the adoption of 'foreign' names). Yet in all this confusion the continuation at the level of the shire of an English community did not merely ease the settlement of the conquerors into their new territories; it also ensured the continuance of English customs and traditions.

It is also noticeable that in Mercian Shropshire more of the 'better men' of King Edward's day survived than appears to be the case in the south and east. There is a high rate of survival in other western shires, notably Warwickshire and Gloucestershire, which suggests that the Mercians were not dispossessed to

pp. 596–7. King David married Matilda, daughter of Earl Waltheof, who was Earl Siward's son.
126 Dr Chibnall (OV iv, p. 277 note) suggests that Edward was the son of Siward Barn, a magnate often confused with Siward son of Æthelgar, but there would be no reason to call Siward Barn a Mercian; he held land in the west but his main estates were in the Danelaw (see also Chapter III above).
127 Michelmore, 'Township and tenure', pp. 251–64. See especially p. 253: 'The prominence of families of native origin in the twelfth century can be explained in two ways. Either there was an upward social movement of Englishmen in the century after the Conquest, or the native aristocracy survived to a greater extent than is at first apparent, *their survival being concealed by the incompleteness of Domesday Book's recording of subinfeudation in 1086, as demonstrated above*' (my italics).
128 Fleming, *Kings and lords in Conquest England*, pp. 132, 143–4.

the same extent as the West Saxons.[129] The same is true of the north where most of 'the great families of whom the English descent is beyond question' are to be found.[130] There is something paradoxical in the fact that the English survived best in those areas where they resisted longest.

[129] For Gloucestershire, see Williams, 'An introduction to the Gloucestershire Domesday', pp. 33–9; for Warwickshire, see Ann Williams, 'A vicecomital family in pre-Conquest Warwickshire', ANS 11 (1989), pp. 286–92.

[130] Stenton, 'English families and the Norman Conquest', p. 333.

Chapter V

THE SERVICE OF THE KING

> Thus, whoever of the conquered race possesses
> lands or anything of the sort, has acquired not
> what he considered due to him by right of
> succession but only what he has earned by his
> services or got by some kind of contract.
>
> *Dialogus de Scaccario.*[1]

DOMESDAY BOOK is the most eloquent testimony to the downfall of the Old English aristocracy. Stenton identified only two Englishmen, Thorkell of Warwick and Colswein of Lincoln, holding 'estates of baronial dimensions' in 1086, and though he might have added Gospatric son of Arnkell and Edward of Salisbury, it is clear that the higher ranks of the nobility were overwhelmingly of foreign extraction.[2]

Of the few Englishmen who held land of the king in 1086 (see Table I), most fall into two categories. First are the surviving kinsmen of Edward the Confessor. Harold, son of the king's nephew, Earl Ralph of Hereford, had been a minor in 1066 in the charge of Queen Edith. He held 36 hides of land in Gloucestershire, Worcestershire and Warwickshire, the remnant of his father's once-great estate.[3] Harold was soon to improve his fortune, for he acquired Ewias Harold, Herefordshire, and its lands, possibly by marrying the daughter of its Domesday lord, Alvred of Marlborough. He was also a protege of Eustace of Boulogne, his grandmother's second husband.[4] Harold's kinswoman, Christina, younger daughter of the ætheling Edward, held two manors in Warwickshire and one in Gloucestershire, assessed at 57¼ hides.[5] She was soon to become a nun at Romsey,

---

[1] *Dialogus*, p. 54.
[2] Stenton, *ASE*, p. 626. For Gospatric see Chapter II above, and for Edward, see below.
[3] GDB, fol. 129v (Ebury, Middx). Harold must have been born between 1050 and 1057, when his father died.
[4] I.J. Sanders, *English Baronies, a study of their origin and descent, 1086–1327* (Oxford, 1960), p. 43; Bates, 'Lord Sudeley's ancestors', p. 44; Tanner, 'The expansion of the power and influence of the counts of Boulogne under Eustace II', p. 276. Ewias Harold takes its name from Harold son of Ralph.
[5] GDB, fol. 238. The other English woman holding in 1086 is Eadgifu, whose land consisted of a single large manor, Chaddesley Corbett, Worcs. (GDB, fol. 178). She may have been related to the earls of Mercia (Williams, 'An introduction to the Worcestershire Domesday', pp. 30–1).

TABLE I. ENGLISH TENANTS-IN-CHIEF, 1086

Edward of Salisbury	312½ hides
Gospatric son of Arnkell	145½ carucates
Thorkell of Warwick	132 hides
Colswein of Lincoln	100 carucates
Christina	57¼ hides
Harold son of Earl Ralph	36 hides
Godric *dapifer*	32 carucates
Colgrim	25¼ carucates
Eadgifu of Chaddesley Corbett	25 hides
Alric the cook	20 hides
Alsige	10 hides
Edgar ætheling	8¼ hides
Alfred, Wigot's nephew	8 hides

where she had charge of her niece Edith, daughter of King Malcolm III and future wife of Henry I. Christina's brother, Edgar ætheling, had been generously endowed by the Conqueror at the outset of his reign, but lost his lands by subsequent rebellion. He was reconciled with William in 1074, but the only lands listed in his name in Domesday are two small manors in Herefordshire, eight and a quarter hides in all. These were held of him by Godwine, perhaps the father of Robert fitzGodwine, who accompanied the ætheling to the Holy Land in 1102 and was martyred for his faith at Ramleh. It may be significant that Edgar withdrew from William's court in 1086 'because he did not have much honour from him'. Any subsequent land which he may have acquired was probably the reward for his service to William Rufus.[6]

In the second category, which comprises the bulk of the English survivors, were royal servants and officials of various kinds. The manor of Steeple Claydon, Bucks, assessed at 20 hides, was held in 1086 by Alric the cook (*coquus*) but had previously belonged to Queen Edith; presumably Alric had been in her service. Three more estates in the same shire, held in 1086 by Alsige, had belonged either to the queen or to her man, Wulfweard White, and in the case of one of these estates, Domesday specifically says that the queen had given it to Alsige with Wulfweard's daughter.[7] Wulfweard White was dead by 1086, but had survived the Conquest in possession of at least some of his lands. He had been a wealthy man, with over 150 hides of land in eleven shires. The bulk of it lay in Buckinghamshire, where he and his wife, Eadgifu, held eight manors assessed at 90 hides.[8] Apart from the estate given to his son-in-law, these manors were

---

[6] For Godwine and his son Robert, and for the career of the ætheling, see Hooper, 'Edgar ætheling', pp. 197–214.
[7] GDB, fol. 153.
[8] GDB, fols 145,147,153. Wulfweard's other manors lay in Kent, Hants, Berks., Dorset,

divided between the bishop of Coutances (who also held Wulfweard's single tenement in Somerset) and Walter Giffard. One of Wulfweard's Middlesex manors went to the count of Mortain and the other to Ernulf de Hesdin, who also held all his lands in Oxfordshire, Berkshire and Gloucestershire. One of his Dorset manors went to William de Falaise, while the other was held by the king. It is likely that Wulfweard was a royal servant whose land reverted to his lord when he died without male heirs.

The fate of his tenancy at Hayling Island, Hants, is particularly revealing. The monks of Winchester possessed a charter, which (if genuine) dates from 1053, claiming that Queen Emma had given half the manor to the Old Minster and half to Wulfweard for his lifetime, with reversion to the same house; Wulfweard had then arranged to hold the Old Minster's half of the vill on a life-lease. King William later gave Hayling Island to the abbey of Jumièges, giving rise to a long dispute settled (in favour of Jumièges) only in the reign of Stephen. In 1066, Wulfweard was, according to Domesday's testimony, holding the manor of Queen Edith, which suggests that his office lay in the household of the queen, rather than the king.[9]

A second ministerial family is represented in Domesday by Alfred nephew of Wigot, who held two manors in Oxfordshire, assessed at eight hides of land. In addition to this land held of the king, he is (for reasons which will emerge) to be identified with Alvred who held 5 hides at Cuxham, Oxon, of Miles Crispin and (in conjunction with Olaf) 10 hides at Harlington, Middx, of Earl Roger of Shrewsbury.[10] Alfred's father may be the Wulfred who preceded him in the two manors which he held in chief in 1086, but his uncle was clearly a more important man. His name (ON Vigot) is uncommon in England, and he is probably to be identified as Wigot (or Wigod) of Wallingford, who held at least 160 hides of land in eight shires before 1066.[11] A Westminster writ 'in which authentic and spurious material has been blended' represents Wigot as a kinsman of King Edward, but the degree of relationship (if it existed) is unknown. Wigot was, however, a member of the royal household, a king's butler (pincerna).[12] His main function was perhaps to act as custodian of Wallingford, where lay the strategic

Middx, Oxon., Glos. and Lincs. (GDB, fols 9, 43v, 62v, 81, 129, 129v, 160, 169, 337). In Wilts. he was a tenant of the bishop of Sherborne and in Dorset of Glastonbury, and in Somerset he held half a hide of the royal manor of Keynsham; his wife still held land there in 1086 (GDB, fols 66, 77v, 87). He is called 'King Edward's thegn' in Middx.

9 Robertson, Charters, pp. 212–13, 462; J.H. Round, Calendar of Documents preserved in France (London, 1899), no. 157, p. 55; no. 1423, p. 526; GDB, fol. 43v.
10 GDB, fols 129, 159v, 160.
11 Sussex, Berks., Wilts., Middx, Herts., Bucks., Oxon., Glos. (GDB, fols 28, 62, 71, 129, 137, 150, 158, 159, 169v). This total includes the 30-hide manor of Great Ogbourne, Wilts., which, though in the king's hands, may have belonged to Wigot; the Wiltshire Geld Roll for Selkley hundred (where Ogbourne lay) describes the king's demesne there as de terra Wigoti (Exon, fols 4, 9, 11; GDB, fol. 65v; VCH Wilts. ii, pp. 61, 119, 199–200).
12 Harmer, Writs, no. 104, pp 368–9, cf. 336; Keynes, 'Regenbald the chancellor (sic)', pp. 206–7.

ford, the last point downstream where the Thames could be crossed without boat or bridge. Wallingford had been fortified by King Alfred and in the eleventh century may have had a permanent military garrison of royal housecarls.[13] It was at Wallingford that Duke William crossed the Thames in 1066 and Wigot's survival has suggested that he assisted the passage of the Norman army.[14] His son Toki was certainly taken into royal service, for he was killed in 1079 at the siege of Gerberoi, while bringing King William a fresh horse. Toki may have been one of William's squires, and had certainly been one of King Edward's housecarls; before 1066 he held land at Brinkworth and Chippenham, Wilts, Ickenham, Middx and Iver, Bucks, amounting to 25 hides in all.[15]

By the time of Toki's death, Wigot's lands had passed into other hands. His manors of Letcombe Bassett, Berks, Tiscott, Herts and Goring, Oxon, belonged to Robert d'Oilly, sheriff of Oxfordshire and castellan of Oxford castle. Robert's wife, Ealdgyth, was an Englishwoman and almost certainly Wigot's daughter; Robert's manor of Iver, Bucks, which had belonged to his wife's fief, had been held by Toki, presumably Wigot's son, before 1066.[16] Since their daughter Matilda was old enough to become the wife of Miles Crispin in 1084, Robert and Ealdgyth may have been married in the immediate aftermath of the Conquest.[17] It is likely that most of the land which Robert d'Oilly held in Oxfordshire had belonged to Wigot, for pre-Conquest tenants are only sporadically recorded in this shire and Wigot is described as Robert's *antecessor* in the Hertfordshire entry.

The largest share of Wigot's estate passed, not to Robert d'Oilly but to Miles Crispin, castellan of the castle built at Wallingford in 1071. He held lands in Wiltshire, Buckinghamshire, Oxfordshire and Gloucestershire which had once belonged to Wigot, and lands in Hampshire and Berkshire which had belonged to Wigot's men, one of whom, Leofweard of 'Langley', Berks, still held of Miles

---

[13] For the strategic significance of Wallingford and the land in the town 'where the housecarls dwelt', see Nicholas Hooper, 'An introduction to the Berkshire Domesday', *The Berkshire Domesday*, ed. Ann Williams and R.W.H. Erskine (London, 1988), pp. 7, 23–4. See also note 19 below for the description of Wigot as 'lord of the *oppidani* of Wallingford'.

[14] Freeman ii, p. 543; Campbell, 'Some agents and agencies of the late Anglo-Saxon state', p. 204, note 18; *GDB*, fol. 50, 137.

[15] *AS Chron*, 1079; *GDB*, fols 71, 73, 129, 149. Brinkworth was held by Miles Crispin in 1086 and Chippenham by Reginald Canute, who also held (of Miles) a manor in Rodbourne which had belonged to Wigot (*VCH Wilts*. ii, p. 146). For Iver, Bucks., see next note. The Middx entry describes Toki as King Edward's housecarl and in Bucks. he is called King Edward's thegn.

[16] *GDB*, fol. 149. The name of Robert's wife is preserved in the cartulary of Oseney Abbey (*The English register of Oseney Abbey*, ed. A. Clark, EETS (1907) p. 6; *VCH Wilts*. ii, p. 102).

[17] See next note. The d'Oillys were well-established in Oxfordshire by 1071, for Earl Edwin had given Ralph d'Oilly the service of Saegeat, a thegn who dwelt (*mansit*) at Bloxham, and did service 'like a free man' (*sicut liber homo*). For the significance of *mansit*, see Chapter VIII below. Bloxham, to which was attached a house in Oxford, had belonged to Earl Ælfgar and then to Edwin (*GDB*, fols 154, 154v).

in 1086. Later tradition made Miles the husband of Matilda, daughter of Robert d'Oilly and Wigot's daughter Ealdgyth. It has been suggested that Miles is more likely to have married a daughter of Wigot himself. If, however, Robert and Ealdgyth were married in 1067, their daughter could herself have been of marriageable age in 1084, when Robert gave a lavish feast at Abingdon, perhaps his daughter's wedding-breakfast, for Miles and the future Henry I.[18]

As with Robert d'Oilly, other estates held by Miles in 1086 may have belonged to Wigot. Domesday states that Whitchurch, Oxon, had been held in 1066 by Leofric and Alwine, but the monks of Abingdon later claimed that the estate had been taken from them by Wigot, 'lord of the townsmen (oppidani) of Wallingford'. They said further that Whitchurch had belonged to the patrimony of Leofric, a monk of Abingdon, who is presumably the Leofric mentioned in Domesday, and perhaps also Leofric the monk, former holder of Miles' manor at Betterton, Berks.[19] Marriage with an English heiress may have enabled Robert d'Oilly and subsequently Miles Crispin to settle into their positions in Oxfordshire and Berkshire. It is noticeable that a number of Miles' tenants, especially in Oxfordshire and Buckinghamshire, were Englishmen, some holding land which had belonged to them, or to their families, before 1066.[20] The Alured who held Cuxham, Oxon, which had belonged to Wigot himself, is probably Wigot's nephew but since the native name Alfred is not easily distinguished from Breton Alvred (both appear as Alured in Domesday) it is impossible to say whether it was Wigot's nephew who held Eaton, Berks, of Miles; it had belonged to Bosi TRE (GDB 61v).

Another of Wigot's nephews held land in 1086, though not of the king; Thorvald, nepos Wigoti, held Meysey Hampton, Gloucs, of Earl Roger of Shrewsbury, and is probably to be identified with the earl's tenant at Penton Mewsey and Houghton, Hants, and Castle Eaton (formerly Eaton Mewsey) and Milston, Wilts, as well as Burpham, Worplestone and Loseley, Surrey. All of these manors, with the exception of Meysey Hampton, were held before 1066 by Osmund, perhaps Thorvald's father.[21] Though only a mesne-tenant, Thorvald was better-off than Alfred, with 42½ hides (the total assessment before 1066 was 49 hides but some reduction had taken place on the Surrey lands) to Alfred's 23 hides. How Thorvald came to enter Earl Roger's service is unknown, but the earl's lands in Middlesex included estates held formerly by Wigot, his son Toki and men

---

18 K.S.B. Keats-Rohan, 'The devolution of the honour of Wallingford, 1066–1148', Oxoniensa 54 (1989), pp. 312–14; for the suggestion that Miles married a daughter of Wigot, see VCH Wilts. ii, p. 102. For Miles' lands, see GDB, fols 50, 71, 150–150v, 159, 169v.
19 GDB, fols 61v, 159; Chron Abingdon i, p. 477. There is an alleged diploma of Æthelred II granting Whitchurch to Leofric minister in 1012 in the same cartular; (S.927, see Keynes, The diplomas of Æthelred II, p. 265).
20 GDB, fols 61v, 71, 149v, 159v.
21 GDB, fols 34v, 44v, 68v, 166v; see Williams, 'An introduction to the Gloucestershire Domesday', p. 39.

commended to him. The *Alured* who, with Olaf, held Harlington, Middx, of the earl in 1086 is probably Wigot's nephew.[22]

Wulfweard White and Wigot of Wallingford were both dead by 1086, but their kinsmen still enjoyed the advantages of their connexion with royal officials. The Norman administrators needed the expertise of the Englishmen who knew how the machinery of government worked and it is clear that the lower ranks of the royal service were filled by natives.[23] Some are visible in 1086, especially in Little Domesday, which is fuller than the revised and abbreviated text of the final version. Richard Poynant, for instance, had been reeve of Earsham, Norfolk, but the estate was actually managed by his sub-reeve (*subpraepositus*) Godwine, and in the same shire Brun, reeve of Roger Bigod, sheriff of Norfolk, was administering the royal manor of Southmere.[24] In the reign of William Rufus, Eadwig, reeve of the sheriff of Oxfordshire, was accused of despoiling the lands of Abingdon Abbey.[25] In 1102–3, the hundred of Andover was commanded by the king to enquire into the possessions of Andover Priory appropriated by Alvric (Ælfric), reeve of Andover; the court met in the house of the former reeve (*veteris prepositi*), Edwin. Both men were clearly English.[26]

Several other Englishmen holding land of the king in 1086 were connected with the royal service and the richer men held the higher posts. Thorkell of Warwick was the son of Æthelwine, sheriff of Warwickshire in King Edward's day and perhaps for some years after. Thorkell may have succeeded his father as sheriff, though by 1086 the post was held by Robert d'Oilly.[27] Thorkell's survival had ensured that of his kinsmen too, but they had to adapt to new conditions of tenure. The kindred seems to have channelled what wealth remained to it through its most powerful member, Thorkell himself, of whom the others held as tenants; a Norman, not an English stratagem. Thorkell's brother Guthmund held Great Packington, and Æthelmaer and Ordric, who were probably uncles of Thorkell, appear among his tenants. The heirs of Guthmund and (probably) of Æthelmaer continued to hold as tenants of Thorkell's descendants, the Ardens, in the twelfth century.[28]

---

[22] GDB, fol. 129.

[23] See W.L. Warren, 'The myth of Norman administrative efficiency', *TRHS* fifth series 34 (1984), pp. 113–132.

[24] LDB, fols 110, 186.

[25] *Chron Abingdon* ii, no. 41; *Regesta* i, no. 390.

[26] Van Caeneghem i, p. 135.

[27] Green, *English sheriffs to 1154*, p. 83. For the family, see Williams, 'A vicecomital family in pre-Conquest Warwickshire', pp. 279–95. Æthelwine was alive in 1072, when he attested, as sheriff, a charter of Robert of Stafford in favour of Evesham (R.W. Eyton, 'The Staffordshire Cartulary', *Collections for a History of Staffordshire*, William Salt Archaeological Society 2 (1881), p. 178).

[28] Guthmund was the ancestor of the le Notte family and Æthelmær may have been the father, or more probably the grandfather of Ketilbjorn of Longdon and his brother Thorkell, who held of Siward of Arden, son of Thorkell of Warwick (Williams, 'A vicecomital family in pre-Conquest Warwickshire', pp. 287–8 and references cited; see also Chapter VIII below).

Thorkell of Warwick seems to have allied himself with several of the incoming Normans in Warwickshire. All but one of the Warwickshire estates of Robert d'Oilly, the Domesday sheriff, had belonged to Thorkell's kinsmen, and five of the six were held as Thorkell's tenant. The single manor which Robert held in chief had been bought from Ælfric, who was probably one of Thorkell's uncles.[29] Thorkell's brother Guthmund held land of William fitzAnsculf and both he and Thorkell, with their brother Ketilbjorn, their father Æthelwine and Ælfric 'the king's knight', who was probably their uncle, witnessed a charter of Robert of Stafford in 1072.[30] Ælfric held of Robert of Stafford at Bubbenhall, Ilmington and Bearley and he and other members of Thorkell's kindred appear among the *taini regis*.[31] The names of Thorkell's kindred (which admittedly are very common) appear among the predecessors of Robert of Meulan, whose brother Henry de Beaumont was made earl of Warwick in 1088.[32] He was given, *inter alia*, the lands of Thorkell of Warwick, but Thorkell's son Siward of Arden, continued to hold of the new earl. Such 'down-grading', from tenant-in-chief to mesne-tenant did not affect only English families; the fiefs of Gilbert Tison and Osbern d'Arches, held in chief in 1086, were incorporated in the honour of Mowbray by Henry I.[33] Indeed, since it seems that Thorkell's ancestors had been men of the earls of Mercia, the Ardens managed to preserve their social status as well as at least some of their land.[34] Moreover many of the mesne-tenants on Thorkell's

---

[29] Robert held only one other manor in Warks., as the tenant of the bishop of Bayeux (*GDB*, fols 238v, 241, 241v, 242). Thorkell's only manor outside Warks. was Drayton, Oxon., a vill in which Robert d'Oilly also had land (*GDB*, fols 158, 160v).

[30] See note 27 above.

[31] Four of the five English *taini* in Warwickshire were probably Thorkell's kin: Ælfric at Barcheston, Alsige at Fillongley, Leofwine at Flecknoe and Ordric at Ettington (*GDB*, fol. 244v).

[32] Some connection between Thorkell and the Beaumonts is suggested by the count of Meulan's tenure of Myton, Warks., of Thorkell's fief (*GDB*, fol. 241v).

[33] *Chron Abingdon* ii, p. 80; Greenway, *Charters of the Honour of Mowbray*, p. xxv.

[34] Williams, 'A vicecomital family in pre-Conquest Warwickshire', pp. 291–2. It has been suggested that Æthelwine the sheriff was the son of Wigot (not Wigot of Wallingford), holder of Wixford, Warks., before 1066 (*GDB*, fol. 239), who is said to have married a sister of Earl Leofric, and that the Arden ancestors were thus kin to the Mercian earls (K.S.B. Keats-Rohan, 'The making of Henry of Oxford: Englishmen in a Norman world', *Oxoniensa* 54 (1989), pp. 301–4). The evidence is, however, late and largely unverifiable and some of the supporting material adduced is clearly spurious. The charter of 'Ufa the Hwede' supposedly Wigot's grandfather, giving Wixford to Evesham (S.1214, dated 962) was probably forged at Evesham in the late eleventh century (Hart, *Early charters of Northern England and the North Midlands*, p. 79, cf. p. 63). Thorkell's second wife, Leveruna (Leofrun), daughter of Earl Ælfgar, is equally dubious; the earliest evidence for a wife of Thorkell of this name comes from an inquest of 1208, in which she is described as the mother of Osbert of Arden (*Curia Regis Rolls* v, p. 241). Osbert of Arden, however, was the grandson, not the son of Thorkell; his father was Siward of Arden and his mother was probably Siward's wife Cecilia (PRO E13/76 m 71r). I am indebted for the last reference to Professor David Crouch, to whom thanks are due for his permission to use his unpublished material on the Arden family.

fief were Englishmen, some holding the same manors which they or their fathers had held before the Conquest; a phenomenon also found on the fief of Robert of Meulan. It seems that the survival of one of the key families in Warwickshire had enhanced the chances of some of the lesser men of the shire. It should be remembered that two members of the old royal kindred, Harold son of Earl Ralph and Christina, Edward ætheling's daughter, were also tenants-in-chief in Warwickshire in 1086.

Another Englishman who survived by virtue of his vicecomital office is Edward of Salisbury, sheriff of Wiltshire. He is, by a long way, the richest of the English survivors (see Table I), so much so that his native origins have been doubted. A fictitious pedigree constructed in the thirteenth century makes him a younger son, born in England, of Walter de Roumare, whose grandson, Robert fitzGerald, held lands in Wiltshire, Dorset and Somerset in 1086.[35] The point of the story is to explain why Richard I gave the county of Roumare to William Longspee, whose wife was a descendant of Edward of Salisbury, and has no value as a statement about Edward's parentage. His name is English and suggests an English origin. His Wiltshire fief (the bulk of his land) came from a large number of predecessors, but one name stands out; that of Wulfwynn, who held three manors, at Chitterne (the later *caput*), Poole Keynes and Winterbourne Earls (17 hides in all). The same woman had held both Edward's Dorset manors, his single manor in Middlesex, all three of his Buckinghamshire estates, one of his two manors in Somerset and a manor in Hertfordshire which was *lænland* of the abbey of St Albans. In all Wulfwynn had possessed, and passed to Edward, just under 100 hides of land in six shires; three-quarters of his land outside Wiltshire (82 hides out of 125) had belonged to her and her holdings determined the general shape of his fief.[36] In Middlesex and Buckinghamshire she is called 'King Edward's man' and in the latter shire she is also called Wulfwynn of Cresslow. At least two men there were commended to her, Almaer, who also held land of her, and an unnamed thegn holding a tenement in Helsthorpe.[37] It seems more than likely that Wulfwynn was Edward's mother. Another possible kinsman is Azur, who preceded Edward on three Wiltshire manors, one at Chitterne; his name is common, but an Azur had held two of Edward's three manors in Surrey.[38] Beorhtric of Trowbridge, who held nearly 51 hides of land in Wiltshire as a *tainus regis* in 1086, may also have been a relation, for his estates formed part of the later honour of Trowbridge, held by Humphrey de Bohun and his wife Matilda, Edward's daughter.[39]

[35] *Monasticon* vi, p. 501; VCH *Wilts* ii, p. 99; GDB, fols 72v, 80v, 86v, 97.
[36] GDB, fols 69v, 80v, 98, 130v, 139, 150v.
[37] GDB, fols 150v, 152.
[38] GDB, fol. 36.
[39] GDB, fol. 73v; Sanders, *English baronies*, p. 91. A Beorhtric preceded Edward of Salisbury at Lus Hill and an Alwig (the name of Beorhtric of Trowbridge's brother) at Winterbourne Stoke, where Alwig's wife still held land of Edward in 1086 (GDB, fol. 69).

No pre-Conquest tenants are recorded for the first three manors of Edward's Wiltshire fief, at Wilcot, Alton Barnes and Etchilhampton.[40] Wilcot seems to have been Edward's chief manor in 1086 for it possessed 'a new church, a very fine house and a good vineyard (*aecclesia nova et domus obtima et vinea bona*)'. These three estates may have belonged to Edward himself in 1066.[41] The strongest evidence for his English origin comes not from Domesday but from the Ramsey Chronicle, which records the settlement of a dispute involving Ramsey Abbey before the shire-court of Lincolnshire, in the presence of Edward of Salisbury 'and many other *fideles* and thegns of the king'. The hearing took place before the Conquest for the land concerned was subsequently seized by Odo of Bayeux *in permutatione regni*.[42] That Edward had some connection with the north is suggested by his role in the foundation of Selby Abbey, Yorks, for (as suggested above) he is likely to be identical with Edward the Rich (*dives*) who helped the founder, Benedict, on his way to the north.[43]

Edward's prosperity would be more easily explained if he had been an official of Edward the Confessor. He was a wealthy man in 1086, with over 300 hides of land in nine shires. In Wiltshire, of which he was sheriff by the early 1070s, Edward was the richest tenant-in-chief.[44] He also appears among the tenants of Glastonbury Abbey and Shaftesbury Abbey and perhaps of other religious houses.[45]

Edward was dead by, at the latest, about 1120, when his son, Walter fitzEdward, was holding his Shaftesbury tenancy.[46] It was Walter who succeeded to his estates and to his office but he may have had a second son, the Edward of Salisbury who attests charters of Henry I between 1114 and 1126; it was presumably this younger Edward who bore the king's banner at the Battle of Bremule in 1119.[47] The

---

[40] GDB, fol. 69; they are assessed at 27½ hides in all. A second holding in Etchilhampton had belonged to the pre-Conquest sheriff, Eadric; his wife still held in 1086 of Ernulf de Hesdin.

[41] He may also be one of the two unnamed thegns who had held 2 hides in Langford of the abbot of Glastonbury in 1066, for both this and a second tenement in Langford, which had belonged to Azur, were in Edward's hands in 1086 (GDB, fols 66v, 69v).

[42] *Chron Ramsey*, pp. 153–4; Hart, *Early charters of Eastern England*, pp. 102–3.

[43] See Chapter II. William I's alleged confirmation charter in favour of Selby is attested, *inter alia*, by Edward of Salisbury (*Regesta* i, no. 178).

[44] GDB, fols 36, 46v, 51, 69–69v, 80v, 98, 130v, 139, 150v, 154, 160. For the shrievalty, see Green, *English sheriffs to 1154*, p. 85. Edward's predecessor, Eadric, was alive in 1067 but is not heard of thereafter and was dead by 1086 when his wife held his house in Malmesbury and his land at Calstone Wellington and Etchilhampton (GDB, fols 64v, 70; she held of Ernulf de Hesdin).

[45] GDB, fols 66v, 67v; see also 65v, 66, 67, 68. The land he held of Shaftesbury was probably at Chicklade, see next note.

[46] The Shaftesbury tenancy at Tisbury (GDB, fol. 67v) was probably at Chicklade, held for 1 knight's fee by Edward's son, Walter fitzEdward, sheriff of Wiltshire, and Walter's son, Patrick, earl of Salisbury (Williams, 'The knights of Shaftesbury Abbey', p. 216).

[47] VCH *Wilts*. ii, p. 107; OV vi, pp. 236–7, note 6. He was one of those who wisely decided not to embark on the White Ship in 1120 (OV vi, pp. 296–7).

younger Edward does not seem to have held any of the elder Edward's estates; he did, however, hold land in Nottinghamshire and Derbyshire which in 1086 belonged to Ralph fitzHubert, and it is possible that his mother, Maud, was Ralph's daughter. Maud's only known husband is Hasculf de Tony, but she may have been previously married to Edward of Salisbury; Edward the younger was her eldest son. He married Adeliza de Rames, thereby acquiring land in Normandy, and was dead by 1130, when Adeliza was married again, to Pain de Houghton. Her daughter by Edward, Leonia, married Robert de Stuteville.[48]

Other ministerial tenants-in-chief are Colswein of Lincoln and Godric *dapifer*. Colswein does not seem to have held any land before 1066. By 1086 he held a sizeable fief, mainly in Kesteven and to the north of Lincoln itself.[49] His main interests seem to be in Lincoln itself, where he held four tofts which had belonged to his nephew Cola, perhaps the *Col* who had preceded him at Barlings. In addition the king had given him a stretch of undeveloped land outside the city, on which he had built 36 houses and two churches. One of them can be identified as St Peter *ad fontem* (*atte welles*), to the east of Lincoln and just beyond the existing suburb of Butwerk.[50] As with Wigot of Wallingford, we do not know what service Colswein had performed for the Conqueror, but he may have been town-reeve of Lincoln. His heir was his son Picot, who apparently died without heirs, and Colswein's lands passed to Robert de la Haye, who married his daughter Muriel. Robert, whose Norman lands centred on La-Haye-du-Puits in the Cotentin, was an official in the service of Henry I; he served as a justiciar in Normandy, and by 1131 was the king's steward.[51] He and his descendants were hereditary constables of Lincoln Castle; his grand-daughter Nicola 'whose heart was not that of a woman', held the castle for John when he rebelled against Richard I in 1191 and again in 1216, when John's own barons rebelled against him.[52]

---

[48] EYC ix, pp. 49–51; for the remarriage of Edward the younger's widow, see PR 31 Hen I, p. 81; Judith Green, *The government of England under Henry I* (Cambridge, 1986), p. 259. An Edward of Salisbury was a benefactor of Saint-Georges de Boscherville, founded by William de Tancarville (Round, *Calendar of documents preserved in France*, nos. 211–12, p. 70). Professor Crouch identifies the benefactor of Saint-Georges, who also attests charters of William de Tancarville, with the elder Edward of Salisbury and suggests that the latter married a kinswoman of William de Tancarville; see also Chapter VIII below (D.C. Crouch, *William Marshal* (London, 1990), pp. 19–20).

[49] GDB, fols 356v–357v; see the map in Sir Francis Hill, *Medieval Lincoln* (Cambridge, 1948, republished Stamford, 1990), p. 49.

[50] GDB, fol. 336v; Hill, *Medieval Lincoln*, pp. 48–50, 133–4, 161. Colswein's son Picot gave St Peter's church to St Mary's, York, with 2 messuages and 4 acres *in campis et le Hevedland*.

[51] Green, *The government of England under Henry I*, pp. 146–7, 258; Sanders, *English baronies*, p. 109. Robert's father, also called Robert, had been seneschal to Robert count of Mortain.

[52] Richard de la Haye succeeded to his father's office in 1155, and in 1166 was holding the land which had been Colswein's (J.C. Holt, 'The carta of Richard de la Haye', 1166: a note on "continuity" in Anglo-Norman feudalism', EHR 84 (1969), pp. 289–97). For

The descendants of the other Englishman holding in Lincolnshire in 1086 were also involved in the king's service. Unlike Colswein, Colgrim had held at least some of his land before 1066. Besides what he held of the king, he appears as the tenant of Crowland Abbey, Robert of Stafford and Count Alan, and held property in Grantham over which he had sake and soke.[53] The lands which he held of the count were part of the honor of Richmond, Yorks, and either Colgrim or his son Osbert acquired a knight's fee at Wensley, Yorks, of the same honor. Osbert's grandson was Nicholas son of Alexander of Ingoldsby (a manor held in chief by Colgrim in 1086), sheriff of Lincoln from 1185 to 1189 and a justice-in-eyre in 1188.[54]

Godric the steward (*dapifer*) was a minor landowner, but his role as a farmer of royal manors gave him considerable status in East Anglia.[55] Most of his own land (some 25 carucates) came from Edwin, a king's thegn and one of an extensive and wealthy kindred (see Genealogical Table VII), known from a series of surviving wills, including those of Edwin himself, his sister Wulfgyth and his nephew Ketel.[56] Ketel's will mentions a brother called Godric, who may be identical with Godric the steward, but the name is common and the lands which Ketel left to Godric his brother (Hainford and Stratton Strawless, Norfolk and Coggeshall, Essex) do not appear in the possession of Godric *dapifer*.[57] Nevertheless Godric and his wife Ingereda did fulfil the bequest of Little Melton to the abbey of St Benet's, Holme, made by Edwin and renewed by Ketel.[58]

It was Godric's position as manager of royal estates in Norfolk, Suffolk, Essex

his eldest daughter Nicola de la Haye, who married Gerard de Camville (d.1215), see *The Chronicle of Richard of Devizes*, ed. John T. Appleby (London, 1963), p. 31. She resigned the castle in 1226 and died in 1230 (Hill, *Medieval Lincoln*, pp. 88–9, 199–201).
53 GDB, fols 370–370v. He is presumably the Colgrim of Grantham whose brother Leofwine held Luddington, Hunts, *ad censum* of Drew de Hastings in Henry I's time (*Cartularium Monasterii de Rameseia* i, p. 131 and see Chapter IV, note 58 above).
54 GDB, fols 346v, 347v, 348, 348v, 368v; Stenton 'English families and the Norman Conquest', pp. 332–3.
55 For Godric's land, see LDB, fols 202–205v (*DB Norfolk*, nos. 12,1–45), 355v–356 (*DB Suffolk*, nos. 13,1–7). It is possible that he is the Godric who gave evidence at the Kentford inquest on the lands of Ely in 1080, with 'many other respected French knights and Englishmen also from the four shires of Essex, Hertford, Huntingdon and Bedford' (van Caeneghem i, p. 45).
56 Dorothy Whitelock, *Anglo-Saxon Wills* (Cambridge, 1930) pp. 31–4; S.1516, 1519, 1531, 1535; Douglas, *Feudal documents*, pp. cxii–cxvi; Richard Mortimer, 'The Baynards of Baynard's castle', *Studies in medieval history presented to R. Allen Brown*, ed. Harper-Bill, Holdsworth and Nelson, pp. 248–50.
57 Hainford, with its berewick at Stratton Strawless, was held by Roger the Poitevin (*LDB*, fol. 243) and Coggeshall belonged to Christ Church, Canterbury (*LDB*, fol. 8; C.R. Hart, *The early charters of Essex*, 2nd edn (Leicester, 1971), p. 26). Ketel was the *antecessor* of Rannulf Peverel and his brother may be the Godric *liber homo* of Ketel who had once held Rannulf's land at East Carleton (*LDB*, fol. 254).
58 D.C. Douglas, *The social structure of medieval East Anglia* (Oxford, 1927), pp. 244, 246; EHD ii, nos. 190, 191, pp. 842–3. The estate was leased to Ralph son of Godric and his wife Lesceline.

GENEALOGICAL TABLE VII. EDWIN THE THEGN

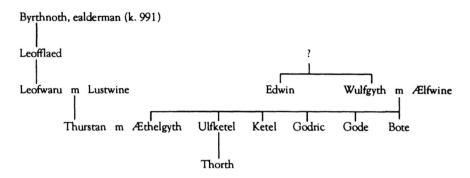

and Cambridgeshire that made him a man of importance. One group of Norfolk manors is headed 'Lands which Godric administers'; most of them had belonged to Earl Ralph Guader and an equivalent group in Suffolk is described as 'Lands of Earl Ralph which Godric administers in Suffolk in the king's hand'. In Essex he held the manor of Great Sampford and in Cambridgeshire that of Exning.[59] There are two references to Godric's 'office' (*ministerium*) and it was by his orders (allegedly) that Robert the crossbowman had appropriated land in Tunstead.[60] Godric had held other royal manors in 1086, of which a half-carucate in Bradenham held by Earl Ralph before his forfeiture is the most interesting; it had been held by Robert Blund and by Godric at farm for 30s *in thesauro regis in brevi suo*.[61]

Godric may originally have been in the service of Earl Ralph, and perhaps of Ralph the staller before him. Some of the free men commended to his predecessor Edwin had been held by Godric 'under Earl Ralph' and some of the lands of Earl Ralph had been held by Godric before the earl's forfeiture. Godric also bore witness that Walter of Dol, one of Ralph's adherents who fell with him, had held Shropham by Ralph's gift.[62] His knowledge of local affairs, however gained, was what made him useful, so much so that he was made sheriff of Norfolk in the reign of William Rufus and his son Ralph attests charters of Henry I.[63]

Most of the Englishmen holding land of the king in 1086 are not given individual entries, but grouped together as *taini regis*. They have never been

59 *LDB*, fols 7v, 119v, 284v; *GDB*, fol. 189v and see above, Chapter III.
60 *LDB*, fols 125, 244.
61 *LDB*, fol. 276v.
62 *LDB*, fols 152, 175v, 188–188v, 189, 200, 277v. Robert Fardenc, Godric's man, claimed Stoke Ash as part of the royal manor of Mendlesham, because Walter of Dol held it when he forfeited (*LDB*, fol. 285v). Godric had farmed this manor at some point, and it seems that his man (a Norman by his name) was still administering it.
63 Green, *English sheriffs to 1154*, pp. 60, 76; idem, 'The sheriffs of William the Con-queror', p. 132.

TABLE II. TAINI REGIS AND OTHERS, 1086

Taini regis	Servientes	'Franci'	Not mentioned
CIRCUIT I			
Surrey			Kent
Hampshire	Hampshire		Sussex
Berkshire			
CIRCUIT II			
Devon	Devon	Devon [Exon]	Cornwall
Somerset	Somerset	Somerset [Exon]	
Dorset	Dorset	Dorset	
Wiltshire	Wiltshire	Wiltshire	
CIRCUIT III			
Hertfordshire			Middlesex
Bucks	[Beds]		Cambs
CIRCUIT IV			
[Oxfordshire]			
Northants	Leics		
Warwickshire	Warwickshire		
Staffordshire			
CIRCUIT V			
Gloucs			Worcs
			Herefordshire
			Shropshire
			Cheshire
CIRCUIT VI			
Hunts			
Derbyshire			
Notts			
Yorkshire			
Lincolnshire			

TABLE III. THE DOMESDAY CIRCUITS

I   Kent, Surrey, Sussex, Hampshire, Berkshire

II   Wiltshire, Dorset, Somerset, Devon, Cornwall [also covered in the circuit return, Exon Domesday]

III   Middlesex, Hertfordshire, Buckinghamshire, Bedfordshire, Cambridgeshire

IV   Oxfordshire, Northamptonshire (with Rutland), Leicestershire, Warwickshire, Staffordshire

V   Gloucestershire, Worcestershire, Herefordshire, Shropshire, Cheshire

VI   Huntingdonshire, Derbyshire, Nottinghamshire, Yorkshire, Lincolnshire

VII   Essex, Norfolk, Suffolk [Little Domesday]

discussed as a whole, though individual *taini* are well-known and there are some regional studies.[64] It is plain from the most cursory glance that the *taini regis* of 1086 are very different in status and in function from the king's thegns of pre-Conquest England, and for that reason have been called by their Latin name in what follows to avoid confusion.[65] The accompanying table (Table II) shows the distribution of *taini regis* and *servientes regis* in 1086.

Most of the *taini* and nearly all the *servientes* are found in the shires of Circuits I and II. This distribution need imply no more than the normal variation in practice between the groups of circuit commissioners, though these are also the shires of Wessex itself, over which the pre-Conquest kings had exercised a more direct authority than in Mercia or Northumbria (for the Domesday circuits, see Table III). Some differences are certainly due to local conditions, rather than procedural idiosyncrasies. For instance, no *taini* are recorded in Cornwall, Shropshire or Cheshire, three shires dominated by their earls, with little or no royal demesne. In each shire, the tenants of those earls include groups of men with English names, who might have been called *taini regis* elsewhere.[66] In Kent, which also has no *taini*, Odo of Bayeux occupied a position similar to that of the three earls in their shires, but no comparable group of Englishmen appears. Here the

---

[64] The Wiltshire *taini* were studied by R.R. Darlington (*VCH Wilts.* ii, pp. 72–8) and Clive Harfield undertook a comparative study of the *taini* of Dorset and Nottinghamshire ('The Conqueror's thegns') which is still unpublished; I am very grateful to Dr Harfield for giving me a copy and allowing me to cite his findings.

[65] The pre-Conquest *cyninges thegnas* were great nobles, the equivalent of the Anglo-Norman baronage (for the equation of *baro* and *tainus*, see *LHP*, chaps 35,1a; 41,1b; 80,9b; 87,5). The *taini regis* were on a par with the *servientes regis* and the later tenants in sergeanty. *Taini* and *servientes* are equated in the Surrey folios, where the text heading *Terrae Oswoldi et aliorum tainorum* (GDB, fol. 36v) appears in the List of Tenants as *Oswold' Teodricus et alii servientes regis* (GDB, fol. 30). The more 'honourable' usage is preserved by Richard of Hexham's reference, in the mid-twelfth century, to David of Scotland's 'thegns, that is barons', see G.W.S. Barrow, *David I of Scotland, 1124–1153: the balance of new and old*, Stenton Lecture (Reading, 1985), p. 10.

[66] GDB, fols 124v–125, 259–259v, 267v.

explanation for their absence is probably to be sought in the tenurial upheaval immediately after the Conquest. The same holds true for Sussex; here the only laymen to hold land outside the rapes were Oda and his brother Ealdred, who appear as *taini* elsewhere.[67]

Outside Wessex *taini* are most consistently recorded in the Danelaw (Circuit VI). They are found in all five shires and the only anomaly is in Lincolnshire, where Svartbrandr and Ketilbjorn are given individual headings in the list of tenants (at the beginning of the county description) but incorporated into the *taini* in the text.[68] It may be, however, that the *taini* of the north are not, like their southern counterparts, royal servants, but merely the successors of those pre-Conquest royal and median thegns who survived the rebellion of 1069–70. In Yorkshire some 330 manors once held by Anglo-Scandinavian thegns were appended to the king's fief because they had been forfeited by their owners.[69]

In the three remaining circuits, covering the east midlands (Circuits III and IV) and Mercia (Circuit V) there is considerable inconsistency in the classification and recording of *taini* and of *servientes*. In Buckinghamshire (Circuit III) the list of tenants announces a section for the *taini regis et elemosinarii*, two groups normally kept separate. The equivalent part of the text is headed *Terra Lewini de Neweham*, though only the first four entries are for the manors of Leofwine of Nuneham Courtenay.[70] In Bedfordshire the place of the *taini* is taken by the *prefecti regis et bedelli et elemosinarii*, preceded by the English burgesses of Bedford.[71] In Hertfordshire the *taini regis* of the text appear in the list of tenants as *Derman et alii anglici regis*.[72] Middlesex and Cambridgeshire have no *taini* or *servientes*, though in Middlesex two widows held land in alms, and Cambridgeshire 'two king's carpenters' (*duo carpentarii regis*) had an unidentified estate, and two manors belonged to Erchenger the baker (*pistor*).[73]

Of the Circuit IV shires, the list of tenants for Oxfordshire has an entry for Richard Engaine *et alii ministri regis* and the equivalent section in the text includes the lands of 24 men, eleven of whom have English names.[74] Likewise in Northamptonshire, the list of tenants includes William [Engaine] *et alii taini* and the relevant section includes, apart from the lands of William himself, those of

---

[67] GDB, fol. 29v and see below.
[68] GDB, fols 337, 370v.
[69] GDB, fols 300–302. These folios were added by the Domesday scribe to the original gathering, see Roffe, 'Domesday Book and northern society', p. 324; Palliser, 'An introduction to the Yorkshire Domesday', pp. 10–11.
[70] GDB, fols 143, 153. For Leofwine, see below.
[71] GDB, fol. 209. In the text (GDB, fol. 218v) the equivalent heading reads *Terra prepositorum et elemosinarium*.
[72] GDB, fols 132, 142. They include, besides Deormann of London, Alwine Dodda's son, Peter the burgess, Baldwin *quidam serviens* and three unnamed priests, one holding jointly with his sister.
[73] GDB, fols 130v, 202, 202v. The widows were Eadgifu wife of Edmund son of Swein (see also below) and Ælfgifu, wife of Hwaetmann of London.
[74] GDB, fols 154, 160v.

Olaf, Doding and Oslac, Englishmen by their names. In Warwickshire too the list of tenants has Richard *et alii taini et servientes regis*, and the corresponding section includes the lands of Richard the forester (who may be Richard Engaine), Richard the huntsman and five Englishmen, four of them the kinsmen of Thorkell of Warwick.[75] Leicestershire has no *taini* but some of the men described as *servientes* have names which may be English.[76]

There are no *servientes* in the Mercian shires (Circuit V) and *taini* are found only in Gloucestershire and Staffordshire; one of the Gloucestershire *taini*, Madoc, has a Welsh name, and one of the Staffordshire *taini*, Richard, has a continental one.[77] Herefordshire has no *taini* but the three manors held respectively by Madoc, Eadric and Almaer are lumped together under one number and appear in the place where *taini* are to be expected.[78] The absence of *taini* in Shropshire and Cheshire had already been mentioned and there are none to be found in Worcestershire, a county dominated by the churches of Worcester, Westminster, Evesham and Pershore.

It is tempting to conclude that the *taini* of 1086 were no more than 'all those miscellaneous little people who had to be listed with the tenants in chief because they were royal servants or did not fit in anywhere else'.[79] Yet the frequency of occupational by-names among the *taini* as well as the *servientes* suggests that the former were connected with the royal administration and the needs of the royal household.[80] It is true that many men with 'occupational' by-names are not included among the *taini* but have individual entries.[81] Some men, moreover, are described in one place as *taini* and elsewhere as tenants-in-chief. Thus Theodoric the goldsmith is among the *ministri* in Oxfordshire and the *taini* in Surrey but is a tenant-in-chief in Berkshire.[82] There is no reason to suppose that this has anything to do with the terms on which the lands were held; variations in the collection and presentation of material are much more likely.[83]

The survival of Exon Domesday, the circuit return for the south-western shires,

---

[75] GDB, fols 238, 244v, and note 31 above.

[76] GDB, fols 230, 236v. *Raven* is ON Hrafn, and *Aschil* and *Turchil* might be either continental Germanic, or the Anglo-Scandinavian names Askell and Thorkell.

[77] GDB, fols 170v, 250v.

[78] GDB, fols 179, 187v. Madoc may be the *tainus* of that name found in Gloucestershire, see previous note.

[79] Susan Reynolds, 'Bookland, folkland and fiefs', ANS 14 (1992), p. 226.

[80] Some examples: *accipitrarius* (falconer), *arbalester* (crossbowman), *aurifaber* (goldsmith), *carpentarius* (carpenter), *equarius* (groom), *granetarius* (granary-keeper), *hostiarius*, *portitor* (doorkeeper), *prebendarius* (purveyor). In Wilts., Leofgyth held land in Knook for making a gold fringe (*aurifrigium*) and Godric the sheriff gave half a hide in Bucks. to Ælfgyth for teaching his daughter gold embroidery (GDB, fols 74, 149).

[81] In Hampshire, for instance: Turstin the chamberlain, Richard the archer, Herbert the chamberlain, Henry the treasurer, Croch the huntsman, Durand the baker and Geoffrey, chamberlain of the king's daughter Matilda (GDB, fol. 73). Croch the huntsman appears as a *serviens* in Wiltshire as does another Hampshire tenant-in-chief, William Belet.

[82] GDB, fols 36v, 63, 160v.

[83] VCH *Wilts*. ii, p. 73.

enables comparison to be made between what the Domesday scribe received and what he did with it. Exon Domesday was compiled in two sections, one for Wiltshire and Dorset, now incomplete, and the other including Somerset, Devon and Cornwall, for which the full text survives. The shire divisions are ignored, and the fiefs of the tenants-in-chief determine the arrangement; thus the land of Robert of Mortain in Devon is immediately followed by his estates in Cornwall and Somerset.[84] The composite entries occur towards the end of the text: the *terrae francorum militum* in Devon and the *terrae francorum tegnorum* in Somerset, followed by the *servientes regis* and English *taini* of both shires.[85] Though the Wiltshire and Dorset section is incomplete in Exon, the Domesday folios suggest that it followed a similar tripartite arrangement. The list of tenants for Wiltshire has entries for Herman *et alii servientes regis*, Oda *et alii taini regis* and Hervey *et alii ministri regis*. In the text, the lands of Herman of Dreux and six others are duly separated from those of Hervey of Wilton and 19 others, though transposition signs in the margins indicate that they should be amalgamated and both sections are headed '(land) of the king's *servientes*'.[86] In Dorset the list of tenants has Hugh d'Ivry *et alii franci*, William Belet *et alii sevientes regis* and Guthmund *et alii taini regis*. These groups appear in the text, though there is no heading for Hugh d'Ivry and his fellows, merely a marginal number, equivalent to that in the list of tenants, placed against the first entry in the section.[87]

Somerset's 'French thegns' have caused some puzzlement. There are fourteen names in the section, only one of which (Ealdred) is English; three individuals (Humphrey the chamberlain, Hugolin the interpreter and Richard the interpreter) have occupational by-names. The Domesday scribe completely revised this section. He removed the lands of Ralph Paynel and Ralph de Limesey and gave them individual entries, and the single manor held by Samson the chaplain of Odo of Bayeux was entered with the bishop's fief.[88] The rest of the land appears on the last of the Somerset folios, under the heading *Item Hunfridi terra et quorundam aliorum*, with transposition signs indicating that the section should be amalgamated with the rest of Humphrey the chamberlain's section on the verso of the preceding folio. This amalgamated section is quite separate from the lands of the *servientes* and *taini*, which correspond to the Exon groupings.[89] The Domesday scribe made similar rearrangements in the Devon material.

---

84 Exon, fols 210–82; that the Wiltshire/Dorset section was also arranged by fiefs is shown by the survival of William de Moyon's only Wiltshire manor, entered immediately before his fief in Dorset. A list of Exon's contents is given by V.H. Galbraith, *Domesday Book: its place in administrative history* (London, 1974), pp. 184–8.
85 Exon, fols 456–467v, 475–494v. The land of Nicholas and others described as crossbowmen occupies fols 468–474v; why they were not included in the 'composite' entries is unclear.
86 GDB, fols 64v, 73–73v, 74v. Herman of Dreux is a tenant-in-chief in Herefordshire (GDB, fol. 187).
87 GDB, fols 75, 83, 84–85. One of the *franci* is David *interpres*.
88 GDB, fols 87v, 96v–97.
89 GDB, fols 98v, 99. The only variation among the *servientes* is that two manors of

It is clear from Exon Domesday that, in the shires of western Wessex, both the Domesday commissioners and the Domesday scribe had trouble classifying the smaller landholders, probably because of their numbers. The circuit return for East Anglia, Little Domesday, was never abbreviated and edited by the Domesday scribe, and we do not know what he would have made of it. What is clear is the difference between Little Domesday and Exon. No headings are found for *taini* or *servientes*; there are composite entries, but the men and women who appear in them seem to be of much lower status.[90] Men, both French and English, with occupational by-names appear among the lesser holders towards the end of each shire-account, and perhaps most or all of these lesser tenants would have been described as *servientes* or *taini regis* elsewhere.[91] Indeed some do appear as *servientes* and *taini* in other shires. Ralph de Feugeres of Osmandiston, Norfolk, is a 'French knight' in Exon; Edmund son of Payne, of Dunham, Norfolk, is a *tainus regis* in Hampshire and a *serviens* in Somerset; and Eadgifu, wife of Edmund son of Swein, who held half a hide in Chafford, Essex, also held land in alms in Middlesex.[92]

What seems to have united *taini*, *servientes*, and some of the lesser tenants-in-chief is that they held their land in return for service; what was later called sergeanty. In Wiltshire, a number of the sergeancies recorded in the thirteenth century were attached to lands held by *taini regis* in 1086, which suggests that 'all the men entered as thegns were in the royal service and that all Englishmen who held estates of the king had survived because they were already or had become royal servants'.[93] The large numbers of *taini* and *servientes* in the shires of central Wessex would be explained by the proximity of the administrative centre of Winchester. Most of the Englishmen named in a writ, issued after 1070 and addressed to the shire-courts of Hampshire and Wiltshire, can be identified as *taini regis*.[94] Oda of Winchester held 38 hides of land in four shires, and is probably

Humphrey the chamberlain at Lytes Cary, which Exon entered among its *servientes*, are removed by the Domesday scribe and entered under Humphrey's name on folio 98v. Next he enrolled the *servientes* and *taini*, and then apparently discovered that the rest of Humphrey's lands appeared in the 'French thegns' section; he had thus to enter them (and the other lands which he left in this section) on folio 99, with transposition signs, as described.

[90] All three shires have headings for *liberi homines* and Suffolk has a group of *vavassores*; in no case are the holdings included even full manors (*LDB*, fols 1, 99; 109, 272–273v; 281, 446–447v.

[91] In Essex: Otto *aurifaber*, Ansger *coquus*, Reginald *balistarius*, Grim *prepositus*, Thorkell *prepositus*; in Norfolk, Eadric *accipitrarius*, Rahel *artifex*; in Suffolk, Gilbert *balistarius*, Ralph *balistarius*.

[92] *LDB*, fol. 263, Exon, fol. 462 (Devon); *LDB*, fol. 264, *GDB*, fols 50v, 98v; *LDB*, fol. 98, *GDB*, fol. 130v and see note 73 above.

[93] *VCH Wilts*. ii, pp. 76, 77–8 and see James Campbell: 'it could be that the sergeancies, as they come to light, or twilight, in the thirteenth century, are the semi-fossilized remnants of important parts of the Anglo-Saxon governmental system' ('Some agents and agencies of the late Anglo-Saxon state', p. 211).

[94] *Regesta* i, no. 267; the Englishmen addressed are Oda, Æthelsige, Saewulf, Ælfsige of Hatch, Cola and Eadric, of whom all except Cola attest William I's grant of Buttermere,

Oda the steward (*dapifer*), tenant of five hides at Micheldever, 'conveniently close to Winchester'.[95] His brother Ealdred (who does not appear in the writ) held 24½ hides in Sussex, Hampshire and Wiltshire, and was a juror for Titchfield hundred. Both of them had property in Winchester, that of Ealdred being a messuage on the High Street, and Oda had property in Southampton and in Calne, Wilts.[96] Ealdred's wife was an embroideress in the employ of Queen Matilda.[97] Ælfsige was a *burcniht* (chamberlain), who in 1086 held land at Enham Alamein and Steventon, having pledged Hatch Warren itself to Oda of Winchester.[98] Cola the huntsman, son of Wulfgeat the huntsman, held land as a *tainus regis* in Hampshire, Berkshire and Wiltshire, and his father Wulfgeat appears in Hampshire, Berkshire and Dorset.[99]

Huntsmen frequently occur among the *taini* and *servientes*. The land of Edwin the huntsman in Hampshire (two hides in Kingsclere Hundred) had been given to him by King Edward and was held *de firma regis*. It can be identified as Edmundsthorp Benham, probably named after Edmund, son of the Domesday holder, commemorated, with his father, his mother Odelina and his brothers Eadulf and Ælfwine, in the *Liber Vitae* of Hyde Abbey. They are presumably the forebears of the Edmundsthorp family, who later held the same land of Ruald de Woodcott.[100] William Engaine, who held Pytchley and Laxton, Northants, as a *tainus* (though he was certainly a Frenchman) was probably a huntsman. By the end of the twelfth century the land belonged to his descendant, Richard Engaine, by the service of hunting hares. The land at Pytchley had been held by the service of the king's hunting from before the Conquest, for it had belonged to Alwine

Wilts., to the Old Minster (1070 x 1087, Pelteret, *Vernacular documents*, no. 32, pp. 67–8). Only Æthelsige cannot be found in Domesday; Saewulf is probably the father of Alwine son of Saewulf, who held East Tytherley, and a *tainus* called Eadric held land in the New Forest (GDB, fols 50, 51v, 53v).

95   GDB, fols 29v, 42v, 49v, 50v, 51v, 52, 63v, 73v; Brian Golding, 'An introduction to the Hampshire Domesday', *The Hampshire Domesday*, ed. Ann Williams and R.W.H. Erskine (London, 1989), p. 24.

96   GDB, fols 29v, 40, 42v, 73v; *Winchester in the early middle ages*, ed. Martin Biddle, Winchester Studies I (Oxford, 1976), p. 42. The brothers may also be identical with Oda son of Eadric and Ealdred the forester, who held land in Devon (GDB, fol. 118; DB Devon, nos. 52,22;26–8 and notes). Round (VCH *Somerset* i, p. 417, VCH *Hampshire* i, p. 427) identified the Devon Ealdred both with Ealdred brother of Oda and with Ealdred of Monksilver, Somerset (GDB, fols 93v, 99; Robertson, *Charters*, pp. 238–9).

97   Dodwell, *Anglo-Saxon Art*, pp. 227, 327 (note 100). Ealdred's land in Micheldever, held of the New Minster, had been her dowry (GDB, fol. 42v).

98   GDB, fols 49v, 50, 50v. Domesday actually uses the English word for Ælfsige's office (*berchenistr*). Ælfsige owed the monks of the Old Minster a pledge of £12 on Enham Alamein.

99   GDB, fols 50, 50v, 63v, 73v, 74, 77v, 84, 84v; Golding, 'An introduction to the Hampshire Domesday', p. 25.

100   GDB, fol. 50v; VCH *Hampshire* iv, p. 260; *Liber Vitae: register and martyrology of New Minster and Hyde Abbey, Winchester*, ed. W. de Gray Birch, Hampshire Record Society (London and Winchester, 1892), p. 67. I owe these references to Dr John Moore.

the huntsman. The same man preceded William's brother, Richard Engaine, on all four of his Northamptonshire manors. Richard Engaine may have been a royal forester, for he claimed 36 hides of the manor of Bampton, Hunts, as part of the royal forest, and his lands were held in 1166 by the royal forester Fulk de Lisures, who had to attend the king not only *equis et armis* but with his hunting-horn slung around his neck. Richard Engaine may well be Richard the forester who held land in Warwickshire.[101] Other hunting sergeancies may go back to Domesday. The manors of Shapley and Skerraton, Devon, were held in 1212 by the render of arrows when the king hunted on Dartmoor, and the tenant, David of Skerraton, claimed that his forbears had held *a Conquestu*; in 1086 the manors were held by Ælfric (no by-name).[102] Edward the huntsman's half-virgate at Gillingham, Dorset, was held in 1212 by William of Hanton for looking after the king's wolfhounds (*per seriancie de luverez*) and Saeweard's land in Purse Caundle descended to John fitzAlan, for the service of nursing the king's dogs which were injured in Blackmore Forest.[103] Some huntsmen were clearly men of importance; William II is described doing justice with 'his bishops, earls, sheriffs, reeves, huntsmen and other officers'.[104]

Most of the *taini* are no more than names, but some are better-documented than others. In Buckinghamshire, Leofwine of Nuneham Courtenay held five burgesses in Buckingham and four manors as a *tainus regis*.[105] One of them lay at Salden, where another tenement was held before the Conquest by a thegn commended to Alwine *de Neuham*, who was presumably a kinsman.[106] Another lay in Beachampton, which suggests that Leofwine of Nuneham is identical with the man of the same name who held a hide in this vill as Roger d'Ivry's tenant.[107] Drayton Parslow had also belonged to Leofwine before the Conquest, and afterwards had been held of him by Ralph Passaquam, but in 1086 the manor

[101] GDB, fols 208v, 229; Round, *Feudal England*, pp. 29–30 and see above.
[102] GDB, fol. 118v: *DB Devon*, nos. 52,44–5 and notes; *The Book of Fees*, HMSO (London, 1920–21) i, p. 98.
[103] GDB, fol. 84v; *VCH Dorset* iii, p. 54; *DB Dorset*, no. 56,55, note.
[104] Van Caeneghem i, 98. Walter Map complains of the loutish and abusive behaviour of the *forestarii* at Henry II's court (*De Nugis Curialium*, trans. James, pp. 5–6).
[105] GDB, fols 143, 153: *DB Buckinghamshire*, nos. B15; 57,1–4; all this had been held by Leofwine TRE. Only in the first entry, for Salden, is he called Leofwine of Nuneham, but presumably he is the holder of the next three manors. He may also be the Leofwine who had a virgate in Wavendon, held of him by Godric the priest, but his name is common and there were several other men called Leofwine in Buckinghamshire (GDB, fols 148v, 152, 153).
[106] It has been suggested that they were brothers, and identical with Æthelwine the sheriff of Warwickshire (who was dead by 1086) and his brother Leofwine (Keats-Rohan, 'Henry of Oxford: Englishmen in a Norman world', pp. 295–6) but the names are very common. There was, for instance, a Leofwine son of Alwine who held land in Nottinghamshire and Lincolnshire (GDB, fols 280v, 337). Since Alwine of *Neuham* does not appear in 1086, I would regard him as the father, rather than the brother of Leofwine of Nuneham, if they were related at all; see also notes 110, 112 below.
[107] GDB, fol. 151v. It had been held TRE by Leofric, a *commendatus* of Azur.

was in the possession of Nigel de Berville.[108] Leofwine had given Nuneham Courtenay, Oxfordshire, described as his patrimony, to Abingdon Abbey. The gift had been confirmed by Odo of Bayeux, but on his fall in 1082 his acts were cancelled, and in 1086 it was held by Richard de Courcy.[109] The mother of Leofwine of Nuneham had held five hides at Mollington, Warks, which passed to Osbern fitzRichard and he himself may be the Leofwine Dodda whose land at Wilmcote in the same shire also went to Osbern.[110] Leofwine may be identical with the *minister* who had held Chinnor (13 hides) and Cowley (4½ hides) of King Edward and continued to hold of King William.[111] This Leofwine in turn might be the ancestor of Henry of Oxford, sheriff of Berkshire (1153–5), who also held land in Cowley.[112]

Alsige of Faringdon took his name from Faringdon, Berks, where in 1086 he held four hides as the king's tenant. Faringdon had belonged to Earl Harold, as had Littleworth, where Alsige held two hides; he continued to hold of King William in 1086.[113] Before 1066, Alsige had a manor of five hides at Longney-on-Severn, Gloucs, where he built a church, consecrated by St Wulfstan (1062–95). The church had a graveyard, in which stood a fine nut-tree, and Alsige's habit of sitting beneath it, drinking and dicing with his friends, aroused the bishop's ire; he cursed the tree, which died.[114]

If this was all Alsige held before 1066 (and his name, which is common, makes it impossible to be certain) he must be counted among the Englishmen enriched

[108] GDB, fol. 151v. Ralph owed two armed men (*loricati*) as castle-guard (*custodia*) at Windsor, but Geoffrey, bishop of Coutances, had dispossessed him and given the manor to Nigel.

[109] *Chron Abingdon* ii, p. 12; GDB, fol. 159. The pre-Conquest tenant is named as Hakon, who presumably held the manor under Leofwine.

[110] GDB, fol. 244: DB *Warwickshire*, no. 37,2;9. The Leofwine who held Wilmcote may have been a son of Dodda, or perhaps Dodda was simply an alternative name. Leofwine of Nuneham (Courtenay) is frequently identified with the Leofwine who appears as the *antecessor* of Geoffrey de la Guerche, holding (*inter alia*) Newnham Paddox, Warks. (GDB, fol. 243v: DB *Warwickshire*, no. 31,11). But this Leofwine is never called *de Neuham/Niweham* and held no land in 1086; indeed he may have been dead for he had a son, Leofric, who was adult and holding land in 1066 (GDB, fol. 235v). In Lincolnshire (fol. 369) Leofric is called *cild*, a sign of high rank. The vill of Mollington was divided between Warwickshire, Oxfordshire and Northamptonshire in 1086 (GDB, fols 157, 226, 244).

[111] GDB, fol. 160v: DB *Oxfordshire*, nos. 58,24–5. He may also be the Leofwine who held 5 hides in Hanwell and had held TRE.

[112] Green, *English sheriffs to 1154*, p. 27. Keats-Rohan ('Henry of Oxford: Englishmen in a Norman world', pp. 294–5, 306) suggests that Henry's father Eilwi (Æthelwig/ Æthelwine) and his grandfather Godwine may have been reeves of Oxford; if Godwine (as argued by Dr Keats-Rohan) was Leofwine of Nuneham's son, then he (Leofwine) belonged to a ministerial family. Dr Keats-Rohan also identifies Leofwine of Nuneham with Leofwine, father-in-law of Geoffrey de la Guerche, but see note 110 above.

[113] GDB, fols 57v, 58.

[114] GDB, fol. 170v; *Vita Wulfstani*, pp. 40–1; Mason, *St Wulfstan of Worcester*, pp. 145–6; Williams, 'An introduction to the Gloucestershire Domesday', p. 35.

by the Conqueror, for by 1086 he held 15 hides of land in Berkshire, Oxfordshire and Gloucestershire. Two of his estates had belonged to Earl Harold, and one is said to have been King William's gift.[115] The king had also given Alsige's son Alwig a messuage (*haga*) in Wallingford, and the young man held a hide in Milton-under-Wychwood, Oxon, of Earl William's fief.[116] Alwig's grandson, Robert of Astrop, gave this land to Bruern Abbey.[117]

To this modest endowment must be added the royal estates which Alsige held at farm: Langford (15 hides) and Shipton-under-Wychwood (8 hides), Oxon and Great Barrington (four hides), Gloucs. The first two had belonged to Earl Harold and the third was held by Tovi the Wend, the earl's housecarl.[118] The rents are not given, but the three manors were worth a total of £33. As with Robert Latimer in Kent, one wonders how Alsige raised the cash; presumably from the proceeds of royal service. In Gloucestershire he was disputing the ownership of three and a half hides at Windrush with the abbey of Winchcombe, and had removed it from Barrington to Salmonsbury Hundred.[119] This act suggests that he had some authority in the shire, and he may have been one of the sheriff's officers.

Alsige may have been one of those who did well out of the Conquest. The vicissitudes which might befall even ministerial kindreds are exemplified by the fate of Eadnoth the staller's family. Eadnoth himself, who was killed in 1068 while defending Somerset against the sons of Harold II, had been a steward (*dapifer*) of Edward the Confessor. He may also have acted as a royal justice, for he is said to have recovered 2½ hides of land at Ugford, belonging to Wilton Abbey, from Earl Godwine.[120] His son Harding was still alive when William of Malmesbury

---

[115] GDB, fols 63v, 160v, 170v. Barcote, Berks. (the gift of King William) and Shipton-under-Wychwood had belonged to Harold.

[116] GDB, fols 56, 161. The other tenant in Milton-under-Wychwood was Rannulf Flambard, soon to become the chief advisor and minister of William Rufus (GDB, fol. 157).

[117] Stenton, 'English families and the Norman Conquest', p. 333.

[118] GDB, fols 154v, 164. Langford had 'a notably lavish church of c.1060–90, incorporating slightly earlier sculpture' (H.M. and J. Taylor, *Anglo-Saxon Architecture* (Cambridge, 1965), i, pp. 364–72; Elizabeth Coatsworth, 'Late pre-Conquest sculptures with the Crucifixion south of the Humber', *Bishop Æthelwold: his career and influence*, ed. Barbara Yorke (Woodbridge, 1988), pp. 173–4, 190).

[119] GDB, fols 165v, 170v.

[120] AS Chron, 'D', 1067. Eadnoth the staller is addressed in a writ of Edward the Confessor, which cannot be dated more closely than 1053 x 1066, relating to land held by Westminster Abbey in Hampshire; his name appears among the witnesses to two Westminster charters, allegedly of 1065, forged by Osbert de Clare (S.1041, 1043, 1129, and see Harmer, *Writs*, pp. 351, 558–9, Keynes, 'Regenbald the chancellor (sic)', p. 207 and note). He is called 'staller' in *Regesta* i, no. 7 (1067), AS Chron, 'D', 1067 and GDB, fol. 58v and *constabulus* in *Chron Abingdon* ii, p. 19; GDB (fols 68v–69) also calls him *dapifer*. For Ugford, see GDB, fols 68, 72v; it was held in 1086 by Osbern Giffard, who had also received Eadnoth's land at Knowle, Somerset (GDB, fol. 98, Exon, fol. 447; for a similar case, involving land in Norfolk, see Chapter VI, p. 144, note 94 below).

was writing the *Gesta Regum* (1118–1125).[121] He is probably to be identified with Harding son of *Alnod*, who in 1086 held six manors (11½ hides) in Somerset as a *tainus regis*. One was held of him by Ceolric, whose name is uncommon, and who can probably be identified with Ceolric, Harding son of Eadnoth's reeve, who was involved in the purchase of a woman at Topsham, Devon, at an unknown date in the reign of William I.[122] All these Somerset lands went to Harding's son Nicholas, brother of Robert fitzHarding of Bristol, whose family claimed descent from Eadnoth the staller.[123] Since Harding's name is not uncommon, it is difficult to identify his estates in Domesday. He is probably the *tainus* who held five hides at Wheatenhurst, Gloucs, in pledge from its former owner, for Robert fitzHarding was a burgess of Bristol, and the family might be expected to have land in the vicinity.[124] He may be the *tainus regis* who held 27½ hides in Wiltshire in 1086, and had held a further 18½ hides then in Earl Aubrey's fief; but this Harding had held the land before 1086, whereas Harding son of Eadnoth's Somerset manors had been in other hands.[125] Eadnoth's son can probably be identified with Harding son of *Alnod* whose daughter became a nun at Shaftesbury Abbey.[126]

Harding did not, however, inherit his father's lands, amounting to nearly 65 hides in Berkshire, Wiltshire, Dorset, Somerset, Devon and Gloucestershire, the

---

121 GR i, p. 313; for the date, see Barlow, *The English church, 1066–1154*, p. 17. Harding and his (unnamed) brothers attest an undated transaction of the late eleventh or early twelfth century (Pelteret, *Vernacular documents*, no. 123, p. 111).

122 GDB, fols 98v–99; for Ceolric, see Exon, fol. 491v (*DB Somerset*, no. 47,4); Pelteret, *Vernacular documents*, no. 123, pp. 110–11. Harding son of Eadnoth himself sold a woman at Topsham (Pelteret, *Vernacular documents*, no. 107, pp. 105–6). Though the names 'Harding' and 'Eadnoth' are not uncommon, it does not seem necessary to postulate two men, both called Harding and both with fathers called Eadnoth, in roughly the same area at the same time; see however the objections of Dr Lewis, 'The formation of the honour of Chester, 1066–1100', pp. 67–8.

123 The most recent study is that of Robert B. Patterson, 'Robert fitz Harding of Bristol: profile of an early Angevin burgess-baron patrician and his family's urban involvement', *Haskins Society Journal* 1 (1989), pp. 109–22. Nicholas was the ancestor of the Meriet family.

124 GDB, fol. 178v.

125 GDB, fols 69, 74. The Wiltshire Harding is presumably Harding of Wilton, who held Cranmore of the church of Glastonbury in 1066 and in 1086 (*GDB*, fol. 90v; *DB Somerset*, no. 8,32 note). He may be identical with Harding the queen's butler (*regine pincerna*), who attests S.1036 and 1042 (dated 1062 and 1065 respectively); see Keynes, 'Regenbald the chancellor (*sic*)', pp. 206–7. Harding the queen's butler is presumably the Harding who held half a hide at Burley, Berks., of Queen Edith, which had belonged to Ælfgifu, and might also be the Harding who had held Bredy Farm, Dorset, before 1066 and continued to hold it at farm of Berengar Giffard in 1086 (*GDB*, fol. 82v; *VCH Dorset* iii, p. 36). Harding of Wilton is probably not identical with Harding son of Eadnoth, since the latter, who was alive and active c.1120, is unlikely to have been old enough to hold land before 1066.

126 BL Harleian Ms 61, fol. 54; Cooke, 'Donors and daughters: Shaftesbury Abbey's benefactors, endowments and nuns, c.1086–1130', pp. 31, 40, 42.

bulk of which passed to Hugh d'Avranches, earl of Chester.[127] Perhaps Eadnoth's connections with Harold Godwineson continued to arouse suspicion, even though he fell in battle against Harold's sons.[128] William of Malmesbury described Harding as 'one more accustomed to sharpen his tongue for litigious ends than to make steel clash on steel in battle'; if his father's land had been denied him, one can see why he acquired this reputation.[129] William's description of Harding's litigiousness is born out by other sources. Domesday records that he had returned Beechingstoke, Wiltshire, which he held for life of Shaftesbury Abbey 'of his own free will' (*sponte sua*) but in the reign of Henry I the abbey had to resort to law to recover it from him.[130] He was also involved in litigation with Abbot Herluin of Glastonbury (1101–20).[131]

What service Harding performed for King William is not known. His Somerset manors, with the exception of Merriott, had belonged to Tovi the sheriff. Among them was Capland, to which was attached half a hide in the royal manor of Curry Rivel, and it may be that Harding had been farming this estate, though he did

---

[127] *GDB*, fols 58v, 60, 68v–69, 80, 91v, 104v, 166v; for Earl Hugh's succession to the lands of Eadnoth the staller, see *Chron Abingdon* ii, p. 19 (cf. *GDB*, fol. 58v). Osbern Giffard held Knowle, Som, and Ugford, Wilts, both of which probably belonged to Eadnoth the staller (*GDB*, fols 72v, 98). This estimate of Eadnoth's holding depends on the suggestion of Freeman (iv, pp. 757–61) that the Alnod (or Elnod), who appears as Hugh's predecessor, should also be identified with Eadnoth (*Ednod*) the staller. The Domesday forms *Alnod* and *Elnod* could represent the name Ealdnoth and confusion between the prefixes *Ead-* and *Eald-* is found elsewhere in Domesday (in Worcestershire, *Eldeve* (Ealdgifu) in the list of tenants is represented by *Eddeva* (Eadgifu) in the text; *GDB*, fols 172, 178). Dr Lewis ('The formation of the honour of Chester, 1066–1100', pp. 48–9, 67–8) has expressed scepticism on this point, though acknowledging a second confusion of *Alnod/Ednod* in Lincolnshire (*GDB*, fols 370, 376. A similar confusion seems to have occurred in Cornwall (*GDB*, fol. 124v), where an estate held by *Ednod* is inserted among the five manors of *Alnod*).

[128] Ann Williams, 'Land and power in the eleventh century: the estates of Harold Godwineson', *ANS* (3) 1981, p. 181.

[129] *GR* i, p. 313.

[130] Domesday (*GDB*, fol. 67v) describes Harding as the pre-Conquest tenant of Beechingstoke, but it may have been held by his father (see Williams, 'The knights of Shaftesbury Abbey', p. 227 and note 65). In Henry I's writ for Shaftesbury (*Regesta* i, no. 309, BL Harleian Ms 61, fols 23, 30) Harding is described as son of Alweald (*filius Aluoldi*) but the compiler of the Shaftesbury Cartulary was notoriously careless and this is probably scribal error.

[131] William of Malmesbury claims that Herluin 'wrested Mells (Somerset) and Lyme (Regis, Dorset) from Harding son of Eadnoth, who was at that time a very powerful man and an advocate (*causidicus*)' (John Scott, *The early history of Glastonbury: an edition, translation and study of William of Malmesbury's De Antiquitate Glastonie Ecclesie* (Woodbridge, 1981), pp. 160–1). What claim Harding had to the estates (if any) is unknown; in 1086 Lyme Regis was held of Glastonbury by Wulfgeat, who had also held TRE from the abbot, and one hide at Mells was held of Glastonbury by Godgifu in succession to her husband; the rest of the 20–hide manor was in the hands of the church, except for 5½ hides given by the king to the bishop of Coutances (*GDB*, fols 77v, 90v).

not do so at the time of Domesday.[132] He may also have had some office in connection with the royal manor and hundred of Topsham, Devon.[133] In 1096 he was one of the magnates (*optimates*) who heard pleas in Devon and Cornwall, and he attests a charter of Henry I in 1105.[134] His lands in Somerset went to his son Nicholas, and his second son, Robert fitzHarding was a prosperous Bristol burgess. Robert's service to Henry II brought him the lands and castle of Berkeley, Gloucestershire, held of the king, and the opportunity to acquire other estates of other lords. One such was Fifehead Magdalen, Dorset, given by Rannulf II, earl of Chester. In 1086, the manor had been held by Earl Hugh, in succession to Eadnoth (*Alnod*) the staller. Thus at least one of their ancestor's estates returned to the family, along with the status which had been theirs before 1066.[135]

Royal service could thus ensure not only the survival of kindreds and the possibility of acquiring fresh lands, but 'could even do something to reverse the decision of the Conquest, and help families to regain something of what they had then lost'.[136] Bernard, a royal scribe active in the 1120s, was, despite his continental name, of English descent. He and his brother Nicholas, another royal scribe, were benefactors of Merton Priory, and the church's register preserves notes on some charters relating to Bernard's land; further details come from a compilation on miracles made by his nephew, Peter of Cornwall.[137] Henry I rewarded Bernard's service with the lands of Gisulf the scribe, drowned in the White Ship disaster of 1120, and confirmed the lands in Cornwall of his grandfather Theodulf, his father Ailsi (Æthelsige) and his uncle Brictric (Beorhtric). Most of the lands named cannot be identified, though *Trecharl* might be *Tregal* (?Tregole), one of five small manors held in 1086 by Beorhtric (presumably Bernard's uncle) of the count of Mortain, and *Botwei* might be Bojorrow (Domesday *Bodeworwei*), a dependency of the royal manor of Winni-

---

132 GDB, fols 88v–89, 98v. A Harding held 5 hides *in firma regis* at Alton, Hants (GDB, fol. 43).
133 GDB, fol. 101; a royal manor in 1086, it had been held by Earl Harold TRE. For Harding son of Eadnoth's connection with Topsham, see note 122 above.
134 Van Caeneghem i, nos. 144, 168, pp. 117–18, 136; F. Barlow, *William Rufus* (London, 1983), p. 208. See also William of Malmesbury's description of him as *causidicus* (advocate), note 131 above.
135 Patterson, 'Robert fitz Harding of Bristol', p. 111; GDB, fol. 80. It is possible that Harding had continued to hold Fifehead as Hugh's tenant; not all mesne-tenants are recorded in Domesday (Williams, 'An introduction to the Gloucestershire Domesday', p. 39, and Chapter VIII below).
136 R.W. Southern, 'The place of the reign of Henry I in English history', *Proceedings of the British Academy* 47 (1962), p. 147, reprinted as 'King Henry I', R.W. Southern, *Medieval Humanism and other studies* (Oxford, 1970), p. 225.
137 A. Heales, *The records of Merton Priory in the County of Surrey* (London, 1898), pp. 8–11 (I owe this reference to Dr John Moore); J.H. Round, 'Bernard the king's scribe', EHR 14 (1899), pp. 417–30; Southern, 'Place of the reign of Henry I', pp. 147–50 (*Medieval Humanism*, pp. 225–8); Green, *The government of England under Henry I*, p. 235. Extracts from Peter's work are translated in G.C. Coulton, *Social life in Britain* (Cambridge, 1919), pp. 221–24.

anton, also held by Beorhtric of the count of Mortain in 1086. It had been held of the fee of Richard de Lucy by Wigan, presumably the father of Ruald fitzWigan, whose property in Launceston was given to Bernard by the same grant. Soon afterwards Ruald fitzWigan gave Bernard the churches on his land, which had belonged to Beorhtric 'the Cornishman' (*Walensis*), who is probably Bernard's uncle; perhaps Beorhtric's estate had passed to Wigan and thence to his son.[138]

Bernard's grandfather Theodulf, whose name is not English, cannot be identified in Domesday. In the 1120s Bernard recovered the land of his grandfather in Launceston Castle from Erchembald the Fleming, which suggests that Theodulf's property (which may not have been large) should be sought among Erchembald's manors in 1086.[139] Bernard's father Ailsi might be the *Alsi* who held *Trelamar* (unidentified, perhaps in Fawton hundred) of the count of Mortain.[140] His grandson, Peter of Cornwall, described Ailsi as a master-builder in the service of the canons of Launceston, with property just outside the town. Henry's grant included the land of Ralph the chancellor in the castlery of Launceston, later specified as a vacant messuage 'between the cess-pit (*puteum*) and the chapel' for Bernard's dwelling (*ad se hospitandum*).[141] This is perhaps the property on which Peter's father, Jordan, dwelt; Peter also had a married sister in Launceston.[142]

Bernard had been involved in considerable legislation to secure his land and

---

[138] Round, 'Bernard the king's scribe', pp. 418, 419–20. Henry's grant also conveyed the lands of Dodda and the land of Ralph (Rannulf) *cancellarius* in the castle (Launceston); the property listed includes the church of Lawhitton (see GDB, fol. 120v, held by the bishops of Exeter TRE and 1086), the land of *Trecharl* (?Tregole), *Menwinnoc* and *Cheulent* of the bishop's fee; the land of *Charbrixi* (see note below) and *Botwei de Wigan* of Richard de Lucy's fee; the land of *Trethu* of William fitzRichard's fee; the land of *Treghestoc* of Roger de Courseulles' fee; the church of Liskeard (GDB, fol. 121v, held 1086 by the count of Mortain in succession to Mærle-Sveinn); the *virgultum castelli* of Ruald fitzWigan's fee; and the land of *Trevalrig* of Andrew de Vitry's fee. For the lands of Beorhtric in 1086, see GDB fols 120 (Mawgan and Bojorrow), 124v (Lesnewth, Tregole, Tregeagle, Trethurffe and Perranuthoe) and see also below, note 142.
[139] Van Caeneghem i, no. 267, pp. 226–7; Round, 'Bernard the king's scribe', p. 422. Erchembald's lands lay at Bodbrane, *Avalda* and Brea (GDB, fol. 124) of which the two last had been held TRE by Dodda, perhaps the Dodda whose land was granted to Bernard by Henry I (see previous note).
[140] GDB, fol. 124v.
[141] Round, 'Bernard the king's scribe', p. 420. Ralph (Rannulf) *cancellarius* was Ralph the priest (presbiter), chancellor of Robert, count of Mortain, who held land at Thorne, near Montacute, and the tithes of nine churches in Dorset and Somerset (GDB, fol. 92, Brian Golding, 'Robert of Mortain', ANS 13 (1991), pp. 138–9).
[142] Southern, 'Place of the reign of Henry I', pp. 149–50 (*Medieval Humanism*, p. 258). In the 1140s, Peter's father Jordan attested a charter of his alleged kinsman, Reginald de Dunstanville, in favour of the canons of Launceston, as Jordan *de Trekarl*, *prepositus* (van Caeneghem i, no. 23, pp. 278–9). Jordan's property at *Trecarrel* is said to have lain 4 miles from Launceston. If this is the *Trecharl* of Henry I's confirmation, the latter cannot be Tregole, which was on the other side of the county. Domesday *Tregal*, held by Beorhtric (GDB, fol. 124v) is unidentified by Oliver Padel, though placed in Stratton

his success was probably due to his position as a royal scribe. The shire-court of Devon had adjudged to Bernard the lands of his grandfather in Launceston against Erchembald the Fleming, and he made good his claim to *Trecharl* (?Tregole) in the bishop of Exeter's court against the son of Elwi (Ælfwig) Gold; another Englishman, Brihtnoth (Beorhtnoth) quitclaimed Bernard of an acre and his houses in *Chambrixi*, and Stephen, then count of Mortain, quitclaimed his rents in *Fleshmangerestrete* (Parchment Street), Winchester.[143] Bernard became a fairly wealthy man, with a following of his own; his esquires Roger and Rannulf (*scutigeri*) and Ralph (*armiger*) attest transactions in which he was involved. Apart from his Cornish lands he held Gisulf's property in Busket Lane, Winchester, and bought a second tenement nearby from Thezo and his wife Rohasia, daughter of Ailric of *Cleindona*; he also had rents in *Fleshmangerestrete* (Parchment Street).[144] Gisulf's inheritance included a house and land in London, and Bernard also held the churches of Cuddington, Surrey, Potterspury, Northants, and *Cliva*, and even acquired land in Normandy, at Mathieu near Douvres.[145]

Since Bernard had no children of his own, his wealth passed to Jordan, presumably his youngest brother, and father of Peter of Cornwall, prior of Holy Trinity, Aldgate (1197–1221), who was born about 1140. Peter describes his father as 'learned in the secular law' and says his advice was often sought in legal matters. Peter also claimed relationship with William fitzRichard of Cardinan, Cornwall, and the latter's son-in-law, Reginald de Dunstanville, an illegitimate son of Bernard's employer, Henry I. Reginald was created earl of Cornwall by his sister the Empress in 1140, and one of his charters is attested by Peter's father, Jordan of Trecharl, described as a *prepositus* (reeve). It is possible that Peter's mother was a kinswoman of Reginald's wife, Beatrice.[146]

hundred (*DB Cornwall*, no. 5,23,2 and note); the identification with Tregole is that of Ian Maxwell, *The Domesday settlements of Cornwall* (Redruth, 1986), p. 15.
[143] Van Caeneghem i, nos. 266, 267, pp. 226–7; Round, 'Bernard the king's scribe', pp. 420, 421; Southern, 'Place of the reign of Henry I', p. 149 (*Medieval Humanism*, pp. 226–7. *Chambrixi*, the *Charbrixi* of Henry I's confirmation, is unidentified, but the second element must be the OE personal name Beorhtsige. A man of this name (*Brixi* in Domesday) held land at Trembraze, an appendage of Winnianton, of the count of Mortain in 1086.
[144] Round, 'Bernard the king's scribe', pp. 423, 424; *Winchester in the early middle ages*, ed. Biddle, pp. 62, 106, 117 (cf. 7 note 3). Note that Thezo's wife, though she has a continental name, was the daughter of an Englishman (OE Æthelric); *Cleindona* is unidentified, but may be Clandon, Surrey (Dr John Moore, personal communication).
[145] Round, 'Bernard the king's scribe', p. 426; Green, *The government of England under Henry I*, p. 151.
[146] Richard Sharpe, 'Peter of Cornwall', *The Dictionary of National Biography, Missing Persons*, ed. C.S. Nicholls (Oxford, 1993), pp. 519–20. William fitzRichard was the son of Richard fitzTurold (or Turolf) one of the richer landholders in Cornwall in 1086, who also held land in Devon (GDB, fols 113v, 122–122v, and see Ian Soulsby 'An introduction to the Cornish Domesday', *The Cornish Domesday*, ed. Ann Williams and R.W.H. Erskine (London, 1988), p. 15; idem, 'Richard fitzTurold, lord of Penhallam, Cornwall',

Englishmen, defined as men with English names, were not uncommon amongst the royal servants of King Henry I's reign, though they are by no means the largest group, nor did they hold positions of first importance.[147] They were minor court dignitaries or local officials, sometimes sheriffs, but more often foresters, huntsmen or sheriff's officers.[148] Some men with continental names whose background is unknown may, of course, have been English; the example of Bernard, and his brothers Nicholas and Jordan, shows that not all men with 'Norman' names were French. The service of the king had certainly enabled some English families to acquire or recover something of their wealth and status. The royal court was dominated by foreigners, but much of the local business in the shires must still have been in the hands of Englishmen.

Medieval Archaeology 20 (1976), pp. 146–8). *Trethu,* of the fee of William fitzRichard, was one of the estates confirmed in Henry I's grant to Bernard, so some early connection between the families is possible. For Jordan *de Trekarl's* attestation, see note 142 above.

[147]Green, *The government of England under Henry I,* pp. 155–6 and the biographical appendix, pp. 226–81. For another English family who profited by service to Henry I, see Hugh Thomas, 'A Yorkshire thegn and his descendants after the Conquest', *Medieval Prosopography* 8 (1987), pp. 1–22.

[148] In 1119, Edward the priest of Cholsey and his son Samuel, who were presumably English, were geld-collectors in Berkshire (van Caeneghem i, no. 215, p. 182).

Chapter VI

HOLY MEN AND WORLDLY GOODS

> Their nationality was their downfall. If they
> were English, no virtue was enough for them to
> be considered worthy of promotion; if they
> were foreigners, the mere appearance of virtue,
> vouched for by their friends, was sufficient for
> them to be judged worthy of the highest
> honour.
>
> Eadmer, *Historia Novorum*, p. 224

THE GENERAL EFFECT OF the Conquest on the church was much the same as its effect on the lay aristocracy. Positions of power and wealth were given to foreign ecclesiastics at the expense of natives, either by deposition or on the death of the incumbents. By 1087 only two bishops remained from the pre-Conquest order: the Lotharingian Giso, bishop of Wells (1060–88) and the Englishman St Wulfstan, bishop of Worcester (1062–1095). Osbern (1072–1103), bishop of Exeter, who succeeded Leofric (1046–72), might be included since, although he was the brother of William fitzOsbern, he had also been one of the Confessor's clerks.[1] All were succeeded by foreigners. Wells was given to John de Villula (1088–1122), a native of Tours and one of William I's physicians, who moved the see to Bath. Worcester went to Samson, who came from a notable episcopal family; his brother Thomas was archbishop of York (1070–1100) and he himself fathered both Thomas II of York (1109–1114) and Richard II of Bayeux (1108–34). Exeter went, after a vacancy, to William Warelwast (1107–37), an agent both of William Rufus and Henry I. Most, though not all, of the English monastic houses were also placed under foreign abbots.

The advent of foreign bishops and abbots, and especially the appointment of the noted reformer, Lanfranc, as archbishop of Canterbury, meant great changes in the English Church which are beyond the scope of this book.[2] So far as the

---

[1] Barlow (*The English Church, 1066–1154*, p. 62) describes Osbern as 'completely anglicized', and the chapter of Exeter continued to use the rule introduced by his predecessor, Leofric, throughout his tenure of office; indeed it remained a conservative and idiosyncratic community well into the twelfth century (see David Blake, 'The development of the chapter of the diocese of Exeter, 1051–1161', *Journal of Medieval History* 8 (1982), pp. 1–11).

[2] For a general view, see Barlow, *The English Church 1066–1154*; Martin Brett, *The English church under Henry I* (Oxford, 1970).

holders of land were concerned, these changes were far less sweeping than the disaster which befell the lay aristocracy. The Church's lands belonged, not to individual bishops and abbots, but to the institutions which they represented and were thus spared, to some extent, the tenurial upheaval which affected the laity. Moreover its personnel, below the level of bishops, abbots and priors, remained largely English. When Bishop Maurice (1086–1107) reorganized the chapter of St Paul's, London, 'a little under half' the canons were recruited from the invaders.[3] The same proportion is seen at Dover, a college of secular canons refounded (possibly by Earl Godwine) in the early eleventh century.[4] Its communal prebends were distributed by Odo, bishop of Bayeux, to individual canons, who are named in Domesday Book; of the twenty-four, twelve are French and eleven English, all of whom had either held the same land before 1066 or had succeeded their fathers, or, in one case, a brother.[5] Some churches thus preserved at least a substratum of English sentiment.

Dover was in origin one of the minsters whose *parochiae* had been the backbone of the early church. As far as the minsters are concerned, the Conquest stands in the middle of a process which had been going on since the tenth century. Their *parochiae*, served by teams of priests, were splitting up into smaller, one-priest parishes, owing residual dues to the mother-church from whose province they had been detached. Many factors affected these developments. Local lords who founded estate-churches were allowed from the time of Edgar to divert a proportion of their tithes to their own establishments, but it was often to the advantage of minster-priests themselves to reorganize their *parochiae* into individual chapelries, and when secular chapters and colleges were disbanded, their members were often compensated with livings in the churches of the old *parochia*.[6]

Not all the minster *parochiae* were affected by these developments. Some

---

[3] C.N.L. Brooke, 'The composition of the chapter of St Paul's, 1086–1163', *Cambridge Historical Journal* 10 (1950), p. 122. St Paul's produced one of the English collections of pre-Conquest law-codes (Cambridge, Corpus Christi College Ms 383, see *EHD* i, p. 328); the other is the *Textus Roffensis*, produced at Rochester, which also had a large proportion of English members. Local families, and kinsmen of the successive bishops, supplied a high proportion of the known canons of Exeter Cathedral, and some families at least (like that of John of Salisbury) were of English or partly English descent (Blake, 'The development of the chapter of the diocese of Exeter, 1050–1161', pp. 7–9).
[4] Tim Tatton-Brown, 'Churches of the Canterbury diocese', *Minsters and parish churches: the local church in transition*, ed. John Blair (Oxford, 1988), p. 110. The community was moved from the hill-top church of St-Mary-in-Castro, now in the castle, to a new church, St Martin's, in the lower town.
[5] *GDB*, fol. 1v; the 24th prebend belonged, before and after 1066, to the abbot of St Augustine's, Canterbury. Of the foreign canons, Will[elmu]s pictav[ensis], who held Sibertswold and Deal, may be the King's panegyrist, William of Poitiers (R.H.C. Davis, 'William of Poitiers and his history of William the Conqueror', *The writing of history in the middle ages: essays presented to Richard William Southern*, ed. R.H.C. Davis and J.M. Wallace-Hadrill (Oxford, 1981), p. 90).
[6] It seems that when the secular canons of Durham were replaced with monks, those

remained as royal free chapels, others were re-organized as Benedictine monasteries, others again survived to be colonized by Augustinian canons in the twelfth century.[7]

These developments often meant the gradual replacement of secular clerks and canons by regular clergy, some of foreign origin. The secular college founded at Clare by the English magnate, Ælfric son of Wihtgar, c.1045 was taken over by Richard fitzGilbert, who acquired Wihtgar's lands after the Conquest. Richard's son Gilbert gave the minster to Bec, and his son, Richard, transformed it into a dependent priory at Stoke by Clare, to which the individual prebends were to revert on the deaths of the incumbents. The effects are clearly displayed in Domesday Book and in the Stoke by Clare cartulary. By 1086, the prebend at Gestingthorpe, Essex, once held by Leodmaer the priest, the community's head, was in the hands of William Pecche, a layman, and by 1090, most of the canons were of foreign extraction.[8]

The minsters which were most successful in retaining their rights were those which, like Leominster, were granted to monasteries.[9] The ones which did worst were those which were used for the endowment of royal chaplains. Christchurch, Hants, was given by William II to his chief minister, Rannulf Flambard, in or soon after 1087. By not replacing canons who died, Rannulf reduced their number from twenty-five to thirteen, and appropriated much of the revenue, though he did use this for the re-building of the church. His successors, however, were more directly abusive, and by the 1140s Christchurch had become 'little more than a single, very rich living for a single clerk, assisted by hired chaplains'. Those canons who remained were distributed as rectors among the dependent churches of the parochia. Nevertheless, when the Winchester clerk, Hilary (later bishop of Chichester), who became dean in the 1140s, attempted to retrieve the situation, there were still two English canons who remembered the constitutions of the original community; Ailmer (Æthelmaer) at Christchurch itself, and Almetus, priest of Carisbrooke and dean of the Isle of Wight. It was on their testimony that the community was reformed, and one or other of them was probably the author of the surviving history of Christchurch commissioned by Dean Hilary.[10]

who did not wish to make their professions were given prebends in Durham's dependent churches (see below, note 136).

[7]   John Blair, 'Introduction: from minster to parish church', Minsters and parish churches, ed. Blair, pp. 1–19; Richard Morris, Churches in the landscape (London, 1989), pp. 228–9.
[8]   LDB, fol. 39; The Stoke-by-Clare Cartulary, ed. Christopher Harper-Bill and Richard Mortimer, 3 vols (Woodbridge, 1982–4), i, pp. 54–8. Seven prebends are recorded in 1090, two held by men with English names. Five of the original seven, with a sixth canon, Lefwin (Leofwine) who must also be English, are mentioned in the charter of Richard fitzGilbert (1114–36) transforming the community into a Benedictine priory.
[9]   Brian Kemp, 'Some aspects of the parochia of Leominster in the twelfth century', Minsters and parish churches, ed. Blair, pp. 83–95.
[10] P.H. Hase, 'The mother churches of Hampshire', Minsters and parish churches, ed. Blair, pp. 49–58.

The minster of Christchurch is unusual in that a written account of its history survives. Most ecclesiastical records of the early medieval period not only emanate from monasteries but are also critical of the secular church, which is thus both under- and mis-represented.[11] The only secular house which can match Christchurch's history is the the college of secular canons at Waltham Holy Cross.[12] The church was re-founded by Tovi the Proud, in the reign of Cnut, but it was Harold, as earl of Wessex, who established a college of a dean and twelve canons, for which he built a new church in the German style.[13] German influence affected more than the architecture of Waltham, for its schoolmaster Adelard was a native of Liege who had studied at Utrecht.[14] Waltham suffered from its association with the defeated king, who was probably buried in the church. Much of its treasure was seized for the enrichment of Saint-Etienne of Caen, and the college itself was given first to Walcher, bishop of Durham, and later (from 1100) became part of the queen's dower.[15] The canons were not, however, expelled until 1177, when Henry II transformed Waltham into an Augustinian house. The deans after Wulfwine, whom Harold appointed, may have been foreigners, but

[11] Pauline Stafford, *Unification and conquest: a political and social history of England in the tenth and eleventh centuries* (London, 1989), p. 181. The secular churches, which produced no books of their own, 'have often left no more than the faintest footsteps in the sands of time' (James Campbell, 'Some twelfth-century views of the Anglo-Saxon past', idem, *Essays in Anglo-Saxon history* (London, 1986), pp. 218–19).

[12] W. Stubbs, *The foundation of Waltham Abbey: the tract 'de inventione sanctae crucis nostrae'* (Oxford, 1861). *De inventione* (hereinafter cited by chapter) was composed by one of the canons dispossessed in 1177, and is partly based on a lost history written in the late eleventh century. The author also knew the anonymous *Vita Haroldi*, completed in 1204 (*Vita Haroldi*, ed. W. de Gray Birch (London, 1885), translated in Swanton, *Three Lives of the last Englishmen*).

[13] P.J. Huggins and K.N. Bascombe, 'Excavations at Waltham Abbey, Essex, 1985–91: three pre-Conquest churches and Norman evidence', *Archaeological Journal* 149 (1992), pp. 287–320. The nave of the present church at Waltham, which closely resembles that of Durham, was probably built in the early twelfth century, when Waltham and Durham were closely associated; the author of *De Inventione Sanctae Crucis* remembered, as a boy, the third translation of Harold's body into the new church. Archbishop Ealdred also turned to Germany for the re-furbishment of Beverley and (possibly) Gloucester (Janet M. Cooper, *The last four Anglo-Saxon archbishops of York*, Borthwick Papers 38 (York, 1970), p. 27; Michael Hare, *The Two Anglo-Saxon minsters at Gloucester*, Deerhurst Lecture 1992, pp. 22–3).

[14] Harold's reforms at Waltham, like those of the bishops Leofric at Exeter, Giso at Wells and Ealdred at Beverley, were influenced by the canonical revival in Lotharingia (Frank Barlow, *The English Church 1000–1066*, 2nd edn (London, 1979), p. 90) For Harold's continental connections, see also Nicholas Rogers, 'The Waltham Abbey relic-list', *England in the eleventh century*, ed. Carola Hicks (Stamford, 1992), pp. 164–7; the earliest part of this list may have been compiled by Master Adelard.

[15] *The early charters of the Augustinian canons of Waltham Abbey, Essex*, ed. Rosalind Ransford (Woodbridge, 1989), pp. xxiii–xxv; Rogers, 'The Waltham Abbey relic-list', p. 163.

some at least of the canons were English, who preserved both the tomb and the memory of the dead King Harold.[16]

Most parish clergy, whether parsons, vicars or hired chaplains, were probably Englishmen from the social level of the free peasantry.[17] Their educational standards may have been modest, but Abbot Samson of Bury, who probably came from the same background, knew Latin and French as well as English. The Bury Chronicler, Jocelin of Brakelond, relates that 'he could read books written in English most elegantly and he used to preach to the people in English, but in the Norfolk dialect, for that was where he was born and brought up'. The English books probably included homiletic works like those produced by Ælfric of Cerne for the use of parochial clergy. Even at Battle Abbey, a house very conscious of its 'French connection', Abbot Odo (1175–1200) was praised for writing and preaching not only in Latin and French (nunc Latine nunc Gallico) but 'often, for the instruction of the ignorant mass, in the mother tongue' (lingua materna), which must, from the context, mean English.[18]

Concern for the education and competence of the parish clergy is evident from the tenth century.[19] In the twelfth it took the form of the impropriation of local churches to bishoprics and monasteries, on the assumption that this would produce more literate and educated priests and advance the cause of clerical celibacy, though it is doubtful whether these ideals were ever fully realised. Lay lords were most unwilling to relinquish control over the churches which they had founded, and ecclesiastical houses were often more interested in income than in raising the standards of the parish clergy. Abbot Walter of Battle (1139–71) was quite prepared to allow Nicholas son of Wihtgar to follow his father as priest

---

16 Few canons are named, but a notification of Queen Matilda II, addressed to her chamberlain Aldwine and Geoffrey the dean, concerns land given to Waltham by the canon Bruning, later confirmed by his son Adam, who inherited his father's prebend. Bruning was the brother of Godwine Overgate, a citizen of London (Early charters of Waltham, ed. Ransford, nos. 11–14, pp. 7–9). The anonymous author of the Waltham history, who entered the church in 1124, was taught as a child by Master Peter, son of the first schoolmaster, Adelard, and could remember the sacristan Thorkell who had seen the body of King Harold brought to Waltham (Stubbs, The foundation of Waltham Abbey, pp. xxii–vii, chapters 20, 25).
17 Barlow, The English church, 1066–1154, p. 263. In 1150 the social group of free men (homines francos) was defined as milites, clericos et frankelengos: knights, clerks and free peasants (franklins); van Caeneghem i, no. 326, p. 283.
18 The Chronicle of Jocelin of Brakelond, ed. H.E. Butler (London, 1949), p. 40, trans. Jocelin of Brakelond, Chronicle of the Abbey of Bury St Edmunds, Diana Greenway and Jane Sayers (Oxford, 1989), p. 37; M.T. Clanchy, From Memory to written record, 2nd edn (Oxford, 1993), pp. 205–6, 243; Chronicle of Battle Abbey, ed. Searle, pp. 306–9.
19 For pre-Conquest attempts to ensure the basic standards of the parish clergy, see the so-called 'Canons of Edgar', actually the work of Archbishop Wulfstan II of York (Wulfstan's Canons of Edgar, ed. Roger Fowler (Oxford, 1972), pp. xlvi–liii); The Law of the Northumbrian priests (Liebermann i, pp. 380–5, EHD i, no. 53, pp. 434–9); Joyce Hill, 'Monastic reform and the secular church: Ælfric's pastoral letters in context', England in the eleventh century, ed. Hicks, pp. 103–117.

of Mendlesham, Suffolk, provided the pension paid to the abbey was increased from 10s to 40s. Another Nicholas, the priest of Tarrant Hinton, Dorset (a manor of Shaftesbury Abbey) in the 1170s, was probably the son of the previous incumbent, Ailric (OE Æthelric). Nor did everyone think that complete celibacy was practicable. When in 1102 the Council of Westminster legislated against married priests, Bishop Herbert Losinga objected that if all the married clergy in his diocese of Norwich were ejected, it would not be possible to serve any of the churches.[20]

The main effect of the Conquest at this level was perhaps to increase the gulf between the great magnates of the church and the local parish clergy. Brihtric (Beorhtric), priest of Haselbury Plucknett, Som., in King Henry I's time, knew only English and, though this was the language he needed for his ministry, his lack of French hampered his relations with the bishop and archdeacon of the diocese.[21] The proliferation of hermits in twelfth-century England may have something to do with this problem. Most, if not all, came from the English strata of society; Christina of Markyate and Robert of Knaresborough came from the urban elite, Wulfric of Haselbury from 'middling English stock (de mediocre Anglorum gente)', and Godric of Finchale had been a merchant. It is possible that such people acted, sometimes quite literally, as interpreters between monolingual Englishmen and their foreign rulers.[22]

Much more is known about the monastic churches. Here there was no clean sweep of the English abbots. Æthelwig retained Evesham until his death in 1077, Sihtric, abbot of Tavistock, survived until 1082, Wulfwold of Chertsey until 1084 and Edmund of Pershore and Beorhtric of Burton until 1085. In 1087 at least six abbeys and cathedral priories had English heads: Ælfsige of Bath, Ingulf of Crowland, Æthelsige of Ramsey, Ælfwold of St Benet's, Holme, Aldwine, prior of Durham and Ælfric, prior of Sherborne.[23] The abbots of Milton, Dorset, and Muchelney, Somerset, are patchily recorded but the names are all English until

---

[20] Christopher Harper-Bill, 'The struggle for benefices in twelfth-century East Anglia', ANS 11 (1989), pp. 113–32; Chronicle of Battle Abbey, ed. Searle, p. 241; Williams, 'The knights of Shaftesbury Abbey', p. 229 (in both cases the families concerned were English); Councils and Synods, ed. Brett, i, part ii, pp. 683–4. For the views of the historian, Henry of Huntingdon, himself a priest's son, see Chapter VIII below.

[21] Barlow, The English Church, 1066–1154, p. 133; John of Ford, The Life of Wulfric of Haselbury, ed. Maurice Bell, Somerset Record Society 47 (1933), pp. xxvi–viii, 28–9, 30–1.

[22] Christopher Holdsworth, 'Hermits and the power of the frontier', Reading Medieval Studies 16 (1990), pp. 55–76; Henry Mayr-Harting, 'Functions of a medieval recluse', History 60 (1975), pp. 337–352.

[23] Ulfkell of Crowland was deposed at Christmas, 1085, but his successor Ingulf (1085–1109), though a monk of Saint-Wandrille, was an Englishman, who persuaded the king to let Ulfkell retire to Peterborough, where he had been a monk (OV ii, pp. 344–7). Bury St Edmunds retained its French but pre-Conquest abbot, Baldwin (1065–97), the Confessor's, and subsequently the Conqueror's physician (Antonia Gransden, 'Baldwin, abbot of Bury St Edmunds, 1065–1097', ANS 4 (1982), pp. 65–76).

1102 and 1114 respectively.[24] The nunnery of Wilton, where Queen Edith lived until her death in 1075, may also have had English abbesses, though no names are recorded between Godgifu (c.1067) and Matilda (c.1093 x 9).[25] Some houses continued, against the prevailing fashion, to elect native heads well into the twelfth century. At Crowland, Ingulf was succeeded by Geoffrey of Orleans (1109–c.1124), prior of Saint-Evroul, but the next abbot was not only a monk of Crowland, but an Englishman, Waltheof, son of Earl Gospatric of Dunbar (formerly of Bamburgh) and thus related to Earl Waltheof, whose cult the monks were enthusiastically promoting.[26] All the priors of Durham between 1083 and c.1138 were Englishmen.[27] Eadwulf, abbot of Malmesbury (1106–18) was presumably English, and the same must be true of Aldwine, abbot of Ramsey: elected in 1091, he was deposed in 1102, but was restored in 1107 and held the abbacy until his death in 1112.[28] After the death of the fearsome Turold in 1098, the monks of Peterborough paid William Rufus 300 marks (£200) for permission to elect Godric, brother of Abbot Brand, but he was deposed for simony in 1102.[29]

In general it was the more important abbeys which were bestowed upon foreigners. The new men appointed their own followers to key offices, but there was no attempt to replace all the English monks; indeed this would have been impossible. Lanfranc made Henry, one of his monks from Bec, prior of Christ Church in place of the Englishman, Godric, and Bishop Walkeline's prior at Winchester was his brother Simeon, but although some Norman and French monks followed their superiors, established communities, as opposed to new foundations, were not colonized wholesale from abroad.[30] As monasteries grew in size after the Conquest, English monks may gradually have become

---

[24] HRH, pp. 56–7. The abbots of Athelney may also have been English, though no names are recorded between 1024/32 and 1125 (HRH, p. 26). Jurisdiction over Athelney and Muchelney was claimed by Glastonbury, and the Glastonbury history has an (apparently apochryphal) story of Lanfranc attempting to depose the abbot of Athelney, but no name is given (The early history of Glastonbury (De antiquitate Glastonie ecclesie), ed. Scott, pp. 154–5).

[25] HRH, p. 222. The same is probably true of Romsey, where Edgar ætheling's sister Christina became a nun (HRH, p. 218). Gunnhild, King Harold II's daughter, and Edith, daughter of Malcolm king of Scots and St Margaret, lived at Wilton, though both denied having taken the veil (Eleanor Searle, 'Women and the legitimisation of succession at the Norman Conquest', ANS 3 (1981), pp. 166–9). Eva, the Wilton nun for whom Goscelin of St Bertin wrote his Liber Confortarius, had a Lotharingian mother and a Danish father: his name, Opi, is rare, but occurs twice among the pre-Conquest tenants in Domesday Book, once in Surrey and once in Bucks. (GDB fols 31v, 151v; Vita Edwardi, p. 92).

[26] OV, ii, pp. 344–7, 350–1; HRH, p. 42.

[27] HRH, p. 43 and see below.

[28] HRH, pp. 55, 62.

[29] Hugh Candidus, pp. 86–7; King, Peterborough Abbey, 1066–1310, p. 12.

[30] Lanfranc's monks, imported from Caen and Bec, 'were a small addition to a predominantly English community' (R.W. Southern, St Anselm and his biographer (Cambridge, 1966), p. 246).

outnumbered. The Benedictines drew their members mainly from the aristoc-racy, and the lack of English families of the first rank probably meant increasing recruitment from the continent, or at least from the Anglo-Norman baronage.[31] Nevertheless, houses which relied primarily on local families of mixed descent for their members might remain 'English' in sympathy, even if their superiors were of foreign extraction. The monks of Evesham, Chertsey and Bath named in a confraternity agreement of 1077 (for which see below) are all English and a list of Worcester monks in the Durham *Liber Vitae*, dated c.1104, includes thirty-one English names, eight 'French' (continental) and twenty-three 'scrip-tural, patristic or classical'. The *Textus Roffensis* supplies the names of thirteen monks at Rochester around the year 1100: all came from local families, six (to judge by their fathers' names) English and seven continental. At Shaftesbury Abbey too, the nuns came from English as well as French families in the early twelfth century.[32]

Tensions, not to say animosities, arose between foreign abbots and their English monks. We have already seen how the Fecamp monk, Turold, had fallen out with the monks of Malmesbury before he was transferred to Peterborough, and he was not remembered kindly in his second house.[33] At Abingdon there was trouble of an unspecified kind during the abbacy of Adelelm, who succeeded the deposed Ealdred in 1071. A letter of Lanfranc informs Adelelm that some of his monks 'have come to me as their own accusers, saying that they have sinned gravely against you and that they are to blame for having withdrawn from their monastery'. He urges Adelelm to receive them 'and show them from now on such fatherly love that God may show mercy to you', which may suggest that there had been faults on both sides.[34] Adelelm's reputation may be judged from a tale in the abbey's chronicle-cartulary which recounts his row with Ælfsige, the king's reeve of Sutton Courtenay. The latter had tried to commandeer the abbey's oxen to cart lead; Adelelm himself had the beasts unloaded and when Ælfsige

---

[31] The history of St Albans (whose abbot, Paul, was Lanfranc's nephew) records that the 'English' were in a minority by 1100 (Knowles, *The Monastic Order in England*, pp. 126–7). For the social background of churchmen, see in general, Alexander Murray, *Reason and Society in the Middle Ages* (Oxford, 1978), pp. 317–415, and for post-Conquest England, Knowles, *The Monastic Order in England*, pp. 423–5.

[32] Mason, *St Wulfstan of Worcester*, p. 222 (all the witnesses to Wulfstan's charters have English names, apart from Prior Thomas); Hirokazu Tsurushima, 'Bishop Gundulf and Rochester Cathedral Priory as an intermediary between English and Normans in Anglo-Norman local society' (State, Church and Society in medieval England: sympo-sium in the Faculty of Education, Kumamoto University, 1992), *The Studies in Western History* 31 (Fukuoka, Japan, 1993), pp. 42–51 (I am very grateful to Mr Tsurushima for sending me a copy of this paper); Cooke, 'Donors and daughters: Shaftesbury Abbey's benefactors, endowments and nuns, c.1086–1130', pp. 31–3.

[33] He used the treasures of Peterborough in an unsuccessful attempt to bribe the canons of Beauvais to elect him bishop and his foreign sacristans stole the gold-embroidered chasuble of Bishop Æthelric and other heirlooms, and took them to the Abbey of Préaux (Hugh Candidus, pp. 84–5; Dodwell, *Anglo-Saxon Art*, p. 220).

[34] *Letters of Lanfranc*, pp. 112–15.

remonstrated he 'was struck with a stick which the abbot happened to be carrying'. On another occasion the unfortunate reeve jumped into the River Ock rather than confront the abbot, who was standing on the bridge. Adelelm was fined for assaulting a royal officer, but the carting-service was not enforced.[35] Nevertheless he was remembered at Abingdon as a spoiler of church land and treasure which he used to enrich his former monastery of Jumièges; he is also said to have denigrated St Æthelwold and to have refused to allow his veneration.

At Christ Church itself the English and French monks initially regarded each other with 'unconcealed hostility' but matters improved in the 1070s. In 1076, soon after the appointment of the Bec monk, Henry, as prior, one of the English brethren, Æthelweard, went mad, attacked the prior, and made a spectacular confession of sexual irregularites, involving among others a young monk held in especial affection by the archbishop himself. The scandal seems to have brought about a change of heart in the community, though Archbishop Anselm was still complaining of the monks' disobedience in the early twelfth century.[36]

There were violent upheavals at St Augustine's, Canterbury in 1088. Abbot Scotland, a monk of Mont-Saint-Michel, had ruled the community without incident since 1070 but the appointment of his successor Guy was bitterly resisted by Prior Ælfwine and his monks. Lanfranc himself had to install Guy by force and when he himself died in 1089 there was further trouble, solved only by the expulsion of the leading monks, who were dispersed into various other communities and replaced by twenty-four monks from Christ Church, one of whom was made prior. The monks' objections were perhaps not to Guy personally but to the fact that he was Lanfranc's protege, and the root of the trouble may have been resentment at Christ Church's dominance in the appointments to St Augustine's. It may be significant that the troubles coincided with the dispute between St Augustine's and Lanfranc's new college of St Gregory over the relics of St Mildryth.[37]

Yet even after 1089 the community remained English in sympathy. It included the anglophile Fleming Goscelin of Saint-Bertin, who had lived in England since before the Conquest; he may have arrived as early as 1058. He had been a protege of Herman, bishop of Sherborne, but fell out with his successor Osmund of Sées,

---

[35] Chron Abingdon, ii, pp. 10–11 (van Caeneghem i, no. 12, p. 35), 278, 282–4.

[36] Osbern of Canterbury, Miraculi Sancti Dunstani, Mem. St Dunstan, p. 148; Osbern himself had previously been sent to Bec, perhaps as a disciplinary measure. Eadmer is much more circumspect about the incident (Mem. St Dunstan, pp. 236–8; see Southern, St Anselm and his biographer, pp. 247–8, 253; Barlow, The English Church, 1066–1154, p. 191).

[37] The section of the Acta Lanfranci which describes the rebellion is printed in Two of the Saxon Chronicles parallel, ed. Charles Plummer and John Earle (Oxford, 1892), i, pp. 290–2. St Gregory's began to make claims to the relics of St Mildryth in 1087 or 1088 (D.W. Rollason, The Mildrith legend: a study in early medieval hagiography in England (Leicester, 1983), pp. 21–5; see also note 65 below. For Lanfranc's foundation of St Gregory's, see Margaret Gibson, Lanfranc of Bec (Oxford, 1978), pp. 188–90.

and wandered from house to house until he finally settled at St Augustine's.[38] William of Malmesbury considered him the best English historian since Bede, and his skill in music was praised by his contemporary at St Augustine's, Reginald of Canterbury. Reginald was a Frenchman, from Faye-la-Vineuse, and a former monk of Noyers, but though he remembered his birthplace with fond affection, he embraced the English as his new nation (gens Anglica nostra) and wrote in praise of the saints of Canterbury.[39]

The worst incident occurred at Glastonbury in 1083, when Abbot Turstin (1078–92) sent in his knights to enforce obedience on his recalcitrant monks. They fled into the church where at least two or three were killed before the altar by archers firing from the galleries. John of Worcester explains that Turstin, who had been a monk of Caen, tried to introduce the chant of Fecamp, but was resisted by the English community, who claimed to use the pure Gregorian music.[40] More may have been involved than liturgical disagreement. Turstin's predecessor, Æthelnoth, had been one of those taken by the king to Normandy in 1067. He is said to have been deposed by a council held at London at Whitsun (28 May) 1078, but issued a charter as abbot of Glastonbury dated Easter Day (24 March) 1079. Perhaps, like Æthelric of Selsey, he contested the deposition for some time and this may have affected the attitude of his monks to the Norman who eventually supplanted him.[41] Orderic seems to hint at some irregularity in Turstin's succession to Æthelnoth. He claims that 'venerable abbots . . . were driven from their cures unjustly, without a hearing in any synod' and replaced by 'hirelings', adding that 'between such shepherds and the flocks committed to their keeping existed such harmony as you would find between wolves and helpless sheep, as all who saw the conduct of Turstin of Caen in Glastonbury Abbey know'.[42] Turstin's hasty action brought about his own downfall, for the king sent him back to Normandy in disgrace, and though he was never deprived of his abbacy, he did not reside at Glastonbury again.

Such incidents were rare and should not necessarily be taken as evidence of racial animosity. The continental rulers who took over the English church were critical of much of its culture, but there was no straightforward rejection of all it stood for.[43] Indeed some characteristic customs were embraced with enthusiasm.

---

[38] Vita Edwardi, pp. 91–109.
[39] A.G. Rigg, A history of Anglo-Latin literature, 1066–1422 (Cambridge, 1992), pp. 24–30.
[40] AS Chron, 1083; FlW, 1083.
[41] For the death of Æthelnoth, on 13 April but in an unknown year, and for a discussion of the charter, see Matthew Blows, 'A Glastonbury obit list', The archaeology and history of Glastonbury Abbey, ed. L. Abrams and J. Carley (Woodbridge, 1991), p. 264. I am grateful to Dr Blows for help on this puzzling episode.
[42] OV ii, pp. 270–1; Orderic then relates the story of the murdered monks, with the explanation, presumably derived from John of Worcester, that the quarrel involved the liturgical chant. John also complains that some abbots were deposed for political rather than ecclesiastical reasons (see Chapter III above).
[43] Eadmer describes how Lanfranc, who 'as an Englishman was still somewhat green'

Monastic cathedral chapters, by the eleventh century confined to England, were not only retained, but increased in number.[44] That Worcester's chapter should remain monastic is not surprising, since its bishop was the Englishman St Wulfstan. Archbishop Lanfranc, however, not only maintained the monastic chapter at Christ Church albeit under a new rule (the *Regularis Concordia* was superseded by Lanfranc's *Monastic Constitutions*) but also encouraged his protege Gundulf bishop of Rochester (1077–1108) to replace his canons with monks. He is also credited with dissauding Walkeline, bishop of Winchester (1070–98) from replacing his monks with canons.[45] It was with Lanfranc's encouragement, moreover, that William of Saint-Calais (1081–96) established a monastic chapter at Durham in 1083.[46]

By the early twelfth century the number of monastic cathedrals had increased from four to nine, out of a total of seventeen. Not all were inspired by a belief in monasticism *per se*. Many of the episcopal sees were poor, especially in comparison with the Benedictine houses, and the takeover of a rich monastery might significantly improve a bishop's finances. After the death in 1087 of Ælfsige, abbot of Bath, John de Villula moved the see of Wells into the monastery. Peter, appointed bishop of Lichfield in 1072, first moved the see to Chester and subsequently attempted to take over Earl Leofric's abbey of Coventry, where his deposed predecessor, Leofwine, was abbot. The community complained to Lanfranc, who commanded Peter to desist in the strongest possible terms.[47] The removal of the see of Chester to Coventry was accomplished by Peter's successor, Robert de Limesey (1086–1117) in 1102, much to the loss of the monks.[48] Herfast,

changed many customs at Christ Church 'often with good reason, but sometimes simply by the imposition of his own authority' (VA, pp. 49–51). Lanfranc's own attitude can be judged from his letter to Pope Alexander II in 1071, seeking guidance on the consecration of a new bishop for Lichfield, after Leofwine's resignation: 'Now I am a novice Englishman (*novus anglicus*), virtually ignorant as yet of English affairs, except for what I learn at second hand'; see also the description of Archbisop Thomas of York as a *novus homo* 'with no experience whatever of English usage' (*Letters of Lanfranc*, pp. 37–9, 40–1).

44 David Rollason, *Saints and Relics in Anglo-Saxon England* (Oxford, 1989), p. 216. Of the four pre-Conquest monastic sees, three survived (Christ Church, Canterbury, the Old Minster, Winchester and Worcester) but the see of Sherborne was moved to Salisbury (Old Sarum) in 1078, where a secular chapter was established.

45 Knowles, *The Monastic Order in England*, p. 130; Eadmer (HN, p. 18) says Walkeline 'had nearly forty clergy assembled, tonsured and arrayed as canons, ready to be installed by him in the church of Winchester as soon as the monks had been ejected'.

46 For Durham see below, pp. 149–53.

47 *Letters of Lanfranc* no. 27, pp. 110–13. Lanfranc rehearses the complaints of the community against Peter: 'you forced an entry into their dormitory and broke into their strongboxes . . . you have robbed them of their horses and all their goods. Furthermore you pulled down their houses and ordered the materials of which these were built to be taken to your own residences; finally you remained in that monastery with your retinue for eight days eating up the monks' provisions.'

48 GR, pp. 388–9; Dodwell, *Anglo-Saxon Art*, p. 220.

bishop of Thetford (1070–85), made determined efforts to take over Bury St Edmunds, whose abbot, Baldwin (1065–1097), appealed to the pope against him. Once more Lanfranc intervened, but the final blow to Herfast's plan was dealt by the king, to whom Baldwin was physician. The attack was renewed by Herbert Losinga (1090–1119), but he too was unsuccessful. Eventually he moved the East Anglian see to Norwich, where he established a monastic chapter.[49] In 1109 the unwieldy diocese of Lincoln was divided by the establishment of a bishopric at the abbey of Ely, causing much disruption to the monastic community.[50]

Other English traditions were adopted as the foreign superiors settled into their communities. It was once believed that the pre-Conquest cults of English saints were regarded with scorn and suspicion by the new ecclesiastical lords but this is not borne out by the evidence.[51] Lanfranc was unsure of the basis of St Ælfheah's canonization, and also encouraged his former chaplain, Abbot Walter of Evesham, to test the relics of his community by fire, but such scepticism should not be regarded as specifically anti-English.[52] Men trained, like Lanfranc, in the disciplines of the new scholasticism were critical of cults, whether English or continental, which appeared obscure, confused and badly-documented; a few years later, Peter Abelard expressed doubts about the relics of Saint Denis.[53] When, in St Ælfheah's case, Lanfranc was convinced by the arguments of Anselm, he commissioned the English monk, Osbern of Canterbury, to compose a *vita* of the saint.[54] At Evesham, the relics of SS Credan and Wigstan survived the test and were re-installed in new shrines. Indeed, Abbot Walter was so impressed with Wigstan's sanctity that, as he took the remains from the fire, his hand trembled so much that he dropped the saint's skull, which was seen to

[49] *Regesta* i, no. 137, ii, no. 394; *Letters of Lanfranc*, pp. 150–3; Gransden, 'Baldwin, abbot of Bury St Edmunds, 1065–1097', pp. 69–72. Lanfranc's letter to Herfast is very sharp in tone; he reproaches Herfast for uttering 'cheap and unworthy remarks' about him and commands him to 'give up the dicing (to mention nothing worse) and the world's amusements' in which he idles away his time.
[50] Miller, *The abbey and bishopric of Ely*, pp. 75–6.
[51] Susan Ridyard, 'Condigna veneratio: post-Conquest attitudes to the saints of the Anglo-Saxons', ANS 9 (1987), pp. 76–83.
[52] Lanfranc's nephew, Paul, abbot of St Albans, 'destroyed the tombs of his venerable predecessors, the noble abbots, whom he used to describe as *rudes et idiotas*', but he showed no such disrespect for St Alban himself (Matthew Paris, *Gesta Abbatum monasterii Sancti Albani*, ed. H.T. Riley, 3 vols, Rolls Series (London, 1867–9), i, p. 62; Ridyard, 'Condigna veneratio', pp. 189–90).
[53] Richard W. Pfaff, 'Lanfranc's supposed purge of the Anglo-Saxon calendar', *Warriors and Churchmen in the High Middle Ages: essays presented to Karl Leyser*, ed. Timothy Reuter (London, 1992), pp. 95–108. For the feast of the Immaculate Conception, see Chapter VII below.
[54] VA, pp. 50–4. Osbern composed a [lost] hymn on St Ælfheah, a *passio* and a *translatio*; see Rosemary Morris and Alexander R. Rumble, 'Translatio Sanct Ælfegi . . . Osbern's account of the translation of St Ælfheah's relics from London to Canterbury, 8–11 June 1023', *The reign of Cnut*, ed. Alexander Rumble (Leicester, 1994), pp.283–315, especially pp. 288–9.

sweat.[55] His confidence in the power of the English patrons of his house was such that in an important law-suit with Wulfstan, bishop of Worcester, he relied wholly (and in the event unsuccessfully) on the production of the relics of St Ecgwine to win his case.[56]

A desire to check the authenticity of relics and provide accurate documentation for those which proved genuine does not indicate hostility to the English cults per se, nor was this a novel attitude in England. The Arundel Psalter, compiled by the Canterbury scribe Eadui Basan in the second decade of the eleventh century, contains far fewer feasts than the Bosworth Psalter.[57] From the late tenth century, more and more saints' lives were composed in England, many by foreign writers specially commissioned, and this activity continued and even increased in the late eleventh and early twelfth centuries.[58] Indeed by 1066, hagiography had become almost professionalized. The Flemish monk Goscelin of St Bertin produced vitae for the houses of Barking, Ely, Ramsey, Sherborne and St Augustine's, Canterbury, and Folcard, another St Bertin's monk, was commissioned by Archbishop Ealdred to write the life of St John of Beverley, and by Walkeline of Winchester to compose a vita of St Botolf.[59] Not all such vitae were regarded with favour. The life of St Mildryth commissioned from the German scholar Bertram by St Gregory's, Canterbury, was intended to support that house's claim to the saint's relics, a claim demolished by Goscelin of St Bertin (see below). Eadmer, who was himself commissioned by the monks of Worcester to write a life of St Oswald, has some scathing remarks on foreigners who wrote lies for money.[60]

It would have been foolish in the extreme for the new bishops and abbots to ignore the spiritual treasures of their churches. The saints of a community were its undying landlords, who guaranteed continued enjoyment of its lands and privileges. Hence it was vital both to ensure that one's own relics were genuine and to combat claims that the real relics actually rested in another place.[61] A

---

55 Chron Evesham, pp. 323–4, 335–6. The vita of St Wistan was composed by Dominic, prior of Evesham, in the early twelfth century (Chron Evesham, pp. 313–17).

56 See below, Chapter VII.

57 Rollason, Saints and relics in Anglo-Saxon England, pp. 227–8. For BL Arundel Mss 155, once thought to be post-Conquest, see Richard W. Pfaff, 'Eadui Basan: scriptorum princeps?', England in the eleventh century, ed. Hicks, pp. 273–6 and for the Bosworth Psalter (BL Add. Ms 37514), see P.M. Korhammer, 'The origin of the Bosworth Psalter', ASE 2 (1973), pp. 173–87.

58 Rollason, Saints and relics in Anglo-Saxon England, pp. 229–30.

59 Vita Edwardi, pp. xlv–lvii, 91–111; Gransden, Historical Writing in England, pp. 107–111.

60 Mem. St Dunstan, p. 415 and see next note. For Eadmer's life of St Oswald, see Gransden, Historical writing in England, p. 129; Southern, loc cit., pp. 283–4.

61 See, for example, Eadmer of Canterbury's angry letter to the monks of Glastonbury, who claimed to have the relics of St Dunstan (Mem. St Dunstan, pp. 412–22; discussed and translated in Richard Sharpe, 'Eadmer's letter to the monks of Glastonbury concerning St Dunstan's disputed remains', The archaeology and history of Glastonbury Abbey, ed. Abrams and Carley, pp. 205–15; see also Chapter VII, note 76 below).

vivid example of this is the vigourous campaign of St Augustine's, Canterbury, to prove that it possessed the relics of St Mildryth, former abbess of Minster-in-Thanet. Her remains had been translated to St Augustine's by King Cnut, and even before 1066 the abbey had seen off a counter-claim by the canons of Dover.[62] In the 1080s another attempt was made to appropriate the relics, this time by the newly-established house of St Gregory, founded c.1085 by Archbishop Lanfranc.[63] The church, which had both pastoral and educational functions, was provided with the relics of St Æthelburh, founder and first abbess of Lyminge, but soon began to claim that it also possessed the remains both of St Eadburh, Mildryth's successor at Minster-in-Thanet, and of Mildryth herself.[64] Among the monks of St Augustine's at this time was the prolific writer of saints' lives, Goscelin of Saint-Bertin; he had already produced a life of Mildryth, and now composed 'a hagiographical polemic' against the claims of St Gregory's.[65]

It was not only St Mildryth's sanctity that made possession of her remains desirable; her property also passed to the holder of her relics.[66] In the eleventh century, Thanet was still an island, divided from the mainland by the Wantsum Channel, whose southern end was dominated by Sandwich.[67] Rights in the port were granted to Christ Church by Cnut, but withdrawn by Harold I Harefoot, who also granted the third penny of Sandwich to St Augustine's. The monks of Christ Church complained to the king, who restored their rights, and a request by Abbot Ælfstan of St Augustine's to build a wharf opposite 'Mildryth's acre' was turned down. This was not the end of the affair, for Odo of Bayeux had designs on Sandwich and, like Harold I, granted rights in the town to St

---

[62] The authenticity of Cnut's writ granting the relics and land (S.990) is not undisputed but the date of the translation was probably 1030 (Richard Sharpe, 'The date of St Mildreth's translation from Minster-in-Thanet to Canterbury', Medieval Studies 53 (1991), pp. 344–54). The Old English memorandum recording the dispute between Abbot Ælfstan and Leofwine the priest (of Dover) refers to Cnut's grant of the saint's relics and 'her uncles' wergeld', i.e. Thanet (S.1472, Robertson, Charters, pp. 190–1, 438–9).

[63] Gibson, Lanfranc of Bec, pp. 186–8. Two masters of St Gregory's school are known by name, the Norman Ebroin and the Englishman Leofwine.

[64] St Gregory's case was set out by Bertram, another foreign hagiographer, this time from Germany (Gransden, Historical Writing in England, p. 107).

[65] Libellus contra inanes sancte virginis Mildrethae usurpatores, see Martin L. Colker, 'A hagiographic polemic', Medieval Studies 39 (1977), pp. 60–108; for the other works of Goscelin on Mildryth and the controversy as a whole, see Rollason, The Mildryth legend, pp. 58–68.

[66] Colker, 'A hagiographical polemic', p. 145; Rollason, The Mildryth legend, p. 67; idem, Saints and relics in Anglo-Saxon England, pp. 196–214. Durham's possession of the relics of SS Baldred of Tyningham, Æbbe of Coldingham and Bede of Jarrow constituted 'the title-deeds to the estates of these monasteries' (Aird, 'St Cuthbert, the Scots and the Normans', p. 9).

[67] See the map of the ancient coastline in Tim Tatton-Brown, 'The towns of Kent', Anglo-Saxon towns in southern England, ed. Haslam, p. 4.

Augustine's, which Lanfranc had to recover.[68] The final settlement of the dispute, in 1127, reveals St Augustine's successful establishment of a rival port at Stonar, whose officials took the tolls from foreign merchants which should have been rendered at Sandwich, and operated a rival ferry 'to carry men and their goods from the island of Thanet, for the abbot had a great multitude of men there'.[69] Thanet was a valuable asset to the abbey, which helps to account for the enthusiastic support of the Norman abbots for its saintly owner. St Augustine's was rich in relics and eager to display its treasures, which in 1091 were translated by Abbot Guy into the new church built by his predecessor Scotland. Indeed they were accorded greater prominence and splendour than in the pre-Conquest building.[70]

The English religious houses needed the protection of their saints in the years following the Norman Conquest. The moveable wealth of the English church was regarded as spoil and vast amounts of gold and silver plate, jewelled reliquaries and books embellished with ornamental covers, gold-embroidered vestments and hangings, and similar treasures, including manuscripts, were seized and used to enrich the abbeys of Normandy and northern France. Some houses were singled out because of their political affiliations, like King Harold's church of Holy Cross, Waltham, despoiled to adorn the Conqueror's monastery of Saint-Etienne, Caen. Others had to sell plate and treasure to pay the heavy gelds imposed by the Conqueror and his son, William II, or to buy the king's favour.[71] In some cases the despoilers were the new abbots themselves; both Turold of Peterborough and Adelelm of Abingdon were remembered as robbers of their abbeys. More typical perhaps is Theodwine, the monk of Jumieges who succeeded Thurstan at Ely in 1072, who refused to take up his office until the king restored all the 'gold and silver and precious stones' which he had previously seized.[72]

Some of these seizures were authorized by the king, but it is clear that his officers abstracted church property as well as the goods which dispossessed laymen had deposited in the monasteries.[73] Moreover the Benedictine houses had also to provide for the new military quotas imposed upon their lands after 1066.[74] It was of course possible, even customary, for the greater ecclesiastics to

---

[68] S.1467, and see Nicholas Brooks, The early history of the church of Canterbury (Leicester, 1984), pp. 292–4.

[69] D.M. Stenton, English Justice from the Conquest to Magna Carta (London, 1965), pp. 116–17; van Caeneghem i, no. 254, pp. 216–19.

[70] Rollason, Saints and relics in Anglo-Saxon England, pp. 230–1.

[71] Dodwell (Anglo-Saxon Art, pp. 216ff) describes the scale of losses as 'unparalleled since the days of the Danish predators' and adds (p. 230) that 'in relation to the enormous losses of Anglo-Saxon objects in precious metal . . . the replacements by the Normans themselves were simply derisory'. For the loss of English manuscripts after 1066, see David Dumville, 'Anglo-Saxon books: treasure in Norman hands?', ANS 16 (1994), pp. 83–99.

[72] Liber Eliensis, pp. 195–7. Theodwine had an inventory made of the restored treasures.

[73] Chron Abingdon i, p. 480 and see Chapter III, p. 45 above.

[74] For the quotas, see Chapter VIII below.

keep knights in their households; but an obvious solution to the problem of maintaining them in sufficient numbers to meet the king's demands was to endow them with land. Churchmen had always provided for the necessary service from their lands by grants of thegnland, used for the endowment of servants and officials, or *lænland*, held for life or a term of lives. Such grants were already familiar in Normandy and their use by the church lords allowed them to reconcile the need to provide for their military obligations with the requirement of canon law that ecclesiastical possessions should not be alienated.[75]

Much land of this kind was already available. Many Englishmen who before 1066 had held thegnland or *lænland* of the church had been dispossessed in the upheavals of the Conquest and their lands were available for re-distribution. It was believed at Abingdon that Abbot Adelelm had endowed his knights with the lands of English thegns killed at the battle of Hastings, and at Worcester Hemming complained of the seizure of the church's *lænlands* by Frenchmen (*francigenae*) who had usurped the inheritances of Englishmen.[76] William Rufus, after Lanfranc's death, created military tenancies on lands belonging to the archbishopric which were thought to have been held by English 'knights' before the Conquest.[77] On the lands of Shaftesbury Abbey, virtually all the known thegnlands of the church were later incorporated into knight's fees, some of which were in existence by the time of Domesday.[78] Just before the time of Domesday, in 1083, Abbot Gilbert Crispin gave William Baynard the berewick of Tothill, part of the manor of Westminster, to hold for life by the service of one knight, 'as well and as freely as the thegn Wulfric Bordewayte held it from the church'. It was to return to Westminster on his death and William had to promise neither to sell, pawn nor otherwise alienate the land.[79]

In many cases, however, the initiative in creating military tenancies did not

---

[75] John Hudson, 'Life grants of land and the development of inheritance in Anglo-Norman England', ANS 12 (1990), pp. 72–3. Whether life-grants were used by lay magnates and to what extent must remain uncertain, given the bias towards ecclesiastical documentation in the surviving sources. There is a similar problem concerning lay leases before 1066, which are mentioned only where the land concerned eventually passed to the church (Lennard, *Rural England*, pp. 166–7).

[76] *Chron Abingdon* ii, p. 3 (see i, 484 for Henry de Ferrers' seizure of the lands held of the abbey by Thorkell and Godric the sheriff); Hemming's Cartulary i, p. 269.

[77] Southern, *St Anselm and his biographer*, p. 156. This is probably the basis of the later belief that Lanfranc had made knights out of the pre-Conquest 'drengs' of the archbishopric (F. M. Stenton, *The first century of English feudalism, 1066–1166* (Oxford, 1932), pp. 145–8; F.R.H. du Boulay, *The lordship of Canterbury* (London, 1966), p. 79).

[78] Williams, 'The knights of Shaftesbury Abbey', p. 225.

[79] EHD ii, no. 219, pp. 895–6; J. Armitage Robinson, *Gilbert Crispin* (Cambridge, 1911), p. 38; Barbara Harvey, *Westminster Abbey and its estates in the Middle Ages* (Oxford, 1977), pp. 73, 75. It appears in Domesday as a 3-hide tenement attached to the manor of Westminster, held by 'Baynard' of the abbot (GDB, fol. 128). No service is recorded, which is not unusual; it is not Domesday but the bishop of Hereford's charter which reveals that Roger de Lacy owed two knight's fees for his tenement at Holme Lacy, also held for life only (GDB, fol. 181v; Galbraith, 'An episcopal land-grant of 1085', pp.

lie with the grantors. Urse d'Abetot, sheriff of Worcester seized lands belonging to the church of Worcester at Greenhill and Eastbury, which the monks then granted him for fear of his power; he subsequently ceased to perform the services.[80] These and other lands taken by Urse were later held by his heirs, the Beauchamps, by knight-service, but the bishops of Worcester never succeeded in obtaining what they considered the full service from them.[81] Some of the best-endowed of the Canterbury knights had once been tenants of Odo of Bayeux, who continued to hold their lands even after Archbishop Lanfranc recovered them from the bishop.[82] The abbot of Ely was forced to allow lands seized from the church to be held as fees; as at Worcester it proved hard to obtain the service, and writs of William I commanding holders of the church's thegn-lands to do the service or lose the land were still being re-iterated by Henry I.[83]

Domesday Book is full of complaints by ecclesiastics against lay magnates who had usurped or appropriated estates belonging to their churches and the same concern is manifested in the litigation of William I's reign. It was not only 'rebellious' houses like Ely which suffered in this way; Christ Church, Canterbury, was also a victim, as was the bishopric of Worcester.[84] Most of the losses affected not the demesne manors, but thegnland, *lænland* or sokeland owing customary service. If one of the church's tenants had had his estates confiscated for rebellion and granted *en bloc* to a continental successor, that successor might attempt to appropriate the lands which his *antecessor* held of the church along with the rest of his property. Peterborough Abbey lost Dunsby, leased by Abbot Brand to his kinsman Halfdane, 'because King William had taken all Halfdan's land from him and had given it to Remigius, bishop of Lincoln and so Remigius himself unjustly took away Dunsby from St Peter's'. Ramsey likewise lost the manors of Hemingford and Yelling, Hunts., leased to Wulfwine son of Alwine, because King William gave Wulfwine's whole inheritance (*totam ipsius haereditatem*) to Aubrey de Vere.[85] Of course this was illegal; but it was not

353–72). For the imposition of knight-service on the Church, see also Chapter VIII below.

[80] Hemming's Cartulary i, pp. 257–8; GDB, fols 172v, 173v.

[81] Christopher Dyer, *Lords and peasants in a changing society: the estates of the bishopric of Worcester, 680–1540* (Cambridge, 1980), pp. 48–9; see also Chapter VIII below.

[82] Du Boulay, *The lordship of Canterbury*, pp. 53–4.

[83] *Liber Eliensis*, p. 217; Miller, *The abbey and bishopric of Ely*, pp. 67–9. For William I's writs, see van Caenegham i, pp. 45–7; for Henry I's writ, see *Regesta* ii, no. 1500. Similar problems were experienced by other churches; for examples, see van Caeneghem i, pp. 36 (Westminster); 89 (Ramsey); 128, 133–4 (Abingdon); 194 (St Augustine's, Canterbury).

[84] For Ely see note 97 below; for Christ Church, see du Boulay, *The Lordship of Canterbury*, pp. 36–43 (cf Gibson, *Lanfranc of Bec*, p. 153) and for Worcester, see Chapter VIII below. The losses of St Benet's, Holme, another 'rebellious' house, are described by Stenton, 'St Benet of Holme and the Norman Conquest', pp. 225–35.

[85] Hugh Candidus, p. 69, GDB, fols 344v, 377; *Chron Ramsey*, pp. 152–3. Wulfwine is presumably the king's thegn who preceded Aubrey de Vere in Cambs., Essex and Suffolk (GDB, fols 199v, LDB, fols 76–77v, 418–419) but Domesday gives a different account

unknown, even before the Conquest.[86] Earnwig, reeve of the manor of Cotheridge, which belonged to the church of Worcester, leased the estate to his
brother Spirites, a royal clerk. In 1065, Spirites was exiled by King Edward and
his property was forfeited; Cotheridge was given, presumably by the king, to his
Norman follower, Richard fitzScrob, even though it should have returned to the
Church of Worcester.[87]

Other encroachments on church land might turn on the fact that the pre-
Conquest tenant was commended to the *antecessor* of a Norman magnate. This
did not in itself confer title to land, but was often made the basis of expropriation.
As we saw in Chapter IV above, Badlesmere in Kent was held in 1086 by Ansfrid
of the bishop of Bayeux's fief, but claimed by St Augustine's, Canterbury. The
local hundred court supported the abbey, and the shire-court of Kent testified
that the abbot had had sake and soke over the pre-Conquest holder, Godric *wisce*.
Godric's son, however, claimed that his father could commend himself (*se
vertere*) where he would; presumably either he or his father had sought the
protection of Ansfrid, who had appropriated the land.[88]

The frequency of such disputes is sometimes put down to Norman bewilder-
ment at 'the confusion of pre-Conquest dependent relationships'.[89] Continental
perceptions about lordship over land and lordship over men might indeed have
differed from those current in England, but this particular 'misunderstanding' is
also found among Englishmen both before and after the Conquest. Let us take
an example already mentioned (see Chapter IV above); the dispute recorded in
Domesday between the bishopric of Worcester and six brothers, the sons of
Beorhtwine, over a tenement at Alvestone, Warks.[90] The brothers acknowledged
that the tenement had owed to Archbishop Ealdred 'sake and soke and toll and
team and churchscot and all judicial forfeitures except the four which the king
has over the whole country', but said they did not know from whom their father
had held the land, whether from the church, or from Earl Leofric, whom he served

---

of Hemmingford and Yelling; these are said to have been leased to Ælfric, who was killed
at the battle of Hastings, and whose lands were then given to Aubrey de Vere (GDB fol.
208, cf. fols 204v, 207 and see Hart, *The early charters of eastern England*, fols 36–7).

[86] The principle that when a man forfeits his estates, his *lænland* reverts to his lord and
his bookland to the king is enunciated in II Cnut 77.

[87] Hemming's Cartulary i, p. 254. Hemming presents this as an act of violence committed by Richard Scrob, but since the king gave Spirites' prebend at Broomfield, Shrops,
to another Norman follower, Robert fitzWymarc, it was presumably by the king's gift
that Richard acquired Cotheridge (GDB, fol. 252v; Barlow, *The English Church
1000–1066*, pp. 131–2, 135, 175).

[88] GDB, fols 10, 12v; *Inquisitio*, pp. 4–5; see also Chapter IV above.

[89] Miller, *The abbey and bishopric of Ely*, 66. It was not only the Normans, however, who
were accused of such misappropriations; on the death of the Englishman Æthelwig of
Evesham in 1077, a group of his commended men complained to the Norman Bishop
Odo that Æthelwig had seized their lands by force; the chronicler asserts that he had
merely paid 'the appropriate price' (*Chron Evesham*, pp. 96–7 and see Chapter I, note
20 above).

[90] GDB, fol. 238v.

(*cui serviebat*); they themselves held from the earl and could commend themselves (*se vertere*) with the land wherever they would. Eventually Bishop Wulfstan recovered the land and restored it to the cathedral priory, complaining, however, that it 'had long been wrongfully possessed by certain powerful men' and had been regained only 'with great labour and expense'.[91] The 'powerful men' may include the Mercian earls, but the sons of Beorhtwine were not without influence; one of them was almost certainly Æthelwine, sheriff of Warwickshire.[92] It is unlikely that he was unfamiliar with English law and custom and disputes of this kind are best regarded, both before and after 1066, as excuses for encroachments based on nothing more than, to quote the Worcester monk Hemming, 'craft and fraud and secular power'. He was speaking of the Danish conquerors, but much the same might be said of the Normans.[93] Even land taken in the process of law by royal officers might be appropriated by their Norman heirs. In Norfolk, Æthelwig of Thetford, an Englishman in King William's employ, seized the land held of St Benet's by the outlawed Ringulf of Oby, but when Æthelwig's possessions passed to Roger Bigod, the latter appropriated Ringulf's land as well, though it should have reverted to St Benet's Holme.[94]

Norman landowners, far from misunderstanding English tenurial custom, were quite able to exploit it to their own advantage when they wished and, in any case, advice from Englishmen was always available. Æthelwig of Evesham's knowledge of secular law was used by the English Bishop Wulfstan as well as by Lanfranc and Abbot Serlo of Gloucester.[95] Abbot Adelelm of Abingdon established his rights with the help of two monks, of whom one (Godwine) was certainly English, and Alfwine, priest of Sutton Courtenay, who 'were so well versed in secular matters and had such a good memory for bygone events that the others [in the shire-court], on every side, easily approved as valid the judgement which they proposed'.[96] The problem was not to secure a court ruling against illegal tenures but to enforce it. The abbots of Ely pursued a series of legal actions throughout the 1070s and 1080s, but the lands adjudged to Ely in these hearings were still being withheld at the time of Domesday.[97] Even when lawsuits

---

91 *The cartulary of Worcester Cathedral Priory*, ed. R.R. Darlington, Pipe Roll Society new ser. 38 (London, 1968), no. 8 (dated 1089).
92 Williams, 'A vice-comital family in pre-Conquest Warwickshire', pp. 282–3, and see Chapter V above.
93 Hemming's Cartulary, i, p. 280.
94 Stenton, 'St Benet of Holme and the Norman conquest', p. 233. For a similar case, see Ugford, Wilts., recovered by Eadnoth the staller for Wilton Abbey, but appropriated by Osbern Giffard after Eadnoth's death (GDB, fols 68, 72v and see Chapter V, note 120 above).
95 See p. 148 and note 116 below.
96 *Chron Abingdon* ii, pp. 1–2; van Caeneghem i, pp. 6–7. The Abingdon account claims that the named monks were only the best among the many English *causidici* in the abbey at that time.
97 Edward Miller, 'The Ely land pleas in the reign of William I', EHR 62 (1947), pp. 438–56; *Liber Eliensis*, pp. 426–32; van Caeneghem i, pp. 43ff.

were successful, the usual outcome was a compromise, in which the land remained with the defendant, who acknowledged that service was due to the church and sometimes even performed it.[98]

The Church's first line of defence against encroachment was its written records. Charters, especially royal charters, were the best evidence of title, which is why, before the Conquest, they were stolen or forged by tenants who wished to claim permanent rights in their lands.[99] Just as the spiritual inheritance (the relics of the saints) was protected by the production of *vitae*, so the worldly wealth of the Church was defended by an overhaul of the surviving archives, and their augmentation by re-copied charters, not all of which were genuine.[100] Once again, the process was enhanced rather than initiated by the Norman Conquest. The earliest surviving English cartulary was written at Worcester in the early eleventh century, perhaps at the behest of Wulfstan Lupus, bishop of Worcester and archbishop of York (1002–23).[101] It was certainly his successor, St Wulfstan, who ordered the compilation of the second cartulary, by the monk Hemming, in the 1090s; the aim was to record all the existing documents which related to the endowment of the church (as opposed to the bishopric), including estates which had been wrongfully appropriated during the whole of the eleventh century, whether by Danes, Englishmen or Normans. Such matters were the concern of all responsible bishops and abbots.[102]

---

[98] Thus, in 1102, Walter Giffard, who had withheld the service on 7 hides at Linford which he held of Abingdon Abbey, was compelled by the king's command to become the abbot's man and render the service of one knight (van Caeneghem i, no. 162, p. 128; *Chron Abingdon* ii, pp. 133–4).

[99] Robertson, *Charters*, pp. 122–3 (S.1457); Patrick Wormald, 'Charters, law and the settlement of disputes in Anglo-Saxon England', *The settlement of disputes in early medieval Europe*, ed. Wendy Davies and Paul Fouracre (Cambridge, 1986), pp. 155–7, 160–1.

[100] Forgery was rife in the late eleventh and twelfth centuries. The activities of Osbert de Clare and his helpers at Westminster are discussed by Emma Mason, *Westminster Abbey Charters, 1066–c.1214*, London Record Society 25 (1968), pp. 8–11 and those of the monks of Worcester by Julia Barrow, 'How the twelfth-century monks of Worcester perceived their past', *The perception of the past in twelfth-century Europe*, ed. Paul Magdalino (London, 1992), pp. 53–74. For Guerno, a professional forger of continental origin, who worked for St Ouen, Rouen and St Augustine's, Canterbury, as well as 'various other churches', see Gransden, 'Baldwin, abbot of Bury St Edmunds, 1065–97', pp. 71–2.

[101] N.R. Ker, 'Hemming's Cartulary: a description of the two Worcester cartularies in Cotton Tiberius A xiii', *Studies in Medieval history presented to F.M. Powicke*, ed. R.W. Hunt, W.A. Pantin and R.W. Southern (Oxford, 1948), pp. 49–75; reprinted in *Books, Collectors and Libraries*, ed. Andrew G. Watson (London, 1985), pp. 31–59. The *Historia de Sancto Cuthberto*, written in the mid-tenth century, when the community was still at Chester-le-Street, contains much information about its land and charters, and was called a *cartula* in the twelfth century (E. Craster, 'The community of St Cuthbert', *EHR* 69 (1954), pp. 177–89; Gransden, *Historical writing in England*, pp. 76–7).

[102] Gibson, *Lanfranc of Bec*, p. 153, citing as examples Archbishop Lanfranc, Giso of Wells and Baldwin of Bury St Edmunds as well as Wulfstan.

Both the compilation of saints' lives and the overhaul of archives required a knowledge of the English past and the English language. Both tasks engaged the interests not only of the largely foreign hierarchy but also of the English monks and clerks under their rule, and encouraged an interest in the pre-Conquest history of the English church and people. This was particularly marked in some houses, for example Peterborough, where the *Anglo-Saxon Chronicle* continued to be compiled until 1154.[103] The exemplar of the surviving manuscript ('E') was at Peterborough by 1121, when it was copied, with interpolations, in the same, English hand which composed the 'first continuation', covering the years 1122 to 1131. Whence and how it came to Peterborough is unknown but it had been at St Augustine's, Canterbury, in the mid eleventh century.[104] Ernulf, abbot of Peterborough from 1107 to 1114, had been prior of Christ Church, Canterbury, and may, though a Frenchman from Beauvais, have been interested in the Old English past.[105] The survival of the Chronicle shows, however, how the traditions of a religious house were carried by the community, rather than its heads, for the subsequent abbots included the foxy Henry of Saint-Angely (1127–32) who is described as living in the abbey as do drones in a hive, and whose arrival coincided with that of the Wild Hunt.[106]

English traditions were also preserved at nearby Crowland, where the cult of Earl Waltheof was earnestly fostered both by the English brethren and their French abbot, Geoffrey of Orleans (1109–c.1124), formerly prior of Saint-Evroul. When the earl's cult was denigrated by the Norman monk, Ouen of St Albans, it was Geoffrey who rebuked him. The mocking monk was struck down for his impudence, and Geoffrey, meditating on his fate, saw in a vision Crowland's patrons, SS Bartholomew and Guthlac, standing by the earl's tomb and proclaiming his sanctity.[107] It should be stressed that there is no sign that the veneration of Waltheof had the political connotations found in earlier cults of murdered princes. His cult was not a focus of English feeling against the Normans, but a local observance in which both English and Norman shared. Hereward's memory was similarly preserved at Ely, whose bishops and priors were largely

---

103 Knowles (*The Monastic Order in England*, p. 424) identifies two particularly 'English' areas; the 'fenland circle' of Ely, Peterborough, Thorney, Ramsey and Crowland, and 'the remoter Wessex houses' of Cerne, Milton, Athelney, Muchelney and Abbotsbury. The houses of the Worcester diocese could be added to the list (see below and also Chapter VII).
104 Clark, *The Peterborough Chronicle, 1078–1154*, pp. xi–xiii, xvi–xviii; idem, 'Domesday Book – a great red herring: thoughts on some late eleventh-century orthographies', *England in the eleventh century*, ed. Hicks, pp. 322–6.
105 Southern, *St Anselm and his biographer*, p. 270. Ernulf became bishop of Rochester in 1114 and was perhaps responsible for the compilation of the *Textus Roffensis*, which contains a notable compendium of Old English material, including the vernacular laws.
106 Henry and the Wild Hunt both turned up during Lent, and the latter continued to haunt the area until Easter (*AS Chron*, 'E', 1127).
107 OV ii, pp. 322–4, 348–51.

French. Even the incipient 'cult' of King Harold II at Waltham Holy Cross was a purely local phenomenon.[108]

It was Wulfwine, the English prior of Crowland, who commissioned Abbot Geoffrey's former colleague, Orderic Vitalis, to write the *vita* of Crowland's founder, St Guthlac. Orderic's work is summarized in his *Ecclesiastical History*, and draws upon the earlier *vita* of Felix. He then adds a history of Crowland's subsequent development, 'from the trustworthy account of the subprior Ansgot and other senior monks'.[109] It is clear that despite the fire of 1091 much earlier material was available at Crowland in the twelfth century, some of it now embedded in the late medieval *Historia Croylandensis* (the Pseudo-Ingulf). Though this is not the work of Abbot Ingulf himself, he may have been responsible for reorganizing and copying earlier materials which had been damaged or lost.[110]

The diocese of Worcester, where Wulfstan retained his see until his death in 1095, was another area with strong links to its pre-Conquest past. Wilstan, a former monk of Worcester, was abbot of St Peter's, Gloucester until 1072, when he died on pilgrimage to Jerusalem.[111] Æthelwig was abbot of Evesham until his death in 1077. Edmund kept the abbey of Pershore until 1085, when he died and was succeeded by Turstin (1085–7), a monk of the same house. Godric of Winchcombe was indeed deposed and replaced by the Frenchman, Galandus, but he was placed in the custody of Æthelwig, who also administered the monastery between the death of Galandus in 1075 and the appointment of Ralph in 1077.

Even the succession of foreign abbots to Gloucester and Winchcombe did not upset the close community of the Worcester houses. In 1077, Serlo of Gloucester and Ralph of Winchcombe, with their monks, were linked in a confraternity established by Bishop Wulfstan which also included the communities of Worcester, Evesham, Pershore, Bath and Chertsey.[112] The terms of the agreement, which stress prayers for the king and queen and the duties of almsgiving, suggest a wish to promote the values of the pre-Conquest church, while the inclusion of Bath and Chertsey, which did not lie in Wulfstan's diocese but did have English abbots, may indicate a deliberate attempt to present a united front against the

---

[108] Rollason, *Saints and relics in Anglo-Saxon England*, pp. 217–20.
[109] OV ii, pp. 322–51; the quotation is on pp. 338–9.
[110] OV ii, pp. xxv–xxix; David Roffe, 'The *Historia Croylandensis*: a plea for re-assessment', *EHR* 110 (1995), pp. 93–108.
[111] For Gloucester's connection with Worcester, see Hare, *The two Anglo-Saxon minsters of Gloucester*, pp. 17–26.
[112] Benjamin Thorpe, *Diplomatarium Anglicum aevi Saxonici* (London, 1865), pp. 615–7; *Two Chartularies of the Priory of St Peter at Bath*, ed. William Hunt, Somerset Record Society 7 (1893), pp. 3–4. The (English) monks of Evesham, Bath and Chertsey are all named and include Godric, the deposed abbot of Winchcombe. The agreement is also attested by Godric, a monk of Malmesbury, with an unnamed companion, and by Wulfweard *Pices brodor* of Taunton.

incomers.[113] The same may be true of the later confraternity between Worcester and Ramsey, which also had English abbots throughout the Conqueror's reign, though the links between these two houses went back to St Oswald's re-foundation of Ramsey in the tenth century.[114]

The key figures in the West Midlands were Wulfstan of Worcester and Æthelwig of Evesham, both of whom were much more than conservers of the old ways. Their careers exemplify both the survival of English tradition and its adaptation to the new order. Both men were utterly loyal to the Norman kings. They were among the commanders of the force which prevented Earl Roger of Hereford crossing the Severn in 1075, and in the rebellion of 1088, it was Wulfstan who held the town of Worcester for William II against the supporters of Robert Curthose. Æthelwig, who, according to the Worcester monk Hem-ming, 'surpassed everyone by his intelligence, his shrewdness and his knowledge of worldly law', was appointed as what amounts to the king's justiciar in the west.[115] His biographer, who wrote soon after his death, claims that earls and sheriffs sought his counsel and he is known to have advised Serlo of Gloucester, Wulfstan of Worcester and Archbishop Lanfranc in legal disputes. His loyalty did not make him the king's lapdog. His relief of the fugitives from the Harrying of the North has already been mentioned, and he also assisted the local nobles who sought refuge at Evesham when they lost their lands in the Norman settlement of the west. Indeed many landowners commended themselves to Æthelwig for protection, a fact which led, after his death, to serious disputes over the ownership of their lands.[116]

Wulfstan was regarded as a saint in his own lifetime, and his cult was promoted in the *vita*, written, in English, by the Worcester monk Colman soon after the bishop's death.[117] The surviving sources therefore lay great stress on his spiritual authority and his worldly concerns are played down. Eadmer saw him as 'the one and only [survivor] of the ancient fathers of the English, a man distinguished in all religious observance and thoroughly imbued with knowledge of the ancient customs'.[118] But Wulfstan was far more than a relic of the past. He was a link between old and new, adapting traditional custom to new influences from the

---

113 Mason, St Wulfstan of Worcester, p. 200.
114 Ælfwine of Ramsey (1043–179/80) was succeeded by Æthelsige (1080–87), for-merly abbot of St Augustine's, Canterbury. For the confraternity agreement, which also guaranteed refuge within each house for brethren of the other at need, see The Cartulary of Worcester Cathedral Priory, ed. Darlington, no. 304.
115 Hemming's Cartulary i, pp. 269–70; Darlington, 'Aethelwig, abbot of Evesham', p. 14. The shires of the 'Mercian law', recorded for the first time in the Leges Henrici Primi (LHP, p. 97) may originate in the sphere of authority granted to Æthelwig at this time (see Mason, St Wulfstan of Worcester, p. 126, note 68).
116 Chron Evesham, pp. 89–92; for the early source of this part of the Evesham Chronicle, see Darlington, 'Aethelwig, abbot of Evesham', 1–5. See also note 89 above, and Chapter I, note 20.
117 Vita Wulfstani; it now exists only in the Latin translation of William of Malmesbury.
118 HN, p. 46.

continent. He sent his monk Nicholas, an Englishman, to study the customs of Christ Church under the guidance of Lanfranc, and the experience enabled Nicholas, as prior of Worcester (before 1116–1124), to promote high standards of observance and learning among his monks.[119] Wulfstan's attitudes are clearly demonstrated in his rebuilding of the church at Worcester in the Romanesque style. William of Malmesbury records how he wept as the old church was demolished, lamenting the destruction of 'the work of saints' and censuring the pretension of the new building, but despite his misgivings, Wulfstan did rebuild in the example of his continental contemporaries. Moreover, though his views on the value of simple and unpretentious architecture seemed antiquated in the eleventh century, they became fashionable once more in the twelfth, when they were re-stated by the Cistercians.[120]

It was not only in architecture that Wulfstan was prepared to adopt a foreign model. In the defence of his church's lands and liberties, he also asserted novel claims based on French, not English prototypes. The triple hundred of Oswaldslow, established (probably) by King Edgar, gave the bishop of Worcester considerable powers. Within the triple hundred, the bishop had sake and soke, and could intercept all dues owed to the king, except for military service and the greater judicial rights. Soon after 1066, Bishop Wulfstan was claiming Oswaldslow as a continental-style liberty, from which the sheriff was excluded, and by the time of the Domesday Inquest he had succeeded in his efforts.[121] Wulfstan's hagiographers emphasized his dove-like innocence, but he was by no means destitute of the serpent's cunning.

Wulfstan's influence extended beyond his own diocese. He administered the see of Lichfield between the resignation of Leofwine in 1071 and the appointment of Peter in 1072, and was a close friend of Bishop Robert of Hereford (1079–95). Robert, a Lotharingian scholar skilled in mathematics and astronomy, brought to England the chronicle of Marianus Scotus, which John of Worcester, one of Wulfstan's monks, used as the basis for his *Chronicon ex Chronicis*. John reports how Wulfstan, after his death, appeared to Robert 'whom he had greatly loved' at Cricklade, and asked him to come to Worcester and bury him.[122] Robert did so, and received his friend's lambskin cloak, the subject of a famous exchange between himself and Geoffrey de Mowbray, bishop of Cou-

---

[119] Mason, *St Wulfstan of Worcester*, pp. 116–17; 219–23. Nicholas was one of the chief informants of William of Malmesbury for the career of Wulfstan; he also supplied material on St Dunstan and Edward the Martyr to the Canterbury historian Eadmer, and advised the latter in his tribulations as bishop-elect of St Andrews (1120–1).

[120] Richard Gem, 'England and the resistance to Romanesque architecture', *Studies in medieval history presented to R. Allen Brown*, ed. Harper-Bill, Holdsworth and Nelson, pp. 129–39. Dominic of Evesham expressed similar sentiments about the destruction of the abbey church, 'one of the most beautiful in all England' (*Chron Evesham*, p. 55).

[121] See Chapter VII, pp. 162–64 below.

[122] *FlW*, 1095.

tances.[123] Robert also took into his service Wulfstan's former tenant, Eadric the steersman, whose lands had been confiscated after the Conquest.[124]

Ancient ties linked the churches of York and Worcester. Both St Oswald (991–92) and Wulfstan Lupus (1002–16) had been bishops of Worcester and archbishops of York, and when Ealdred was elected to York in 1060, he did not expect to relinquish Worcester, though Pope Nicholas insisted that he did.[125] Ealdred solved the problem by having his prior, Wulfstan, elected as bishop of Worcester and by retaining a number of the manors of Worcester Cathedral in his own hands. Moreover he actually consecrated Wulfstan, although the diocese lay in the province, not of York, but of Canterbury. In Wulfstan's Vita the obvious excuse is given, that Wulfstan did not wish to receive consecration from the dubious authority of Stigand.[126] Whatever the circumstances, Ealdred's arrangements caused considerable problems after his death, for his successor, Thomas, appropriated the estates and claimed jurisdiction over the diocese. Wulfstan upheld Lanfranc's rights to the see of Worcester, and in return Lanfranc supported Wulfstan's claims to the lands held by Ealdred. The dispute did not end the links between York and Worcester. Thomas was eventually compensated with the lands of the minster of St Oswald, Gloucester, held until 1070 by Archbishop Stigand.[127] This maintained the territorial link, while Wulfstan acted at need as Thomas' assistant. In 1073 he attended Thomas in the consecration of Ralph as bishop of the Orkneys, and acted again in the same capacity in 1081, at the consecration of William of St Calais as bishop of Durham; on both occasions he had the permission of Archbishop Lanfranc.[128]

These connections between Worcestershire and York are the background to the renaissance of monasticism in the north, which was achieved by men from the western diocese.[129] It was a genuinely Anglo-Norman venture, whose first

123 GP, p. 302. Geoffrey, who was noted for the richness of his apparel, chided Wulfstan for wearing sheepskins, rather than one of the more expensive furs, such as catskin: Wulfstan replied that he had often heard men speak of the lamb of God, but never of the cat of God (Vita Wulfstani, p. 46; GP, pp. 282–3).
124 See Chapter IV above.
125 Whitelock, 'The dealings of the kings of England with Northumbria', pp. 73–6.
126 Vita Wulfstani, p. 190.
127 GDB, fol. 164v. St Oswald's was a particularly apt endowment for an archbishop of York. It was founded by the lords of Mercia, Æthelred and his wife Æthelflaed, King Alfred's daughter, who in 909 translated the relics of Oswald, king of Northumbria, from Bardney; the king's head, of course, lay in the coffin of St Cuthbert, between the hands of the saint (Hare, The two Anglo-Saxon minsters at Gloucester, pp. 4–7). The intention was almost certainly to prepare the way for the conquest of Viking York, which did in fact submit to Æthelflaed in 918 (Rollason, Saints and relics in Anglo-Saxon England, pp. 153–4). Both she and her husband were buried at St Oswald's.
128 Mason, St Wulfstan of Worcester, pp. 114–16.
129 HR, 1074; HDE, chaps 56–66; R.H.C. Davis, 'Bede after Bede', Studies in medieval History presented to R.Allen Brown, ed. Harper-Bill, Holdsworth and Nelson, pp. 103–116; Anne Dawtry, 'The Benedictine revival in the north: the last bulwark of Anglo-Saxon monasticism?', SCH 18 (1982), pp. 87–98.

mover was Reinfred, a knight in the service of William de Percy. While visiting his lord's manor at Whitby, he was struck by the ruins of the old monastery of *Streonashalh* and decided to enter the religious life. He chose to go to Evesham, for reasons which are unspecified, but may be connected with Reinfred's likely participation in the Harrying of the North; it was at Evesham that the refugees from this devastation had been sheltered. There he met Aldwine, prior of Winchcombe, and Ælfwig, a monk of Evesham itself, who taught him of the golden age of Northumbria, as described in Bede's *Historia Ecclesiastica*. The three men conceived the idea of reviving the houses celebrated by Bede. They travelled north in the simplest style, with their belongings packed on a single donkey, and (like Benedict of Selby) sought the help of the sheriff of Yorkshire, Hugh fitzBaldric, who directed them to Monkchester (Newcastle). When Walcher, bishop of Durham, learnt of their presence, he invited them to the episcopal manor of Jarrow, 'where were to be seen many buildings of the monks, of which the remains scarcely indicated what their original condition had been'.[130]

At Jarrow, the companions were joined by Turgot (Thorgod) *lagr* (the short), the Lincolnshire clerk who had fled England in 1069, and had subsequently returned to enter the service of Bishop Walcher.[131] Walcher also gave them the manor of Tynemouth to establish a priory, later appropriated by Robert de Mowbray, earl of Northumbria, and given to St Albans.[132] From Jarrow the companions set out to revive other Bedan monasteries. In 1078 Reinfred fulfilled his ambition of restoring Whitby (*Streonashalh*), with the help of his former lord, William de Percy, whose brother and nephew became, respectively, the last prior and the first abbot of the new house.[133] The abbey of St Mary's, York, was an offshoot of this community and retained close links with Evesham.[134] Aldwine and Turgot went to Melrose, but this site was under the control of Malcolm Canmore, king of Scots, and neither the secular nor the ecclesiastical authorities were willing to see links established between Northumbria and Scotland. Ald-wine and Turgot were recalled and sent to Wearmouth, where Turgot finally took his monastic vows. The church there had been burnt down by Malcolm in 1070 and 'nothing more than the half-ruined walls' – and presumably the extant pre-Conquest tower – were standing.[135]

In 1080 Bishop Walcher was murdered at Durham. His successor was William of Saint-Calais, formerly prior of Saint-Vincent-des-Pres (Le Mans) and a prominent figure in the royal administration. On the advice of Lanfranc, William

---

[130] *HR*, 1074; the remains must have included the chancel of the Bedan church, which is still standing.
[131] See Chapter II above.
[132] In the Durham Cartulary, the original gift is attributed to Earl Waltheof, whose cousin Morcar was a monk of Jarrow, but quite apart from the unsatisfactory nature of the charter itself (see above Chapter III note 97) Tynemouth was an episcopal, not a comital estate (Offler, *Durham episcopal charters 1071–1152*, pp. 4–6).
[133] *HRH*, p. 78.
[134] *Chron Evesham*, p. 256, Knowles, *The Monastic Order in England*, p. 171.
[135] *HR*, 1070.

decided to replace the secular clerks of Durham with monks, a move sanctioned by Bede's account of the original community at Lindisfarne. Where better to look than in the newly-restored houses at Monkwearmouth-Jarrow, Bede's own home? In 1083, the newly-established communities were removed to Durham and the secular canons compensated with positions elsewhere.[136] Aldwine became prior of the new chapter, and on his death in 1087 was succeeded by Turgot. It is possible that another member of the community was the English scribe of Domesday Book.[137]

To house the community, Bishop William began to build the magnificent cathedral on its rock above the Wear. Its foundation-stone was laid on 11 August 1093 by Turgot the prior, assisted by Malcolm, king of Scots.[138] The work was completed by William's successor, Rannulf Flambard (1099–1128), another royal servant who had been chief minister to William II. He presided over the opening of St Cuthbert's tomb in 1104, the prelude to the saint's translation into his shrine in the newly-completed choir. Soon afterwards the community commissioned Simeon, one of their number, to write the history of the church.[139] Simeon's work emphasises the English saints of Durham, Oswald, Aidan and Cuthbert himself. Cuthbert's relics, and the head of Oswald, who established Aidan as bishop at Lindisfarne, were the link which bound the twelfth-century community to its illustrious past, and guaranteed their power and possessions. When William of Saint-Calais called the monks to Durham, he commended them 'to Mary the most blessed mother of God and to his most holy patron Cuthbert . . . and he bound them by a link which could not be severed to the

---

136 HDE, chapter 62; David Rollason, 'Simeon of Durham and the community of Durham in the eleventh century', England in the eleventh century, ed. Hicks, pp. 191–2. Simeon claims that only the dean agreed to take monastic vows and the rest were expelled from the community, but the transition may have been more gradual (see Aird, 'St Cuthbert, the Scots and the Normans', p. 19).

137 Pierre Chaplais, 'William of Saint-Calais and Domesday Book', Domesday Studies, ed. Holt, pp. 65–77.

138 HDE, chap. 77; HR, 1093. Alexander, Malcolm's son, is the only layman recorded at the opening of St Cuthbert's tomb in 1104 (HR, 1104; Historia Translationum Sancti Cuthberti, Symeonis . . . Collectanea i, p. 195). Five years later, Alexander, now king of Scots, made Turgot bishop of St Andrews but his tenure of the see was bedevilled by disputes about the primacy of York over St Andrews, which Turgot seems to have accepted but Alexander not, and since 'he could not rightly exercise his episcopal office in difficult cases', he returned to Durham, where he died in 1115 (HR, 1074, cf. 1109, 1115; Hugh the Chantor, pp. 31, 35). It is possible, though not certain, that Turgot was the author of the Vita of Margaret of Scotland (Derek Baker, ' "A nursery of saints": St Margaret of Scotland reconsidered', Medieval Women, ed. Derek Baker, SCH Subsidia i (1978), pp. 129–31; Lois L. Huneycutt, 'The idea of the perfect princess: the Life of St Margaret in the reign of Matilda II (1100–1118)', ANS 12 (1990), p. 116 note 71).

139 A.J. Piper, 'The first generations of Durham monks and the cult of St Cuthbert', St Cuthbert, his cult and community to AD 1200, ed. Gerald Bonner, David Rollason and Clare Stancliffe (Woodbridge, 1989), pp. 438–43.

body of the most holy father Cuthbert'.[140] The tie between a community and its saint could not be better expressed.

Despite its English roots, the monasticism of the northern revival was no antiquarian exercise. At Durham William imposed the *Monastic Constitutions* of Lanfranc as the new rule and equipped his church with the latest in continental scholarship, though he also gave a copy of Bede's *Ecclesiastical History*, still to be seen in the treasury of Durham Cathedral. The northern houses represent a fusion of English and Norman elements, producing 'a monasticism which was truly Anglo-Norman in its outlook'.[141] Even though the primitive and ascetic life sought by the founders of the movement was inspired by the writings of Bede, the desire for a purer form of Benedictinism was itself the local expression of a more general yearning.[142] Aldwine and his associates have been described as 'an English example of that widespread movement towards a simpler, more solitary form of religious life which . . . was at the very moment about to develop at Tiron, Savigny, Citeaux and the Grande Chartreuse'.[143] The same temper can be seen in Wulfstan of Worcester, and one of the key figures in the birth of the Cistercian movement was another Englishman, Stephen Harding, whose career began as a monk of Sherborne.[144] There was an intimate relation between the houses of the northern revival and the earliest Cistercian colonies in England. Fountains was founded from St Mary's, York, and Maurice, the second abbot of Rievaulx, had been sub-prior of Durham.[145] His successor Ailred (1147–69) was the son of Eilaf, hereditary priest of Hexham, grandson of Eilaf *larwe* (schoolmaster), treasurer of Durham, and great-grandson of Alfred Westou, who translated the remains of Bede from Jarrow to Durham. The same amalgam of Englishmen and Normans which characterized the northern revival is found amongst the English Cistercians.

The northern revival is marked by a community of interest between Normans and English. It has been argued that the Norman sponsors of the movement were inspired by political, rather than religious motives, and were more concerned with removing the clerks of Durham, with their dangerous local connections, than reviving Old English traditions.[146] This may be so, and it is probably true

---

[140] *HDE*, chapter 62.
[141] Dawtry, 'The Benedictine revival in the north', p. 98.
[142] Davis, 'Bede after Bede', p. 109.
[143] Knowles, *The Monastic Order in England*, p. 167.
[144] Knowles, *The Monastic Order in England*, p. 199.
[145] *HRH*, pp. 132, 140.
[146] Rollason, 'Simeon of Durham and the community of Durham in the eleventh century', pp. 183–98; Ted Johnson-Smith, 'The Norman Conquest of Durham: Norman historians and the Anglo-Saxon community of St Cuthbert', *Haskins Society Journal* 4 (1993), p. 95. The pretext for the expulsion of the clerks may have been an alleged connection with the Bamburgh family, some of whose members were involved in Walcher's murder (see Chapter III above), but there is little evidence for any close ties between Durham and the Bamburgh earls; rather the reverse (see Aird, 'St Cuthbert, the Scots and the Normans', pp. 15–20).

that to the Northumbrians the monks from Evesham and Winchcombe were as much 'foreigners' in the land of the *Haliwerfolc* as their Norman patrons. Nevertheless, they drew their inspiration from the remote past, the golden age of Northumbrian monasticism, which vanished before the West Saxon kings began to bring all England under their authority. Their source was a book, the *Ecclesiastical History of the English nation*, which had first articulated the idea of an English *gens*.[147] In the twelfth century, Bede's work, always popular, was copied and recopied, and became the model and source for a new generation of historians, whose view of the English past became a vital factor in the forging of a new English nation.

---

[147] Patrick Wormald, 'Bede, the *Bretwaldas* and the origin of the *gens Anglorum*', *Ideal and reality in Frankish and Anglo-Saxon society*, ed. Patrick Wormald, Donald Bullough and Roger Collins (Oxford, 1983), pp. 99–129.

Chapter VII

REMEMBERING THE PAST

> It will not be a waste of time for you young
> heroes to listen to an old man who, through the
> chances of time, the changes of kings, and the
> variable issues of war, has learned to reflect on
> the past, weigh up the present, and surmise
> about the present from the past, the future from
> the present.
>
> Walter Espec at the Battle of the Standard, 1138[1]

IN 1070 THOMAS, archbishop-elect of York, presented himself at Canterbury for
consecration by his colleague, Archbishop Lanfranc. When, however, Lanfranc
asked him for a written profession of obedience and an oath of loyalty, Thomas
replied that 'he would never do that until he could read evidence of the claim
and could see witnesses testifying to its antiquity' and departed unconsecrated.
King William, believing that Lanfranc 'was trying to get more than his due', was
annoyed but Lanfranc

> calmed his anger with an explanation of the case and completely per-
> suaded the *transmarini* who were there that right was on his side. As for
> the English, who already understood the matter, they testified very firmly
> in support of his claim in all respects.

This was the beginning, not the end, of the primacy dispute between Canterbury
and York, the complications of which are beyond the scope of this study.[2] The
point to notice is the stress laid on the testimony of the English; indeed Thomas's
objections were attributed to his ignorance of English customs. In both the
church and the field of lay government, the law to be followed was that of the
English, conceived as the customs observed in the time of King Edward.[3] Thus

---

[1] According to Ailred of Rievaulx, *Relatio de Standardo* (*Chronicles of the reigns of
Stephen, Henry II and Richard I*, ed. Richard Howlett, Rolls Series 82 (London, 1886),
p. 185); quoted in Derek Baker, 'Ailred of Rievaulx and Walter Espec', *Haskins Society
Journal* 1 (1989), p. 94.
[2] *Letters of Lanfranc*, pp. 40–1; Gibson, *Lanfranc of Bec*, pp. 116–31; Southern, *St Anselm
and his biographer*, pp. 127–42.
[3] A writ of William I for Ely (van Caeneghem i, p. 49) specifies that the abbey's

Henry I, in his coronation charter, restored 'the law of King Edward, with such emendations to it as my father made with the counsel of his barons'.[4]

One problem with this theory was the absence of any law-code issued by Edward the Confessor. The 'law of King Edward' was in fact, as far as written law was concerned, the laws of Cnut, drafted by Archbishop Wulfstan of York before 1023.[5] In the early twelfth century efforts were made to rectify the lack of recent legislation, and the reign of Henry I saw 'a remarkable revival of legal writing'.[6] Indeed much of the existing corpus of pre-Conquest law is found only in compilations of this period, notably the *Textus Roffensis*, produced at Rochester, and a similar collection made at St Paul's, London. Both are in English, and have been interpreted as exercises in nostalgia, but the fact that Latin translations and compilations were also made at this time points to a more practical purpose.[7] The legal collection in the *Textus Roffensis*, which contains enactments of Henry's reign as well as the Old English texts, was compiled for Bishop Ernulf (1115–24), probably in 1122–24.[8] Ernulf had been a pupil of Ivo of Chartres and was consulted as an expert on canon law, but his position as bishop of Rochester

opponents were to plead 'as they would have done in the time of King Edward'; see Stenton, *English Justice between the Norman Conquest and Magna Carta*, pp. 6–25; George Garnett, ' "Franci et Angli": the legal distinctions between peoples after the Conquest', *ANS* 8 (1986), p. 135.

4 *EHD* ii, p. 402; text in Liebermann i, p. 522, A.J. Robertson, *The laws of the kings of England from Edward the Elder to Henry I* (Cambridge, 1925), pp. 282–3.

5 *Quadripartitus* (see note 12 below) notes that 'the laws that go by King Edward's name derived from the institutes of Cnut in the first place' (*leges quas dicunt Edwardi regis ex Cnudi primum institutione*), and describes how when Edward returned from exile in 1042, the English thegns would not accept him unless he swore to uphold the laws of Cnut (Richard Sharpe, 'The prefaces of "Quadripartitus" ', *Law and government in medieval England and Normandy: essays in honour of Sir James Holt*, ed. Garnett and Hudson, pp. 162, 164; see also John Hudson, 'Administration, family and perceptions of the past in twelfth-century England: Richard fitzNigel and the Dialogue of the Exchequer', *The perception of the past in twelfth-century Europe*, ed. Magdalino, p. 97). The *Consiliatio Cnuti* (see note 10 below) is described, in an addition to the text, as *leges que vocantur Edwardi*. For Archbishop Wulfstan's authorship of Cnut's laws, and the collection of legal texts at Worcester which is probably connected with him, see *EHD* i, pp. 322–3; Dorothy Whitelock, 'Wulfstan's authorship of Cnut's laws', *EHR* 70 (1955), pp. 72–85.

6 Green, *The government of England under Henry I*, p. 97.

7 R.W. Southern, 'Historical writing in the twelfth century: the sense of the past', *TRHS* fifth series 23 (1973), p. 253; idem, 'The place of England in the twelfth-century renaissance', *Medieval Humanism*, p. 161; against this 'antiquarian' interpretation, see Green, *The government of England under Henry I*, pp. 97–100, and the articles by Patrick Wormald cited in notes 8 and 9 below.

8 Patrick Wormald, '*Laga Eadwardi*: the *Textus Roffensis* and its context', *ANS* 17 (1995), forthcoming. Sawyer's date of 1122–3 for the Textus Roffensis is incorrect, and Liebermann's date of the 1130s ('Notes on the Textus Roffensis', *Archaeologia Cantiana* 23 (1898) pp. 101–12) is too late, as is the date of 1125–30 for the St Paul's collection (Cambridge, Corpus Christ College Ms 383, see *EHD* i, pp. 328–9). I am very grateful to Patrick Wormald for help on the dating and context of the Henrician collections, and for his advice on their purpose and use; any remaining errors are, of course, my own.

would have required some secular expertise as well, which the collection in *Textus Roffensis* might be intended to supply. The St Paul's collection probably served the same purpose; Maurice, bishop of London from 1086 to 1107, had been William I's chancellor and his successor, Richard de Beaumais, had a reputation for legal knowledge.[9]

At about the same time as the English collections, two Latin translations based on Cnut's codes, but containing other pre-Conquest enactments, were made; the *Instituta Cnuti*, which must be earlier than the *Textus Roffensis* (in which it appears), and the *Consiliatio Cnuti*.[10] Like the other Latin compilations of Henry's reign, the 'Ten Articles' of William I (also contained in the *Textus Roffensis*), the *Leges Edwardi Confessoris*, and the *Leis Willelme*, which also exists in French, the authors are anonymous, but there is no indication that they were monks, and they may have been clerks in royal or episcopal service. Their purpose may have been to familiarize those whose native tongue was not English with the workings of English law. A demand for such texts is implied by the survival of 'five different assertions in the in the early decades of the twelfth century of the relevance of the Anglo-Saxon legal heritage, each an attempt to give it order and system'.[11]

The largest Latin collection of pre-Conquest laws is the *Quadripartitus*. The author may have begun work on this compilation in the later years of William Rufus, and completed his task some time between 1108 and 1118, probably closer to the earlier than the later date.[12] He was also responsible for the *Leges Henrici Primi*, which relies on the *Quadripartitus* for its knowledge of the pre-Conquest codes. Though he could read and translate Old English, his mistakes suggest that he was not an Englishman, but he does identify England as his *patria* and the

---

A full discussion of the Henrician collections will appear in Patrick Wormald, *The Making of English Law, King Alfred to the Norman Conquest*, forthcoming.

[9] Patrick Wormald, '*Laga Eadwardi*: the *Textus Roffensis* and its context', forthcoming; idem, 'Quadripartitus', *Law and government in medieval England and Normandy: essays in honour of Sir James Holt*, ed. Garnett and Hudson, p. 142. For a brief account of Ernulf, Maurice and Richard de Beaumais, see Barlow, *The English Church, 1066–1154*, pp. 64, 81, 82–3, 168–9.

[10] *Consiliatio Cnuti*, ed. F. Liebermann (Halle, 1893). The *Instituta Cnuti* appears on fols 58–80 of the *Textus Roffensis*, followed by the Ten Articles of William I (fols 80–81v); it is printed by Liebermann (i, pp. 612–17) and discussed in idem, 'On the Instituta Cnuti aliorumque regum Anglorum', *TRHS* new series 7 (1893), pp. 77–107. Liebermann dated the *Instituta* to 1103–20 and the *Consiliatio* to 1110–30 (Liebermann iii, pp. 330, 333–4), but these dates are probably too late.

[11] Wormald, 'Quadripartitus', p. 145: the texts are the Rochester and St Paul's collections, the *Instituta Cnuti*, the *Consiliatio Cnuti* and *Quadripartitus* itself. See also Green, *The government of England under Henry I*, pp. 98–9; H.G. Richardson and G.O. Sayles, *Law and legislation in England from Æthelberht to Magna Carta* (Edinburgh, 1966), pp. 45–6.

[12] *Quadripartitus* is the sole authority for a number of pre-Conquest texts which do not appear in the English compilations (*EHD* i, pp. 329–30). Its context and purpose is examined by Wormald, 'Quadripartitus', pp. 111–47. For the date, see Sharpe, 'The prefaces of "Quadripartitus" ', pp. 150–1.

English as his *gens*, and shows particular feeling for Winchester and Hampshire.[13] In the *Leges* he refers to *nostra professio*, which implies a 'claim to a special level of legal expertise', and he 'must have served in some judicial capacity'.[14] The *Leges* has been criticized by modern historians for its confusion and disorganization, but when it is seen as a literary production, in the long tradition of early medieval legal codes, its purpose becomes more understandable. The *Leges* contains the famous statement on the pre-eminent authority of the king, 'the formidable authority of the royal majesty which we stress as worthy of attention for its continual and beneficial pre-eminence over the laws'.[15] The *Quadripartitus* also emphasizes this theme ('the king of England is lord over his dominion with a unique majesty') showing 'an awareness of the ideological dimension of written law as a statement of the ideals as well as the practice of kingship'.[16] The 'formidable authority of the royal majesty' rested on the accumulated prestige of the Old English past.[17]

Law was enshrined not only in the law-codes of the English kings, but also in the collective memory of the English. Determining the law entailed consultation with those who remembered the times of King Edward.[18] When Lanfranc began proceedings to recover the alienated lands of Christ Church, Canterbury, the shire-court of Kent at Penenden Heath was advised by Æthelric, *quondam* bishop of Selsey, who was knowledgeable in the 'old legal customs'.[19] About the same time, Abbot Adelelm of Abingdon relied on the expertise of English *causidici* to establish the privileges of Abingdon over its lands.[20] Likewise when Baldwin of Bury St Edmunds was defending his abbey's liberty against Bishop Herfast of East Anglia, 'testimony going back to the time of King Cnut was proffered by Abbot Ælfwine of Ramsey, then in the fullness of his days and an old man, which was confirmed by the voice of the nine counties', before whom

---

13 Wormald, 'Quadripartitus', pp. 139–40; *LHP*, pp. 12–28.

14 Wormald, 'Quadripartitus', pp. 143–4.

15 *LHP*, chapter 6, 2a.

16 Sharpe, 'The prefaces of "Quadripartitus" ', p. 169; Green, *The government of England under Henry I*, p. 99. The *Instituta Cnuti* too contains a section on 'the customary rights of kings among the English' (Liebermann, 'On the Instituta Cnuti aliorumque regum Anglorum', pp. 97–9; this section is drawn mainly from II Cnut).

17 H.R. Loyn, 'De iure domini regis: a comment on royal authority in eleventh-century England', *England in the eleventh century*, ed. Hicks, pp. 17–24. Cf. Garnett, 'Franci et Angli', p. 111: 'one of the few departures from pre-Conquest practice in the formulation of [William I's] Latin writs was to specify that he was "king of the English". Anglo-Saxon kings had been content, in writs, with the unadorned royal title'.

18 The twelfth-century text known as the *Leges Edwardi Confessoris* represents William I, in the fourth year of his reign (1069–70) summoning 'noble Englishmen, wise and learned in their law, so that he might hear from them their customs' (Liebermann i, p. 627).

19 Van Caeneghem i, p. 9. Bishop Æthelric was also consulted by Eadmer when writing the *Vita* of St Dunstan (*Mem. St Dunstan*, p. 164).

20 *Chron Abingdon* ii, pp. 1–2; van Caeneghem i, pp. 6–7 (see also Chapter VI above).

the case was heard.[21] A writ of William I commands the shires which have heard the complaints of Ely Abbey to be recalled, and orders that 'several of those Englishmen who know how the lands . . . lay on the day when King Edward died' be elected to give their sworn evidence.[22]

The shire-courts, whether engaged in considering local affairs or convened by royal justices, were a meeting-place for Normans and Englishmen. It was not only tenants-in-chief and their immediate mesne-tenants who were required to attend. The *Leges Henrici Primi* specifies bishops, earls, sheriffs and their deputies (*vicarii*), hundredmen and aldermen, stewards and reeves, barons, vavassors, village reeves (*tungrevi*) and 'lords of lands' (*terrarum domini*); and the king's judges included not only 'the barons of the county' but also those who held 'free lands' (*qui liberas terras tenent*).[23] Clearly some of these suitors must have been English. A shire-court held in Kent in 1127 included not only the sheriff, the archbishop, the bishop of Rochester, the king's constable and the Norman landholders of the locality, but also three Englishmen, Wulfric, Geldwine and Leofwine, of uncertain status.[24] Free men were required to attend both the shire and the hundred courts; indeed attendance at the hundred courts was obligatory both for free men and sokemen, unless their soke had been transferred elsewhere.[25] Only villeins, cottagers, farthingmen (those who held a quarter of a virgate) and other 'base and poor persons' (*viles et inopes persone*) were excluded.[26]

The criteria for attendance at the shire-court are not entirely clear, but may have included possession of a tenement of appropriate size.[27] William II forbade the men of Bury St Edmunds to attend the shire and hundred unless they had

---

[21] Mem. St Edmunds i, p. 65; van Caeneghem i, no. 9, pp. 24–9, esp. 27.

[22] Van Caeneghem i, p. 47.

[23] LHP, chapters 7,2; 29, 1; cf. 27, 1, for 'vavassors who have free lands (*liberas terras*)'. See also Henry I's writ addressed to all barons, vavassors and 'lords who hold lands' (*dominis qui terras tenent*) in Well Wapentake, Lincs. (van Caeneghem i, no. 279, p. 236). The *domini terrarum* 'are evidently those landholders, whatever their status in the feudal hierarchy, who . . . also owe suit of court' (LHP, p. 315); they may be the *ruricole* (?local men) who, according to Richard fitzNigel, knew 'what are the counties [shires] hundreds and hides' (*Dialogus*, p. 64; Hudson, 'Administration, family and perceptions of the past in late twelfth-century England: Richard fitzNigel and the Dialogue of the Exchequer', p. 87). For the meaning of 'free land', see above, Chapter IV.

[24] See note 42 below.

[25] The suitors of the hundred included all free men, whether householders (*hurthfest*) or *folgarii*, those in the households of others (LHP, chapter 8,1, repeating II Cnut 20). A Ramsey writ, attributed to King Edward but probably of twelfth-century date, conveys to the abbey jurisdiction over the mootworthy men of the hundred of Clackclose (Harmer, Writs, no. 61, pp. 259–62 and see also pp. 475–6). For the jurisdiction of the hundred, see Green, *The government of England under Henry I*, pp. 111–12.

[26] LHP, chapter 1a. In the Bury case quoted above (note 21) Bishop Herfast was able to produce only 'the testimony of some base persons who were not even lawful men' (*vilium testimoniis personarum, etiam non legalium*); one of his witnesses was a man who had been keeper of dogs to Herfast's predecessor, Bishop Æthelmaer. See also GDB, fol. 44v for the testimony of *villanis et vili plebe et de preposito*.

[27] Raftis, The estates of Ramsey Abbey, p. 47.

the amount of land which would have made them 'worthy' (*digni*) in King Edward's time.[28] Little Domesday records that at Fersfield and Winfarthing, Norfolk, holders of 30 acres were justiciable in the hundred court, while those with smaller tenements attended the manorial court.[29] On the lands of Shaftesbury Abbey in the twelfth century, it was usually the larger holdings which owed suit to the shire and hundred. Only four men are said to owe suit of court in the earliest survey (c.1130), of whom one held half a hide, one a hide and the two others 1½ hides each; one of the latter held by knight-service. In the second survey, of c.1170, suit of court is recorded more frequently, but again is due mainly from the men with the larger holdings. Examples include Guy of Hinton St Mary, Dorset, whose one-hide tenement was held by knight-service, and three men at Dinton, Wilts., described as franklins, holding five virgates, a hide, and three virgates respectively; one of them, William fitzOsiet (Osgeat) is clearly of English descent.[30] Such tenants were probably the 'better men (*meliores*) of the vill', who, with the priest and reeve, represented their lord if neither he nor his steward could attend.[31] References to the testimony of juries empanelled by the shire-courts are frequent and in some cases, the individual jurors are named. The account of the Ely pleas of the 1070s names some of the *plurimi milites probati francigene et Angli* of the shires of Essex, Hertford, Huntingdon and Bedford in the 1070s. Hardwin, Guy (Wido), Wimer, Wichumer and Odo are presumably French; Godric, Northmann, Colswein and Godwine are probably English.[32] This mixture of English and French is also found in the hundred juries of Cambridgeshire and Huntingdonshire who swore to the Domesday material, but the jurors who perjured themselves in the Isleham case, heard before the shire-court of Cambridgeshire between 1077 and 1086, were all English.[33]

Two generations of York lawmen (*lagamen*) are recorded in suits relating to the privileges of the archbishopric. In the 1080s (perhaps in 1086) the 'Rights and Laws' of the archbishop were determined by a sworn jury of twelve named Englishmen and six named Frenchmen.[34] Some of the Englishmen can be

---

[28] Douglas, *Feudal documents*, no. 16, pp. 59–60; *Regesta* i, no. 393.

[29] *LDB*, fol. 130v.

[30] BL Harleian Ms 61, fols 38, 41v, 42, 65–65v, 74v and see Williams, 'The knights of Shaftesbury Abbey', pp. 230–2. Some virgaters owed suit to the shire and hundred, but there may have been special circumstances, at least in some cases; for instance, Robert, who held a virgate at Dinton for 6s. rent and suit of the shire and hundred courts, was reeve (*praefectus*) of the estate (BL Harleian Ms 61, fol. 73).

[31] *LHP*, chapter 7,7b.

[32] *Liber Eliensis*, pp. 199–200, 427; van Caeneghem i, no. 18, pp. 43–50. Godric might be Godric the steward (see Chapter V) and Colswein the Domesday juror of Armingford hundred (see Chapter IV).

[33] *Textus Roffensis*, fols 175–175v; van Caeneghem i, no. 19, pp. 50–1 and see Chapter IV above. Six of the twelve jurors are named; the others may of course have been Frenchmen. Were they omitted because they escaped the charge of perjury brought against the English jurors?

[34] F. Liebermann, 'An early English document of about 1080', *Yorkshire Archaeological*

identified in Domesday. Arngrim the monk (of St Mary's, York) held land in Kirby Underdale and Painsthorpe as a *tainus regis*; *Ouderbem* may be the *tainus* Authbjorn who held land in North Dalton; *Hardolf* (Heardwulf) held land as a *tainus* in Burnsall; *Beornolf* is probably the Beornwulf (or Bjornulfr) who retained most of his lands as a tenant of Count Alan.[35] A generation later the lawmen of York were still English. When in 1106 the privileges of the archbishop of York were challenged by Osbert the sheriff, a commission sent by the king to inquire into the matter convoked the shire-court and 'asked the wisest Englishmen of that city by the fealty which they owed the king to say the truth about those customs' which the archbishop claimed. The twelve named jurors are described as hereditary lawmen of York (*hereditario jure lagaman civitatis*).[36] Where they can be identified, they come from the same stratum of sub-tenants and baronial officers as the hundred jurors of the Domesday survey. Uhtred son of Alwine attested a charter of Gilbert Tison in favour of Selby Abbey and probably held at least some of the estates of his his father, Alwine son of Northmann, as Tison's tenant.[37] Gamall son of Orm may be the son of Orm Gamallson of Kirkdale, whose land went to Hugh fitzBaldric, and Morcar son of Ligulf's father is presumably the man whose murder precipitated that of Walcher, bishop of Durham in 1080.[38] William son of Ulfr is perhaps son of the Ulfr who appears as a juror in the 1080s.

In the earlier inquest the French and English jurors apparently gave testimony in their respective languages.[39] The jurors of 1106 evidently spoke in English, for they had an interpreter, Ansketil of Bulmer, then reeve of the North Riding.[40] Ansketil was steward to Robert Fossard, and later (about 1115) succeeded Osbert as sheriff of York; he was presumably of Norman descent, but clearly spoke and understood English.[41] A fuller description of court procedure appears in the account of the plea of 1127 which decided the dispute between Christ Church

---

Journal 18 (1905), pp. 412–16; the date may be contemporary with the Domesday survey, see Palliser, *Domesday York*, pp. 6–8, 25. See also Pelteret, *Vernacular documents*, no. 148, p. 122.

[35] GDB, fol. 331, *DB Yorkshire*, Appendix 3 (Arngrimr); GDB 330v; GDB, fol. 331v; GDB, fols 311, 311v, 312, *DB Yorkshire*, Appendix 3 (Bjornulfr).

[36] Van Caeneghem i, no. 172, p. 139.

[37] See Chapter II note 109.

[38] For Orm Gamallson, see GDB, fol. 327v; *DB Yorkshire*, no. 23,N19, Appendix 3; he rebuilt St Gregory's minster, Kirkdale 'in the days of King Edward and in the days of Earl Tostig (Elizabeth Okasha, 'The English language in the eleventh century', *England in the eleventh century*, ed. Hicks, pp. 333–45). For Morcar son of Ligulf, see Chapter III above.

[39] Palliser, *Domesday York*, pp. 6–7.

[40] The references to interpreters in the late eleventh and early twelfth centuries suggests that English may have been widely used; Orderic claimed that William I attempted to learn English 'so that he could understand the pleas of the conquered people without an interpreter' (OV ii, pp. 256–7).

[41] Green, *English sheriffs to 1154*, pp. 89–90; idem, *The government of England under Henry I*, pp. 200, 238–9. Compare the position of Robert Latimer (*latinarius*, interpreter) as a sheriff's officer (*minister*) in Domesday Kent (above, Chaper IV).

and St Augustine's over the market of Sandwich.[42] Testimony was given by the twelve king's men (*homines regis*) of Dover and twelve from the neighbourhood of Sandwich: all were, to judge by their names, English.[43] The first to swear was Wulfwig son of Beornwig, 'standing in the midst of the multitude and holding in his hand the book of the holy gospels'. His words, though given in Latin, were presumably spoken in English. A similar procedure is seen in Dorset in 1122, when a dispute over land at Burton Bradstock between Saint-Etienne of Caen and the king's men (*homines regis*) of Bridport was settled before a court of seven hundreds: sixteen jurors were chosen, three from Bridport, three from Burton Bradstock and ten from 'the neighbourhood' (*de vicinis*). Three have continental (French) names and the rest insular (English) names.[44]

English testimony was required to establish English law, but that law was not unchanging. One of the advantages of customary law was precisely the selective memory of the law-worthy men, which enabled out-of-date ideas and practices to be discarded and more appropriate – or more desirable – procedures to be introduced.[45] The re-definition of the liberty belonging to the bishopric of Worcester is a celebrated example of this. From the tenth century the bishops of Worcester had enjoyed considerable privileges over the triple hundred of Oswaldslow, including the right to take the profits of its court. By 1086, the contemporary incumbent, St Wulfstan, was claiming much more than this. His return to the Domesday commissioners claims that 'no sheriff can have any claim (*querelam*) there, either in any plea or in any other matter' and adds 'the whole shire testifies to this'.[46] The reputations both of St Wulfstan and of the Domesday

---

[42] Stenton, *English Justice between the Norman Conquest and Magna Carta*, pp. 19–21, 116–23; van Caeneghem i, no. 254, pp. 216–18, and see above, Chapter VI.

[43] King Henry I's writ specified a recognition by the oath of 'twelve lawful men of Dover and twelve lawful men of the neighbourhood of Sandwich' (*per sacramentum duodecim legalium hominium de Douorre et duodecim legalium hominium de provincia de Sandewico*) and the jurors are described as 'wise old men full of years and having good testimony' (*maturi sapientes senes multorum annorum bonum testimonium habentes*); Stenton, *English Justice between the Norman Conquest and Magna Carta*, pp. 118–19; van Caeneghem i, p. 217. In 1123 the 'old and reliable men' (*antiqui et autentici viri*) of the area swore to the extent of the *parochia* of Leominster, when it was granted to Reading Abbey (*Reading Abbey Cartularies*, ed. Brian Kemp, Camden Society 4th series 31 (1986), pp. 287–8). One of the tenants at Leominster in 1086 was Leofwine Latimer (*latinarius*) see GDB, fols 180, 180v and compare the role of Ansketil of Bulmer, above.

[44] Stenton, *English Justice between the Norman Conquest and Magna Carta*, p. 21; van Caeneghem i, no. 232, p. 197. One seems to be an Englishman with a continental name, Richard son of *Living* (Lyfing, Leofing). For the distinction between continental and insular personal names, see Chapter VIII below.

[45] Clanchy, *From memory to written record*, p. 296. Such emendation was not always favourably regarded. The *Leges Henrici Primi* complain (chap. 6,3a) that 'the laws of the counties differ very often from shire to shire, according as the rapacity of the evil and hateful practices of lawyers (*professorum*) have introduced into the legal system more serious ways of inflicting injury'. Downer interprets *professores* as 'persons claiming special skill or knowledge' (*LHP*, pp. 313–14).

[46] GDB, fol. 172v.

survey have ensured that this claim has been taken at face value but it has always been (to say the least) difficult to show that such privileges were exercised before 1066. The charter which purports to record the origin of the liberty is a twelfth-century forgery and it is significant that although William I's writ to Prior Ælfstan does include an exclusionary clause, the earlier writ of Edward the Confessor does not.[47]

It seems in fact that the 'liberty' of Oswaldslow, in so far as the exclusion of the sheriff and his officers is concerned, is a creation of William I's reign.[48] That the bishop's powers within Oswaldslow and indeed within the shire of Worcester were extensive need not be doubted; indeed they are amply demonstrated in the law-suit between Bishop Wulfstan and Abbot Walter of Evesham. It concerned the manors of Hampton and Bengeworth, held by Evesham but claimed as part of the triple hundred of Oswaldslow, and thus owing the same services as those due from the other tenants of the church.[49] In support of his claim Wulfstan produced the testimony of witnesses who had seen the service performed before 1066, including Eadric of Hindlip, his former steersman, Cyneweard, one-time sheriff of Worcestershire, Siward *dives* of Shropshire, Osbern fitzRichard Scrob and Thorkell of Warwick; all Englishmen by the current definition, for Osbern, though the son of a foreign favourite of King Edward, had held his land before 1066.[50] Abbot Walter produced only the relics of Evesham's founder, St Ecgwine, but, seeing the opposition ranged against him, yielded the case.

The appearance of Cyneweard among the bishop's supporters is particularly significant. He had been sheriff of Worcestershire before 1066 and probably held office until the advent of Urse d'Abetot in 1069. Moreover he was not only a tenant of the bishop of Worcester, but almost certainly a member of the family of Wulfstan Lupus, bishop of Worcester and archbishop of York.[51] To say that the pre-Conquest sheriff of Worcestershire was in the bishop's pocket may be excessive, but their close relations cannot have done the bishop's authority any harm. King William's dispositions in the west upset this cosy relationship; Abbot Æthelwig of Evesham became (perhaps in 1068) the king's local justiciar, and in 1069 Urse d'Abetot was made sheriff of Worcestershire. These developments

[47] S.731 ('Altitonantis'), printed in *The Cartulary of Worcester Cathedral Priory*, ed Darlington, no. 1, pp. 4–7 (see also note 53 below); *Regesta* i, no. 252; Harmer, *Writs*, pp. 409, 411–12.
[48] Patrick Wormald, 'The Oswaldslow "immunity": a proposition with discussion', forthcoming. I have to thank Mr Wormald for allowing me to read and cite his paper in advance of publication.
[49] Hemming's Cartulary i, pp. 80–3; van Caeneghem i, pp. 37–41. The service is specified as sake and soke, burial rights and churchscot, *requisitiones* (pleas), *omnes consuetudines*, and the king's geld and service and military service by land and sea.
[50] For Eadric and Siward, see Chapter IV above; for Thorkell of Warwick, see Chapter V above. For the pre-Conquest Norman settlers as *anglici*, see Chapter I above.
[51] Williams, 'An introduction to the Worcestershire Domesday', pp. 24–6. 'Fixing' of juries by powerful magnates was not unknown either in pre- or post-Conquest England, see Robin Fleming, 'Testimony, the Domesday Inquest and Domesday Book', forthcoming.

'gave Wulfstan the strongest of motives for institutionalizing his position' especially as 'he was excellently well-placed to square the evidence submitted by the
shire community to the Domesday commissioners'.[52] Hence its testimony on the
immunity of Oswaldslow, which was represented, against all the evidence, as 'a
custom of ancient times'.[53] It was not long before similar 'ancient' privileges were
claimed by other English religious houses, including Evesham itself.[54] However
new it was, however, the law was always seen as old. The *murdrum* fine,
introduced by William I, had by the time of Henry I's accession become part of
the 'law of King Edward', so that the law remained 'English' law even when it
was adapted to new circumstances.[55]

The twelfth century saw a transformation in English law which is beyond the
scope of this book.[56] In this process the remembrance of the past may play only
a small part, but that part is nevertheless worthy of notice. It preserved a link,
albeit increasingly tenuous, with indigenous traditions. In this sense the collections of old English laws – and the manufacture of codes in the names of
pre-Conquest kings – are the counterparts of the saints' lives discussed in the last
chapter. Just as the hagiographies justified the veneration of their subjects' cults,
the legal collections vindicated the existence of a common English law. Law in
this sense was, with 'descent, manners and language', one of the distinguishing
marks of a nation; and the English had felt themselves to be a nation since the
establishment of the West Saxon supremacy in the tenth century, and perhaps
since the days of Bede.[57] Though they now had a foreign hierarchy and a foreign
ruler, the law which bound rulers and ruled remained a link with the pre-
Conquest past. It was 'English law', however little that owed to pre-Conquest
customs, which was exported to Ireland after 1171, to shape the self-perceptions
of the 'English' conquerors.[58]

The past is particularly the business of historians and it is no accident that

---

[52] Wormald, 'The Oswaldslow "immunity" ', forthcoming.
[53] *Altitonantis*, forged in the 1140s, extended this 'ancient custom' back to the reign of
Edgar (S.731; Barrow, 'How the monks of Worcester perceived their past', pp. 53–74).
[54] D.C. Cox, 'The Vale estates of the Church of Evesham, c.700–1086', *Vale of Evesham
Historical Society Research Papers* 5 (1975), pp. 37–8. Before the Conquest, rights similar
to those enjoyed by the bishop of Worcester over Oswaldslow had belonged to the abbots
of Evesham, Pershore and Westminster (Williams, 'An introduction to the Worcestershire Domesday', pp. 15–18).
[55] Garnett, '*Franci et Angli*', pp. 136–7: 'whilst the fine was entirely new, it was
constructed from English materials. But despite its origins it, too, had to be shown to be
impeccably English'.
[56] See R.C. van Caeneghem, *The birth of the English common law* (Cambridge, 1973);
Green, *The government of England under Henry I*, pp. 99–116.
[57] Susan Reynolds, *Kingdoms and communities in western Europe, 900–1300* (Oxford,
1984), pp. 257, 262–4.
[58] 'The Old English state ... afforded the political basis on which later generations could
build the Common Law' (van Caeneghem, *The birth of the English Common Law*, p. 93);
Robin Frame, ' "Les Engleys nees en Irlande": the English political identity in medieval
Ireland', *TRHS* 6th series 3 (1993), pp. 85–7.

there was a renaissance in historical writing in England after the Conquest. The English and Anglo-Norman historians of the early twelfth century have received lavish praise, not least because their achievements arose almost *ex nihilo*.[59] Though Bede's *Ecclesiastical History* was well-known in pre-Conquest England, no one had been inspired to emulate it. Apart from Asser's *Life of Alfred* and a few saints' lives (often composed by foreigners), historical interests had been focused only on the *Anglo-Saxon Chronicle* in its several versions. It took the trauma of conquest to make their past a matter of burning interest to the English.

The writing of history was a logical development of the effort to preserve local cults and traditions, and many of the twelfth-century historians were also hagiographers, often commissioned by religious houses other than their own. The search for written records of all kinds, whether saints' lives or charters, with which to defend the spiritual and secular wealth of the Church not only stimulated interest in the past but also provided the means to discover it. It is not surprising that the old Benedictine houses should be the chief centres for historical research and historical writing in the early twelfth century.

Outstanding among the Benedictine historians are Eadmer at Canterbury, John of Worcester, Orderic Vitalis and William of Malmesbury. Eadmer was interested in contemporary history and his *Historia Novorum* is the secular counterpart to his *Vita Anselmi*. John of Worcester, using the world chronicle of Marianus Scotus as a foundation, based his *Chronicon ex Chronicis* on the *Anglo-Saxon Chronicle*. Orderic, inspired by the example of Bede, concerned himself with the story of the Norman *natio*, while William of Malmesbury, in his *Gesta Regum* and *Gesta Pontificum*, tackled the whole history of the English, from the beginnings to the present day; he also wrote on contemporary history in the *Historia Novella*. Differences in emphasis and purpose notwithstanding, there is much common ground between these men. Eadmer and John of Worcester were Englishmen, while William of Malmesbury and Orderic were half-French and half-English. Their feelings and opinions are almost the only evidence for contemporary English attitudes to the Norman settlement and the importance of preserving what was good in the English past.

Of the four, Eadmer, the only one to have been born before the Conquest, is the most outspoken.[60] He was born about 1060, probably in Kent. His mother may have been the poor widow to whom Lanfranc gave a pension; his sister's son

---

[59] See R.W. Southern ('Aspects of the European tradition of historical writing, 4: The sense of the Past', TRHS 23 (1973), p. 256): '. . . they created the image of a phase of English history which would scarcely have existed without their efforts: substantially they were responsible for bringing Anglo-Saxon history into existence'; James Campbell ('Some twelfth-century views of the Anglo-Saxon past', *Essays in Anglo-Saxon history*, p. 209): 'the greatest advances in the study and understanding of Anglo-Saxon history made before the nineteenth century were those of the twelfth'. They are discussed as a group by R.R. Darlington, *The Anglo-Norman historians*, Inaugural Lecture, Birkbeck College (London, 1947).
[60] For Eadmer's life and background, see Southern, *St Anselm and his biographer*, pp. 229–40.

Haimo was a monk of Christ Church c.1115 and Henry, another kinsman with a continental name, was living c.1130.[61] Kent had experienced great upheavals during the Conquest and it is likely that Eadmer came from a family of impoverished local gentry, which would explain why he cannot bring himself to speak of the treatment meted out to those English nobles who survived the battles of 1066.[62] This sense of catastrophe is voiced by another Kentish writer, Æthelnoth (Ælnoth) of Canterbury, who laments the fall of Anglorum gens nobilissima, slain or scattered or reduced to public servitude.[63]

Eadmer entered Christ Church as a child oblate; he could remember the old church destroyed in the fire of 1067. The initial response of the Christ Church monks to Lanfranc and his followers had been hostile, though eventually the parties were reconciled, and Eadmer was devoted to Archbishop Anselm, whose vita he composed. Nevertheless Christ Church remained English in sympathy, even experiencing a resurgence of native traditions in the twelfth century.[64] Osbern, an older contemporary of Eadmer, wrote lives of the former archbishops Ælfheah and Dunstan, complaining, as did William of Malmesbury, of the Latinity of earlier writers.[65] Eadmer himself began as a hagiographer, composing vitae of Dunstan and Oda, and the Historia Novorum itself is largely an account of the secular career of Anselm. It opens with a eulogy of the 'golden age' of Edgar and Dunstan, when king and church were at one, and the Benedictines universally admired; from this point Eadmer records a steady decline, not sparing the reign of Edward the Confessor, when the monasteries which had escaped earlier depredations were finally destroyed.[66] Edgar is clearly Eadmer's mirror of kingship, and when he records the marriage of Edith/Matilda to Henry I, it is to Edgar specifically that he traces her pedigree.[67]

Eadmer's English sympathies emerge in many ways. In 1097 at the Council of Bari, he met the archbishop of Benevento, who was wearing a magnificent embroidered cope, 'richer than that of any other of those present in the assembly'. Eadmer remembered the older monks of Christ Church describing how Arch-

61 HN, pp. 13–14; Southern, St Anselm and his biographer, p. 231.
62 HN, p. 9: 'What treatment he (the Conqueror) meted out to those leaders of the English who survived the great slaughter, as it could do no good, I forbear to tell'. See also his story of the accusation of poaching brought against fifty survivors of the Old English nobility (ex antiqua Anglorum ingenuitate) 'who in those days [the reign of William Rufus] seemed still blessed with some traces of wealth' (HN, p. 102).
63 For Æthelnoth (Ælnoth) see Chapter III above.
64 Southern, St Anselm and his biographer, pp. 252–5. Rollason (Saints and relics in Anglo-Saxon England, pp. 230–39) discusses the restoration – and even creation – of English cults in the twelfth century.
65 For Osbern, see Southern, St Anselm and his biographer, pp. 248–53; he died in or soon after 1093. His vita of Dunstan and his collection of the saint's miracles are printed in Mem. St Dunstan, pp. 69–128, 129–61. For his criticism of earlier writers, see Chapter VIII, note 153 below.
66 HN, p. 5; William of Malmesbury is also critical of the Confessor.
67 HN, p. 121. In William of Malmesbury's estimation, too, Edgar was 'the honour and delight of the English' (GR i, p. 164).

bishop Æthelnoth had given such a cope to a previous archbishop of Benevento, from whom Queen Emma bought the arm of St Bartholomew for Christ Church. He determined, by asking the present wearer, that it was the same cope, and told Anselm of his discovery. Eadmer's pride in the fact that the most beautiful garment in the assembly was of English workmanship is evident in the space allocated to this anecdote.[68] His love for his country appears also in his meditation on his guardian angel, when 'far from my native soil and from my compatriots and friends'.[69] Two of Anselm's miracles concern English individuals. In c.1106, a 'noble and rich Englishman' (*Anglus quidam vir nobilis quidem et dives*) was cured of an unspecified illness by eating bread blessed by Anselm. No details are given by which this nobleman can be identified, but the second, posthumous miracle is more specific. It occurred when Eadmer was bishop-elect of St Andrews (1120–1), when Eastrilda, a woman of noble English stock (*matronam de nobili Anglorum prosapia ortam*) was cured by St Anselm's belt.[70] This lady is presumably Estrild of Dunfermline, an Englishwoman resident in Scotland, listed in a thirteenth-century Christ Church obituary list.[71]

Also characteristically English is Eadmer's devotion to the cult of the Virgin.[72] In his treatise on the feast of the Immaculate Conception, written c.1125, Eadmer complains that in its abandonment after the Conquest, 'the simplicity of the poor was despised', though he does not directly criticize Lanfranc or the church hierarchy. In fact the devotees of this obscure feast were about to be vindicated, as its veneration began to spread all over Europe.[73] Nevertheless the cult of the Virgin remained particularly strong in England. Archbishop Anselm's nephew and namesake, Anselm, abbot of Bury (1121–48), made a collection of miracles attributed to the Virgin, as did Dominic, prior of Evesham; both works were used by William of Malmesbury in his collection of her miracles.[74]

---

[68] *HN*, pp. 107–10.

[69] Southern, *St Anselm and his biographer*, p. 297.

[70] *VA*, pp. 138, 163.

[71] The same text records another Englishwoman, Liviga (Leofgifu) holding land in the Dunfermline area. She and Estrild may well have been Kentish in origin, for the church of Holy Trinity, Dunfermline, had been founded by Queen Margaret and staffed with Christ Church monks led by the (presumably English) monk Goldwine (Barrow, *Kingdom of the Scots*, pp. 193–8).

[72] The earliest known representation in the west of Mary crowned as Queen of Heaven is that in the Benedictional of St Æthelwold (R. Deshman, 'Christus rex et magi reges: kingship and Christology in Ottonian and Anglo-Saxon art', *Frühmittelalterliche Studien*, 10 (1976), pp. 397–9).

[73] Southern, *St Anselm and his biographer*, pp. 287–96; compare St Wulfstan's 'anticipation' of Cistercian architectural ideals (see Chapter VI above).

[74] R.W. Southern, 'The English origin of the Miracles of the Virgin', *Medieval and Renaissance Studies* 4 (1958), pp. 176–216; Peter Carter, 'The historical content of William of Malmesbury's Miracles of the Virgin', *The writing of History in the Middle Ages*, ed. Davis and Wallace-Hadrill, pp. 137–8. The first major continental collections were made by Guibert of Nogent and Herman of Laon (Rigg, *A history of Anglo-Latin literature, 1066–1422*, p. 35).

It is natural that Eadmer should have been aggrieved at the lack of advancement for Englishmen in the post-Conquest period. In the 1120s he complains that English nationality alone is enough to debar men, however worthy, from high office in the church, while for foreigners 'the mere appearance of virtue, vouched for by their friends, was sufficient for them to be judged worthy of the highest office'.[75] About the same time, in a savage letter to the monks of Glastonbury, who claimed to have the relics of St Dunstan, he expressed amazement that Englishmen should utter such blatant falsehoods: 'why did you not consult some foreigner – one of those experienced and knowledgeable men from beyond the sea, who could have invented some likely lie on such an important matter, which you could have bought?'.[76] With these passages should be contrasted Eadmer's picture of Wulfstan of Worcester, 'the one sole survivor of the old Fathers of the English people, a man eminent in all the religious life and unrivalled in his knowledge of the ancient customs of England'.[77]

Eadmer owed a particular debt to Worcester and to the monks whom Wulfstan had trained and instructed. When he was composing the life of Dunstan, the Worcester monk Nicholas, like Eadmer an Englishman, sent him material on his hero Edgar; Nicholas was to advise Eadmer again during his stormy tenure of the see of St Andrews in 1120–1.[78] Eadmer is known to have visited Worcester, and he and Nicholas would in any case have met at Canterbury, where Nicholas studied for a while under Lanfranc.[79] It was perhaps at Nicholas' request that Eadmer composed a *vita* of St Oswald of Worcester.

Whether Eadmer was also personally known to John of Worcester is uncertain, but John certainly used the *Historia Novorum*, a text not widely circulated in the twelfth century, as his main authority for the years 1102 to 1121.[80] All that is known of John is that he was an Englishman, who entered the monastery at Worcester as a boy; he was perhaps there by 1088, when Wulfstan orchestrated the defence of the city against the rebellious supporters of Robert Curthose. Since he died in or after 1140, he may have been quite young at Wulfstan's death in

---

[75] HN, p. 224. The passage occurs in the later section of the work, begun in 1119 (Southern, *St Anselm and his biographer*, p. 299).

[76] Mem. St Dunstan, p. 415; Sharpe, 'Eadmer's letter to the monks of Glastonbury concerning St Dunstan's disputed remains', pp. 210–11; Southern, *St Anselm and his biographer*, p. 232.

[77] HN, p. 46.

[78] Nicholas' letter is printed in *Mem. St Dunstan*, pp. 422–4; for his life and career, see Mason, *St Wulfstan of Worcester*, pp. 116–17, 218–24. He was prior of Worcester from 1113/6–1124. Eadmer also acknowledges the assistance of the Worcester monk Ægelredus (Æthelred), one-time subprior and precentor at Christ Church but this is probably Nicholas under his layman's name (Mason, loc.cit., p. 117 and note 36; the name *Edred* which appears c.1104 in the Durham *Liber Vitae* represents OE Eadred, and cannot be, as suggested, an 'abbreviation' for Æthelred. Nor can *Ægelredus* be Archdeacon Æthelric (*Agelric, Alric*), as suggested in *Mem. St Dunstan*, p. 163, note 3).

[79] See Chapter VI above.

[80] For John's life and work, see Martin Brett, 'John of Worcester and his contemporaries', *The writing of history in the middle ages*, ed. Davis and Wallace-Hadrill, pp. 101–26.

1095, yet it was Wulfstan (according to Orderic) who commanded John to undertake his history.[81] Its basis was the universal chronicle of Marianus Scotus, brought to England by Wulfstan's friend, Robert of Hereford. For English history John used the works of Bede and Asser, various saints' lives (including Colman's life of Wulfstan himself) and an *Anglo-Saxon Chronicle*, as well as Eadmer's work.[82]

It was not a format which encouraged the expression of personal opinions, but some hints of John's feelings can be deduced from his treatment of particular events. The treatment of Harold is particularly revealing. John specifically states that Harold was crowned by Archbishop Ealdred after being nominated by King Edward and elected by all the nobles of England, and he praises the king for his reverence to the Church, his devotion to justice and his severity to evil-doers. He makes no mention of Harold's journey to Normandy in 1064, nor to any oath taken by him to Duke William, nor to the judgement of God in the battle of Hastings. Indeed in the *Chronicula*, his own abbreviation of the *Chronicon*, he praises Harold as 'another Maccabeus', and 'a great and true king, had God willed it'.[83] In this he differs greatly from Eadmer and Orderic, who regard Harold as a perjurer, though Orderic praised his courage, good looks and wit.[84] John's views are presumably those of his companions at Worcester, where Harold was regarded as a friend and benefactor.[85]

The historical tradition of Worcester was based on the archives of the church, which included the pre-Conquest cartulary and the charters collected by Hemming in the second cartulary, compiled at the command of Bishop Wulfstan. Clearly there was much other documentation of interest to historians at Worcester, upon which both John and William of Malmesbury appear to have drawn.[86]

---

[81] OV ii, pp. 186–7; Mason, *St Wulfstan of Worcester*, p. 144. The earlier part of John's chronicle, up to the year 1118, was once attributed to the monk Florence, who died in this year and whose assistance John acknowledged.

[82] Brett, 'John of Worcester and his contemporaries', pp. 110–11; Gransden, *Historical writing in England*, p. 145. Subsequent revisions drew on other works, notably Simeon of Durham's *History of the Church of Durham*, the work of the continental historian Hugh of Fleury, and William of Malmesbury's *Gesta Pontificum* (Brett, loc.cit., pp. 117–24).

[83] Brett, 'John of Worcester and his contemporaries', p. 123: this and the accompanying verses on Edward and Wulfstan 'reflect the strong ties with the Saxon past which Worcester retained long after the Conquest'. Judas Maccabeus was a popular hero in the middle ages, 'defender of the Jewish people' in the place of his dead father (*William Thorne's Chronicle of Saint Augustine's Abbey*, translated A.H. Davis (Oxford, 1934), p. 122; I owe this reference to Hirokazu Tsurushima).

[84] HN, pp. 8–9; OV ii, pp. 135–9. Herman of Bury describes Harold coming to the kingdom by cunning and force (*callida vi veniens ad regnum*) and Henry of Huntingdon is noticeably hostile both to Harold and to his family (*Mem. St Edmunds* i, p. 57).

[85] See the *Vita Wulfstani*, p. 13, where Harold 'claimed the kingdom by his noble qualities'. It is not possible to say whether these were the views of Colman or William of Malmesbury, for whom see below.

[86] Brett, 'John of Worcester and his contemporaries', pp. 113–117. This material included the collection of pre-Conquest laws compiled for or by Archbishop Wulfstan

These resources allowed Nicholas to undertake research for Eadmer, and later for William of Malmesbury, both of whom in turn contributed to John's work.[87] John's chronicle was 'constructed out of materials which were the objects of an active traffic between Canterbury, Malmesbury, and Worcester' and this co-operation led to further exchanges, recalling 'at a much higher level of intellectual activity . . . the circulation of draft annals among the various compilers of the Anglo-Saxon chronicle before the Conquest'.[88]

It is no surprise that Worcester should be such a hive of historical activity. For nearly a century after the death of Wulfstan, its bishops were seculars, often royal servants, and relations between them and the community were not always happy.[89] Moreover the effects of the Gregorian reform movement were, by the early twelfth century, altering the balance between the episcopacy and the old Benedictine abbeys. Bishops and their agents, principally the archdeacons, were seeking to impose their authority on their dioceses, and to restrict monastic activity to the walls of their own monasteries. In response the Worcester monks concocted a series of forgeries, culminating in the celebrated 'foundation-charter', *Altitonantis*, fathered on King Edgar, by which they vindicated the existence of their monastic chapter and laid claim to their share of the liberties of Oswaldslow.[90]

Worcester, like Canterbury, looked back to the golden age of Edgar; but Wulfstan himself was an important asset. His *vita* was written soon after his death by his chancellor, Colman; it is typical of the atmosphere at Worcester that he chose to write, not in Latin but in English. Wulfstan's cult, though locally popular, spread only gradually. William of Malmesbury recorded miracles at his tomb in the *Gesta Pontificum*, completed in 1125, and helped to spread knowledge of his cult in learned circles by translating Colman's *vita* into Latin at the request of Prior Warin (1124–1140/2). By 1131 Henry of Huntingdon, who seems to have had no direct connection with Worcester, could style him *sanctus*, but his official canonization had to wait until 1203.[91]

(see note 5 above); it is noteworthy that Cnut's Letter of 1027 to the English people is preserved only by John and by William of Malmesbury (*EHD* i, p. 416).

[87] William is very complimentary to Nicholas, who, in his opinion, should have undertaken the life of his mentor, Wulfstan (Mason, *St Wulfstan of Worcester*, p. 223).

[88] Brett, 'John of Worcester and his contemporaries', pp. 117, 125. The Durham *Historia Regum* depends upon John for the period between 848 and 1118, and copies of John's chronicle were made for Abingdon, Bury, Gloucester and Peterborough (Gransden, *Historical writing in England*, p. 148).

[89] Samson (1096–1112), brother of Archbishop Thomas I of York, was a married man, father of Archbishop Thomas II of York and Richard, bishop of Bayeux; he had been a canon of Bayeux, as had his successor Theulf (1115–23), a royal clerk, whose rule was found oppressive. His successor, Simon (1125–50) had been chancellor to Queen Adeliza, and was well-thought-of by John and by William of Malmesbury (Barlow, *The English church, 1066–1154*, pp. 71–2, 83, 86).

[90] Barrow, 'How the twelfth-century monks of Worcester perceived their past', pp. 54, 73; Brett, 'John of Worcester and his contemporaries', pp. 125–6.

[91] For the development of the cult, see Mason, *St Wulfstan of Worcester*, pp. 254–85.

William of Malmesbury had close connections with Worcester. Born c.1095, of mixed English and Norman parentage, William entered the monastery at Malmesbury at an early age.[92] Since he had received some education and was able to collect books at his own expense, his family were perhaps well-to-do, but he tells us nothing of his kinsmen.[93] Like Orderic Vitalis, who was also of mixed parentage, he was clearly brought up in an English-speaking environment, and could read Old English fluently, for not only did he translate Colman's *vita* of Bishop Wulfstan into Latin, but also consulted pre-Conquest works, including an *Anglo-Saxon Chronicle* and St Æthelwold's English version of the Benedictine rule. Indeed he warns his readers that the life of St Aldhelm by Faritius of Abingdon is inaccurate, because its author was ignorant of the English language.[94]

Like John of Worcester, William's career as an historian began early. About 1115, the monks of Malmesbury provided Queen Matilda II, at her own request, with a written genealogy showing her relationship, through the West Saxon kings, to their most famous son, St Aldhelm. The queen then commissioned a more detailed work on her illustrious ancestors, which was entrusted to the young monk, William.[95] Why he was selected for the task is unknown, but the breadth of his interests and his literary talents, as evidenced in his later work, may already have been manifest.[96] It was probably with Matilda's support that William undertook the extensive travels whose fruits are obvious both in the *Gesta Regum*, part of which was already complete at the queen's death in 1118, and in the *Gesta Pontificum*, finished in 1125.[97] His visits to Worcester brought him into contact with Nicholas and probably with John, and at Canterbury he met Eadmer, for

---

[92] For William's life and work, see R. Thomson, *William of Malmesbury* (Woodbridge, 1987).

[93] GR i, p. 103.

[94] Thomson, *William of Malmesbury*, p. 45; GP, p. 331. William showed great interest in English writers, both those who wrote in the vernacular, and those who used Latin, though the elaborate style popular in the tenth century did not please him; see his strictures on the language of Ealdorman Æthelweard the Chronicler, whose purpose, nevertheless, he approved (GR i, pp. 1, 3).

[95] Thomson, *William of Malmesbury*, pp. 34–5: William, however, did not believe in Aldhelm's kinship with the West Saxon kings. All the Anglo-Norman historians lay stress on Edith/Matilda's descent from what the *Anglo-Saxon Chronicle*, sub anno 1100, calls 'the royal race of the English'. William of Malmesbury records the contrary opinions of those Normans who declared for Robert Curthose, who derided the marriage, calling the royal couple 'Godric and Godgifu' (GR ii, p. 47).

[96] William's connections with the royal family continued after the queen's death. Copies of the completed *Gesta Regum* were sent to her brother, David of Scotland and her daughter, the Empress, and the *Historia Novella* was dedicated to her step-son, Robert of Gloucester.

[97] Thomson, *William of Malmesbury*, pp. 15, 34–5, 72–5. 'The evidence suggests a number of journeys through southern England, concentrating especially on religious houses and cathedrals in the neighbourhood of Malmesbury and the east, plus at least one journey to the far north'.

whose work he had a great regard. He also had a high opinion of Goscelin of Saint-Bertin, who ended his days at St Augustine's, Canterbury, and whom William praised as the best historian since Bede, and second only to Osbern of Canterbury in his musical skill.[98]

William's pride in his English ancestry appears in the preface to the *Gesta Regum*, written 'for love of my country' (*propter patriae caritatem*). It was framed, on the model of Bede, as a 'continuous history of the English' (*continuam Anglorum historiam*), from the *adventus Saxonum* to the reign of Henry I, in which the Norman Conquest appears as an event in English history.[99] William prided himself, however, that his ancestry allowed him to view the English and the Normans with impartiality. He observes of William I that Norman writers 'have praised him to excess, extolling to the utmost his good and his bad actions alike', whereas Englishmen, 'out of national hatred, have laden their conqueror with undeserved reproach'. He, however, born of both strains, will steer a middle course.[100] This even-handedness is shown in his treatment of Harold. He considered that the English claim that Harold was nominated to succeed by the Confessor was advanced 'more through regard [for Harold] than through sound judgement', for why should Edward promote a man of whose power he had always been jealous? He adds, however, that Harold 'would have governed the kingdom with prudence and courage . . . had he undertaken it lawfully', and records the raising of Battle Abbey on the spot where Harold fell *pro patriae caritate*.[101] William makes the Conqueror return the king's corpse, unransomed, to his mother Gytha, for burial at Waltham, which directly contradicts the account in William of Poitiers and the *Carmen*.[102] In his treatment of the Conquest in

---

[98] 'He [Eadmer] described things so lucidly that they seem to take place under our very eyes' (GP, p. 74); for Goscelin, see GR ii, p. 389. Eadmer's *Historia Novorum* was one of William's sources for the *Gesta Regum* (GR i, pp. 1–2).

[99] GR i, p. 2; ii, p. 518; cf. i, p. 103, where he describes how he came to study the history of 'our nation' (*nostra gens*). William's English sympathies have been investigated by David James Friendenthal, 'The Englishness of William of Malmesbury', submitted as a London MA dissertation. I have to thank Mr Friedenthal for allowing me to read this unpublished paper.

[100] GR ii, p. 283: *ego autem, quia utriusque gentis sanguinem traho, dicendi tale temperamentum servabo*.

[101] GR i, p. 280; GP, p. 207; these sentiments are very close to those of John of Worcester. The *Vita Wulfstani* (p. 22), which as we have it is William's re-working of Colman's text, shows the same balance in blaming King Edward for leaving the matter of the succession in doubt, and giving both views of Harold's succession, 'either obtaining the crown by seeking support or seizing it by force' (*vel favore impetrata vel vi extorta corona*).

[102] GR ii, p. 306; for the claims of the canons of Waltham to have Harold's body, see *De Inventione Sanctae Crucis*, chapter 21. William of Poitiers says the duke refused Gytha's offer of its weight in gold for Harold's body, and that 'it was said in mockery to be appropriate to leave him as the keeper of the sea and shore which he had so recently sought to defend in his insanity' (WP, p. 208); the *Carmen* (pp. 38–9) expands this into an actual burial on the sea-cliffs.

general, William steers a middle course. He sees the Norman victory as a merited punishment for the sins of the English, but the fourteenth of October is still 'a fatal day for England, a melancholy havoc of our dear country', and he praises the stand of the English troops 'few in number but brave in the extreme' who laid down their lives for their country.[103] Later he remarks that the English, though defeated at home, were invincible abroad, and seems to regard Tinchebrai, fought forty years later to the day, as a kind of revenge for Hastings.[104]

The West Saxon dynasty, which 'flourished with unconquerable vigour, even to the coming of the Normans' receives lavish praise: 'one more magnificent and lasting Britain never beheld'.[105] William gives some details of the career of Edgar ætheling, the last direct male representative of the West Saxon royal kin. He records the ætheling's pilgrimage to the Holy Land in 1102, and his eventual return to live on his estates, somewhere in England. William regarded the ætheling's return to his homeland as foolish, remarking that 'the love of their country deceives some men to such a degree, that nothing seems pleasant to them unless they can breathe their native air'. This has often been taken to mean that William regarded any English patriotism as itself misguided, but his own expressed opinions (cited above) contradict such an assumption. His criticism of Edgar is linked with the ætheling's refusal of honours more appropriate to his rank and birth, offered both by the Greek and German emperors.[106]

In 1100 the ætheling's niece, Edith, married Henry I and changed her name to Matilda. The birth of their son William raised hopes that 'the prediction of King Edward would be verified in him, and it was said that now it would be expected that the hopes of England, like the tree cut down, would through this youth again blossom and bring forth fruit'. These hopes, however, were dashed with William's death in the wreck of the White Ship.[107] Edward had prophesied that the woes of England should endure until 'a green tree, if cut down in the middle of its trunk, and the part cut off carried the space of three furlongs from the trunk, shall be joined again to its trunk . . . and begin once more to push leaves and bear fruit'.[108] William interpreted this as a reference to the Conquest and used it as an occasion for complaint on the exclusion of Englishmen from high office:

England is become the residence of foreigners and the property of strangers; at the present time there is no Englishman who is either earl,

---

[103] GR ii, p. 304 (*illa fuit dies fatalis Angliae, funestum excidium dulcis patriae*); i, p. 282.
[104] GR ii, pp. 316, 475.
[105] GR i, p. 19.
[106] GR ii, pp. 309–10. Details of Edgar's career after the Conquest are given variously in the *Anglo-Saxon Chronicle*, John of Worcester and Orderic Vitalis, as well as William, but none have a full account; the most favourably disposed is the 'D' version of the chronicle (Hooper, 'Edgar ætheling', p. 197).
[107] GR ii, pp. 495–6.
[108] *Vita Edwardi*, p. 76; 2nd revised edn, pp. 118–19.

bishop or abbot; strangers all, they prey upon the riches and vitals of England.

Osbert de Clare, the Westminster monk who revised the anonymous *vita* of King Edward in 1138, interpreted the prophecy in the same way and complained in almost the same terms.[109] A similar bitterness appears in the grotesque story of the Siamese twins, one of whom had died, which for William symbolised the living England sustaining with her taxes and tributes the moribund Normandy.[110]

William shows a particular feeling for his own region, western Wessex and south-west Mercia. Something of Eadmer's pride in the English origin of the Archbishop of Benevento's cope appears in his account of Stephen Harding, the monk of Sherborne who became one of the leading lights of the Cistercian order: 'it redounds to the glory of England to have produced this distinguished man . . . to us he belonged and in our schools he passed the earlier part of his life'.[111] Equally striking are his descriptions of the English landscape, especially the Vale of Gloucester; a land enriched both by nature and the hand of man, with its apple-orchards and vinyards, better than those of any other region of England, though their wines were less sweet than those of France, and watered by the Severn, which surpassed all other English rivers in its breadth, the violence of its eddying waters and its abundance of fish.[112]

In his description of the Vale, William particularly specifies its outstanding monasteries. These ancient houses were the home of a distinctive culture, whose roots went back before the Conquest into the Old English past, and of which William was one of the most distinguished products.[113] History was one of its characteristic elements and historians from elsewhere were attracted to the region by its wealth of historical material. Eadmer's researches at Worcester have already been discussed; another visitor was Ordericus Vitalis. Unlike William, he tells us in some detail about his family and early life. He was born on 16 February 1075, at Atcham, near Shrewsbury, and baptized by Ordric, priest of St Eata's, whose name he received. Though his father, Odelerius of Orleans, was a Frenchman, Orderic claims that when he was sent to St Evroul as a child of ten, he could not understand French; he describes himself as a foreigner and exile (*advena*) among the monks of that house and regularly calls himself *angligena*.[114]

---

[109] GR ii, pp. 277–8; *Vita Edwardi*, pp. 89–90, 2nd rev. edn, pp. 131–2. It may be significant that Osbert does not say that there are no English abbots in his time. For Ailred of Rievaulx's treatment of the prophecy, see below.
[110] GR i, pp. 259–60.
[111] GR ii, p. 380. Stephen was presumably the name taken by Harding when he went to France, as Orderic added the name Vitalis at St Evroul; he was clearly an Englishman.
[112] GP, pp. 291–2. William was not moved only by his own region, describing Thorney in similar terms though at shorter length (GP, p. 98).
[113] Thomson, *William of Malmesbury*, p. 2; R.W. Hunt, 'English learning in the late twelfth century', *Essays in medieval history*, ed. R.W. Southern, pp. 106–28, especially pp. 110, 114–18.
[114] For Orderic's life, see OV i, pp. 1–6, 24–32, iii, pp. 142–51.

Presumably his mother was English, though he says nothing about her, probably because of the stigma which was becoming attached to married clergy. Odelerius was a chaplain of Roger de Montgomery, earl of Shrewsbury, who gave him the church of St Peter's, Shrewsbury, where Orderic received his early education from the 'noble priest' Siward.[115] Odelerius persuaded Earl Roger to transform St Peter's into a Benedictine abbey, a process which was just begun at the time of the Domesday survey.[116] By this time Orderic was at St Evroul, where he added the continental name Vitalis to his own English name, which the French considered barbarous.

Orderic returned to England only as a visitor. At some time between 1114 and 1123 he met John at Worcester and saw his chronicle in progress. He was presumably collecting material for his projected *Ecclesiastical History*, on which he worked from 1123 to 1141. His inspiration was Bede, whose *Historia Ecclesiastica* he copied out at St Evroul, and his ambition was to produce a history of the Norman *gens*, as Bede had done for the English.[117] Pre-Conquest English history does not figure largely in his work, but naturally the post-Conquest period is an important element in his theme. In his treatment of England and the English, he expresses views similar to those of Eadmer and William of Malmesbury; for instance, he presents the reign of Edgar as a golden age of monasticism.[118] He regards the Conquest as a just judgement on the sins of the English in general and Harold in particular, but deplores many of its effects. His criticism of King William is delivered obliquely, most notably in the language he puts into the mouth of the monk Guitmund, refusing ecclesiastical office in England as 'the spoils of robbery':

I cannot see what right I have to govern a body of men whose strange customs and barbarous speech are unknown to me, whose beloved ancestors and friends you have either put to the sword, driven into bitter exile, or unjustly imprisoned or enslaved. Read the scriptures, and see if there is any law to justify the forcible imposition on a people of God of a shepherd chosen from among their enemies.[119]

Like Eadmer and William, he complains of the lack of honour shown to men of English birth: 'foreigners grew wealthy with the spoils of England, whilst her own

---

[115] OV iii, pp. 6–9 and see also Chapter IV above. It was presumably Siward who taught Orderic to write Old English letter-forms (OV i, pp. 5, 202).
[116] OV iii, pp. 142–51; GDB, fols 252, 252v.
[117] Davis, 'Bede after Bede', p. 116: 'He, it seems, was the one person who understood what Bede was intending . . . because he was concerned . . . with a different people at a similar stage of religious and political development'.
[118] OV ii, pp. 242–5.
[119] OV ii, pp. 272–3; for Orderic's criticism of one who accepted and abused office, see his comments on Turstin of Glastonbury, Chapter VI above. See also the list of complaints attributed to the rebels of 1075 (OV ii, pp. 312–13).

sons were either shamefully slain or driven as exiles to wander hopelessly through foreign kingdoms'.[120]

Orderic also shows some attachment to his own particular birthplace, the north-west midlands. He describes himself as a boy 'from the remoter parts of Mercia', and his partiality for men of Mercian origin has already been remarked. It is natural that he should admire Siward son of Æthelgar, the original patron of his father's church, but he is also concerned to show Earl Edwin and his brother Morcar in a sympathetic light, in marked contrast to the indifference shown by John of Worcester, and the hostility of William of Malmesbury. He excuses Edwin's rebellion in 1068 by claiming that 'envious and greedy' followers of the king had provoked him, and describes him and his brother as 'zealous in the service of God . . . remarkably handsome, nobly connected . . . and well-loved by the people at large'.[121] Treachery is also alleged in 1071, when 'King William, ill-advisedly relying on evil counsellors, brought great harm to his reputation by treacherously surrounding the noble Earl Morcar in the Isle of Ely, and besieging a man who had made peace with him and was neither doing nor expecting any harm'. As Waltheof was to do in 1075, Morcar trusted the king and led his men out of the isle, but William, 'fearing that Morcar might wish to avenge all the wrongs that he and his fellow-countrymen had endured, and might foment further hostile risings in the realm of Albion, flung him into fetters without any open charge'. Orderic places Edwin's death after Morcar's capture, and attributes his rebellion to a wish to free his brother; his epic description of Edwin's final stand, among his men, has already been described.[122] Orderic's mention of the 'wrongs' which Morcar might wish to avenge recalls his strictures on the 'Harrying of the North' which, as we have seen, go far beyond other writers, the Durham *Historia Regum* excepted.[123]

Though each has his own particular viewpoint, Eadmer, John, William and Orderic have much in common, not least a feeling for their English birth and origins, and a vein of bitterness at the fate of their countrymen, past and present. So far as can be seen, they came from similar backgrounds among the lesser families, who followed and served the greater nobles. The opinions and feelings which they express are perhaps those found in that stratum of minor English and Anglo-Norman families which, but for them, is largely voiceless. That more is involved than mere monkish nostalgia for a less fraught past is shown by the appearance of similar views in the works of writers who were not members of the Benedictine order; Henry of Huntingdon, Geoffrey Gaimar and Ailred of Rievaulx.

Henry of Huntingdon, born before 1089, was the son of Nicholas, canon of Lincoln and, like Odelerius of Orleans, a married clerk.[124] Nicholas' nationality

---

120 OV ii, pp. 266–7.
121 OV ii, pp. 216–17.
122 OV ii, pp. 256–9; see Chapter III above.
123 See Chapter II above.
124 For Henry, see Nancy F. Partner, *Serious entertainments: the writing of history in*

is unknown, though he is assumed to have been of continental origin, but the family seems to have been settled in the region of Huntingdonshire or Cambridgeshire. They may have been tenants of Ramsey, for Henry calls Abbot Aldwine (1091–1102; 1105–1112) *dominus meus*, and Henry himself and his descendants certainly held of the abbey.[125] Nicholas received the archdeaconry of Huntingdon from Remigius, bishop of Dorchester, who moved the see to Lincoln, and Henry was brought up in the household of Robert Bloet, bishop of Lincoln. When Nicholas died in 1110, Henry succeeded to his father's office as archdeacon of Huntingdon. Like his father, Henry was a married man, as were his son Adam, his grandson Aristotle and his great-grandson Nicholas; 'a respectable, prosperous, ecclesiastical family that suffered no penalty for its uncanonical succession of generations'.[126] Indeed Henry's masters were in no position to complain of such irregularities. Robert Bloet (1094–1123), in whose household Henry had been raised, was a married man, who promoted his son Simon to be dean of Lincoln. He came from the Norman aristocracy, had risen through royal service to be William II's chancellor, and 'lived in ostentatious splendour' both before and after his elevation to the episcopate.[127] His successor Alexander, though not married himself, came from the most powerful of curial families; he was a nephew of the justiciar, Roger bishop of Salisbury, a married man, whose sons and nephews held both ecclesiastical office and positions of power in the royal administration.[128]

As archdeacon of Huntingdon, Henry belonged to a group of men particularly maligned by laymen and monks alike. Archdeacons were responsible for ecclesiastical discipline within their provinces, and received the same kind of contumely levelled at their lay counterparts, the royal reeves. It says much for Henry's courtesy and tact that he seems to have been on good terms with the local monasteries, and that he always spoke well of monks.[129] His office ensured that he had more knowledge than the regulars about the mutability of fortune, and both his patrons suffered great vicissitudes; the *Historia Anglorum* is full of

twelfth-century England (Chicago and London, 1977), pp. 11–48; Diana Greenway, 'Henry of Huntingdon and the manuscripts of his *Historia Anglorum*', ANS, 9 (1987), pp. 103–126.

[125] Henry held Stewkley, where he built and endowed a church dedicated to St Martin, at farm of the abbey, and his son Adam, who also held land at Gidding and Abbot's Rypton, succeeded to him (Partner, *Serious entertainments*, p. 15; *Cartularium Monasterii de Rameseia*, ed. William Henry Hart, 3 vols, Rolls Series (London, 1884–86), pp. 392, 396).

[126] Partner, *Serious entertainments*, p. 15. Henry archdeacon of Huntingdon witnessed a grant to Sawley Abbey, in company with his son Adam and his nephew Alexander (Edmund King, 'Dispute settlement in Anglo-Norman England', ANS 14 (1992), p. 128).

[127] Barlow, *The English Church*, 1066–1154, pp. 70–1. William of Malmesbury denounced his encroachments on monastic liberties (GP, p. 314).

[128] Barlow, *The English Church*, 1066–1154, p. 86; Green, *The government of England under Henry I*, pp. 185, 263, 273–4.

[129] Partner, *Serious entertainments*, pp. 13–14.

reflections on the emptiness of worldly glory.[130] Yet despite the differences in background, Henry's expressed views have much in common with his Benedictine contemporaries. He agreed with William of Malmesbury that it is disgraceful to know nothing about one's country.[131] For Henry the knowledge of the past is what distinguishes rational from irrational beings; 'brutes, whether they be men or beasts, neither know nor wish to know whence they come, nor their own origin, nor the events and deeds of their own country (*patriae suae casus et gesta*)'.[132] It is possible that Henry was English on his mother's side, though he says nothing about her. His summing-up of William I's reign, when 'all the English were brought to a reluctant submission, so that it was a disgrace to be called an Englishman' recalls the sentiments of Eadmer, William and Orderic.[133] Certainly he could read English, for he used a version of the *Anglo-Saxon Chronicle*, and so admired the poem on the battle of Brunanburh that he translated it, 'so that . . . we may thoroughly learn through the dignity of the language the dignity of the deeds and minds of that people (*gens*)'. His version betrays some unfamiliarity with Old English poetic vocabulary (he renders hæleð, 'men, heroes' as 'health') but he does attempt to reproduce, here and elsewhere, the rhythm, and even the alliteration of pre-Conquest verse.[134] His comments on the vanished Picts, whose 'very language, the gift of God in the origin of their nation, is quite lost' show a consciousness of the vital part played by one's own tongue in the making of nationhood.[135]

Whatever his origins, Henry seems to have regarded England as his *natio*. In his dedication to the *Historia Anglorum*, addressed to Bishop Alexander, Henry promises to write of 'the events of the kingdom and the origins of our *gens*'.[136] Alexander was a nephew of Roger, bishop of Salisbury, a Norman from Avranches, who sent Alexander and his brother Nigel to study at Laon. Alexander has been associated, either as author or as patron, with a collection of Old English legal terms, and it is possible that one or other of his parents was English. Nigel's wife, the mother of his sons, Richard fitzNigel (author of the *Dialogus de Scaccario*) and William 'the Englishman', was an Englishwoman, and Roger's wife, Matilda of Ramsbury, may have also have been of English origin.[137]

---

130 Partner, *Serious entertainments*, pp. 27–40.
131 GP, p. 4.
132 HH, p. 2.
133 HH, p. 208.
134 *Ut pene de verbo in verbum eorum interpretantes eloquium, ex gravitate verborum gravitatem actuum et animorum gentis illius condiscamus* (HH, pp. 159–60; Partner, *Serious entertainments*, p. 21); see the analysis of Henry's technique in Rigg, A *history of Latin literature, 1066–1422*, pp. 37–8 and Chapter VIII, note 150 below.
135 HH, p. 12.
136 *Regni gesta et nostrae gentis origines* (HH, p. 3). Compare the language of the author of *Leges Henrici Primi*, pp. 157–8 above. Alexander was also a patron of Geoffrey of Monmouth, see Chapter VIII below.
137 Green, *The government of England under Henry I*, p. 162; Hudson, 'Administration, family and perceptions of the past in twelfth-century England: Richard fitzNigel and the

To judge by the speech which he places in the mouth of Ralph, bishop of Orkney, before the Battle of the Standard in 1138, Henry regarded English nationality as more than a question of ethnic origin. Ralph began with the words 'Brave nobles of England, Norman by birth' (*proceres Angliae clarissimi Norman-nigenae*) and was greeted with rapturous applause by 'all the English', and in the ensuing struggle, 'the whole people, Normans and English, stood fast round the Standard in one solid body' (*tota namque gens Normannorum et Anglorum in una acie circum Standardo conglobata persistebant immobiliter*).[138] It seems that Henry saw the English *natio* as an amalgam of the English and Norman *gentes*. It was a perception shared by John of Worcester, who refers to 'our men' (*nostri*) in his account of the Battle of the Standard, meaning both English and Normans.[139]

Like William and, to a lesser extent, Orderic, Henry betrays a partiality for his own region of England. In his praise-poem on England's cities he singles out Lincoln for its outstanding inhabitants (*Lincolnia gens infinita decorum*) but it is Huntingdon and the Fenland which he especially favours.[140] He gives the correct etymology of Huntingdon's name ('the hill of the hunters') and describes the town as 'remarkable for the two castles aforementioned, and for its sunny exposure, as well as for its beauty, besides its contiguity to the Fens and the abundance of wildfowl and animals of the chase'.[141] The Fens themselves 'are of wide extent and the prospect is beautiful, for they are watered by numerous flowing streams varied by many lakes, both great and small, and are verdant in woods and islands'.[142]

Just as Henry admires the local scenery of his region, so he is interested in its traditions, and particularly in its Danish past. He knew some stories about Earl Siward, Waltheof's father, which probably come from a popular saga and claims to have heard accounts of the massacre of St Brice's Day from some 'very old persons', who would have been ancient indeed if they were eye-witnesses.[143] Certainly his treatment of the massacre is very different from that of the

Dialogue of the Exchequer', pp. 78–81. Roger of Salisbury's wife, Matilda of Ramsbury, is named only in Orderic Vitalis, in what appears to be an addition to the text (OV vi, pp. 532–5 and 533 note 2); Roger of Ramsbury, a canon of Salisbury and archdeacon of Wiltshire c.1130–60, might be her brother (E.J. Kealey, *Roger of Salisbury* (Berkeley, Los Angeles and London, 1972), pp. 22–3, 186, 272–4). Kealey makes Alexander a son of Roger's brother Humphrey and a woman called Ada, who held land in Winford, Dorset, in 1130 (Kealey, loc. cit., p. 272; PR 31 Hen I, p. 15).

[138] HH, pp. 262, 263, 264. Ailred of Rievaulx gives a similar account but with significant difference of emphasis, see below p. 185.

[139] FlW, 1138; I owe this reference to John Gillingham. For the idea of a *natio* as a group of *gentes*, see Graham Loud, 'The *gens Normannorum*: myth or reality', ANS, 4 (1982), pp. 109–10.

[140] HH, p. 11.

[141] HH, p. 178.

[142] HH, p. 165.

[143] HH, p. 174. For the 'Siward saga' see C.E. Wright, *The cultivation of saga in Anglo-Saxon England* (London, 1939), pp. 127–35; R.M. Wilson, *The lost literature of medieval England*, 2nd ed (London, 1970), pp. 56–7.

Anglo-Saxon Chronicle. Henry describes it as a treacherous slaughter of peaceable folk, and accuses Æthelred II of breach of faith, whereas the Chronicle explains that the king had been told of a plot against him by the resident Danes.[144] The roles which Eadmer and William gave to the West Saxon line and Edgar are bestowed by Henry on the Danish kings and Cnut. Cnut reigned 'with more glory than any of his predecessors'; 'before him was never so great a king of England'. His greatness was fitly coupled with humility, exemplified in the story of Cnut and the waves, interpreted as an expression of the king's submission to the power of God and his contempt for lying flatterers.[145] William of Malmesbury also admired Cnut for his just laws, but it is perhaps significant that the king's stock was particularly high at Bury St Edmunds, where he was regarded as the founder, and at Ramsey, of which Henry was holding land. Indeed the Ramsey Chronicler, writing early in Henry II's reign, echoes Henry's judgement on Cnut, 'inferior to none of his royal predecessors in virtue or strength of arms'. Thus Henry's views on Cnut may be those current in the east midlands generally.[146]

More unusual is his treatment of Cnut's two sons, who do not usually appear as likeable figures. Henry presents Harold I as a legitimate king, chosen by the English 'in order to preserve the kingdom for his brother Harthacnut, who was then in Denmark'. In this he is merely following his source, the *Anglo-Saxon Chronicle,* but he departs from it when he describes Harold as the son of Cnut by Ælfgifu, Ealdorman Ælfhelm's daughter, for all surviving versions of the Chronicle deny this, and John of Worcester repeats the slander that Harold and his brother Swein were children neither of Cnut nor of Ælfgifu.[147] Notable also is Henry's description of Harthacnut as *munificus* (generous) for the Chronicle describes him as grasping, treacherous and tyrannical and declares that 'he did nothing worthy of a king as long as he ruled'. Henry's partiality for Danes was not shared by William of Malmesbury, who thought that habitual drunkenness was their only legacy to the English.[148]

---

144 AS *Chron,* 1002.

145 *HH,* pp. 188–9, 220, and see Greenway, 'Henry of Huntingdon and the manuscripts of his *Historia Anglorum*', p. 103.

146 *GR* i, p 224; *Chron Ramsey,* pp. 125, 155; *Mem. St Edmunds,* i, pp. 46–7, 65, 126 and see *GP,* 154; Hudson, 'Administration, family and perceptions of the past in twelfth-century England: Richard fitzNigel and the Dialogue of the Exchequer', p. 96.

147 *HH,* p. 189. In the 'C' and 'D' versions of the Chronicle Harold 'said that he was the son of Cnut and the other Ælfgifu, though it was not true'; in 'E' 'some men said about Harold that he was the son of King Cnut and of Ælfgifu, the daughter of Ealdorman Ælfhelm, but it seemed incredible to many men'. John says (*FlW* 1035) that Swein was the son of a priest and Harold of a shoemaker, and that both were smuggled as infants into Ælfgifu's chamber, so that she could pretend to have given birth to them; the story, so far as Harold is concerned, is also found in the *Encomium Emmae Reginae* (ed. A. Campbell, Camden Society third series 72 (1949), pp. 39–41).

148 *HH,* pp. 190, 213; AS *Chron,* 'C', 'D', 1040; *GR* i, p. 165. See also Hemming's strictures on the greediness of Sigmund the Dane of Crowle, who coveted the other estate of Crowle, belonging to the monks of Worcester, 'as the men of his race are wont to do' (Hemming's Cartulary i, 265).

The local traditions and stories of eastern England are also to be found in the work of Geoffrey Gaimar. Gaimar was 'probably a secular clerk of Norman origin', but virtually nothing is known of his background and origin.[149] His only surviving work is *Lestorie des Engles*, a French poem on English history, probably written in 1136–37.[150] This in itself is worthy of note, but the genesis of the work is even more significant. It was commissioned by Constance, wife of the Lincolnshire landowner, Ralph fitzGilbert. Her husband had borrowed a copy of Geoffrey of Monmouth's *Historia Regum Britanniae*, and Constance asked Gaimar to translate it into French verse. His version is lost, but *Lestorie des Engles* was originally conceived as the central portion of a trilogy, comprising a history of the Britons, a history of the English, and a history of contemporary events.[151]

Gaimar wrote in French and could, presumably, have written Latin had he chosen; more noteworthy is his knowledge of English. The basis of the *Lestorie* is the *Anglo-Saxon Chronicle*, of which he had two copies (or versions): 'the Winchester history' and 'a certain English Book from Washingborough'.[152] To this he added a wealth of legends and folk-tales, many of which concern the Danes. Gaimar is the first to tell the story of Havelock, later celebrated both in a French lay and an English romance.[153] He also has Henry of Huntingdon's story of Cnut and the waves, and the romantic tale of 'Buern butsecarl', whose wife was seduced by his lord, the king of Northumbria, a version of which occurs in

---

[149] For Gaimar see M. Dominica Legge, *Anglo-Norman literature and its background* (Oxford, 1963), pp. 27–36, 276–8; Gransden, *Historical writing in England*, pp. 209–12; *Lestoire des Engleis by Geffrei Gaimar*, ed. Alexander Bell, Anglo-Norman Texts Society (Oxford, 1960), pp. ix–xi, 14–16.

[150] The standard edition is *L'Estoire des Engleis*, ed. Bell (see previous note); the poem is also printed and translated in *Lestorie des Engles*, which is the text cited here. For the date, see Ian Short, 'Patrons and polyglots: French literature in twelfth-century England', *ANS* 14 (1991), p. 244. Another history of England in French verse, which is now lost, belonged to Reginald of Cornhill, who lent it to King John (*Rotuli Litterarum Clausarum* i, p. 29b (dated 29 April 1205); see also Chapter VIII, note 110 below).

[151] Legge, *Anglo-Norman literature*, pp. 28–9, 277. The third part was never written, since, as Gaimar says, Henry I's reign had been covered in a work commissioned by Queen Adeliza from one David; this is lost, but Gaimar's patron Constance had paid a silver mark for a copy, which she kept and read in her private chamber.

[152] *Lestorie des Engles* i, p. 276, lines 6468–70; Short, 'Patrons and polyglots', pp. 243–4. One of the chronicles may have been 'E' (the Peterborough Chronicle) or a variant of it. Washingborough was an ancient central vill, perhaps a comital manor, see David Roffe, 'Lady Godiva, the Book and Washingborough', forthcoming.

[153] The French lay is printed and translated in *Lestorie des Engles* i, pp. 290–327, ii, pp. 216–46; for the English poem, see *Havelock the Dane*, ed W.W. Skeat and Kenneth Sisam, *EETS*, 1950. The hero is loosely based on Olafr Cuaran Sigtryggson, king of York (941–943; 949–952): 'a central feature of the plot of the romance, namely, the death of Havelock's father while Havelock was still an infant, and the flight of Havelock from Denmark to England, may represent a distorted memory of the flight of the young Olafr from York to Dublin on the death of Sigtrygg in 927' (A.P. Smyth, *Scandinavian York and Dublin* (Dublin, 1979), ii, pp. 108, 122).

the same manuscript from Sawley Abbey which contains the Durham *Historia Regum*.[154]

The most noteworthy of these local stories is that of Hereward. The development of this legend has already been discussed; the remarkable thing about Gaimar's treatment is his presentation of Hereward, a rebel who opposed the ancestors of his patroness and her husband, as a hero fighting oppression. His death, after he had come to terms with the king, is the result of treachery, and his killers are made to reflect that 'if he had not been killed thus, he would have driven them out of the country'.[155] Of great interest too is Gaimar's treatment of the English revolt. In his version, the king sends Archbishop Ealdred to York to demand the submission of the northern nobles, promising confirmation of their lands to those who obeyed and safe conduct to those who were unwilling to do so. When, however, they came to the king, all were imprisoned and their lands given to the French.[156] This bias must reflect what was felt about the Conqueror by those who had suffered from his wrath and it is particularly significant that it is found in a French work associated with a family presumably of Norman descent. It suggests that Constance, 'born in England but French-speaking' was 'motivated by an intellectual curiosity to understand the Insular world in which she lived'.[157] She and those like her were beginning, like Henry of Huntingdon, to look on England as their 'nation', regardless of their origins.

If Gaimar's work represents one half of an Anglo-Norman rapprochement, the other is exemplified in the life and writings of Ailred of Rievaulx. Ailred was born at Hexham about 1110, 'of fine old English stock'. Like Henry of Huntingdon, he came from 'a long line of married priests, learned, respectable, conscientious'.[158] His great-grandfather, Alfred Westou, nicknamed *larwe* (schoolmaster), had been sacristan of Durham, whither he conveyed from Jarrow the relics of Bede. Alfred's wife claimed descent from Hunred, one of those who had borne St Cuthbert's coffin in its journeyings. Their son Eilaf, also surnamed *larwe*, was treasurer of Durham Cathedral until the expulsion of the canons in 1083, when he refused to become a monk. He was compensated with the living of Hexham, which he removed from the jurisdiction of Durham to that of York. Eilaf *larwe*'s son, also called Eilaf, succeeded his father as priest of Hexham and retained his

---

154 Wilson, *The lost literature of medieval England*, pp. 34–5; Peter Hunter Blair, 'Some observations on the 'Historia Regum' attributed to Symeon of Durham', *Celt and Saxon*, ed. Nora K Chadwick (Cambridge 1964), p. 69; *Lestoire des Engles* i, pp. 328–38.
155 *Lestorie des Engles* i, pp. 231–42, lines 5457–5700.
156 *Lestorie des Engles* i, pp. 228–9, lines 5375–5403.
157 Short, 'Patrons and polyglots', p. 244. See also Southern's comment on Gaimar's work ('England's first entry into Europe', *Medieval Humanism*, pp. 154–5): 'Here the Anglo-Saxon past has been appropriated by the new aristocracy'. Constance's origins are unknown; her husband's lands in Hampshire may have been her marriage portion, but whether she was of Norman, Anglo-Norman or English descent is uncertain.
158 *Walter Daniel's Life of Ailred, abbot of Rievaulx*, ed. F.M. Powicke (London, 1963), pp. xxxiii, xxxiv. The first quotation, cited by Powicke (p. xxxiii), is from the *Life of St Waldef* of Jocelyn of Furness.

interest in the church and its endowment even after Archbishop Thomas established Augustinian canons there in 1113. Eilaf II eventually became a monk at Durham, bequeathing to the community his land at Cocken, County Durham.[159]

Ailred probably received his early schooling from the canons of Hexham. He regarded the first prior, Anketil (1113–30) with gratitude as 'an elegant and kind man', and it was Ailred whom the canons invited to preach when, in 1155, the Hexham saints were translated into the new church.[160] He also studied at Durham, but was sent, while still young, to the court of David king of Scots (1124–53) and received, about 1131, a place in the king's household.[161] The effects of this upbringing are clear in Ailred's subsequent writings. He himself was an Englishman, and, more importantly, a Northumbrian, with a deep attachment to the saints of Hexham and to St Cuthbert, lord of the *Haliwerfolc*. Life at David's court emphasized aspects of Northumbrian society with which Ailred must already have been familiar. The whole of the north, Northumbria, Cumbria and southern Scotland, was in the twelfth century a melting-pot, not merely of English and Norman, but also Scandinavians, Norse, Britons and Celts.[162] King David himself exemplifies this process. Born about 1085, he was the youngest son of Malcolm III Canmore and Margaret, whose ancestry went back to the royal West Saxon line.[163] David had been brought up in the court of William II, who established his brother, Edgar, on the Scottish throne. In 1100, his sister married Henry I, and in 1113 or 1114, Henry bestowed on David one of the richest English heiresses, Matilda, widow of Simon de St Liz. She in turn was the daughter of Earl Waltheof and the Conqueror's niece Judith and with her came her father's earldom of Huntingdon, as well as a link with the survivors of the native house of Bamburgh. David also had custody of Waldef (Waltheof),

[159] Offler, *Durham episcopal charters, 1071–1152*, no. 28, pp. 22–3, 121; H.E. Craster, 'Some Anglo-Saxon records of the see of Durham', *Archaeologia Aeliana*, 4th series, 1 (1925), pp. 191–3. Eilaf II gave a life of St Bridgid to Lawrence of Durham, who re-wrote it in more elegant Latin (Rigg, *A history of Anglo-Latin literature, 1066–1422*, p. 54).
[160] Marsha L. Dutton, 'The conversion and vocation of Aelred of Rievaulx', *England in the twelfth century*, ed. Daniel Williams (Woodbridge, 1990), p. 38; the substance of Ailred's sermon is probably the basis of *De Sanctis Ecclesiae Haugustaldensis*, his work on the saints of Hexham (Powicke, *Ailred of Rievaulx*, p. xcii).
[161] His office is described as *oeconomus* or *dapifer* (Powicke, *Ailred of Rievaulx*, p. xl); Professor Barrow has suggested he was a colleague or subordinate of Alfwin macArchill, hereditary *rannaire* ('distributor of food') to David and subsequently to Malcolm IV (*Regesta Regum Scottorum I*, pp. 32–3). Since he entered Rievaulx in 1134, at the age of about 24, he probably did not hold office long.
[162] R.K. Rose, 'Cumbrian society and the Anglo-Norman Church', SCH 18 (1982), pp. 119–135; G.W.S. Barrow, *The Anglo-Norman era in Scottish history* (Oxford, 1980), pp. 5–6; idem, 'Northern English society in the twelfth and thirteenth centuries', *Northern History* 4 (1969), pp. 1–28, especially pp. 5–9.
[163] For David's career, see Barrow, *David I of Scotland, 1124–53: the balance of new and old*. Margaret's consciousness of her descent is shown in her choice of names for her four older sons: Edward, Edmund, Æthelred and Edgar.

the younger of her sons by Simon de St Liz; it was with Waldef and Henry, Matilda's son by David, that Ailred was brought up.

David learnt much from his sojourn with the Norman kings of England, and determined to apply what he had learnt in his own kingdom. He recruited young men, mostly younger sons, to his household and his military entourage. Most were Norman or French, but some were English, especially from the families of Yorkshire and Northumbria.[164] He also built up a network of relationships within northern England itself.[165] He did not, however, attempt to displace the native Celtic and Scottish aristocracy as a class. Scotland in David's time saw the amalgamation of native and foreign families and traditions; he himself was 'a man of two worlds, conscious that the roots of his own kingship lay far back in the past of Scotland, but even more aware that in Norman England and on the continent there was being demonstrated a quite different kind of kingship which he had to imitate if he and his dynasty were to survive'.[166] Ailred admired David greatly, not least because of his descent from the West Saxon kings, and this same sense of the need to adapt and assimilate, while retaining a sense of identity, can be seen in his writings.

Ailred is best known for his contribution to the Cistercian ideal but he also wrote three historical pieces, the tracts on the genealogy of the English kings and the Battle of the Standard, and a vita of Edward the Confessor. The first, the Genealogia regum Anglorum, was written for Henry duke of Normandy in 1153 or 1154, and traces Henry's English ancestors back to Woden. All are praised, even Æthelred II, who appears as strenuissimus rather than unræd. The purpose of the tract, which is 'redolent with pride in Englishness', is to show the young duke 'that his true national identity is as Henry the Englishman, Henry the English king'.[167] The same theme is pursued in the vita of Edward the Confessor, composed in 1162 or 1163 for Laurence, abbot of Westminster, Ailred's kinsman.[168] In this work, a re-writing of the life by Osbert de Clare, Ailred reinterprets the Confessor's prophecy of the Green Tree as foreshadowing Henry's kingship: 'the tree flowered when the Empress Matilda was born . . . it came to fruit when of her was born our Henry, rising like the morning star, the cornerstone of both peoples'. In a direct departure from Osbert de Clare's lament on the lack of advancement for Englishmen (also found in William of Malmesbury's interpretation of the prophecy) Ailred continues: 'now England has a king of English

---

164 Barrow, The Anglo-Norman era in Scottish history, pp. 5–6, 106–7, 112–16; see also the case of Edward son of Siward, Chapter IV above.

165 Judith Green, 'Aristocratic loyalties on the northern frontier of England, c.1100–1174', England in the twelfth century, ed. Williams, pp. 94–5.

166 G.W.S. Barrow, Kingship and unity: Scotland 1000–1306 (Edinburgh, 1981), p. 35.

167 Rosalind Ransford, 'A kind of Noah's Ark: Aelred of Rievaulx and national identity', SCH 18 (1982), pp. 137–46. Wace, on the other hand, a Jerseyman whose career was spent in Caen, stresses Henry's 'Norman' descent from Rollo (Matthew Bennett, 'Poetry as history? The "Roman de Rou" of Wace as a source for the Norman Conquest', ANS 5 (1983), pp. 22–4).

168 For their relationship, see Powicke, Ailred of Rievaulx, xxxvi, pp. xlviii, 41.

race, she has from the same people bishops and abbots, princes, knights and magnates, who, sprung from both seeds, confer honour on the one and give consolation to the other'.[169] Here Ailred expresses the same idea of a *natio* composed of both the Norman and the English *gentes* which we have seen in the work of Henry of Huntingdon and John of Worcester. Whether the Angevin Duke Henry was impressed by Ailred's rhetoric scarcely matters; it is the opinions expressed which are significant.

The *Genealogia* is also concerned with the descent of the Scottish kings from West Saxon royalty. This is probably a reflection of opinions common in the north, where loyalty might be given on either or both sides of the Anglo-Scottish frontier. Such loyalties might be sorely tested when the kings of the English and the Scots fell out, as they did after 1135, when Stephen seized the English crown in despite of the Empress, David's niece. David's response was to invade the north, ostensibly in support of Matilda's cause, but also in pursuit of the reunification of Scotland, Cumbria and Bernician Northumbria which had been the ambition of his forefathers.[170] Matters came to a head in 1138. The English resistance was organized by the aged Thurstan, archbishop of York, who rallied not only the Norman baronage but also the local English levies, led by their parish priests. The loyalties of these disparate elements were engaged by the Standard itself, which consisted of the banners of York's patron, St Peter, St John of Beverley and St Wilfrid of Ripon and a silver pyx containing the consecrated Host, all raised upon a ship's mast. The Standard is a striking example of the power of local cults to foster a sense of common identity among different ethnic groups.

The choice before those northern magnates who had entered into relation-ships of friendship and fealty with David is the theme of Ailred's *Relatio de Standardo*.[171] Robert de Brus, who held lands in Scotland as well as Northumbria and owed fealty both to David and to Stephen, was in a particularly difficult position and Ailred makes him the spokesman for the English army. Robert urges David to call off the battle, reminding him that he owes his position to 'English advice and Norman arms', and that he has more in common with the English and the Normans than with the wilder elements in his own kingdom.[172] In this speech 'English' and 'Norman' are interwoven, recalling the account of Bishop Ralph's exhortation in Henry of Huntingdon.[173] When, however, Walter Espec, founder of Rievaulx, (to whom Ailred gives Bishop Ralph's role) addresses the army, it is *Normannitas* that predominates. Walter exhorts the assembled barons and knights to remember their Norman origins, and the warlike deeds of their

---

[169] All three passages, from William of Malmesbury, Osbert de Clare and Ailred, are printed by Barlow (*Vita Edwardi*, pp. 89–90; 2nd rev. edn, pp. 131–2).
[170] Barrow, *David I of Scotland*, pp. 18–9; Green, 'Aristocratic loyalties', pp. 83–4.
[171] Baker, 'Ailred of Rievaulx and Walter Espec', pp. 91–107. The date of the *Relatio* is uncertain; it is usually assigned to 1155–57, but may be as early as 1141–42.
[172] Ransford, 'A kind of Noah's Ark: Aelred of Rievaulx and national identity', p. 139.
[173] See above, p. 179.

ancestors in Normandy, England, South Italy and the Holy Land.[174] The difference of emphasis between Henry and Ailred should not be pushed too far, but it is interesting that Ailred, of pure English descent, should remind the Normans of their glorious heritage, while Gaimar, presumably a Norman, should relate the legends of the Danelaw and praise the English hero Hereward.

Ailred exhibits a secure sense of English identity coupled with acceptance of the Norman settlers and their culture; 'a sense of community transcending racial diversity, allied to a strong sense of historical continuity'.[175] Acceptance of the new without abandoning the old is characteristic of the Anglo-Norman historians. Eadmer, despite his resentment at the lack of honour shown to his countrymen in their own land, was a devoted follower of Anselm, the Italian from Bec who became archbishop of Canterbury. Orderic, half-English, half-French, was inspired by Bede to write the story of the Norman gens, without loss of his English feelings and his sense of belonging to 'the remoter parts of Mercia'. William of Malmesbury considered his mixed birth a positive blessing, and Henry, whatever his origins, saw England as a natio embracing both the English and the Norman gentes. It has been argued that Bede, in his Historia ecclesiastica gentis Anglorum, created the first image of a unified English people. In the same way, his twelfth-century admirers, by presenting the pre-Conquest past as part of a 'continuous history of England', helped to weld English and Normans into a new English nation.

174 R.H.C. Davis, The Normans and their Myth (London, 1976), pp. 66–7; Baker, 'Ailred of Rievaulx and Walter Espec', pp. 94–5.
175 Baker, 'Ailred of Rievaulx and Walter Espec', p. 97; cf. Powicke, Ailred of Rievaulx, pp. xlii–xliii: 'There was nothing insular or parochial in the attitude of Englishmen like Ailred . . . the more conscious they were of their past, the more confidently could they join in the welcome to new ideas and new enterprises'.

Chapter VIII

LIVING IN THE PRESENT

> Nowadays, when English and Normans live
> close together and marry and give in marriage
> to each other, the nations are so mixed that it
> can scarcely be decided (I mean in the case of
> the free men) who is of English birth and who
> of Norman.
>
> Richard fitzNigel, *Dialogus de Scaccario*

THE INSTALLATION OF a foreign hierarchy meant that the conventions of English society were set by an elite with strong ties to northern France, to which Englishmen who wished to survive and prosper had to conform. Herman of Bury put the matter succinctly: King William 'implanted the customs of the French throughout England and began to change those of the English'.[1] Change is to be expected, but it is all too easy to exaggerate the differences between pre-Conquest England and pre-Conquest Normandy and to forget, in the search for the 'origins' of post-Conquest institutions, the extent to which both nations shared in a common inheritance. This is not to say that the two societies were identical, nor that the differences between them were not important; but the amalgamation of Normans and English in the century after the Conquest drew upon the experience of both peoples, and was made possible by their similarities as much as by the imposition of one set of customs on another. Indeed some post-Conquest expedients were derived neither from pre-Conquest England, nor from pre-Conquest Normandy, but developed in response to the problems of the Norman settlement itself.

Contemporaries are rarely specific about the distinguishing customs of English and Normans, and their testimony is not always unambiguous. Opinions on fashion and taste are notoriously unreliable, since they are coloured by personal preferences. The most obvious changes (borne out by the archaeological record) were architectural; the construction of castles, as opposed to the defensible manor-houses built by the English nobility, and the re-building of all the major English cathedrals and abbeys.[2] William of Malmesbury commented that the

---

[1] *Mem. St Edmunds* i, p. 58. One of the customs changed by the advent of the Normans seems to have been the ethic of war (see Introduction).

[2] For pre-Conquest secular buildings, see Derek Renn, '*Burhgeat* and *gonfanon*', ANS 16 (1994), pp. 177–86; Ann Williams, 'A bell-house and a *burhgeat*: lordly residences in

English 'consumed their whole substance in mean and despicable houses, unlike the Normans and French who live with frugality in noble and splendid mansions.' If the evidence from church furnishings may be applied to lay dwellings, this might in fact be true, for although the churches and cathedrals built after the Conquest were larger and more splendid than anything the English had produced, they were less lavishly provided with wall-paintings, tapestries, gold-embroidered vestments and goldsmith's work.[3] Even in the field of architecture, however, it is necessary to be cautious, for post-Conquest builders in England drew on areas other than Normandy for the elements of their style, including the insular tradition.[4]

In the matter of dress and appearance, the evidence is conflicting. Orderic Vitalis describes the markets of both village and town 'filled with displays of French wares and merchandise', so that the English, 'who had previously seemed contemptible to the French in their native dress, [were] completely transformed by foreign fashions'.[5] This recalls a similar passage in the *Vita* of Margaret of Scotland, who 'caused merchants to come by land and sea from various regions and to bring very many precious wares that were still unknown in Scotland', and compelled the Scots 'to buy clothing of different colours and various ornaments of dress'. The *Vita* is contradicted, however, by the *Anglo-Saxon Chronicle*, which lists the gifts of Malcolm Canmore to Edgar ætheling in 1074, too early, surely for Margaret's influence to have had much effect: they included 'many treasures, consisting of skins covered with purple cloth, and robes of marten's skin and of grey fur and ermine, and costly robes and golden vessels and silver'.[6]

For a contradiction of Orderic's words, we need look no further than his source,

England before the Norman Conquest', *Medieval Knighthood* 4 (1992), pp. 221–40. Some of the modifications (notably in the matter of improved defences) which Normans made to the manorial buildings of their English predecessors are discussed by Morris (*Churches in the landscape*, pp. 258–64), and by Guy Beresford ('Goltho manor, Lincolnshire: the buildings and their surrounding defences', ANS 4 (1982), pp. 13–36). Paul Everson ('What's in a name? Goltho, "Goltho" and Bullington', *Lincolnshire History and Archaeology* 23 (1988), pp. 93–9) argues for a revision of Beresford's dating of the successive levels at Goltho, but without change to the overall picture.

[3] GR ii, p. 305; Dodwell, *Anglo-Saxon art*, pp. 226–32; especially pp. 231–2: 'the interest of the Normans was in spaciousness: that of the Anglo-Saxons was in fine and costly objects'.

[4] Eric Fernie, *The architecture of the Anglo-Saxons* (London, 1982), pp. 163–73. The problem is greatest in local churches built or re-built in the second half of the eleventh and the early twelfth centuries, whose architectural features are neither 'Anglo-Saxon' nor 'Norman' but a combination of both (Richard Gem, 'The English parish church in the eleventh and early twelfth centuries: a great rebuilding?', *Minsters and parish Churches*, ed. Blair, pp. 21–30).

[5] OV ii, pp. 256–7.

[6] *Early sources of Scottish history, AD 500–1286*, ed. Alan Orr Anderson (Edinburgh, 1922, reprinted Stamford, 1990), ii, p. 68; AS Chron, 'D', 1074; Barrow, *The kingdom of the Scots*, pp. 315–16. Marten-skins were being imported into Chester before 1066, and the king's reeve had the first refusal of them (GDB, fol. 262v).

William of Poitiers. Describing the Conqueror's gifts to Saint-Etienne, Caen he observes that

> The women of the English race excel in embroidery and cloth of gold, the men in all kinds of craftsmanship. For this reason the Germans, who are expert in similar arts, are accustomed to dwell among them. The merchants also who voyage to distant lands bring in works of art.[7]

William goes on to describe the Easter feast held at Fécamp in 1067 and tells how, when the French guests (among whom was the French king's father-in-law) 'saw the apparel of the king and his followers woven and worked with gold, they thought anything they had seen before vile'. They were also amazed at the many gold and silver vessels. The robes and vessels in question were English artefacts from the Confessor's treasury.[8] In fact there seems to have been little difference between the normal dress of the English and that worn in northern France.[9]

William also says that both French and Normans 'looked with curiosity at the long-haired sons of the northern world . . . as beautiful as girls', and indeed on the Bayeux Tapestry the English are regularly presented with hair low on the neck, in contrast to the crop-headed Normans and Frenchmen.[10] The *Carmen* turns this into an insult, describing Harold II's entourage as 'champions with combed, anointed hair, effeminate young men'.[11] Excessive combing of the hair could be regarded as a Danish characteristic; it was by such underhand means as combing their hair daily, bathing every Saturday and frequently changing their clothes that the Danes made themselves more attractive than Englishmen to the English ladies of King Æthelred II's time.[12] Indeed long hair might be regarded

[7] *WmP*, pp. 256–9.

[8] *WmP*, pp. 260–3; Dodwell, *Anglo-Saxon art*, p. 175 and note 44 (p. 297); for the equivalent passage in the *Historia Ecclesiastica*, see OV ii, pp. 198–9. Dodwell discusses the work of English embroidresses (loc. cit., pp. 182–7, 227–9) and goldsmiths (loc. cit., pp. 188–215); for some individual needlewomen, see GDB, fols 74v, 149 and Dodwell, *Anglo-Saxon art*, p. 327 (note 100).

[9] D.M. Wilson, *The Bayeux Tapestry* (London, 1985), pp. 219–20; Gale Owen, *Dress in Anglo-Saxon England* (Manchester, 1986), pp. 149–73.

[10] *WmP*, pp. 260–1: Owen, *Dress in Anglo-Saxon England*, pp. 168–9. William of Malmesbury on the contrary says (GR ii, p. 305) that the English cut their hair short. He also says that their arms were 'laden with golden bracelets', a custom which Herman of Bury apparently regarded as Danish; see his description of Osgod Clapa, wearing bracelets on both arms 'in the Danish manner', and with a gilded axe hanging from his shoulder (*Mem. St Edmunds*, i, p. 54).

[11] *Carmen*, pp. 22–3. Wulfstan of Worcester also fulminated against long hair (*Vita Wulfstani*, p. 23).

[12] John of Wallingford's Chronicle, *The church historians of England* (London, 1854), ii, part ii, pp. 558–9. The Chronicle was written after John moved from Wallingford to St Albans in 1246–7; he died in 1258 (R. Vaughan, 'The chronicle of John of Wallingford', *EHR* 73 (1958), pp. 66–77).

as a fashion adopted from the English by the Normans, to judge by Eadmer's strictures on William Rufus' court, whose dandies were accustomed 'to grow their hair long like girls; then, with locks well-combed, glancing about them and winking in ungodly fashion, they would daily walk abroad with delicate steps and mincing gait'.[13] Presumably they were hampered by their shoes, which (according to Orderic Vitalis) had long points like scorpions' tails; the style was originally developed by Fulk le Rechin, count of Anjou, to hide his bunions.[14]

Such anecdotes, though entertaining, tell us little about interaction between newcomers and natives in post-Conquest England, nor do they touch the deeper changes and compromises which both groups were compelled to make. The imposition of a foreign aristocracy involved more than manners, more even than a change of personnel. It produced a different way of reckoning status. In pre-Conquest society, the status of the thegn was defined primarily by his relationship with the king. Earls stood at the pinnacle of the structure, governing their *sciras* as the king's deputies; next in rank were the king's thegns, answerable directly to the king, and the median thegns, subject to the authority of some other lord. The title of earl was retained after 1066 for the topmost rank of society, but the context was utterly different. Post-conquest earls lost much of their administrative power to the sheriffs, who became correspondingly more powerful than their pre-Conquest predecessors. Though the earls still bore 'territorial' titles, now usually confined to a single shire, these titles were indicators of rank, not function, and rapidly became hereditary. Below the rank of earl, the word 'thegn', as we have seen, lost any connotation of high status and thegnage was soon assimilated into tenure by sergeanty.[15] For landowners below the rank of earl, the continental term baron was introduced; as before 1066, those who owed suit to the king were *barones regis*.[16]

Earls and barons held their English lands of the king as fiefs, or (to use the commoner term) as honors; whereas in Normandy, the bulk of their lands were alods (inherited family estates).[17] Of course alodial land owed service, but it belonged to the family, not to the lord. It was this which distinguished alods from *beneficia* or fiefs (*feuda*), lands granted from the lord's estate in return for service.[18]

---

13 HN, p. 48; Dodwell, *Anglo-Saxon art*, pp. 222–3.

14 OV iv, pp. 186–91; for Orderic's and William of Malmesbury's elaboration of Eadmer's complaints, see Barlow, *William Rufus*, pp. 102–8.

15 For the title of earl, see Lewis, 'The early earls of Norman England', pp. 207–23; only in Stephen's reign were the earls active in local administration and the sheriffs correspondingly demoted (R.H.C. Davis, *King Stephen* pp. 32–3, 129–32) For the status of *tainus*, see the discussion of the *taini regis* of 1086, above, Chapter V.

16 For the word *baro* and its ramifications, see D.C. Crouch, *The image of aristocracy in Britain, 1000–1300* (London, 1992), pp. 106–122, and for the equation of *baro* and *tainus*, LHP, chapters 35,1a; 41,1b; 80,9b; 87,5.

17 J.C. Holt, 'Feudal society and the family in early medieval England II: notions of patrimony', TRHS 5th series 33 (1983), p. 210.

18 David Bates, *Normandy before 1066* (London, 1982), p. 124. The word *beneficium* is replaced by the word *feudum* (fief) in the second half of the eleventh century.

The distinction between alod and *beneficium* has some similarities with that between bookland and *lænland* in England. Bookland, like patrimonial land, was heritable; indeed by the eleventh century any distinction between the two had probably disappeared.[19] Nevertheless bookland owed service, specifically military service. The lord who held bookland discharged his obligation not merely by personal service, but by providing a contingent of armed men in proportion to the hidage of his estates.[20] The household retinue probably accounted for part of the required contingent, but the lord could endow some of his men with *lænland*, held for a fixed term in return for service.

There is an obvious resemblance between *lænland* and the continental *beneficium*, though it is the differences between the two which have exercised modern writers. Both types of tenure owed services, but those due from *lænland* have been characterized as 'miscellaneous', with military service at most incidental; whereas the *beneficium* owes specific, clearly-defined military service.[21] When eleventh-century *læns* are compared with contemporary *beneficia*, the distinction is not quite so evident. The obligations of *beneficia* are rarely defined, and it is clear that some were held for non-military services. At the time of the Conquest it seems that neither the word *beneficium*, nor its successor the *feudum* (fief) 'had acquired any meaning more specialized than that of an estate held in order to provide some form of service'.[22] On the other hand, the military obligations owed by holders of *lænland* have been underplayed. It has been argued that military service was a public obligation on all land, not an obligation owed by the tenant of *lænland* to his lord; but the evidence suggests that the lord was responsible for the tenants' service and could levy fines on defaulters and, in extreme circumstances, confiscate their lands.[23] This may still fall short of military service owed

[19] Reynolds, 'Bookland, folkland and fiefs', pp. 219–20; see also Roffe, 'From thegnage to barony', *ANS* 12, p. 166.
[20] Landowners were also responsible for the military service of other fyrd-worthy landholders whose soke belonged to them, see Richard P. Abels, *Lordship and military obligation in Anglo-Saxon England* (Berkeley, Los Angeles and London, 1988), pp. 116–31; Reynolds, 'Bookland, folkland and fiefs', pp. 220–1.
[21] Stenton, *First century of English feudalism*, pp. 122–30. See, however, J.C. Holt, 'Feudal society and the family in early medieval England: I The revolution of 1066', *TRHS* 5th series 82 (1982), pp. 202–3.
[22] Bates, *Normandy before 1066*, pp. 122–3; Reynolds 'Bookland, folkland and fiefs', p. 223. Among the examples cited by Professor Bates is an *eques* in charge of a piece of pasture (*equitem cum sua terra qui eadam pratam custodit*), who might be compared with the retainers (*cnihtas*) associated with the park and stud at Ongar, whom Stenton interpreted as 'a group of hunt servants quartered by their master's park' and used to demonstrate the non-military service of English *cnihtas* (Stenton, *First century of English feudalism*, p. 135).
[23] The man who deserts his lord and his comrades in battle 'is to forfeit all that he owns and his own life; and the lord is to succeed to the possessions and to the land which he previously gave him'; conversely if a man falls before his lord, the heriot is remitted and the lord is to supervise the just division of his property between his heirs (II Cnut, 77; 77.i; 78); for the lord's right to levy fines, see GDB, fol. 172. These and other indications

to the lord rather than the king, but the distinction was probably not noticeable in practice.[24]

This is not to say to that ideas about land-holding and the services due from it were identical in pre-Conquest England and pre-Conquest Normandy; merely that they were sufficiently similar to be familiar to men from both regions.[25] Domesday Book can speak of the lands of a pre-Conquest landholder as his *feudum*, meaning, presumably, that he had owed service from his estates.[26] In other contexts, *feudum* is apparently used of *lænland*, and in the shires of Circuit I (the south-east) the words *alodium* and *alodiarius* are used, again in a pre-Conquest context, for lands owing service to a lord but owned by the family.[27] No doubt such usages cover many differences of detail but the fact that they are used implies some perceived similarities.

Just as William I was heir to Edward the Confessor, and through him to all the rights pertaining to the Old English kingship, so his followers held their land in England with all the rights, and with all the obligations, of the king's thegns. Whether their fiefs came from one or more English *antecessores*, or were newly-created by grants which disrupted earlier patterns of lordship, the terms on which they were held go back to the pre-Conquest period. The post-Conquest barons enjoyed the same rights over their estates as those which their predecessors, the king's thegns, had exercised over their booklands.[28]

Bookland had always owed military service; but after 1066 the rate at which it was discharged was established for each fief or honor at a fixed quota of knights, which eventually came to be expressed in units of tenure as knight's fees.[29] These

of military service owed by holders of *lænland* to their lords are discussed in Abels, *Lordship and military obligation in Anglo-Saxon England*, pp. 116–131; 149–59.

[24] Beorhtric son of Ælfgar, who held land at Bushley, Worcs, of the bishop of Worcester, 'rendered to the bishop's soke whatever he owed for the king's service' (*GDB*, fol. 173); for this and other indications of 'the blurring of the distinction between obligations of different origins', see Dyer, *Lords and peasants in a changing society*, pp. 42–4.

[25] I have left it to others to decide whether either society was, or was not 'feudal'. The debate on this topic is in danger of becoming a 'battle over words' (F.W. Maitland, *Domesday Book and beyond* (Cambridge, 1897), p. 295); for some of its ramifications, see John Gillingham, 'The introduction of knight service into England', *ANS* 4 (1982), pp. 43–64 and for a general discussion of 'feudalism', Elizabeth A.R. Brown, 'The tyranny of a construct: feudalism and historians of medieval Europe', *AmHR* 79 (1974), pp. 1063–88).

[26] The holding of Geoffrey de Mandeville's *antecessor*, Esger the staller, is described both as his honor and as his fief (*LDB*, fols 411, 412v).

[27] Blaecmann held Chilton, Berks, *in alodium* and Leverton *in feudo*; both estates were claimed by the abbey of Abingdon, but Chilton had belonged to Blaecmann (he 'could go where he would') and owed *consuetudines* to the abbey, whereas Leverton was presumably the abbey's land, held on a lease or by some form of service (*GDB*, fol. 59v; *Chron Abingdon* i, p. 484; see Maitland, *Domesday Book and beyond*, pp. 153–55 and Chapter IV above).

[28] Roffe, 'From thegnage to barony', pp. 157–76, especially pp. 165–75; Reynolds, 'Bookland, folkland and fiefs', pp. 226–7.

[29] J.C. Holt, 'The introduction of knight-service in England', *ANS* 6 (1984), pp. 105–6;

quotas were unrelated to the size of the honor, in contrast to the pre-Conquest custom of assessing military service in relation to hidage.[30] It might be thought that the system originated in Normandy and was introduced into England by the Conqueror, but it seems that 'there was no defined general service of quotas of knights before the Conquest in Normandy'.[31] Quotas had been imposed on the oldest Norman churches, those founded before 1035; these may originate in Carolingian demands for military service, like the quotas owed to the German emperor from the East Frankish churches in the tenth century.[32] The general quotas of post-Conquest England, however, look like a response to the military and political problems of the Norman settlement. The uncertainties of William's early rule necessitated the maintenance of constant armed vigilance, which both the king and his barons understood; hence the willingness of the latter to accept the high levels of service imposed upon their lands.[33] It seems more than likely that systematic quotas originated in post-Conquest England, and were thence introduced to Normandy.[34]

It was the imposition of quotas upon the post-Conquest honors which led to new forms of tenure and service. The king's barons could, of course, fulfil their quotas by maintaining armed men in their households but it was more conven-ient to enfeoff their vassals with land and pass on some part of the quota as a condition of tenure. It is at this level of enfeoffment that the 'tenurial revolution' of the Conquest took place. The rights of the tenant-in-chief vis-à-vis the king were shared by his own vassals in their relations with him, so that they were possessed of 'all the essential rights to which the king's thegn was entitled'.[35] Before the Conquest only the king could issue landbooks and bookland had been held only by the church and the king's thegns, so that this extension of bookright created a new level of society. Like their lords, the *barones regis*, the mesne-

Hirokazu Tsurushima, 'Feodum in Kent, c.1066–1215', forthcoming (I am very grateful to Mr Tsurushima for allowing me to read this paper before publication).

[30] 'Military service began to be levied by units of tenure – that is, by lordships, through their lords – rather than by shires through their sheriffs' (Reynolds, *Kingdoms and communities in western Europe, 900–1300*, p. 227). The researches of Dr Abels (see notes 20 and 23 above) suggest that matters were moving in this direction even before 1066.

[31] Chibnall, *Anglo-Norman England*, p. 28; see also idem, 'Military service in Normandy before 1066', ANS 5 (1983), pp. 65–77; Bates, *Normandy before 1066*, pp. 122–7; Reynolds, 'Bookland, folkland and fiefs', pp. 258–9.

[32] D.J.A. Matthew, *The Norman Conquest* (London, 1966), pp. 60–65; the East Frankish quotas are recorded in the *Indiculus loricatorum* of 980/981 (Gillingham, 'The introduc-tion of knight-service into England', p. 63).

[33] Holt, 'The introduction of knight-service in England', pp. 89–106, esp. pp. 105–6; Reynolds, 'Bookland, folkland and fiefs', p. 225. In some cases the quotas may have led to a reduction of military obligations, see the quota of the bishopric of Worcester, at note 38 below.

[34] Reynolds, 'Bookland, folkland and fiefs', pp. 224–7.

[35] Roffe, 'From thegnage to barony', pp. 175–6. Henry I's coronation charter specifies that the rights he confirms to his barons are to be extended by them to their own men.

tenants expected to inherit their estates.[36] The effects can be seen on the ecclesiastical honors. Try as they might to insist that land was granted only temporarily, for the term of the grantee's life, the ecclesiastical lords were unable to prevent the establishment of hereditary fees.[37]

One of the best-documented ecclesiastical estates is that of the bishop of Worcester. Here what is striking is not the quota demanded, nor the enfeoffment of tenants to supply it, nor the kind of service required from the bishop's tenants. The bishop's service may in fact have been reduced, for his quota of 50 (or 60) knights was laid on the whole estate of some 580 hides, whereas before 1066 he owed a shipfull (usually estimated at 60 warriors) from the 300 hides of Oswaldslow alone. The land which he used to provide for the quota was by and large the church's *lænland*, and the terms on which it was granted remained the same.[38] Even the concentration of *lænland* in the hands of a few men, notably Urse d'Abetot, sheriff of Worcester, and his brother Robert Despenser, can be paralled before 1066.[39] What is new is the expectation of the post-Conquest tenants. Even before the Conquest, even for the bishop of Worcester, it had often proved difficult to recover the church's *lænland* at the end of the term.[40] After the Conquest it proved impossible. The heirs of Urse d'Abetot, the Beauchamps, still held of the bishopric and admitted service (though less than that required). To describe them as 'tenants', however, is a distortion of the facts. Hereditary sheriffs of Worcester, castellans of Worcester Castle, the Beauchamps were the bishop's rivals, not his men.[41]

The social and political impact of the honorial landholders, who formed the most numerous group within the Anglo-Norman aristocracy, was probably even greater than that of their often absent lords.[42] With the honor came the honorial court, perhaps the most significant innovation in post-Conquest England.[43] Before 1066 rights of sake and soke had included jurisdiction but it is debateable

---

[36] The problems of inheritance before and after 1066 are discussed in J.C. Holt, 'Feudal society and the family in England: II notions of patrimony', TRHS 5th series 33 (1983), pp. 193–219. The present state of opinion seems to be that although the notion of a legal right of inheritance may not have existed until the late twelfth or early thirteenth centuries, inheritance was already established *de facto* in pre-Conquest Normandy.

[37] Hudson, 'Life-grants of land and the development of inheritance in Anglo-Norman England', pp. 67–80; see also Chapter VI, p. 141 and note 79 above.

[38] Dyer, *Lords and peasants in a changing society*, p. 45; for the services, see GDB, fol. 172v.

[39] See, for instance, the lands granted before 1066 to Æthelric, brother of Bishop Brihtheah, and his family, discussed in Williams, 'An introduction to the Worcestershire Domesday', pp. 24–26.

[40] Ann Williams, 'The spoliation of Worcester in the eleventh century', forthcoming.

[41] For the Beauchamps, see Emma Mason, *The Beauchamp Cartulary Charters, 1100–1268*, Pipe Roll Society (London, 1980), pp. xviii–xxv, xlviii–lii.

[42] 'The king and the earls set the fashion for feudal society at large; but it can be argued that in the long run it was the honorial barons rather than these who were the main shapers of feudal custom' (Barlow, *William Rufus*, pp. 174–5).

[43] Stenton, *First century of English feudalism*, pp. 44–50; Chibnall, *Anglo-Norman England*, pp. 167–74.

whether this implied the right to hold a court independent of the shire and hundred, as opposed to merely taking the profits of justice. In Normandy, however, lords regularly held courts for the settlement of disputes among their vassals, and expected to do so in England. Though the honorial courts had political and ceremonial aspects, the dispensing of justice was their most important function, and some of the writs of the Norman kings are concerned with defining their jurisdiction vis-à-vis that of the shire and hundred. As a forum for negotiation and settlement of disputes, they played a major part in the development of legal custom until their role was appropriated by the royal justices in the time of Henry II.[44]

The military tenants were a heterogeneous group. Within most honors, the bulk of the service was devolved onto a group of men, each responsible for several knights, leaving the remainder apportioned among men owing only the service of a single knight, or a fraction of a knight's service. Some of the men who owed several knights' service might be wealthier than some who were *barones regis*, nor was it unusual to hold land both of the king in chief and of some other lord as well. Stenton coined the term 'honorial baronage' to describe the greater mesne-tenants.[45] The *Leges Henrici Primi* speak of 'the barons of the king or of other lords' who could acquit, in the shire court, all their lands held in demesne in that county.[46] Between 1124 and 1136, Richard de Clare made a grant to Stoke-by-Clare Priory at the petition of his barons, knights and free men (*liberi homines*); elsewhere he specifies barons and 'men' without distinction, 'as if the fundamental division is between "barons" and "the rest" '.[47] It seems clear that there was some awareness that gradations of wealth implied gradations in rank. Nevertheless the term 'honorial baron', useful though it may be as a rule of thumb, does not correspond to any contemporary distinction, and should be used with caution.[48]

The lesser tenants of the honor, holding a single fee or less, still held by knight-service, as did the greater 'barons'. In the eleventh century the term *miles* did not in itself imply any social distinction and could be applied to men of greatly varying status.[49] William of Poitiers characterised Duke William's followers as

---

[44] Records of the proceedings in honorial courts are rare; most survivors are *conventiones* (agreements) brought about by mediation, often cast as chirographs, a form widely-used in pre-Conquest England and again from the later twelfth century but rare in the Anglo-Norman period (King, 'Dispute settlement in Anglo-Norman England', pp. 115–30 and see note 135 below; Crouch, *The Beaumont Twins*, pp. 155–62).

[45] Stenton, *First century of English feudalism*, pp. 50; 96–9.

[46] LHP, chapter 7,7.

[47] Richard Mortimer, 'Land and service: the tenants of the honour of Clare', ANS 8 (1986), p. 180.

[48] Crouch, *The image of aristocracy in Britain, 1000–1300*, pp. 106–22, especially pp. 111–12; despite his reservations, Professor Crouch used the concept of the honorial baron in discussing the greater tenants of Breteuil and Leicester in *The Beaumont Twins*, pp. 101–38.

[49] Stenton, *First century of English feudalism*, pp. 142–5.

milites mediae nobilitatis atque gregarii; both knights of middling rank and ordinary soldiers.[50] In the generation of the Conquest, the English did not hesitate to identify the mounted followers of the incomers as *cnihtas* (retainers) and it may be significant that the name stuck, in contrast to the rest of Europe, where a knight is distinctively a horseman (*chevalier*, *ritter*).[51] The range of duties performed by the English *cnihtas* and the household retainers of the Normans was probably not dissimilar.[52] The ranks of the *milites* recorded in Domesday Book probably encompass 'men whom most historians would not label as knights', including infantrymen, who formed a large (and important) part of Duke William's army at Hastings.[53] Some of them were English. Examples include five English *milites* at Chesterton, Warks (the land was held of the Englishman, Thorkell of Arden), a *miles anglicus* at Pirton, Herts, and an Englishman (*anglicus*) at Isleworth, Middx, described as a *miles probatus*.[54] Of course at this date *anglicus* could describe a Frenchman settled in England before 1066; the *anglicus* at Potterne, Wilts., who had become a *miles* by the king's command was the nephew of the Lotharingian Herman, bishop of Sherborne (1058–78). Little Domesday, however, specifically says that there were Englishmen as well as Frenchmen among the 34 *milites* quartered in Bury St Edmunds.[55]

On the other side of the equation, there were Frenchmen among the free tenants. The *francigenae* of Domesday Book have been seen as sergeants, holding by some specialized service, like the seven *francigenae* at Castle Bytham, Lincs., who had two ploughs and three ironworks (*fabricas ferri*) rendering 40s 8d.[56] As with *miles* the word *francigena* need have no precise meaning, and may signify no

---

50 WmP, pp. 232–3; Stenton, *First century of English feudalism*, p. 143.
51 See AS Chron, 1083, 1086, 1088, 1090, 1094. Only twice does the Chronicle use the word *ridere*; in 1086 William *dubbade his sunu Henric to ridere* and in 1090 William Rufus garrisons his castles in Normandy with *rideras*; in the last case the word seems to be equivalent to the *cnihtas* whom William placed in the castles of St Valery and Aumale.
52 Peter Coss, *The knight in medieval England, 1000–1400* (Stroud, Gloucs, 1993), pp. 12–13.
53 Donald Fleming, 'Landholding by *milites* in Domesday Book', ANS (13) 1991, pp. 93–8; for the infantry at Hastings, see WmP, pp. 184–5.
54 GDB, fols 130, 138, 241v (Abels, *Lordship and military obligation in Anglo-Saxon England*, pp. 135, 144).
55 GDB, fol. 66, Stenton, *First century of English feudalism*, p. 147 (for this use of *anglici*, see Chapter 1 above); LDB, fol. 372 (*modo xxxiiii milites inter franci et angli et sub eis xxii bordarii*) and compare the 25 houses in Westminster belonging to the abbot's *milites* and other men, which rendered 8s. per annum (GDB, fol. 128). See note 85 below.
56 GDB, fol. 360v; Stenton (*First century of English feudalism*, p. 144) saw *francigena* as 'a vague word, which will cover sergeants and household officers as well as knights and their squires'; Crouch (*The image of aristocracy in Britain, 1000–1300*, pp. 171–3) suggests it was equivalent to the Norman *vavassor*, 'a lesser free landowner'. In Suffolk, the lands of a group of minor free men, most with English names, are entered under the heading *Terra Vavasorum*; they are followed by another group, with the sub-heading *isti sunt liberi homines de Sudfulc qui remanent in manu regis* (LDB, fols 446–447v). The word vavassor appears only twice in Domesday: a vavassor with 2 cows dwelt at Adgestone, Isle of Wight, and two vavassors at Caldecote, Bucks, paid 32s6d (GDB, fols 53, 146v).

more than 'Frenchman'.[57] In Circuit V, however, where *francigenae* are system-
atically recorded, they seem to be equivalent to the free tenants (radmen,
radcnihts, *homines* and *liberi homines*) who also abound in Domesday's account
of the West Midlands.[58] Their successors are probably to be found among the
liberi homines of Richard de Clare's charter. The same association of knights and
free men occurs a little earlier, when Drew de Hastings gave his land at
Luddington, Hunts., to Ramsey Abbey before a group of witnesses *de curia eius*,
specified as his wife Mahalda, his son Helias and 'many of his knights and men'
(*multis militibus eius et hominibus*); it appears again in the knights and *francolani*
of Nassaburgh, who were concerned in the disafforestation of the soke of
Peterborough in 1215, and the *homines francos*, defined as knights, clerks and
frankelengi, who gave testimony in a Warwickshire agreement of 1150.[59] By the
twelfth century *francolanus* (franklin) meant 'a free man', and the group must
have included those free peasants recorded in the estate surveys of the twelfth
century, like the *liberi feudati* on the manors of Ramsey Abbey.[60]

   The rising status of knighthood sharpened the distinction between knightly
and free tenure, without entirely eroding it. Before the Conquest the line
between the lesser thegns and the upper ranks of the peasants had been a narrow
one, despite differences in legal status, because of the similarities in service owed
by both. In much the same way, the free tenants of the twelfth century, holding
their lands on the same terms as their pre-Conquest counterparts, were economi-
cally comparable to the lesser knight-tenants.[61] Nor does the social distinction
seem to have been impervious. It is not uncommon in the twelfth century to find
men and families holding land both by knight-service and in socage (or, in Kent,

---

[57] At Bottesford, Leics, six small tenements were held by individuals with continental
names and a seventh by four *francigenae* (GDB, fol. 234).
[58] Williams, 'An introduction to the Worcestershire Domesday', pp. 6–7; idem, 'An
introduction to the Gloucestershire Domesday', p. 5.
[59] *Cartularium Monasterii de Rameseia* i, p. 131 (dated 1114 x 19); King, *Peterborough
Abbey, 1086–1310*, pp. 36, 72–4, 172–9; van Caeneghem i, no. 326b, p. 283. Of the five
men named in the last case, four have English names.
[60] J.A. Raftis, *The estates of Ramsey Abbey* (Toronto, 1977), pp. 47–51; for the Shaftesbury equivalents, see Williams, 'The knights of Shaftesbury Abbey', pp. 230–2. Professor
Raftis suggests that the Ramsey *liberi feudati* may be the successors of the abbey's
pre-Conquest thegnly tenants (see also next note).
[61] R.H. Hilton, 'Freedom and villeinage in England', *P&P* 31 (1965), pp. 174–80, esp
p.179; du Boulay, *The lordship of Canterbury*, p. 93. Professor Hilton suggested that some
of the free tenants were successors of pre-Conquest thegns, and it may be significant that
traces of thegnly heriots can still be found in the thirteenth century: a sokeman of Ely
owed his riding-horse and harness, if he had it, and his heir was quit of relief *propter
predictum herietum*; in Kent, the heir of Walter of Bensham, whose free tenement owed
one-twentieth of a knight's fee, was quit of relief by rendering his father's riding-horse
and harness and his sword and arms, if he had any (Miller, *The abbey and bishopric of Ely*,
p. 116; du Boulay, *The lordship of Canterbury*, pp. 80, 339; compare II Cnut, 71,2).

gavelkind), nor is it rare for knightly tenures to be converted to free tenures and vice versa.[62]

It is at this level of society that the intermixture between English and Norman becomes most evident. When the household knights of the eleventh century were enfeoffed with land, a rapprochement between them and the lesser thegns and free men, the most likely group of English landholders to survive the settlement, is only to be expected. The 'marrying and giving in marriage' remarked by Richard fitzNigel must have begun as soon as the first recipients settled into their fees. Little Domesday preserves the story of a man in the following of Wihenoc, a Breton in the service of Ralph Guader, who fell in love with a woman at South Pickenham, Norfolk, and married her, thereby acquiring her land.[63] Soon after the time of Domesday, William Pecche, a minor tenant in Essex, Norfolk, Suffolk and Cambridgeshire, took an Englishwoman called Ælfwynn as his first wife.[64] On the other side of the country, Bishop Wulfstan of Worcester gave the daughter of his thegn, Sigref of Croome, in marriage to one of his *milites*, who was to care for Sigref's widow and perform the service for the land. A similar stipulation was made by Abbot Reginald of Ramsey (1114–33), when he gave land at Brancaster, Norfolk, to Baldwin and Leofwynn, who had been the wife of Cnut; they were to hold Cnut's land for the same service which Cnut had performed, on condition that it should pass with Cnut's daughter, on her marriage, in such a way that the abbot heard no complaint about it.[65] As time passes, English knights, or at least knights of English descent become commonplace. Adam of Cockfield, a particularly well-documented example, was a tenant of Bury St Edmunds; in the time of Abbot Anselm (1121–48), he was permitted to hold in heredity and by the service of one knight the lands of his father *Lemmer* (OE Leofmaer) and his grandfather, Wulfric of Groton.[66] It should be noticed that Adam's English origins are known only because his father is named; by this

[62] Chibnall, *Anglo-Norman England*, pp. 186–7; King, *Peterborough Abbey, 1086–1310*, pp. 35–6. For 'the easy compatibility of holding by knight service with holding by the tenure of gavelkind' (OE *gafol*, rent) in Kent, see du Boulay, *The lordship of Canterbury*, pp. 67–72.
[63] *LDB*, fol. 232: *unus homo Wihenoc amavit quandam feminam in illa terra et duxit eam et postea tenuit ille istam terram*. His successors continued to hold the land.
[64] In 1086 William held small amounts of land from Aubrey de Vere, Roger Bigod, and (most importantly) Richard fitzGilbert (*LDB*, fols 39, 77, 105v, 175, 390, 395v). In 1088, he and his wife Ælfwynn received a life-grant at Over, Cambs, from Ramsey Abbey (*Cartularium Monasterii de Rameseia*, i, pp. 123–7; Hudson, 'Life-grants of land the development of inheritance in Anglo-Norman England', pp. 67–70). William's heir, Hamo Pecche, was the son of his second wife.
[65] *GDB*, fol. 173; *Cartularium Monasterii de Rameseia* i, pp. 129–30.
[66] Douglas, *Feudal documents*, p. 121; *EHD* ii, p. 925. Subsequent Cockfields were involved in a long but apparently amicable dispute with Bury over the service and heritability of their lands (Greenway and Sayers, *Jocelin of Brakelond, Chronicle of the Abbey of Bury St Edmunds*, pp. 122–3, discussed by Holt, 'Feudal society and the family: II notions of patrimony', pp. 193–8).

time 'continental' names were replacing English ones, and many knight-tenants of English descent are probably hidden from our view.

Marriage between the incoming Normans and native English families was probably more common than the surviving sources permit us to see. At the lower levels of society, marriages are unlikely to be recorded at all; especially clerical marriages, which were regarded with disfavour by the hierarchy. We know of the marriage of Odelerius of Orleans only because his son Orderic was a gifted historian, who recorded the names of his father and brothers, though not – the omission is significant – that of his English mother. Henry of Huntingdon, a secular as opposed to a monk, is one of the few writers to refer to the wives (*uxores*) of clerics; most describe them as concubines or use some euphemism.[67] Mahald, wife of Ralph son of Algot, canon of St Pauls, appears as *socia eius* in the *Liber Vitae* of Durham.[68] These marriages should not be forgotten; they were entered into not only by the lesser clergy but by also by bishops. Rannulf Flambard, bishop of Durham (1099–1128), had numerous children by Alveva (Ælfgifu), who came from the same burgess family of Huntingdon which produced the hermit Christina of Markyate; he later arranged Alveva's marriage with a Huntingdon worthy, and often stayed at their house on his journeys to and from the north. Ranulf took care to provide for his sons and nephews, and his descendants are found holding lands in the north in the thirteenth century.[69]

Despite the lack of evidence it is likely that intermarriage took place, to a greater or lesser extent, at all levels of society. William of Malmesbury, himself the son of a mixed marriage, regarded such unions as commonplace and saw in them an example of the Normans' lack of prejudice.[70] Post-Conquest fashions in personal names may be significant in this context. From the moment of settlement, continental names began to replace native names, until by 1250 the indigenous name-stock was almost completely superseded.[71] But there is a gender

[67] Partner, *Serious entertainments*, p. 14. In the *Liber Vitae* of Thorney Abbey, the wives of priests are described as *uxores* (John Moore, 'Family-entries in English *Liber Vitae*, c.1050–c.1530: part two', forthcoming).
[68] *Liber Vitae Dunelmensis*, ed A.H. Thompson, Surtees Society 136 (1923), fol. 42; I owe this reference to Dr John Moore. Ralph was an Englishman (his mother *Leouerun* (Leofrun) and his brother Edmund appear in the same entry) but gave his sons, Thomas and William, continental names. He was an alderman of London and a member of the London cnihtengild (Brooke, 'The chapter of St Paul's, 1086–1163', p. 123). Ralph also held land in Essex and may have been related to Edmund son of Algot, who in 1086 held two manors in Essex of the king and a mill in Middlesex of the bishop of London (*PR 31 Hen.I*, p. 59; *LDB*, fol. 93v, *GDB*, fol. 127v).
[69] R.S. Southern, 'Ranulf Flambard', *Medieval Humanism*, pp. 201–2. See also C.N.L. Brooke, 'Married men among the English higher clergy', *Cambridge Historical Journal* 12 (1956), pp. 187–8.
[70] *GR* ii, p. 306; see also *OV* ii, p. 256.
[71] Cecily Clark, 'Onomastics', *The Cambridge history of the English language, volume II: 1066–1476*, ed. Norman Blake (Cambridge, 1992), pp. 551–3; idem, 'Willelmus rex? vel alius Willelmus?', *Nomina* 11 (1987), pp. 7–33. Some of the peasants in the Bury St Edmunds survey of c. 1100 already have continental names, though on the lands of

difference in this general pattern; women's names changed less rapidly than men's. This time-lag could indicate 'a paucity of women, and so of feminine name-models among the post-Conquest French settlers'; and this in turn might suggest that the newcomers sought English women as wives.[72]

In the immediately post-Conquest period, marriage with an English heiress might help to secure possession of her family's lands. The union of Henry I and Edith, 'of the true royal line of England', is a case in point.[73] It is significant, however, that on her marriage, Edith changed her name to Matilda, just as a hundred years earlier, Emma of Normandy had become Ælfgifu on her marriage to Æthelred II. The greatest lords, who had been magnates in Normandy before ever they came to England, chose their wives from France, but among those whose fortunes were made in England, English wives might well be an advantage. The marriage of Robert d'Oilly and Ealdgyth, daughter of Wigot of Wallingford, and the subsequent marriage of their daughter Matilda to Miles Crispin, resulted in the reconstruction of Wigot's pre-Conquest estate in the hands of Miles' daughter, also called Matilda, and her husband Brian fitzCount.[74] Mixed marriages in the d'Oilly family continued in the next generation, for Robert d'Oilly II married Edith, daughter of the northern magnate Forne son of Sigulf. The lady had already caught the eye of Henry I and had born him a son, Robert, a fact which may have influenced the king's grant of the honor of Greystoke to her father.[75]

English men with foreign wives (or rather wives with foreign names) are even rarer in the surviving sources. Mahald wife of Ralph son of Algot has already been mentioned, but most of the recorded examples come from the north, the area where the native aristocracy seems most tenacious. The Nevilles of Raby, for instance, go back in the male line to Uhtred son of Meldred and his son Dolfin, who held Staindrop of the monks of Durham in the 1120s; in the 1220s, Dolfin's grandson Robert married Isabel de Neville of Raby and took her

Shaftesbury Abbey, the change took place between the dates of the first and second surveys (c. 1130 and c. 1170). I have adopted Cecily Clark's terminology, using 'continental' and 'insular' instead of 'Norman' and 'English', since the former includes names of Biblical and continental Germanic origin and the latter names derived from the Scandinavian settlement.

[72] Cecily Clark, 'Women's names in post-Conquest England: observations and speculations', *Speculum* 53 (1978), pp. 223–51; the quotation appears on p. 251.

[73] Eleanor Searle, 'Women and the legitimization of succession at the Norman Conquest', *ANS* 3 (1981), pp. 159–71; the quotation is from the *Anglo-Saxon Chronicle*, 1100. See also Chapter I above.

[74] Keats-Rohan, 'The devolution of the honour of Wallingford', pp. 311–18 and see Chapter V above.

[75] David Postles, 'The foundation of Oseney Abbey', *Bulletin of the Institute of Historical Reseach* 53 (1980), pp. 242–4; idem, '*Patronus et advocatus noster*: Oseney Abbey and the Oilly family', *Historical Research* 60 (1987), pp. 100–102. Robert II was the son of Robert I's brother Nigel. For the barony of Greystoke, see Sanders, *English baronies*, p. 50.

surname.[76] Edward of Salisbury may have taken a Norman bride, as his son Walter certainly did; he married Sybil, daughter of Patrick de Chaworth (an anglicization of Sourches, arr. Le Mans), lord of Kempsford, Gloucs, and their daughter, another Sybil, became the second wife of John Marshal and mother of that celebrated paladin, William Marshal. At a lower social level, Edwin the huntsman, a Hampshire *tainus*, had a wife called Odelina.[77]

The descendants of Robert d'Oilly and Edward of Salisbury might well fall into that category of 'Anglo-Norman' families of whom Richard fitzNigel wrote.[78] Others appear in the agreement made in 1153 between the fitzHardings of Bristol, descended from the Englishman, Eadnoth the staller, and the Berkeleys, descended from the Norman reeve and castellan, Roger de Berkeley.[79] Robert fitzHarding had rendered loyal support to the Empress in the civil wars of Stephen's reign, while Roger (III) de Berkeley had been at best luke-warm; Henry II rewarded Robert by the gift of the great manor of Berkeley, confiscated from Roger. The transfer was sealed by the marriage of Robert's eldest son Maurice with Roger's eldest daughter, Alice; but Roger was pacified by the marriage of Robert's daughter Helena to his own son, Roger (IV), with a marriage portion at Dursley, Glos. Robert's other children, two sons and two daughters, also married into baronial families.[80] Examples could be multiplied, most of them among the lesser barons and knightly tenants.[81]

Orderic Vitalis, who spent his early boyhood in Shrewsbury, sets such marriages in an urban context. He says that, at a time which seems to be the 1070s (he was born in 1075), English and Normans were living together in boroughs, towns and cities (*in burgis, castris et urbibus*) and were intermarrying with each other (*conubiis alteri alteros mutuo sibi coniungentes*).[82] Orderic's words are borne out by Domesday Book. French settlers appear at Southampton, Wallingford,

---

[76] Offler, *Durham episcopal charters, 1071–1152*, pp. 75–7; this and other examples of northern lords with 'French' wives is cited in Clark, 'Women's names in post-Conquest England', pp. 226–7.
[77] Sanders, *English baronies*, pp. 112 (Chitterne), 125 (Kempsford); VCH *Dorset* iii, pp. 57–8; for the problem of the 'two Edwards', see Chapter V above. The younger Sybil was sister to Patrick, earl of Salisbury (Crouch, *William Marshall*, pp. 14–15, 34–7). For Edwin the huntsman, see Chapter V, note 100 above.
[78] *Dialogus*, p. 53, see the chapter-heading above.
[79] For Roger I de Berkeley, see Williams, 'An introduction to the Gloucestershire Domesday', pp. 38–9.
[80] Patterson, 'Robert fitzHarding of Bristol', *Haskins Society Journal* 1 (1989), pp. 113–14, 115–16.
[81] The researches of Dr John Moore into the Anglo-Norman family are about to be published in *Nomina* (see also footnote 67 above), and will provide many more examples of couples one of whom has a continental, the other an insular name. For a preliminary survey and a discussion of the evidence, see John S. Moore, 'The Anglo-Norman family: size and structure', *ANS* 14 (1992), pp. 153–96. I am grateful to Dr Moore for allowing me to see his unpublished material and for much help and advice on families and marriage in the Anglo-Norman period.
[82] OV ii, pp. 256–7.

Hereford and Shrewsbury and (by implication) at Cambridge.[83] An update made about 1100 to the Domesday accounts of Gloucester and Winchcombe distinguishes between burgesses dwelling on inherited tenements and those who have recently bought their dwellings, and at Gloucester some of the latter were French.[84] The description in Little Domesday of the new borough at Norwich is headed *Franci de Norwic* (the Frenchmen of Norwich). The borough was founded by Earl Ralph (II) and the king and originally housed 36 burgess and six Englishmen (*anglici*) but by 1086 there were 41 French burgesses on the king's land alone and another 83 on the lands of other lords, besides an unoccupied messuage; there was also a church, founded by Earl Ralph.[85] There were new boroughs at Nottingham and Northampton as well, the former including houses built by Hugh fitzBaldric, sheriff of York.[86]

It may be that French colonists were offered favourable terms to induce them to settle in English towns. At Hereford, the French burgesses were quit of all judicial fines except breach of the peace, *heimfara* (housebreaking) and *foresteall* (highway robbery). Ironically it is from Orderic's Shrewsbury that the most explicit complaint about French exemption arises:

The English burgesses say that it is very hard on them that they themselves render as much geld as they rendered TRE, although the earl's castle has occupied [the site of] 51 messuages and another 50 messuages are waste, and 43 *French burgesses hold messuages paying geld* TRE, and the earl himself has granted to the abbey which he is building there 39 burgesses formerly paying geld . . . altogether there are 193 messuages which do not pay geld.

Since there were only 252 houses and as many burgesses in 1086, their attitude is understandable.[87] Nor are such complaints rare, especially those concerning castle-building, which affected virtually every major town in England. At Norwich, 22 of the 1,320 burgesses had left for Beccles, Suffolk, and three more for Thorpe St Andrew; 'those who fled and the rest who remained are utterly

[83] GDB, fols 52, 56v, 179, 252. At Cambridge (fol. 189) Count Alan had five burgesses who pay nothing and nine 'in the land of the English'.
[84] This is the survey from Evesham Abbey known as Evesham K, see DB *Gloucestershire*, Appendix.
[85] LDB, fol. 118. The customary dues went to the king from all the land *tam militum quam burgensium*; cf the French and English *milites* at Bury St Edmunds and the *milites* and other men of the abbot of Westminster at Westminster (note 55 above).
[86] GDB, fols 219, 280. At Lincoln Colswein, who may have been town-reeve, had built 36 houses and two churches on waste land beyond the city's eastern boundary (see Chapter V above).
[87] GDB, fols 179, 252. Susan Reynolds suggested that the French 'used their position as members or camp-followers of an occupying force to evade payment of the dues which their defeated neighbours owed' ('Towns in Domesday Book', *Domesday Studies*, ed. Holt, pp. 308-9).

ruined (*vastati*), partly because of Earl Ralph's forfeiture, partly by fires, partly by the king's geld and partly because of Waleran'.[88] At Lincoln the citizens were more circumspect; after complaining that 166 messuages had been destroyed to make way for the castle they added that 'the remaining 74 have been destroyed outside the castle boundary, not because of the oppression of the sheriff and his officers, but because of misfortune and poverty and the ravages of fire'.[89] The immediate effect of the Conquest on English towns was detrimental, though most eventually recovered.

Town property is described in Domesday in terms of its landlords. The king and the Church usually predominate, but town houses and burgesses were often attached to rural estates, and some manors included both urban and rural elements. Here, as in the rest of England, the English magnates of 1066 have vanished, to be replaced by foreigners. Thus the hall at Lincoln which had belonged to Toki son of Auti had passed, like the rest of his land, into the hands of Geoffrey Alselin and his nephew Ralph, who held it in 1086.[90] Domesday is not concerned with the actual occupants of the messuages held, first by Toki and then by Geoffrey and Ralph. Such people are only rarely recorded. An agreement of Archbishop Anselm's time (1093–1109) names the men who 'sat' (OE *sittan*) on nine messuages (*hagan*) in Canterbury over which Christ Church had sake and soke; only one (William) has a continental name.[91] The use of the verb *sittan* implies the actual occupants of the property, rather than the lords to whom renders were made.[92]

Though the landlords might be French, the burgesses and others who occupied property in the borough were largely English. Only for Colchester does Domesday

---

[88] *LDB*, fol. 117v; Waleran was a royal officer, whose son and nephew, both called John, were holding land in East Anglia in 1086 (R. Welldon Finn, *Domesday Studies: The eastern counties* (London, 1987), pp. 13, 29).

[89] *GDB*, fol. 333v.

[90] *GDB*, fol. 336; Hill, *Medieval Lincoln*, pp. 45–6, 131–3. Half Toki's property in Lincoln (30 messuages) had been given, presumably by the king, to Remigius, bishop of Lincoln, and Geoffrey had received no compensation.

[91] William Urry, *Canterbury under the Angevin kings* (London, 1967), p. 385. The agreement, the original of which does not survive, is a copy of one part of a chirograph, and is in Old English.

[92] The Canterbury tenants may be compared with the *milites* Wade and Leofwine *feirage*, who 'sat' (*sedeat*) on the lands at Bodsham Green and Wilderton given by their lord Æthelric Bigga to St Augustine's (S.1502) and the Kentish free men, Godric who lived (*mansit*) at Solton and held 20 acres as his *allodium*, and Altet, who lived (*mansit*) at Leveberga and had two acres in alodium (*GDB*, fol. 11). See also the case of Saegeat the thegn who dwelt (*mansit*) at Bloxham, Oxon, and *serviebat sicut liber homo*, whom Earl Edwin gave to Ralph d'Oilly (Chapter V, note 17 above). The same idea of 'occupiers' as opposed to owners of land is expressed in the *Anglo-Saxon Chronicle*'s account of the great Lammas assembly at Salisbury in 1086: 'There came to [King William] his witan and *ealle þa landsittende men þe ahtes wæron ofer eall Engleland wæron þæs mannes men þe hi wæron*: 'and all the people occupying land who were of any account all over England, no matter whose men they might be'.

supply a list of burgesses and then only for the king's land.[93] Of the 276 names recorded, only 16 are continental as opposed to insular, and five of these are of the kind which might have been in use before 1066 (Ainulf, Filiman, Hardekin, Sunegod and Tesco). The remaining eleven seem to be post-Conquest immigrants; this is certainly true of Ralph *pinel*, a minor landowner in Essex and Suffolk, William Pecche and Demiblanc, a tenant of Aubrey de Vere.[94] Not all the holders of land were necessarily resident in the town. Ralph *pinel*, for instance, held four houses outside the walls and five acres of land; Hardekin held 10½ houses and 20 acres; Ælfric the priest, 3 houses and 2 acres.

The same mixture of Englishmen and immigrants is found in later sources, though there is an increasing difficulty in determining origin because of the adoption by English families of fashionable continental names. Battle is of particular interest since it was a 'new town', established to serve the needs of the Conqueror's Battle Abbey. The Battle Chronicle describes how 'a great number of men were recruited, many from neighbouring districts and even some from across the Channel' (*ex transmarinis etiam partibus*).[95] The names of the householders are recorded in a survey of c.1110, and suggest that most of the colonists were English, 'native to East Sussex and speaking its dialect'. The English settlers were profoundly affected not merely by the abbey itself, staffed by monks from Marmoutiers in Anjou, but also by the *transmarini* who were their neighbours.[96] Nevertheless it is the English strain which was eventually dominant. The same is true of Canterbury, whose social mix is illuminated by a series of rentals of Christ Church property dating from the second half of the twelfth century.[97] There is a steady diminution in the proportion of insular names recorded, which contrasts with the overwhelmingly English place-names (including streetnames). Analysis of these, and of the insular and continental bynames recorded suggests that though both French and English were spoken in Canterbury, the dominant vernacular was English, of the local Kentish variety.[98]

Domesday Book is silent on the subject of Winchester, the 'capital' of the West

---

[93] *LDB*, fols 101–106. Culling, one of the holders of land in Ipswich, is described as a burgess (*LDB*, fol. 290) and some of the Bedford burgesses (their names are all English) appear in the Bedfordshire survey, although only their lands outside the borough are described (*GDB*, fol. 218).
[94] Ralph *pinel* had received some of the land of the East Anglian thegn, Brihtmaer, and, though he held in chief, was apparently connected with Geoffrey de Mandeville (*LDB*, fols 97–97v, 437); William Pecche, see note 64 above; Demiblanc, see *LDB*, fol. 77. The other names are Arthur, Blanc, Calebot (perhaps an error for Talbot), Dullel (Dublel, 'twin'), Lorce the Breton (*brito*), Roger, Rossell and William (*DB Essex*, no. B3a and notes).
[95] *The Chronicle of Battle Abbey*, ed. Searle, pp. 50–1.
[96] Cecily Clark, 'Battle c.1110: an anthroponymist looks at an Anglo-Norman new town', *ANS* 2 (1980), pp. 21–41; the quotation is on p. 30.
[97] They are printed in Urry, *Canterbury under the Angevin kings*, pp. 221–315.
[98] Cecily Clark, 'People and languages in post-Conquest Canterbury', *Journal of Medieval History* 2 (1976), pp. 1–33.

Saxon kings. Some compensation is afforded by the survival of two twelfth-century surveys, the earlier of which is more or less contemporary with the Battle survey, and refers back to an even earlier record of c.1057. Even before 1066, men with French (and German, and Lotharingian) names could be found in the city, of whom Godwine the Frenchman (*francigena*) is particularly striking.[99] By 1110 the foreigners, many of whom were connected with the royal administration, had colonized the more important streets, and English occupancy of these had been reduced, but there is no suggestion that English tenants as such were of lower status. Many of the more important burgesses were Englishmen, including virtually all the moneyers working for Henry I; indeed some moneyer families can be traced, holding the same property, from the time of Edward the Confessor to that of Stephen.[100] At Lincoln too, Englishmen are found at the highest levels of urban society. Of the twelve lawmen with lands and rights in 1066, five had by 1086 been succeeded by sons, and two by other Englishmen; only two had been replaced by Normans.[101] As at Winchester the Lincoln moneyers who struck coins for William I had also been employed by Edward the Confessor and Harold II, and their successors were men with English or Scandinavian names; the first 'French' names appear in Stephen's reign, when they are no longer a sure guide to national origin.[102] A list of some Lincoln citizens in 1191 still includes some insular names, though their use was about to become 'a noticeable eccentricity'. This does not, of course, mean that those who bore continental names were not of English stock. The first known mayor of Lincoln, Adam (1210–16) was of English descent. His grandparents were Eilwi (Æthelwig) of Wigford and his wife Alviva, who typically gave their five sons continental names: David, Thomas, William, Roger and Reginald, Adam's father.[103]

London has no surveys such as those which survive for Canterbury and Winchester, and only the upper ranks of the London burgesses can be seen in the surviving material; it is thus even more remarkable that their English origins are so marked.[104] As at Lincoln, the first mayor was an Englishman, Henry fitzAilwin (d.1212). His grandfather Leofstan may have been the brother of

---

[99] The surveys are printed in *Winchester in the early Middle Ages*, ed. Biddle, pp. 33–141; the earlier survey is c. 1110 and the later dates from 1148. The personal-names are analyzed by Olof von Feilitzen (loc. cit., pp. 145–229); Godwine *francigena*, see loc. cit., p. 43.

[100] *Winchester in the early Middle Ages*, ed. Biddle, pp. 396–422, 476.

[101] GDB, fol. 336; for the lawmen of York, who were also English into the twelfth century, see Chapter VII above.

[102] Hill, *Medieval Lincoln*, pp. 52–3. The retention of English moneyers after the Conquest is a general trend, see M. Dolley, *The Norman Conquest and the English coinage* (London, 1966), pp. 12–14, 29; *English Romanesque Art, 1066–1200*, ed. George Zarnecki, Richard Gem and Christopher Brooke (London, 1984), pp. 324–37.

[103] Hill, *Medieval Lincoln*, pp. 188, 397, 384.

[104] Susan Reynolds, 'The rulers of London in the twelfth century', *History* 57 (1972), pp. 337–57; even the Bucuinte and Buckerel families, often claimed to be Italian, may have been English.

Deormann of London, whose family supplied moneyers for Edward the Confessor, Harold II, William the Conqueror, William Rufus and Henry I.[105] In 1086 Deormann held property in Middlesex, Hertfordshire and Essex, and may already have acquired the land at Keston, Kent, which he held of Archbishop Lanfranc for the service of half a knight.[106] Deormann gave his Hertfordshire manors of Watton and Walkern to his brother Leofstan, but the king confiscated them and bestowed them on Eudo *dapifer*; by the 1160s, however, they had been regained by Leofstan's grandson, Henry fitzAilwin, presumably the future mayor.[107] Deormann's Essex property eventually passed to Westminster Abbey, into whose confraternity his three daughters were accepted.[108] His land at Islington, Middx, had previously belonged to Algar, who may have been the London moneyer of that name who was active from 1049 to 1072; since Deormann named one of his sons Algar, the elder Algar may even have been Deormann's father. The names of all four of Deormann's sons appear as London moneyers; Algar (1089 x 1104/07), Edwin (1089 x 92), Ordgar (1092 x 1101) and Theodoric (1095 x 98); Theodoric and Algar (a canon of St Paul's) had previously been minting at Hertford. Theodoric or Tierri had a grandson of the same name, who married Matilda, a kinswoman of Gilbert de Clare, earl of Pembroke; he was justiciar of London and Middlesex (1143–52) and died in 1162. His son Bertram of Barrow (Suffolk) held Newington Barrow, in Islington, and his daughter married William, brother of Gervase of Cornhill. Gervase's father Roger was sheriff of London under Henry I and Gervase himself held the same office under Stephen and into the reign of Henry II.[109] He took his byname, however, from his English father-in-law, Edward of Cornhill, when he married the latter's daughter, Agnes. Edward of Cornhill himself had married Godeleve (Godlufu), daughter of Edward of Southwark. The family was prominent both in local and royal administration: Reginald of Cornhill, who possessed a history of the English in French verse, was one of Gervase's grandsons.[110]

It is much easier to trace families, even of lesser landholders, after 1066 than before. In part this is due to the increasing enrollment of records from the early twelfth century; but it also has to do with naming-customs. One of the most

---

[105] Pamela Nightingale, 'Some London moneyers and reflections on the organization of the English mints in the twelfth and thirteenth centuries', *Numismatic Chronicle* 142 (1982), pp. 34–50, esp. pp. 38–42.

[106] GDB, fols 130, 142, LDB, fol. 105 (a house in Colchester); *Domesday Monachorum*, pp. 94, 105.

[107] VCH *Herts* i, pp. 285–6, iii, p. 159; C.N.L. Brooke and Gillian Keir, *London: the shaping of a city, 800–1216* (London, 1975), pp. 346–9.

[108] Harvey, *Westminster Abbey and its estates in the Middle Ages*, p. 373.

[109] Green, *English sheriffs to 1154*, p. 59; Brooke and Keir, *London: the shaping of a city, 800–1200*, pp. 346–7.

[110] Clark, 'Women's names in post-Conquest England', p. 249; J.H. Round, *Geoffrey de Mandeville: a study of the Anarchy* (London, 1892), pp. 304–12. For Reginald, see J.E.A. Jolliffe, *Angevin Kingship* (London, 1955), pp. 289–93, and for the French poem, Chapter VII, note 150 above.

striking, and uncontentious, results of the Norman Conquest is the almost complete replacement of the insular name-stock with names of continental origin. It is obvious even in William I's reign among the upper ranks of society and continues throughout the twelfth century among townsmen, free villagers and dependent peasants, until by c.1250 the process is complete. It was not, however, only the name-stock which was changed. Before 1066, each individual was identified by a single, distinctive name (an idionym). This contrasts very strongly with the present-day system of naming, which consists of at least two components, a 'first-name' plus a surname 'denoting a patrilinear family group'.[111] There is ample evidence of the use of bynames of various kinds in pre-Conquest England, but they are not used consistently nor are they hereditary. After the Conquest, bynames become increasingly common and regularly used, until they eventually develop into true surnames, defining the family to which the individual belongs.

Many modern surnames developed from patronymics, preserving Old English idionyms no longer used as baptismal names.[112] For the upper ranks of landholders, toponymic bynames (derived from place-names) are of particular significance. They accompany a change in family structure common to all the lands of north-western Europe which had been part of the Carolingian Empire. The great aristocratic families of the early middle ages were not 'dynasties in the modern sense, families which can be traced from generation to generation', but extended kindreds, defined by descent from a common ancestor.[113] Like the English aristocracy before 1066, they were defined not by inherited family names, but by recurring idionyms favoured by a particular kindred. It is this which makes individuals and their families so difficult to identify in the early middle ages.

Within the kindreds there were probably always more compact groups, or lineages, which enjoyed prior rights to inherit.[114] It is extremely difficult to determine how inheritance worked in pre-Conquest England, since it was largely governed by custom and not set down in writing. The wills of Old English nobles give little guidance, since it is never clear whether the lands included in the will constitute all the testator's property, or whether there was other land whose descent was determined by unwritten custom. The Secular Code of Cnut does, however, include a revealing clause on intestacy; if a man dies intestate, his lord

[111] Clark, 'Onomastics', p. 551.

[112] Examples include Aylmer, Edrich, Goodwin and Wooldridge (OE Æthelmaer, Eadric, Godwine and Wulfric), see Clark, 'Onomastics', pp. 555–6; Aldridge, Elphick, Liversedge and Utteridge (OE Ealdred, Ælfheah, Leofsige and Uhtric), see P.H. Reaney, *The origin of English surnames* (London, 1967), pp. 97–127.

[113] Karl Leyser, 'The German aristocracy from the tenth to the twelfth centuries: a historical and cultural sketch', *Medieval Germany and its neighbours, 900–1250* (London, 1982), pp. 168–9 (the article first appeared in *P&P* 41 (1968), pp. 25–53).

[114] For pre-Conquest England, see T.M. Charles-Edwards, 'The distinction between land and moveable wealth in Anglo-Saxon England', *Medieval Settlement: continuity and change*, ed. P.H. Sawyer (London, 1976), pp. 183–4; idem, 'Kinship, status and the origins of the hide', *P&P* 56 (1972).

is to supervise the distribution of his property 'very justly' between his widow, his children and his near kinsmen 'each in the proportion which belongs to him'.[115] Clearly there were inner groups of kin within the greater.

From the eleventh century these more restricted families acquire greater and greater prominence. In Normandy, where the crucial period seems to be between c.1020 and c.1050, 'the whole process was one which was basically the transformation of any one family from a large amorphous kin-group, which identified itself with no fixed residence and did not think in terms of ancestry transmitted in a direct male line, into a lineage tenacious of its rights over generations'.[116] Such families began to identify themselves in terms of continued possession of a specific estate, transmitted intact from generation to generation; a patrimony, which in normal circumstances would go to the eldest son, whereas younger siblings would receive lands acquired by their father, or hold in parage, tenurially dependent on the senior line. The chief estate of the family supplied its name. Thus with the Normans, 'the toponymic was not name but title, title to be preserved by all the descendants of the founder of the family's fortunes, only to be surrendered in the junior branches if some new title, the consequence of marriage or the accidents of succession or the exercise of royal patronage, became available'.[117]

The use of toponymic bynames thus has consequences not only for personal naming, but for family structure and inheritance. Of course the process was no-where near complete even in Normandy by 1066, but it was far advanced there in comparison with the situation in England; indeed though there are a few examples of sons bearing their father's bynames, the link between land and lineage seems quite absent.[118] The effects of Norman practice can be seen almost immediately. The fief of Thorkell of Warwick (also known as Thorkell of Arden) was composed at least in part of lands which had belonged to his family before

---

[115] II Cnut, 70,1; see H.R. Loyn, 'Kinship in Anglo-Saxon England', ASE 3 (1974), p. 207.

[116] Bates, *Normandy before 1066*, p. 113. These developments did not, of course, mean that the more remote kin were forgotten; much depended on the context in which kindred was defined and for some purposes the relationships involved might be fairly distant (J.C. Holt, 'Feudal society and the family in early medieval England: III politics and patronage', TRHS 5th series 34 (1984), pp. 14–15).

[117] Holt, 'Feudal society and the family: I the revolution of 1066', p. 200. See, for example, Nigel d'Aubigny, a 'landless younger son of a minor Norman baron', to whom Henry I gave the divorced wife of Robert de Mowbray, who had forfeited his lands for rebellion. Maud brought Nigel the Norman fief of Mowbray (Montbray), and Nigel therefore took the name of her ex-husband. The extensive lands which the king granted Nigel in England thus came to be called the honor of Mowbray (Greenway, *Charters of the honour of Mowbray*, pp. xvii–xx).

[118] Æthelwold the fat had a son called Æthelmaer the fat, and Æthelric bigga's son was called Esbearn bigga; Æthelweard meaw ('seagull') had a son called Ælfgar meaw, though Ælfgar's son Beorhtric is never called Beorhtric meaw (Robertson, *Charters*, pp. 387, 436; Williams, 'An introduction to the Gloucestershire Domesday', p. 22). See also Alfred *larwe* and his son Eilaf *larwe*, Chapter VII above.

1066. The original wealth of the family cannot now be reconstructed; what it possessed in 1086 was what Thorkell and his father Æthelwine, sheriff of Warwickshire, had managed to preserve, or gain, by service to King William. What is striking is Thorkell's dominant position among his surviving kinsmen, two brothers and six uncles. Though some of them held land from the king, or from other lords, most of their property was held of Thorkell himself. Such a situation, where the bulk of the family land is held by a single individual, of whom the rest hold as tenants, conforms to Norman, not to English custom. Moreover the descendants of Æthelmaer of Longdon, Thorkell's uncle, and Guthmund, Thorkell's brother, were still holding land of Thorkell's heirs, the Ardens, in the twelfth century.[119]

The Arden family survived by adapting to Norman custom but many families were not so fortunate. Whatever the precise rules governing inheritance, it was not only sons and brothers (or daughters and sisters) who benefitted on the death of kinsmen. Holders of bookland had freedom of bequest and (in the absence of specific limitation to the contrary) could leave it to whomever they wished. Thus cousins, uncles and others, of the maternal as well as the paternal kin, might receive bequests of land. The forfeiture of members of the kindred did not therefore affect only their immediate family. More distant rights of inheritance were overridden by the Norman settlement, most of them permanently, unless the heirs could attach themselves to the new lords.[120]

So far we have looked at the influence of the incomers on the natives. What of the reverse process? Some have doubted whether the English exercised any influence over the Normans. This view was expressed in its most extreme form by Professor le Patourel: 'I cannot see how the Norman nobility, having destroyed the English landowning class and having estates in Normandy as well as in England and constantly journeying between the two countries, could pick up many of the characteristics of the Old English social organization at its higher levels that were of any great significance'.[121] This might be true of the earls and the greater barons, but not all the settlers had cross-channel estates. Some of the lesser magnates and the knightly tenants had little or nothing in Normandy and every reason to identify themselves with their new fiefs in England. Intermarriage and the survival of at least some socially acceptable families of English descent must have had an effect. Toponymic bynames provide some hints in this respect.

---

[119] Williams, 'A vice-comital family in pre-Conquest Warwickshire', pp. 287–90. About half Thorkell's fief (62 hides out of 132) had come from men related to him.
[120] Fleming, *Kings and lords in Conquest England*, pp. 139–44. Holt ('Feudal society and the family in early medieval England: I the revolution of 1066', p. 198) sees the main difference in 'changes in the capacity to bequeathe to laymen, in particular to kinsmen . . . resulting from the canalisation of the inheritance to a restricted category of heirs'. The development of primogeniture in twelfth-century England (but not in twelfth-century Normandy) meant the virtual disinheritance of younger sons (Crouch, *William Marshall*, pp. 26–8).
[121] John le Patourel, 'The Norman Conquest, 1066, 1106, 1154?', *ANS* 1 (1979), p. 111.

The greater barons took their toponymics from the lands in Normandy which had long provided their families' identity; some even transferred the Norman toponyms to their English estates.[122] Some men, however, (usually not of the higher ranks) took their names from their English lands; Alvred of Marlborough, Judhael of Totnes, Roger of Berkeley. In so doing they 'were surely doing more than indicate their home'; more even than 'staking out title' to inheritance of the land.[123] It seems at least probable that they were also identifying their fortunes, and those of their heirs, with their new country.

Another pointer to the assimilation of Norman families to their new land is provided by their choice of burial place. The newly-enriched settlers were generous donors to the Church, though the beneficiaries were not, on the whole, the English Benedictine houses. Grants of property in England, usually in the form of tithes or churches rather than manors or large tracts of land, were made to religious houses in Normandy and elsewhere in France.[124] Two new abbeys date from the Conqueror's reign, William I's own house at Battle and the Cluniac priory of Lewes, founded by William de Warenne and his wife Gundrada. To these must be added the old minsters transformed, like St Peter's, Shrewsbury, into Benedictine abbeys, or, increasingly throughout the twelfth century, Augustinian priories. Even some new secular colleges were founded, though the vogue for such establishments was passing.[125] Most families patronized more than one church, which makes their choice of burial place significant.

Burial cements the relationship between the church where it takes place and the family whose members are interred there; it ensures future donations for the church and memorial services for the family. Many of the first generation of Norman landholders, especially those of the highest rank, chose to be buried in their Norman foundations. Some did not; the Warennes were interred in their priory at Lewes. The next generation sees some shifting allegiances; for instance, Walter Giffard I, who died in 1102, was buried at Longueville in Normandy, whereas Walter Giffard II, died 1164, chose Nutley in Sussex. Relatively few of those whose place of burial is known were laid to rest in Normandy. The fact that 'so many Norman lords chose to await the Last Judgment in English monasteries suggests a degree of spiritual and cultural assimilation to their adopted land that should not be ignored'.[126]

The wholesale replacement of insular by continental personal names is not

---

[122] The most obvious example is Montgomery, Powys, named after Montgommery in Calvados, the Norman home of Roger de Montgomery, earl of Shrewsbury. See also the example of Cause, Shrops, below.

[123] J.C. Holt, 'What's in a name? Family nomenclature and the Norman Conquest', The Stenton Lecture 1981 (Reading, 1982), p. 21.

[124] See for example S.F. Hockey, OSB, 'William fitzOsbern and the endowment of his abbey of Lyre', ANS 3 (1981), pp. 96–105.

[125] M.J. Franklin, 'The secular college as a focus for Anglo-Norman piety: St Augustine's, Daventry', *Minsters and parish churches*, ed. Blair, pp. 97–104.

[126] Brian Golding, 'Anglo-Norman knightly burials', *Medieval Knighthood* (Proceedings of the Strawberry Hill Conference) 1 (1986), pp. 35–48.

repeated in place-names. In this field French influence is slight.[127] A very few examples are known of pre-existing English names being superseded by names of continental origin. Cause, Shrops, appears as *Alretone* in Domesday, when it was held by Roger fitzCorbet, who may have come from Caux in Normandy.[128] Similarly Miserden, Gloucs (*Grenhamstede* in Domesday) takes its name ('Musard's') from the family of Hascoit Musard, the Domesday holder.[129] Some post-Conquest settlements were given names of French origin. Battle, Sussex, from the abbey of *La Batailge*, is the most famous, but we also find (for instance) Devizes, Wilts, which grew around the castle founded by Roger, bishop of Salisbury, and Pleshey, Essex, round that of Geoffrey (I) de Mandeville.[130]

More common are place-names with French affixes, used to distinguish settlements which shared the same toponym. Most are derived from the name of the family which owned them; Higham Ferrers, Northants, Milton Keynes, Bucks., Worth Matravers, Dorset. Sometimes the affix precedes the settlement name, as in Helion Bumpstead, Essex.[131] Such formations belong to the thirteenth century rather than to the twelfth. The 'Englishness' of post-Conquest place-names reflects the dominance of English as the mother-tongue of most of the population.

The year 1066 has traditionally marked the frontier between Old and Middle English. Middle English is distinguished from its predecessor by numerous technical details, of which the most comprehensible to non-specialists are the loss of grammatical inflexions and the consequent increase in the use of prepositions. Since the earliest Middle English texts date from the twelfth century, it would be natural to regard its emergence as a result of the Norman settlement, but this is not so. The changes which produced Middle English were far advanced in 1066, and owe more to the Scandinavian settlements of the tenth century than to the advent of the Normans.[132] What the Norman Conquest did was displace the written standard developed in tenth-century Winchester, to which

[127] Cecily Clark, 'Onomastics', pp. 588–92; Margaret Gelling, *Signposts to the past* (London, 1978), pp. 236–40.
[128] Eilert Ekwall, *The concise Oxford dictionary of English place-names*, 4th edn (London, 1960), p. 91; Kenneth Cameron, *English place-names* (London, 1979), p. 88.
[129] Ekwall, *Dictionary of English place-names*, p. 328; Margaret Gelling, *Signposts to the Past* (London, 1978), p. 238.
[130] GDB, fol. 17v, and see AS Chron, 1094 for *þa mynster æt þære Bataille* (Earle and Plummer, *Two of the Saxon Chronicles parallel*, p. 229). Devizes (OFr *devise*, Lat *divisae*, 'boundary'), first recorded in 1139, stands on the boundary between the royal manor of Potterne, and that of Bishops Cannings, belonging to the bishopric of Salisbury (Adrian Room, *Dictionary of place-names in the British Isles* (London, 1988), p. 111); Pleshey, founded c.1100, comes from OFr *plessis*, 'enclosure', found also in the castle and village of Le Plessis-Grimoult in Normandy (Cameron, *English place-names*, pp. 88–9).
[131] From Hellean, Brittany; the 1086 holder was Tihel the Breton or Tihel de Hellean (Ekwall, *Dictionary of English place-names*, p. 74).
[132] David Burnley, *The history of the English language* (London, 1992), pp. 63–6; idem, 'Lexis and semantics', *Cambridge history of the English language*, II, 1066–1472, pp. 414–32. The French impact on English was chiefly on vocabulary: 'in quantitative terms

modern scholars give the name of Standard Old English. This was based on West Saxon, but was not, even in Wessex, a spoken dialect, but 'a standard literary language which extended as far as the authority of the English kings'.[133] It is the language of most surviving Old English texts, irrespective of the dialects actually spoken by their authors and scribes.

Since Standard Old English must have seemed almost a foreign language in some parts of England, its maintenance required not only the political control of the West Saxon kings but also an active educational programme for training scribes in the monastic centres.[134] The collapse of the English hierarchy after 1070 meant that this could no longer be sustained, nor did it suit the needs of French speakers accustomed to Latin as the normal medium of writing.[135] From about 1070, Latin replaced English in royal writs, though some beneficiaries continued to produce bi-lingual writs into the reign of Henry I. This did not mean that English ceased to be used in the local courts, merely that English texts were no longer provided.[136] The Northamptonshire Geld Roll of the 1070s is in English; the south-western rolls of 1086 in Latin. The decline of English as a language of record can be seen in David Pelteret's collection of post-Conquest vernacular texts; most date from the late eleventh and early twelfth centuries and those compiled after 1135 are more a tribute to the conservatism of certain scriptoria (notably those of Christ Church, Canterbury and St Andrew's, Rochester) than a living tradition.[137]

The collapse of Standard Old English ended 'a tradition which had taught scribes to observe distinctions in writing which they did not observe in speech', and freed them to create new literary forms out of their spoken dialects.[138] The process can be seen at work in the 'E' version of the Anglo-Saxon Chronicle, the

---

[it was] the most substantial source of new words in written Middle English' (Burnley, loc. cit., p. 423).

133 Clanchy, From memory to written record: England 1066–1307, p. 211. For the development of the standard see Helmut Gneuss, 'The origin of Standard Old English and Æthelwold's school at Winchester', ASE 1 (1972), pp. 63–83; Walter Hofstetter, 'Winchester and the standardization of Old English vocabulary', ASE 17 (1988), pp. 139–61.

134 William of Malmesbury complained that southerners like himself could scarcely understand the speech of northerners, especially in York, and presumably the reverse applied (GP, p. 209); see also Clanchy, From memory to written record, p. 212.

135 Though the conventiones (agreements) formalized in the honorial courts used the chirograph form normal before the Conquest, they were now written in Latin, not English (King, 'Dispute settlement in Anglo-Norman England', ANS 14 (1992), pp. 126–8).

136 Clanchy, From memory to written record, pp. 212–13 and see the discussion on spoken and written language on pp. 206–11.

137 Pelteret, Vernacular documents, nos. 50–55, 60, pp. 76–82, 85; for the 'conservatism' of the Canterbury scribes, see Clark, 'People and languages in post-Conquest Canterbury', pp. 24–6.

138 J.A. Burrow, Medieval writers and their work: Middle English literature and its background 1100–1500 (Oxford, 1982), p. 3; Clanchy, From memory to written record, p. 212.

surviving text of which was written at Peterborough in the twelfth century. For the annals up to and including 1121, it is a copy of a manuscript produced somewhere in south-eastern England, probably in Kent, with various interpolations relating to the history of Peterborough. The copyist himself then composed the entries for the years 1122–31 and finally, in 1155, another scribe continued the chronicle down to 1154.[139] When copying his exemplar, the scribe wrote Standard Old English, but his language in the annals for 1122 to 1131 (the First Continuation) 'is strongly marked by the the the dialect of the district where it was written', and this is even more evident in the language of the annals for 1132 to 1154 (the Second Continuation).[140] In both Continuations language and style are 'magnificently alive'; this is already a literary language.[141]

This use of the local vernaculars produces the diversity of language which is the most striking characteristic of Middle English.[142] The only attempt at uniformity (known as the AB language) is localized in the west midlands, whose Benedictine houses were such a vital repository of English tradition. It was here, perhaps in Herefordshire, that the *Ancrene Wisse* (Anchorites' Guide) was written, in the early thirteenth century.[143] The language and spelling are related to those of the ninth-century English gloss to the Vespasian Psalter, written by 'someone who had received training in a Mercian scriptorium and so wrote consistently in a Mercian dialect'.[144] Moreover the same conventions are found in another thirteenth century manuscript written in a different hand, which contains a collection of saints' lives known as the *Katherine* group. Taken together these manuscripts imply 'a continuous scribal tradition which was not disrupted by the Norman Conquest to the same degree that it was elsewhere'.[145]

Though English was displaced for most purposes by Latin, preaching and teaching in the vernacular had long been the custom in pre-Conquest England and this tradition survived the advent of the Normans.[146] Abbot Samson of Bury St Edmunds, a Norfolk man, considered that sermons should be delivered in French, or better still in English, 'so as to be edifying rather than showily learned'.[147] This was also the opinion of Ælfric of Cerne, whose work may have

---

[139] Clark, *The Peterborough Chronicle, 1070–1154*, pp. xi–xiii; idem, 'Domesday Book: a great red herring', *England in the eleventh century*, ed. Hicks, pp. 322–7.

[140] Clark, *The Peterborough Chronicle*, pp. xl, lviii.

[141] Clark, *The Peterborough Chronicle*, pp. lxvi–lxx.

[142] James Milroy, 'Middle English dialectology', *Cambridge History of the English language vol ii, 1066–1472*, p. 156.

[143] For the date of its composition and revision (1215–1230), see E.J. Dobson, 'The date and composition of the *Ancrene Wisse*', *Proceedings of the British Academy* 52 (1966), pp. 181–208.

[144] Burnley, *The history of the English language*, p. 8.

[145] Milroy, 'Middle English dialectology', p. 158; Burnley, *History of the English language*, pp. 97–8.

[146] Burrow, *Middle English writers and their works*, pp. 3–4; Norman Blake, 'Introduction', *The Cambridge history of the English language, vol II, 1066–1472*, p. 7.

[147] See his response to the prior-elect, Herbert, who lamented that he could not preach

been familiar to Samson.[148] Ælfric and his contemporary, Archbishop Wulfstan Lupus of York, were the most notable figures in a long tradition of homiletic prose. Though Old English had ceased to be a medium of composition, pre-Conquest texts continued to be copied throughout the twelfth and thirteenth centuries, and the works of Ælfric were especially popular. Both Ælfric and Wulfstan wrote rhythmical prose, using many of the techniques, including alliteration, found in Old English poetry. Since there seems to have been little interest in Old English verse (at least not in the 'heroic' vein) in post-Conquest England, it may be that the alliterative poetry of the Middle English period was developed from this rhythmical prose tradition.[149] Very little 'heroic' verse survives from the eleventh century and the form seems to have been declining even before 1066.[150]

It was Latin which replaced English as the normal written language, if indeed replaced is the correct word; even before 1066 the volume of works in Latin exceeded that in English.[151] Twelfth-century authors had a poor opinion of their predecessors' Latinity. William of Malmesbury says of one of his sources that 'he rambles beyond credulity in his praise of Athelstan, in that sort of writing which Cicero, the king of Roman eloquence, called "bombastic" in his *Rhetorica*'.[152] William also complains of the style of Æthelweard the Chronicler and the tenth-century Frankish scholar Frithegod, and Osbern of Canterbury uses the same passage in the *Rhetorica* in his criticism of the pre-Conquest *vitae* of St Dunstan: 'they fell into that style of writing which the prince of Roman

in Latin; Herbert was 'fluent in everday French, being a Norman' (Greenway and Sayers, *Jocelin of Brakelond, Chronicle of the Abbey of Bury St Edmunds*, pp. 113–14). Abbot Odo of Battle could also preach in English, see Chapter VI note 18 above.
148 Ælfric says, in his introduction to the *Catholic Homilies*, that he has chosen not obscure words but clear and simple English (*nec obscura posuimus verba sed simplicem Anglicam*), so that his meaning will reach the hearts of his hearers (cited in Michael Lapidge, 'The hermeneutic style in tenth-century England', ASE 4 (1975), p. 101).
149 Norman Blake, 'The literary language', *Cambridge history of the English language, vol. II, 1066–1472*, pp. 508–13. Layamon's *Brut*, though preserving the alliterative form, employs none of the elaborate diction found in Old English poetry.
150 A preference for simpler and more direct language is seen in some religious verse even before 1066, see M.S. Griffith, 'Poetic language and the Paris Psalter', ASE 20 (1991), pp. 167–86. A lack of familiarity may account for Henry of Huntingdon's difficulties with the 'poetic' language of *The Battle of Brunanburh*, (see Chapter VII above).
151 Angus Cameron, 'The boundaries of Old English literature', *The Anglo-Saxons: synthesis and achievement*, ed. J. Douglas Woods and David A.E. Pelteret (Waterloo, Ontario, 1985), pp. 35–6.
152 GR i, p. 144; the work in question is no longer attributed to Cicero (Michael Lapidge, 'Some Latin poems as evidence for the reign of Athelstan', ASE 9 (1981), pp. 77–83). In contrast, William praised Osbern's *Vita* of St Dunstan for its 'Roman elegance' and regarded Osbern as 'second to none in our time for style, certainly without controversy the first of all in relation to music' (GR i, p. 166; Osbern of Canterbury, '*Translatio Sancti Ælfegi . . .*', p. 289, and note 26).

eloquence calls "bombastic", a style which brings more tedium to the reader than profit to the listener'.[153] These strictures are directed against the hermeneutic style, characterized by the use of recondite words (often Greek) and convoluted sentences. Once popular throughout western Europe, it had fallen out of fashion in the eleventh century, in favour of a more 'classical' Latin. In pre-Conquest England, however, it was practised by almost all the Anglo-Latin writers; the only dissenting voice was that of Ælfric of Cerne. William of Malmesbury's low opinion of the hermeneutic style has been shared by modern scholars but 'it was none the less a vital and pervasive aspect of Late Anglo-Saxon culture'.[154]

Before 1066, educated Englishmen lived in a bi-lingual culture, which became tri-lingual after the settlement of a French-speaking elite. In the twelfth century, English scholars, many of whom were trained in the schools of continental Europe and the university of Paris, were competent in Latin, French and English.[155] Their choice of which language to use was influenced by their subject-matter and intended audience. For most purposes Latin was the first choice, though increasingly challenged by French, which had a virtual monopoly in the field of verse romance. For some purposes, however, especially for homiletic works, English might be most appropriate. It is important to remember that authors might write both in Latin and the vernacular; 'the basic training of the schools was in the use of language, and the techniques learned there could be applied from Latin to the more difficult task of creating styles for writing vernaculars'.[156] The monolingual culture of modern Britain has led to neglect of the Anglo-Latin writers. English literature is defined as works written in English, rather than by English authors. This definition may hold true today but is inadequate for the medieval period. Bede's *Historia Ecclesiastica gentis Anglorum* is no less 'English' because its author chose to write in Latin, the common tongue of Christendom; indeed it is a landmark in the development of English nationality. The dearth of literary works in English in the twelfth and (to a lesser extent) the thirteenth centuries is more than balanced by the output of Anglo-Latin

---

[153] GR i, pp. 1–3; GP, p. 22; Mem. St Dunstan, p. 70. For Frithegod, see Michael Lapidge, 'A Frankish scholar in tenth-century England: Frithegod of Canterbury and Fredegaud of Brioude', ASE 17 (1988), pp. 45–65.
[154] Lapidge, 'The hermeneutic style in tenth-century Anglo-Latin literature', ASE 4 (1975), pp. 67–111; the quotation appears on p. 102.
[155] English (and German) masters and scholars consituted one of the four 'nations' into which the university of Paris was divided (A.B. Cobban, *The medieval universities: their development and organization* (London, 1975), pp. 87–90). Nigel of Whiteacre described the English scholars of Paris as much given to drinking and wenching; 'wassail' and 'drink hail' were their favourite toasts, which suggests that they normally conversed in English (*Speculum Stultorum*, ed. J.H. Mozley and R.R. Raymo (Berkeley and Los Angeles, 1960), lines 1503–53; Rigg, *Anglo-Latin literature*, p. 103; M.T. Clanchy, *England and its rulers, 1066–1272* (London, 1983), p. 167). A more responsible picture of student life at Paris is given by its most distinguished English alumnus, John of Salisbury (*The Metalogicon of John of Salisbury*, ed. Daniel D. McGarry (Gloucester, Mass, 1971), pp. 95–100).
[156] Clanchy, *From memory to written record*, p. 215.

writers, who 'achieved in that period a reputation across Europe that their vernacular counterparts never rivalled, before or since'.[157]

The Anglo-Norman authors have been neglected by historians of French, as well as English literature.[158] In contrast to Latin, there are very few works in French before the twelfth century. Most of the earliest texts were in fact produced in England, and England's long vernacular tradition may have helped to stimulate the development of French as a written language.[159] The precocity of the Anglo-Norman writers has been attributed to England's trilingual culture, in which French had the advantage of being the language of the elite, the obvious source of patronage.[160] Many of the early patrons of French works were women. About 1106, Queen Matilda commissioned the monk Benedict li apostoiles to translate the Latin Navigatio Sancti Brendani into French rhyming couplets.[161] Since Matilda was herself of English descent, her choice of language is particularly revealing. After her death in 1118, the dedication was transferred to Henry I's second wife, Adeliza of Louvain. She in turn was the patron of Philippe de Thaon's Bestiary, a translation of the Latin Physiologus, and after her husband's death commissioned a life (now lost) from David 'the Scot'. A copy of this work was made for Constance, patron of Gaimar's Lestorie des Engles, who paid a silver mark for it. Like Benedict's St Brendan, the Bestiary was rededicated after 1154 to Eleanor of Aquitaine, and Philippe also wrote a Livre de Sibile for the Empress Matilda.[162]

Philippe de Thaon also wrote a treatise on the computus, in 'the most excruciating hexasyllabic rhyming couplets in Medieval French literature'.[163] It was dedicated to Philippe's uncle, Humphrey de Thaon, chaplain to Eudo dapifer, sheriff of Essex and Henry I's steward. Its stated purpose is 'to enable priests to keep the laws of the Church' but it can scarcely have been of much use to the predominantly English-speaking parish clergy, and the upper echelons of the hierarchy would surely have preferred Latin texts. One of Philippe's sources was a Latin Computus, no longer extant, written by Thurkil, an English clerk of the Exchequer, and it may be that the Comput was intended for the French-speaking

157 Their work is surveyed in Rigg, A history of Anglo-Latin literature, 1066–1422, pp. 1–156; the quotation appears on p. 2.
158 Short, 'Patrons and polyglots', pp. 229–30; an exception (among English scholars) is Susan Crane, Insular romance: politics, faith and culture in Anglo-Norman and Middle English literature (Berkeley, Los Angeles and London, 1986). The corpus of Anglo-Norman literature is surveyed in Legge, Anglo-Norman literature and its background.
159 Clanchy, From memory to written record, pp. 216–17.
160 Short, 'Patrons and polyglots', pp. 229–49. 'Anglo-Norman' is the term used by modern scholars for French written and spoken in England (Clanchy, From memory to written record, pp. 213–14).
161 Matilda was the patron of other vernacular poets, and of William of Malmesbury (GR ii, p. 494; Legge, Anglo-Norman literature, p. 9). See also Chapter VII above.
162 Short, 'Patrons and polyglots', pp. 237–8; Clanchy, From memory to written record, pp. 216–17.
163 Short, 'Patrons and polyglots', pp. 241–2.

clerks of the king's household, though this explanation implies a poor standard of Latin in these circles. At least Philippe's translation serves as a reminder of the increasing use of French as an administrative language in the twelfth century.[164]

The close relationship between Latin and vernacular works is exemplified in Geoffrey of Monmouth's History of the Kings of Britain. Geoffrey was probably a Welshman or at least of Welsh descent; he spent most of his life as a canon of St George's, Oxford, and in 1151 was elected bishop of St Asaph's.[165] He claims to have translated his history from a Welsh book lent to him by Walter, archdeacon of Oxford, and though doubts have been expressed as to this volume's existence, his Prophecies of Merlin may be based on Welsh sources.[166] The Historia was completed by 1139, when Henry of Huntingdon, on a visit to Bec, was shown a copy by Robert of Torigny; it was dedicated to Robert, earl of Gloucester, son of Henry I, and Waleran of Meulan. The Prophecies of Merlin, which was probably composed about 1135, was commissioned by Henry of Huntingdon's patron Alexander, bishop of Lincoln, and Geoffrey's last work, the Vita Merlini, was dedicated to Alexander's successor, Robert de Chesney (1148–67), once Geoffrey's fellow-canon at St George's, Oxford. Since he claimed to be writing history, Geoffrey composed his works in Latin. The stated aim of the Historia is to repair the omissions of Bede and Gildas, who had so little to say about 'the kings who lived here before the Incarnation of Christ, or indeed about Arthur and all the others who followed on after the Incarnation'.[167] Geoffrey's 'literary bequest was the whole corpus of Arthurian literature'; whatever stories about Arthur may have been current in Wales and Brittany, it was Geoffrey who spread his fame over all Europe.[168]

Geoffrey's work was soon translated into the vernacular. The earliest version was probably that of Gaimar, who seems to have used two copies (or versions) of the original, one borrowed from Walter Espec of Helmsley, and the other from Walter of Oxford, from whom (allegedly) Geoffrey had obtained his Welsh book. Gaimar's version is lost but another was made in 1155 by Wace, a Jerseyman who spent much of his career in Caen. This, the Roman de Brut, was the basis for the English version by Layamon, composed about 1200, in alliterative verse; according to Layamon, Wace's poem was dedicated to Eleanor of Aquitaine, queen of

[164] Legge, Anglo-Norman literature, pp. 18–21; Short, 'Patrons and polyglots', pp. 242–3; Clanchy, From memory to written record, pp. 218–23.
[165] Geoffrey's life and work are summarized in Rigg, A history of Anglo-Latin literature, 1066–1472, pp. 41–8.
[166] Rigg, A history of Anglo-Latin literature, 1066–1472, p. 44. Gaimar claims that the book lent by Walter Espec to Ralph fitzGilbert had been translated from the Welsh at the command of Robert of Gloucester, one of the dedicatees of the Historia Regum Britanniae (Lestorie i, p. 275, lines 6448–6457; Short, 'Patrons and polyglots', p. 244).
[167] Geoffrey of Monmouth, The history of the kings of Britain, trans Lewis Thorpe, Penguin Classics (Harmondsworth, 1966), p. 51.
[168] Rigg, A history of Anglo-Latin literature, 1066–1472, p. 41.

Henry II.[169] Little is known about Layamon apart from what he himself tells us in his introduction to the *Brut*. He was the son of Leovenath (OE Leofnoth) and lived at Areley Kings, Warwickshire, 'a noble church on the river Severn'. As well as Wace, Layamon used Geoffrey's own *Prophecies of Merlin*, and claims to have used Bede's *Ecclesiastical History*, apparently both in the Latin version and the Old English translation.[170]

We do not know who commissioned Layamon's English *Brut*, nor for what audience it was intended. It is sometimes assumed that works in English were meant for a lower social stratum than those in French.[171] This assumes a rigid distinction between English and French speakers for which there is little evidence. Certainly French seems never to have percolated down into the lower ranks of society, at least in the countryside; in the towns, a degree of bilingualism may have existed from the beginning.[172] But it does not follow that because the lower orders spoke only English that their betters spoke only French. Intermarriage must have produced families which spoke both languages, and by the last quarter of the twelfth century, the point in time when the aristocracy begin to describe themselves as English, English must have been the first language of most Anglo-Normans.[173] The emergence of an English-speaking aristocracy and the emergence of literary texts in English may not be coincidental; 'people whose grandparents had listened to Wace's *Brut* in French in the 1150s could, by 1210, have been natural listeners to Layamon's Middle English version of it'.[174]

Latin and English had lived together as literary languages for centuries; there was no reason why English and French should not do the same, to their mutual profit.[175] Layamon, though he took his matter from French and Latin models, wrote in alliterative verse, but a contemporary English poem, *The Owl and the Nightingale*, perhaps composed by Nicholas of Guildford, was based on French metres.[176] By the thirteenth century, French was the dominant culture in Europe,

---

169 Legge, *Anglo-Norman literature*, p. 45. Brutus the Trojan was the legendary founder of Britain. Whereas Gaimar followed up his lost *Brut* with *Lestorie des Engles*, Wace, the Norman writer, went on to write a history of the Norman nation, the *Roman de Rou*.
170 Burrows, *Medieval writers and their work*, pp. 27–8, 331–3, 339; Michael Swanton, *English literature before Chaucer* (London, 1987), pp. 175–87.
171 See, for instance, the discussion of the English romance of Havelok the Dane in Swanton, *English literature before Chaucer*, pp. 194–203.
172 Burnley, 'Lexis and semantics', p. 424; Clark, 'Battle c. 1100: an anthroponymist looks at an Anglo-Norman new town', pp. 26–9; idem, 'People and languages in post-Conquest Canterbury' p. 21.
173 Burnley, 'Lexis and semantics', pp. 424–5; Short, 'Patrons and polyglots', pp. 246–7. Most notable are the descriptions of the Anglo-Norman conquerors of Ireland as 'English', see also Chapter VII, note 58 above.
174 Short, 'Patrons and polyglots', p. 248; see also Crane, *Insular Romance*, pp. 9–10.
175 For the influence of English accent and stress on Anglo-Norman verse, see R.C. Johnston, 'On scanning Anglo-Norman verse', ANS 5 (1983), pp. 151–64.
176 *The Owl and the Nightingale*, ed Eric Gerald Stanley (London, 1960); Burrow, *Medieval writers and their works*, pp. 5, 39–40; Clanchy, *England and its rulers, 1066–1272*, pp. 172–5.

and its literary forms were emulated not just in England, but in Germany as well. This has little to do with the Norman Conquest *per se*. The Normans did not conquer Iceland, but some of the finest of the Icelandic sagas, including *Laxdæla saga*, were influenced both in content and in style by the French chivalric romances.[177] Even without the Conquest, England would have been influenced by French culture in the thirteenth century, but the introduction of a French-speaking aristocracy and the consequent prestige of French as the language of courtly society made the reception of that culture so much the easier.

[177] *Laxdæla Saga*, trans. Magnus Magnusson and Hermann Palsson, Penguin Classics, (Harmondsworth, 1969), p. 38. *Tristram's saga* is the earliest known translation of a French romance into Old Norse; it was made in 1226 at the behest of Hakon the Old, king of Norway, possibly by an Englishman.

WORKS CITED AND CONSULTED

PRIMARY SOURCES

[Abingdon Abbey] *Chronicon Monasterii de Abingdon*, ed. Joseph Stevenson, 2 vols, Rolls Series (London, 1858).

Adam of Bremen, *History of the Archbishops of Hamburg-Bremen*, ed. F.J. Tschan (New York, 1959).

Ælnoth of Canterbury, *Gesta Swenomagnum et filiorum eius et Passio gloriosissimi Canuti regis et martyris, Scriptores Rerum Danicarum*, ed. Jacob Langebek, vol. 3 (Copenhagen, 1774).

Anderson, A.O., *Early sources of Scottish history, A.D. 500–1286*, 2 vols (Edinburgh, 1922, republished Stamford, 1990).

The Anglo-Saxon Chronicle: a revised edition, ed. Dorothy Whitelock, David C. Douglas and Susie L. Tucker (London, 1961)

[Anglo-Saxon Chronicle] *The Peterborough Chronicle, 1070–1154*, ed. Cecily Clark (Oxford, 1955).

[Anglo-Saxon Chronicle] *Two of the Saxon Chronicles parallel*, ed. Charles Plummer and John Earle (Oxford, 1892).

[Anselm, archbishop] *Sancti Anselmi Opera Omnia*, ed. F.S. Schmitt (Edinburgh, 1949).

Barlow, Frank, ed., *The life of King Edward who lies at Westminster* (London, 1962; 2nd rev. edn Oxford, 1992).

Barrow, G.W.S., ed., *Regesta Regum Scottorum I: The acts of Malcolm IV, king of Scots, 1153–1165* (Edinburgh, 1960).

[Bath Priory] *Two Chartularies of the Priory of St Peter at Bath*, ed. William Hunt, Somerset Record Society 7 (1893).

The Battle of Maldon, ed. D.G. Scragg (Manchester, 1981).

[Battle Abbey] *The Chronicle of Battle Abbey*, ed. Eleanor Searle (Oxford, 1980).

The Bayeux Tapestry, ed. D.M. Wilson (London, 1985).

The Book of Fees, HMSO, 3 vols (London, 1920–21).

[Burton Abbey] *Charters of Burton Abbey*, ed. P.H. Sawyer, Royal Historical Society (London, 1979).

[Bury St Edmunds] *Memorials of St Edmund's Abbey, Bury*, ed. Thomas Arnold, 3 vols, Rolls Series (London, 1890–96).

[Canterbury, Christ Church] *The Domesday Monachorum of Christ Church, Canterbury*, ed. David C. Douglas (London, 1944).

[Canterbury, St Augustine's] Adolphus Ballard, 'An eleventh-century Inquisition of St Augustine's, Canterbury', *British Academy Records of the social and economic history of England and Wales* iv (1920).

The Carmen de Hastingi Proelio of Guy, bishop of Amiens, ed. Catherine Morton and Hope Muntz (Oxford, 1972).

Complete Peerage of England, Scotland, Ireland, Great Britain and the United Kingdom, 13 vols in 14 (London, 1910–1959).

Curia Regis Rolls, Richard I – 1 John, HMSO (London, 1922).
Domesday Book, seu Liber Censualis Willelmi Primi Regis Angliae, ed. Abraham Farley, vol ii [Little Domesday], Record Commission (London, 1783).
Domesday Book, seu Liber Censualis Willelmi Primi Regis Angliae, Additamenta [Exon Domesday], Record Commission (London, 1816).
Great Domesday: facsimile, ed. R.W.H. Erskine, Alecto Historical Editions (London, 1986).
Dominic of Evesham, *Vita Sancti Wistani, Chron Evesham*.
Douglas, D.C., *Feudal documents from the Abbey of Bury St Edmunds* (London, 1932).
Douglas, D.C. and Greenaway, George, *English Historical Documents, 1042–1189* (London, 1961).
Dugdale, William, Monasticon Anglicanum, ed. J. Caley, H. Ellis and B. Bandinel, 6 vols in 8 (London, 1817–30).
Durham Episcopal Charters, 1071–1152, ed. H.S. Offler, Surtees Society 179 (1968).
[Durham] *Liber Vitae Dunelmensis*, ed. A.H. Thompson, Surtees Society 136 (1923).
Eadmer, *Epistola Eadmeri ad Glastonienses, Mem. St Dunstan*; translation, see Sharpe, Richard, below.
Eadmer, *Historia Novorum in Anglia*, ed. M. Rule, Rolls Series (London, 1884).
Eadmer's History of Recent events in England, trans. Geoffrey Bosanquet (London, 1964).
[Eadmer] *The life of St Anselm, archbishop of Canterbury, by Eadmer*, ed. Sir Richard Southern (Oxford, 1962).
Eadmer, *Vita Sancti Dunstani archiepiscopi Cantuariensis, Mem. St Dunstan*.
Encomium Emmae Reginae, ed. A. Campbell, Camden Society third series 72 (1949).
[Ely Abbey] *Liber Eliensis*, ed. E.O. Blake, Camden Society 3rd series 92 (1962).
[Evesham Abbey] *Chronicon Abbatiae de Evesham*, ed. W. Dunn Macray, Rolls Series (London, 1863).
Farrer, William and C.T. Clay, *Early Yorkshire Charters*, Yorkshire Archaeological Society Record Series, extra series, 12 vols (Edinburgh, 1913–65).
[Gaimar] *Lestoire des Engleis*, ed. Alexander Bell, Anglo-Norman Texts Society (Oxford, 1960).
[Gaimar] *Lestorie des Engles solum la translacion Maistre Geffrei Gaimar*, ed. Thomas Duffus Hardy and Charles Trice Martin, 2 vols, Rolls Series (London, 1888).
Galbert of Bruges, *The Murder of Charles the Good, count of Flanders*, ed. James Bruce Ross (New York, 1967).
Geoffrey of Monmouth, *The history of the kings of Britain*, translated Lewis Thorpe, Penguin Classics (Harmondsworth, 1966).
Goscelin of Saint Bertin, *Libellus contra inanes sancte virginis Mildrethae usurpatores*, Martin L. Colker, 'A hagiographical polemic', *Medieval Studies* 39 (1977).
Greenway, D.E. ed., *Charters of the Honour of Mowbray, 1107–1191* (Oxford, 1972).
Harmer, F.E., *Anglo-Saxon Writs* (Manchester, 1952; republished Stamford, 1989).
Vita Haroldi, ed. W. de Gray Birch (London, 1885).
Havelock the Dane, ed. W.W. Skeat and Kenneth Sisam, EETS (1950).
Hemingi Chartularium Ecclesiae Wigornensis, ed. Thomas Hearne, 2 vols (Oxford, 1723).
[Henry of Huntingdon] *Henrici archidiaconi Huntendunensis Anglorum Historia*, ed. Thomas Arnold, Rolls Series (London, 1889).
The Chronicle of Henry of Huntingdon, trans. Thomas Forrester (London, 1909).

[Hereward] *Gesta Herewardi, Lestorie des Engles.*

Herman of Bury, *Miracula Sancti Eadmundi*, in *Mem. St Edmunds.*

Historia Regum, Symeonis . . . Opera.

Howlett, Richard, ed., *Chronicles of the reigns of Stephen, Henry II and Richard I*, Rolls Series (London, 1886).

[Hugh Candidus] *The Chronicle of Hugh Candidus, a monk of Peterborough*, ed. W.T. Mellows (Oxford, 1949).

The Peterborough Chronicle of Hugh Candidus, trans. and ed. W.T. Mellows (Oxford, 1941).

Hugh the Chantor, *The History of the Church of York, 1066–1127*, ed. Charles Johnson (London, 1961).

[Ingulf, abbot of Crowland], The History of Ingulf, *The Church Historians of England*, ed. Joseph Stevenson, ii, part ii (London, 1854).

Inquisitio Eliensis, Domesday Book seu Liber Censualis Willelmi Primi Regis Angliae, Additamenta, (London, 1816).

Inquisitatio Comitatus Cantabrigiensis, ed. N.E.S.A. Hamilton (London, 1876).

[Jocelin of Brakelond] *The chronicle of Jocelin of Brakelond*, ed. H.E. Butler (London, 1949).

Jocelin of Brakelond, *Chronicle of the Abbey of Bury St Edmunds*, ed. Diana Greenway and Jane Sayers (Oxford, 1993).

John of Ford, *The Life of Wulfric of Haselbury*, ed. Maurice Bell, Somerset Record Society 47 (1933).

John of Salisbury, *The Metalogicon of John of Salisbury*, ed. Daniel D. McGarry (Gloucester, Mass, 1971).

[John of Wallingford], The Chronicles of John Wallingford, *The Church Historians of England*, ed. Joseph Stevenson, ii, part ii (London, 1854).

[John of Worcester] *Florence of Worcester, Chronicon ex Chronicis*, ed. B. Thorpe, 2 vols, English Historical Society (London, 1848–9).

[John of Worcester] *Florence of Worcester, A history of the kings of England*, Llanerch Enterprises (Lampeter, n.d).

[Lanfranc] *The Letters of Lanfranc, Archbishop of Canterbury*, ed. Helen Clover and Margaret Gibson (Oxford, 1979).

Laxdæle Saga, ed. and trans. Magnus Magnusson and Hermann Pallson, Penguin Classics (Harmondsworth, 1969).

Leges Henrici Primi, ed. L.J. Downer (Oxford, 1972).

Liebermann, F., *Die Gesetze der Angelsachsen*, 3 vols, (Halle, 1903–16).

Mason, Emma, *The Beauchamp Cartulary Charters, 1100–1268*, Pipe Roll Society (London, 1980).

Matthew Paris, *Gesta abbatum monasterii Sancti Albani*, ed. H.T. Riley, 3 vols, Rolls Series (London, 1867–9).

[Merton Priory] A. Heales, *The records of Merton Priory in the County of Surrey* (London, 1898).

Nigel of Whiteacre, *Speculum Stultorum*, ed. J.H. Mozley and R.R. Raymo (Berkeley, Los Angeles and London, 1960).

Orderic Vitalis, *The ecclesiastical history of Orderic Vitalis*, ed. Marjorie Chibnall, 6 vols (Oxford, 1969–80).

Osbern of Canterbury, *Vita Sancti Dunstani*, Mem. *St Dunstan.*

Osbern of Canterbury, *Translatio Sancti Ælfegi Cantuariensis archiepiscopi et martiris:*

*Osbern's account of the translation of St Ælfheah's relics from London to Canterbury,
8–11 June 1023*, Rosemary Morris and Alexander Rumble, *The reign of Cnut*, ed.
Alexander Rumble (Leicester, 1994).

[Oseney Abbey] *The English register of Oseney Abbey*, ed. A. Clark, EETS (1907).

The Owl and the Nightingale, ed Eric Gerald Stanley (London, 1960).

Pelteret, David A.E., *Catalogue of English post-Conquest vernacular documents* (Woodbridge, 1990).

[Ramsey Abbey] *Cartularium monasterii de Rameseia*, ed. W.H. Hart and P.A Lyons,
Rolls Series, 3 vols (London 1884–93).

Chronicon Abbatiae Rameseiensis, ed. W. Dunn Macray, Rolls Series (London, 1886).

Reading Abbey Cartularies, ed. Brian Kemp, Camden Society fourth series 31 (1986).

Regesta Regum Anglo-Normannorum, i, ed. H.W.C. Davis, ii, ed. C. Johnson and H.A.
Cronne, iii, ed. H.A. Cronne and R.H.C. Davis (Oxford, 1913–1968).

Richard fitzNigel, *Dialogus de Scaccario*, ed. Charles Johnson (London, 1950),
reprinted with corrections by F.E.L. Carter and D.E. Greenway (Oxford, 1983).

[Richard of Devizes] *The Chronicle of Richard of Devizes*, ed. John T. Appleby (London, 1963).

Robertson, A.J., *Anglo-Saxon Charters* (Cambridge, 1956).

Robertson, A.J., *The laws of the kings of England from Edward the Elder to Henry I*
(Cambridge, 1925).

Round, J.H., *A calendar of documents preserved in France* (London, 1899).

Sawyer, P.H., *Anglo-Saxon Charters: an annotated list and bibliography*, Royal Historical
Society (London, 1968).

Saxo Grammaticus, *Danorum Regum Heroumque Historia*, i, ed. Eric Christiansen,
BAR International Series 84 (1980)

[Selby Abbey] *The Coucher Book of Selby Abbey*, ed. J.T. Fowler, *Yorkshire Archaeological Society* 10 (1891).

[Shaftesbury Abbey] British Library, Harleian Manuscript 61 [Cartulary of Shaftesbury Abbey].

[Shrewsbury Abbey] *The Shrewsbury Cartulary*, ed. Una Rees (Aberystwyth, 1975).

Simeon of Durham, *Historia Dunelmensis Ecclesiae, Symeonis . . . Opera*.

[Simeon of Durham] *The historical works of Simeon of Durham, The Church historians
of England*, trans. Joseph Stevenson, vol. iii, part ii (London, 1855).

Symeonis Dunelmensis Opera et Collectanea, ed. Hodgson Hinde, Surtees Society 51
(1868).

Symeonis monachi Opera Omnia, ed Thomas Arnold, 2 vols, Rolls Series (London,
1882–5).

The Stoke-by-Clare Cartulary, ed. Christopher Harper-Bill and Richard Mortimer, 3
vols (Woodbridge, 1982–4).

Stubbs, William, ed., *Memorials of Saint Dunstan, archbishop of Canterbury*, Rolls
Series (London, 1874).

Stubbs, William, *Select charters and other illustrations of English constitutional history*,
ninth edn (Oxford, 1921).

Swanton, Michael, *Three Lives of the Last Englishmen*, Garland Library of Medieval
Literature, series B, vol. 10 (New York and London, 1984) [Harold II, Hereward,
St Wulfstan].

Textus Roffensis, ed. P.H. Sawyer, 2 vols, Early English Manuscripts in facsimile 7, 11
(Copenhagen, 1957–62).

[Thorne, William] *William Thorne's Chronicle of Saint Augustine's Abbey*, translated A.H. Davis (Oxford, 1934).

Thorpe, Benjamin, *Diplomatarium Anglicum aevi Saxonici*, 3 vols (London, 1865).

Van Caeneghem, R.C., *English lawsuits from William I to Richard I*, 2 vols, Selden Society 106–7 (1990–91).

Van Caeneghem, R.C., *Royal writs in England from the Conquest to Glanville*, Selden Society 77 (London, 1959).

Walter Daniel's Life of Ailred, abbot of Rievaulx, ed. F.M. Powicke (London, 1950, reprinted 1963).

Walter Map, *De Nugis Curialium*, ed. T. Wright, Camden Society 50 (1850); trans. *Walter Map's 'De Nugis Curialium'*, ed. M.R. James and E. Sidney Hartland, Cymmrodorion Record Series 99 (1923).

[Waltham Abbey] *The early charters of the Augustinian canons of Waltham Abbey, 1062–1230*, ed. Rosalind Ransford (Woodbridge, 1989)

[Waltham Abbey] William Stubbs, *The foundation of Waltham Abbey: the tract 'De Inventione Sanctae Crucis nostrae'* (Oxford, 1861).

Westminster Abbey Charters, 1066–c.1214, ed. Emma Mason, London Record Society 25 (1988).

Whitelock, Dorothy, *Anglo-Saxon Wills* (Cambridge, 1930).

Whitelock, Dorothy, ed., *English Historical Documents, c. 500–1042* (London, 1955).

Whitelock, Dorothy, M. Brett and C.N.L. Brooke, ed., *Councils and Synods, with other documents relating to the English Church, 871–1204*, 2 vols (Oxford, 1981)

William of Jumieges, *Gesta Normannorum Ducum*, ed. J. Marx, Societe de l'histoire de Normandie (1914).

[William of Malmesbury] Scott, John, *The early history of Glastonbury: an edition, translation and study of William of Malmesbury's De Antiquitate Glastonie Ecclesiae* (Woodbridge, 1981).

William of Malmesbury, *De gestis pontificum Anglorum*, ed. N.E.S.A. Hamilton, Rolls Series (London, 1870).

William of Malmesbury, *De gestis regum Anglorum*, ed. W. Stubbs, Rolls Series (London, 1887).

William of Malmesbury, *The History of the kings of England*, The Church historians of England, trans. Joseph Stevenson, vol iii, part i (London, 1854).

William of Malmesbury, *The Vita Wulfstani of William of Malmesbury*, ed. R.R. Darlington, Camden Society 3rd series 40 (1928).

William of Poitiers, *Gesta Guillielmi*, ed. R. Foreville (Paris, 1952).

[Winchester, New Minster] *Liber Vitae: register and martyrology of New Minster and Hyde Abbey, Winchester*, ed. W. de Gray Birch, Hampshire Record Society (London and Winchester, 1892).

[Worcester Cathedral] *The cartulary of Worcester Cathedral Priory*, ed. R.R. Darlington, Pipe Roll Society new series 38 (London, 1968).

[Wulfstan, archbishop] *Wulfstan's Canons of Edgar*, ed. Roger Fowler (Oxford, 1972).

[York Cathedral] *Anonymous Chronicle of the Church of York*, in *Historians of the Church of York*, ed. J. Raine, Rolls Series (London 1879).

SECONDARY WORKS

Abels, Richard, 'Bookland and fyrd-service in late Saxon England', ANS 7 (1985).

Abels, Richard, Lordship and military obligation in Anglo-Saxon England (Berkeley, Los Angeles and London, 1988).

Abels, Richard, 'An introduction to the Bedfordshire Domesday', The Bedfordshire Domesday, ed. Ann Williams and G.H. Martin (London, 1991).

Abels, Richard, 'An introduction to the Hertfordshire Domesday', The Hertfordshire Domesday, ed. Ann Williams and G.H. Martin (London, 1991).

Aird, William, 'St Cuthbert, the Scots and the Normans', ANS 16 (1994).

Baker, Derek, 'A nursery of saints: St Margaret of Scotland re-considered', Medieval Women, ed. Derek Baker, SCH Subsidia i (1978).

Baker, Derek, 'Ailred of Rievaulx and Walter Espec', Haskins Society Journal 1 (1989).

Barlow, Frank, The English Church, 1000–1066 (London, 1963; 2nd edn, 1979).

Barlow, Frank, Edward the Confessor (London, 1970).

Barlow, Frank, The English Church, 1066–1154 (London, 1979).

Barlow, Frank, William Rufus (London, 1983).

Barrow, G.W.S., 'Northern English society in the twelfth and thirteenth centuries', Northern History 4 (1969).

Barrow, G.W.S., The kingdom of the Scots (London, 1973).

Barrow, G.W.S., The Anglo-Norman era in Scottish history (Oxford, 1980).

Barrow, G.W.S., Kingship and unity: Scotland 1000–1306 (Edinburgh, 1981).

Barrow, G.W.S., David I of Scotland, 1124–1153: the balance of old and new, The Stenton Lecture, 1984 (Reading, 1985).

Barrow, Julia, 'How the twelfth-century monks of Worcester perceived their past', The perception of the past in twelfth-century Europe, ed. Paul Magdalino (London, 1992).

Bates, David, 'Odo of Bayeux', Speculum 50 (1975).

Bates, David, 'The land pleas of William I's reign: Penenden Heath re-visited', Bulletin of the Institute of Historical Research 51 (1978).

Bates, David, Normandy before 1066 (London, 1982).

Bates, David, 'The origins of the justiciarship', ANS 4 (1982).

Bates, David, 'Lord Sudeley's ancestors: the family of the counts of Amiens, Valois and the Vexin in France and England during the eleventh century', The Sudeleys, Lords of Toddington, The Manorial Society (London, 1987).

Bates, David, 'Normandy and England after 1066', EHR 104 (1989).

Bates, David, William the Conqueror (London, 1989).

Beech, George, 'England and Aquitaine in the century before the Norman Conquest', ASE 19 (1991).

Bennett, Matthew, 'Poetry as history? The Roman de Rou of Wace as a source for the Norman Conquest', ANS 5 (1983).

Beresford, Guy, 'Goltho manor, Lincolnshire: the buildings and their surrounding defences', ANS 4 (1982).

Biddle, Martin, ed., Winchester in the early middle ages, Winchester Studies I (Oxford, 1976).

Blair, John, 'Introduction: from minster to parish church', Minsters and parish churches: the local church in transition, 950–1200, ed. John Blair (Oxford, 1988).

Blake, David, 'The development of the chapter of the diocese of Exeter, 1051–1161', Journal of Medieval History 8 (1982).

Blake, Norman, 'Introduction', *The Cambridge History of the English language, volume II: 1066–1472* (Cambridge, 1992).

Blake, Norman, 'The literary language', *The Cambridge History of the English language, volume II: 1066–1472* (Cambridge, 1992).

Blows, Matthew, 'A Glastonbury obit list', *The archaeology and history of Glastonbury Abbey*, ed. L. Abrams and J. Carley (Woodbridge, 1991).

Brand, Paul, 'Time out of mind: the knowledge and use of the eleventh- and twelfth-century past in thirteenth-century litigation', *ANS* 16 (1994).

Brett, Martin, *The English church under Henry I* (Oxford, 1970).

Brett, Martin, 'John of Worcester and his contemporaries', *The writing of history in the middle ages: essays presented to Richard William Southern*, ed. R.H.C. Davis and J.M. Wallace-Hadrill (Oxford, 1981).

Brooke, C.N.L., 'The composition of the chapter of St Paul's, 1086–1163', *Cambridge Historical Journal* 10 (1950).

Brooke, C.N.L., 'Married men among the English higher clergy, 1066–1200', *Cambridge Historical Journal* 12 (1956).

Brooke, C.N.L. and Gillian Keir, *London: the shaping of a city, 800–1216* (London, 1975).

Brooks, Nicholas P., 'Arms, status and warfare in late-Saxon England', *Ethelred the Unready: papers from the millenary conference*, ed. David Hill, BAR British series 59 (1978).

Brooks, Nicholas P., *The early history of the Church of Canterbury* (Leicester, 1984).

Brooks, Nicholas P. and the late H.E. Walker, 'The authority and interpretation of the Bayeux Tapestry', *ANS* 1 (1978).

Brown, Elizabeth A.R., 'The tyranny of a construct: feudalism and the historians', *AmHR* 79 (1984).

Brown, R. Allen, *Origins of English feudalism*, Historical Problems: Studies and Documents 19 (London, 1973).

Brown, R. Allen, *The Norman Conquest*, Documents of Medieval History 5 (London, 1984).

Brown, R. Allen, *The Normans and the Norman Conquest*, 2nd edn (Woodbridge, 1985).

Brown, R. Allen, *Castles from the Air* (Cambridge, 1989).

Brown, Shirley Ann, 'The Bayeux Tapestry: why Eustace, Odo and William?', *ANS* 12 (1989).

Burnley, David, *The history of the English language: a source book* (London, 1992).

Burnley, David, 'Lexis and semantics', *The Cambridge history of the English language, volume II: 1066–1472* (Cambridge, 1992).

Burrow, J.A., *Medieval writers and their work: Middle English literature and its background* (Oxford, 1982).

Cam, Helen, 'The English lands of the Abbey of St Riquier', *EHR* 31 (1916).

Cam, Helen, 'The "private" hundred in England before the Norman Conquest', *Studies in medieval history presented to Sir Hilary Jenkinson*, ed. J. Conway Davies (Oxford, 1957); reprinted in *Law-finders and law-makers in medieval England* (London, 1962)

Cam, Helen, 'The quality of English feudalism', *Law-finders and law-makers in medieval England* (London, 1962).

Cameron, Angus, 'The boundaries of Old English literature', *The Anglo-Saxons, synthesis and achievement*, ed. J. Douglas Woods and David A.E. Pelteret (Waterloo, Ontario, 1985).

Cameron, Kenneth, *English place-names* (London, 1979).

Campbell, Alistair, *Skaldic verse and Anglo-Saxon history*, The Dorothea Coke Memorial Lecture (London, 1970).

Campbell, James, 'Some twelfth-century views of the Anglo-Saxon past', *Peritia* 3 (1984), reprinted in James Campbell, *Essays in Anglo-Saxon History* (London, 1986).

Campbell, James, 'Some agents and agencies of the late Anglo-Saxon state', *Domesday Studies*, ed. J.C. Holt (Woodbridge, 1987).

Carter, Peter, 'The historical content of William of Malmesbury's Miracles of the Virgin', *The writing of history in the middle ages: essays presented to Richard William Southern*, ed. R.H.C. Davis and J.M. Wallace-Hadrill (Oxford, 1981).

Chaplais, Pierre, 'William of Saint-Calais and Domesday Book', *Domesday Studies*, ed. J.C. Holt (Woodbridge, 1987).

Charles-Edwards, T.M., 'Kinship, status and the origins of the hide', *P&P* 56 (1972).

Charles-Edwards, T.M., 'The distinction between land and moveable wealth in Anglo-Saxon England', *Medieval Settlement: continuity and change*, ed. P.H. Sawyer (London, 1976).

Chibnall, Marjorie, 'Military service in Normandy before 1066', *ANS* 5 (1983).

Chibnall, Marjorie, *Anglo-Norman England, 1066–1166* (Oxford, 1986).

Clanchy, Michael, *England and its rulers, 1066–1272* (London, 1983).

Clanchy, Michael, *From Memory to Written Record, England, 1066–1307*, 2nd edn (Oxford, 1993).

Clark, Cecily, 'People and languages in post-Conquest Canterbury', *Journal of Medieval History* 2 (1976).

Clark, Cecily, 'Women's names in post-Conquest England: observations and speculations', *Speculum* 53 (1978).

Clark, Cecily, 'Battle, c. 1100: an anthroponymist looks at an Anglo-Norman new town', *ANS* 2 (1980).

Clark, Cecily, 'British Library Additional Ms 40,000, ff. 1v–12r', *ANS* 7 (1985).

Clark, Cecily, 'Willelmus rex! vel aliud Willelmus?', *Nomina* 11 (1987).

Clark, Cecily, 'Domesday Book – a great red herring: thoughts on some late eleventh-century orthographies', *England in the eleventh century*, ed. Carola Hicks (Stamford, 1992).

Clark, Cecily, 'Onomastics', *The Cambridge History of the English language, volume II: 1066–1476*, ed. Norman Blake (Cambridge, 1992).

Clarke, Peter A., *The English nobility under Edward the Confessor* (Oxford, 1994).

Coatesworth, Elizabeth, 'Late pre-Conquest sculptures with the Crucifixion south of the Humber', *Bishop Æthelwold: his career and influence*, ed. Barbara Yorke (Woodbridge, 1988).

Cobban, A.B., *The medieval universities: their development and organization* (London, 1975).

Cooke, Kathleen, 'Donors and daughters: Shaftesbury Abbey's benefactors, endowments and nuns', *ANS* 12 (1990).

Cooper, Janet M., *The last four Anglo-Saxon archbishops of York*, Borthwick Papers 38 (York, 1970).

Coss, Peter, *The knight in medieval England, 1000–1400* (Stroud, Gloucs, 1993).

Coulton, G.C., *Social life in Britain* (Cambridge, 1919).

Cowdrey, H.E.J., 'The Anglo-Norman *Laudes Regiae*', *Viator* 12 (1981).

Cox, D.C., 'The Vale estates of the Church of Evesham, c. 700–1086', *Vale of Evesham Historical Society Research papers* 5 (1975).

Crane, Susan, *Insular romance: politics, faith and culture in Anglo-Norman and Middle English literature* (Berkeley, Los Angeles and London, 1986).

Craster, H.E., 'The Red Book of Durham', *EHR* 40 (1925).

Craster, H.E., 'Some Anglo-Saxon records of the see of Durham', *Archaeologia Aeliana* fourth series 1 (1925).

Craster, H.E., 'The community of St Cuthbert', *EHR* 69 (1954).

Crouch, David, *The Beaumont Twins: the roots and branches of power in the twelfth century* (Cambridge, 1986).

Crouch, David, *William Marshal: court, career and chivalry in the Angevin Empire, 1147–1219* (London, 1990)

Crouch, David, *The image of aristocracy in Britain, 1000–1300* (London, 1992).

Dalton, Paul, *Conquest, Anarchy and Lordship: Yorkshire, 1066–1154* (Cambridge, 1994).

Darlington, R.R., 'Aethelwig, abbot of Evesham', *EHR* 48 (1933).

Darlington, R.R., *The Anglo-Norman historians*, Inaugural Lecture, Birkbeck College (London, 1947).

Darlington, R.R., 'Anglo-Saxon Wiltshire' and 'The Domesday survey of Wiltshire', *Victoria History of the County of Wiltshire* volume ii, ed. R.B. Pugh and Elizabeth Crittall (Oxford, 1955).

Davis, R.H.C., *King Stephen* (London, 1967).

Davis, R.H.C., *The Normans and their Myth* (London, 1976).

Davis, R.H.C., 'William of Poitiers and his history of William the Conqueror', *The writing of history in the middle ages: essays presented to Richard William Southern*, ed. R.H.C. Davis and J.M. Wallace-Hadrill (Oxford, 1981).

Davis, R.H.C., 'Bede after Bede', *Studies in medieval history presented to R. Allen Brown*, ed. Christopher Harper-Bill, Christopher Holdsworth and Janet L. Nelson (Woodbridge, 1989).

Dawtrey, Anne, 'The Benedictine revival in the north: the last bulwark of Anglo-Saxon monasticism?', *SCH* 18 (1982).

Deshman, R., '*Christus rex et magi reges*: kingship and Christology in Ottonian and Anglo-Saxon art', *Frühmittelalterliche Studien* 10 (1976).

Dickins, Bruce, 'Fagaduna in Orderic (A.D. 1075)', *Otium et negotium, studies presented to Olof von Feilitzen*, ed. Folke Sandgren (Stockholm, 1973).

Dobson, E.J., 'The date and composition of the *Ancrene Wisse*', *Proceedings of the British Academy* 52 (1966).

Dodwell, C.R., *Anglo-Saxon Art* (Manchester, 1982).

Dolley, Michael, *The Norman Conquest and the English coinage* (London, 1966).

Douglas, D.C., *The social structure of medieval East Anglia* (Oxford, 1927).

Douglas, D.C., 'Odo, Lanfranc and the Domesday survey', *Historical essays in honour of James Tait*, ed. J.G. Edwards, V.H. Galbraith and E.F. Jacob (Manchester, 1933).

Du Boulay, F.R.H., *The lordship of Canterbury* (London, 1966).

Duby, Georges, *The Three Orders: Feudal society imagined* (London, 1980).

Dumville, David, 'Anglo-Saxon books: treasure in Norman hands?', *ANS* 16 (1994).

Dutton, Marsha L., 'The conversion and vocation of Aelred of Rievaulx', *England in the twelfth century*, ed. Daniel Williams (Woodbridge, 1990).

Dyer, Christopher, *Lords and peasants in a changing society: the estates of the bishopric of Worcester, 680–1540* (Cambridge, 1980).

Eales, Richard, 'An introduction to the Kent Domesday', *The Kent Domesday*, ed. Ann Williams and G.H. Martin (London, 1992).

Ekwall, Eilert, *The concise Oxford dictionary of English place-names*, fourth edn (Oxford, 1960).

Everson, Paul, 'What's in a name? Goltho, "Goltho" and Bullington', *Lincolnshire History and Archaeology* 23 (1988).

Eyton, R.W., *Antiquities of Shropshire*, 12 vols (London, 1854–60).

Eyton, R.W., 'The Staffordshire Cartulary', *Collections for a history of Staffordshire*, William Salt Archaeological Society 2 (1881).

Farmer, D.H., *The Oxford dictionary of Saints* (Oxford, 1978).

Faull, Margaret L and Marie Stinson, *Domesday Book: Yorkshire*, 2 vols, ed. John Morris (Chichester, 1986).

Feilitzen, Olof von, *Pre-conquest personal names of Domesday Book* (Uppsala, 1937).

Fell, Christine, 'The Icelandic saga of Edward the Confessor: its version of the Anglo-Saxon emigration to Byzantium', *ASE* 3 (1973).

Fernie, Eric, *The architecture of the Anglo-Saxons* (London, 1982).

Fernie, Eric, 'The effect of the Conquest on Norman architectural patronage', *ANS* 9 (1987).

Finberg, H.P.R., *Tavistock Abbey* (Cambridge, 1951).

Finberg, H.P.R., 'The making of a boundary', *Lucerna* (Leicester, 1964).

Finn, R. Welldon, *Domesday Book: the eastern counties* (London, 1967).

Fleming, Robin, 'Domesday estates of the king and the Godwines: a study in late Saxon politics', *Speculum* 58 (1983).

Fleming, Robin, 'The tenurial revolution of 1066', *ANS* 9 (1987).

Fleming, Robin, *Kings and Lords in Conquest England* (Cambridge, 1991).

Fleming, Robin, 'Testimony, the Domesday Inquest and Domesday Book', *ANS* 17 (1995).

Frame, Robin, ' "Les Engleys nees en Irlande": the English political identity in medieval Ireland', *TRHS* sixth series 3 (1993).

Franklin, M.J., 'The secular college as a focus for Anglo-Norman piety: St Augustine's, Daventry', *Minsters and parish churches: the local church in transition, 950–1200*, ed. John Blair (Oxford, 1988).

Freeman, E.A., *The history of the Norman Conquest of England*, 6 vols (Oxford, 1870–79).

Friedenthal, David James, 'The Englishness of William of Malmesbury', unpublished MA dissertation.

Galbraith, V.H., 'An episcopal land-grant of 1085', *EHR* 44 (1929).

Galbraith, V.H., *The Making of Domesday Book* (Oxford, 1961).

Galbraith, V.H., *Domesday Book: its place in administrative history* (Oxford, 1974).

Garnett, George, 'Coronation and propaganda: some implications of the Norman claim to the throne of England in 1066', *TRHS* fifth ser. 36 (1986)

Garnett, George, ' "Franci et Angli": the legal distinctions between peoples after the Conquest', *ANS* 8 (1986).

Gelling, Margaret, *Signposts to the Past* (London, 1978).

Gem, Richard, 'The English parish church in the eleventh and early twelfth centuries: a great re-building?', *Minsters and parish churches: the local church in transition, 950–1200*, ed. John Blair (Oxford, 1988).

Gem, Richard, 'England and the resistance to Romanesque architecture', *Studies in medieval history presented to R. Allen Brown*, ed. Christopher Harper-Bill, Christopher Holdsworth and Janet L. Nelson (Woodbridge, 1989).

Gibson, Margaret, *Lanfranc of Bec* (Oxford, 1978).

Gillingham, John, 'The introduction of knight-service into England', *ANS* 4 (1982).

Gillingham, John, 'Conquering the barbarians: war and chivalry in twelfth-century Britain', *Haskins Society Journal* 4 (1992).

Gillingham, John, '1066 and the introduction of chivalry into England', *Law and government in medieval England and Normandy: essays in honour of Sir James Holt*, ed. George Garnett and John Hudson (Cambridge, 1994).

Gillingham, John, 'Henry of Huntingdon and the twelfth-century revival of the English nation', forthcoming.

Gneuss, Helmut, 'The origin of Standard Old English and Æthelwold's school at Winchester', *ASE* 1 (1972).

Godfrey, John, 'The defeated Anglo-Saxons take service with the Byzantine Emperor', *ANS* 1 (1978).

Golding, Brian, 'Anglo-Norman knightly burials', *Medieval Knighthood* 1 (1986).

Golding, Brian, 'An introduction to the Hampshire Domesday', *The Hampshire Domesday*, ed. Ann Williams and R.W.H. Erskine (London, 1989).

Golding, Brian, 'Robert of Mortain', *ANS* 13 (1991).

Gransden, Antonia, *Historical Writing in England from c. 550 to 1300* (London, 1974).

Gransden, Antonia, 'Baldwin, abbot of Bury St Edmunds, 1065–1097', *ANS* 4 (1982).

Green, Judith, *The government of England under Henry I* (Cambridge, 1986).

Green, Judith, 'Aristocratic loyalties on the northern frontier of England, c. 1100–1174', *England in the twelfth century*, ed. Daniel Williams (Woodbridge, 1990).

Green, Judith, *English sheriffs to 1154* (London, 1990).

Greenway, Diana, 'Henry of Huntingdon and the manuscripts of the *Historia Anglorum*', *ANS* 9 (1987).

Griffith, M.S., 'Poetic language and the Paris Psalter', *ASE* 20 (1991).

Hare, Michael, *The two Anglo-Saxon minsters at Gloucester*, Deerhurst lecture (Deerhurst, 1992).

Harfield, Clive, 'The Conqueror's thegns', unpublished.

Harper-Bill, Christopher, 'The struggle for benefices in twelfth-century East Anglia', *ANS* 11 (1989).

Hart, C.R., *Early charters of Wessex* (Leicester, 1964).

Hart, C.R., *Early charters of Eastern England* (Leicester, 1966).

Hart, C.R., *Early charters of Essex*, 2nd edn (Leicester, 1971).

Hart, C.R., *Early charters of northern England and the north Midlands* (Leicester, 1975).

Hart, C.R., 'Hereward "the Wake" and his companions', *The Danelaw*, ed. C.R. Hart (London 1992).

Harvey, Barbara, *Westminster Abbey and its estates in the Middle Ages* (Oxford, 1977).

Hase, P.K., 'The mother-churches of Hampshire', *Minsters and parish-churches: the local church in transition, 950–1200*, ed. John Blair (Oxford, 1988).

Haslam, Jeremy, 'Saxon Exeter', *Anglo-Saxon Towns in Southern England*, ed. Jeremy Haslam (Chichester, 1984).

Hayward, John, 'Hereward the outlaw', *Journal of Medieval History* 14 (1988).

Hill, Joyce, 'Monastic reform and the secular church: Ælfric's pastoral letters in context', *England in the eleventh century*, ed. Carola Hicks (Stamford, 1993).

Hill, Sir Francis, *Medieval Lincoln* (Cambridge, 1948; republished Stamford, 1990).

Hilton, R.H., 'Freedom and villeinage in England', *P&P* 31 (1965); reprinted *Peasants, knights and heretics: studies in medieval social history*, ed. R.H. Hilton (Cambridge, 1976).

Hockey, S.F., OSB, 'William fitzOsbern and the endowment of his abbey of Lyre', *ANS* 3 (1981).

Hofstetter, Walter, 'Winchester and the standardization of Old English vocabulary', *ASE* 17 (1988).

Holdsworth, Christopher, 'Hermits and the power of the frontier', *Reading Medieval Studies* 16 (1990).

Holt, J.C., 'The carta of Richard de la Haye, 1166: a note on "continuity" in Anglo-Norman feudalism', *EHR* 84 (1969).

Holt, J.C., 'Feudal society and the family in early medieval England: I the revolution of 1066', *TRHS* fifth series 32 (1982).

Holt, J.C., *What's in a name? Family nomenclature and the Norman Conquest*, The Stenton Lecture, 1981 (Reading, 1982).

Holt, J.C., 'Feudal society and the family in early medieval England: II notions of patrimony', *TRHS* fifth series 33 (1983).

Holt, J.C., 'Feudal society and the family in early medieval England: III politics and patronage', *TRHS* fifth series 34 (1984).

Holt, J.C., 'The introduction of knight service in England', *ANS* 6 (1984).

Honeycutt, Lois L., 'The idea of a perfect princess: the *Life of St Margaret* in the reign of Matilda II (1100–1118)', *ANS* 12 (1990).

Hooper, Nicholas, 'Edgar ætheling, Anglo-Saxon prince, rebel and crusader', *ASE* 14 (1985).

Hooper, Nicholas, 'An introduction to the Berkshire Domesday', *The Berkshire Domesday*, ed. Ann Williams and R.W.H. Erskine (London, 1988).

Hudson, Ben, 'The family of Harold Godwineson and the Irish Sea province', *Journal of the Royal Society of Antiquaries of Ireland* 109 (1979).

Hudson, John, 'Life-grants of land and the development of inheritance in Anglo-Norman England', *ANS* 12 (1990).

Hudson, John, 'Administration, family and perceptions of the past in twelfth-century England: Richard fitzNigel and the Dialogue of the Exchequer', *The perception of the past in twelfth-century Europe*, ed. Paul Magdalino (London, 1992).

Huggins, P.J. and K.N. Bascombe, 'Excavations at Waltham Abbey, Essex, 1985–91: three pre-Conquest churches and Norman evidence', *Archaeological Journal* 149 (1992).

Hunt, R.W., 'English learning in the late twelfth century', *Essays in medieval history*, ed. R.W. Southern (London, 1968).

Hunter Blair, Peter, 'Some observations on the *Historia Regum* attributed to Symeon of Durham', *Celt and Saxon*, ed. Nora K. Chadwick and others (Cambridge, 1964).

Jennings, J.C., 'The writings of Prior Dominic of Evesham', *EHR* 77 (1962).

WORKS CITED AND CONSULTED

Johnson-Smith, Ted, 'The Norman Conquest of Durham: Norman historians and the Anglo-Saxon community of St Cuthbert', *Haskins Society Journal* 4 (1993).

Johnston, R.C., 'On scanning Anglo-Norman verse', *ANS* 5 (1983).

Jolliffe, J.E.A., *Angevin kingship* (London, 1955).

Kapelle, William E., *The Norman Conquest of the North: the region and its transformation, 1000–1135* (London, 1979).

Kealey, E.J., *Roger of Salisbury* (Berkeley, Los Angeles and London, 1972).

Keats-Rohan, K.S.B., 'The devolution of the Honour of Wallingford. 1066–1158', *Oxoniensa* 54 (1989).

Keats-Rohan, K.S.B., 'The making of Henry of Oxford: Englishmen in a Norman world', *Oxoniensa* 54 (1989).

Keats-Rohan, K.S.B., 'The Breton contingent in the non-Norman Conquest', *ANS* 13 (1991).

Keen, Laurence, 'An introduction to the Dorset Domesday', *The Dorset Domesday*, ed. Ann Williams and R.W.H. Erskine (London, 1990).

Kemp, Brian, 'Some aspects of the *parochia* of Leominster in the twelfth century', *Minsters and parish churches: the local church in transition, 950–1200*, ed. John Blair (Oxford, 1988).

Ker, N.R., 'Hemming's Cartulary: a description of the two Worcester cartularies in Cotton Tiberius A xiii', *Studies in medieval history presented to F.M. Powicke*, ed. R.W. Hunt, W.A. Pantin and R.W. Southern (Oxford, 1948); reprinted in *Books, collectors and libraries*, ed. Andrew G. Watson (London, 1985).

Keynes, Simon, *The diplomas of Æthelred II, 'the Unready', 978–1016* (Cambridge, 1980)

Keynes, Simon, 'Regenbald the Chancellor (sic)', *ANS* 10 (1988).

Keynes, Simon and Michael Lapidge, *Alfred the Great*, Penguin Classics (Harmondsworth, 1983).

King, Edmund, *Peterborough Abbey, 1066–1310* (Cambridge, 1973).

King, Edmund, 'Dispute settlement in Anglo-Norman England', *ANS* 14 (1992).

King, Peter, 'English influence on the Church of Odense in the early middle ages', *Journal of Ecclesiastical History* 13 (1962).

Korhammer, P.M., 'The origin of the Bosworth Psalter', *ASE* 2 (1973).

Knowles, David, *The Monastic Order in England, 940–1216*, 2nd edn (Cambridge, 1963).

Knowles, David, C.N.L. Brooke and Vera C.M. London, *Heads of Religious Houses in England and Wales, 940–1216* (Cambridge, 1972).

Kristjansson, Jonas, *Eddas and Sagas*, trans Peter Foote, 2nd edn (Reykjavik, 1992).

Lapidge, Michael, 'The hermeneutic style in tenth-century England', *ASE* 4 (1975).

Lapidge, Michael, 'Some Latin poems as evidence for the reign of Athelstan', *ASE* 9 (1981).

Lapidge, Michael, 'A Frankish scholar in tenth-century England: Frithegod of Canterbury and Fredegaud of Brioude', *ASE* 17 (1988).

Legge, M. Dominica, 'Anglo-Norman as a spoken language', *ANS* 2 (1980).

Legge, M. Dominica, *Anglo-Norman literature and its background* (Oxford, 1963).

Lennard, Reginald, *Rural England, 1066–1135* (Oxford, 1959).

Le Patourel, J., 'The date of the trial on Penenden Heath', *EHR* 61 (1946).

Le Patourel, J., 'The reports of the trial of Penenden Heath', *Studies in medieval history presented to F.M. Powicke*, ed.R.W. Hunt, W.A. Pantin and R.W. Southern (Oxford, 1948).

Lewis, C.P., 'The Norman settlement of Herefordshire under William I', ANS 7 (1985).

Lewis, C.P., 'An introduction to the Herefordshire Domesday', *The Herefordshire Domesday*, ed. Ann Williams and R.W.H. Erskine (London, 1988).

Lewis, C.P., 'An introduction to the Cheshire Domesday', *The Cheshire Domesday*, ed. Ann Williams and R.W.H. Erskine (London, 1989).

Lewis, C.P., 'The earldom of Surrey and the date of Domesday Book', *Historical Research* 63 (1990).

Lewis, C.P., 'An introduction to the Shropshire Domesday', *The Shropshire Domesday*, ed. Ann Williams and R.W.H. Erskine (London, 1990).

Lewis, C.P., 'The early earls of Norman England', ANS 13 (1991).

Lewis, C.P., 'The formation of the honour of Chester, 1066–1100', *Journal of the Chester Archaeological Society* 71 (1991).

Lewis, C.P., 'An introduction to the Lancashire Domesday', *The Lancashire Domesday*, ed. Ann Williams and G.H. Martin (London, 1991).

Lewis, C.P., 'The Domesday jurors', *Haskins Society J.* 5 (1993).

Leyser, Karl, 'The German aristocracy from the tenth to the twelfth centuries: a historical and cultural sketch', *P&P* 41 (1968); reprinted *Medieval Germany and its neighbours, 900–1250* (London, 1982).

Liebermann, F., *Consiliatio Cnuti* (Halle, 1893).

Liebermann, F., 'On the *Instituta Cnuti aliorumque regum Anglorum*', TRHS new series 7 (1893).

Liebermann, F., 'Notes on the *Textus Roffensis*', *Archaeologia Cantiana* 23 (1898).

Liebermann, F., 'An early English document of about 1080', *Yorkshire Archaeological Journal* 18 (1905).

Loud, Graham, 'The *gens Normannorum*: myth or reality', ANS 4 (1982).

Loud, Graham, 'An introduction to the Somerset Domesday', *The Somerset Domesday*, ed. Ann Williams and R.W.H. Erskine (London, 1988).

Loyn, H.R., 'Kinship in Anglo-Saxon England', ASE 3 (1974).

Loyn, H.R., *Anglo-Saxon England and the Norman Conquest*, 2nd edn (London, 1991).

Loyn, H.R., '*De iure domini regis*: a comment on royal authority in eleventh-century England', *England in the eleventh century*, ed. Carola Hicks (Stamford, 1992).

Lund, Niels, 'The armies of Swein Forkbeard and Cnut: "leding" or "lið"?', ASE 15 (1986).

Maitland, F.W., *Domesday Book and beyond* (Cambridge, 1897; reprinted 1987).

Mason, Emma, 'Change and continuity in eleventh-century Mercia: the experience of St Wulfstan of Worcester', ANS 8 (1986).

Mason, Emma, *St Wulfstan of Worcester* (Oxford, 1990).

Mason, J.F.A., 'Eadric of Bayston', *Transactions of the Shropshire Archaeological Society* 55 (1954).

Mason, J.F.A., 'Barons and their officials in the later eleventh century', ANS 13 (1991).

Matthew, D.J.A., *The Norman Conquest* (London, 1966).

Maund, Kari, 'The Welsh alliances of Earl Ælfgar of Mercia and his family in the mid-eleventh century', ANS 11 (1989).

Maxwell, Ian, *The Domesday settlements of Cornwall* (Redruth, 1986).

Mayr-Harting, Henry, 'Functions of a medieval recluse', History 60 (1975).

Michelmore, D.S.H., 'Township and tenure', West Yorkshire: an archaeological survey to AD 1500, ed. M.L. Faull and S.A. Moorhouse (Wakefield, 1981).

Miller, Edward, 'The Ely land pleas in the reign of William I', EHR 62 (1947).

Miller, Edward, The abbey and bishopric of Ely (Cambridge, 1951, reprinted 1969).

Milroy, James, 'Middle English dialectology', The Cambridge History of the English language, volume II: 1066–1472 (Cambridge, 1992).

Morris, Richard, Churches in the Landscape (London, 1989).

Moore, John S., Domesday Book: Gloucestershire, ed. John Morris (Chichester, 1982).

Moore, John S., 'The Anglo-Norman family: size and structure', ANS 14 (1992).

Moore, John S., 'Family-entries in English Libri Vitae, c. 1050–c. 1530: part I', Nomina 16 (1994), pp. 99–128.

Moorhouse, S.A., 'Castles and administrative centres', West Yorkshire: an archaeological survey to AD 1500, ed M.L. Faull and S.A. Moorhouse (Wakefield, 1981).

Morgan, Philip, Domesday Book: Kent, ed. John Morris (Chichester, 1983).

Morgan, Philip and Caroline Thorn, Domesday Book: Lincolnshire, ed. John Morris, 2 vols (Chichester, 1986).

Morris, Christopher J., Marriage and murder in eleventh-century Northumbria: a study of 'De Obsessione Dunelmi', Borthwick Papers 82 (London, 1992).

Mortimer, Richard, 'The beginnings of the honour of Clare', ANS 3 (1981).

Mortimer, Richard, 'Land and service: the tenants of the honour of Clare', ANS 8 (1986).

Mortimer, Richard, 'The Baynards of Baynard's Castle', Studies in medieval history presented to R. Allen Brown, ed. Christopher Harper-Bill, Christopher Holdsworth and Janet L Nelson (Woodbridge, 1989).

Munby, Julian, Domesday Book: Hampshire, ed. John Morris (Chichester, 1982).

Murray, Alexander, Reason and Society in the middle ages (Oxford, 1978).

Nightingale, Pamela, 'Some London moneyers and reflections on the organization of the English mints in the twelfth and thirteenth centuries', Numismatic Chronicle 142 (1982).

Okasha, Elizabeth, 'A supplement to Handlist of Anglo-Saxon non-runic inscriptions', ASE 11 (1983).

Okasha, Elizabeth, 'The English language in the eleventh century', England in the eleventh century, ed. Carola Hicks (Stamford, 1992).

Owen, Gale, Dress in Anglo-Saxon England (Manchester, 1986).

Palliser, D.M., Domesday York, Borthwick Paper 78 (York, 1990).

Palliser, D.M., 'Domesday Book and the "Harrying of the North" ', Northern History 29 (1993).

Palliser, D.M., 'An introduction to the Yorkshire Domesday', The Yorkshire Domesday, ed. Ann Williams and G.H. Martin (London, 1992).

Partner, Nancy F., Serious entertainments: the writing of history in twelfth-century England (Chicago and London, 1977).

Patterson, Robert B., 'Robert fitzHarding of Bristol: profile of an early Angevin burgess-baron patrician and his family's urban involvement', Haskins Society Journal 1 (1989).

Pelteret, David, 'Two Old English lists of serfs', Medieval Studies 48 (1986).

Pfaff, Richard W., 'Eadui Basan: scriptorum princeps?', England in the eleventh century, ed. Carola Hicks (Stamford, 1992).

Pfaff, Richard W., 'Lanfranc's supposed purge of the Anglo-Saxon calendar', *Warriors and Churchmen in the High Middle Ages: essays presented to Karl Leyser*, ed. Timothy Reuter (London, 1992).

Piper, A.J., 'The first generations of Durham monks and the cult of St Cuthbert', *St Cuthbert, his cult and community to AD 1200*, ed. Gerald Bonner , David Rollason and Clare Stancliffe (Woodbridge, 1989).

Postles, David, 'The foundation of Oseney Abbey', *Bulletin of the Institute of Historical Research* 53 (1980).

Postles, David, '*Patronus et advocatus noster*: Oseney Abbey and the Oilly family', *Historical Research* 60 (1987).

Raftis, J.A., *The estates of Ramsey Abbey* (Toronto, 1957).

Ransford, Rosalind, 'A kind of Noah's Ark: Aelred of Rievaulx and national identity', *SCH* 18 (1982).

Raraty, D.G.J., 'Earl Godwine of Wessex: the origins of his power and his political loyalties', *History* 74 (1989).

Reaney, P.H., *The origin of English surnames* (London, 1967).

Reaney, P.H., *A dictionary of British surnames*, 2nd edn (London, 1976).

Renn, Derek, '*Burhgeat* and gonfanon: two sidelights from the Bayeux Tapestry', *ANS* 16 (1994).

Reynolds, Susan, 'The rulers of London in the twelfth century', *History* 57 (1972).

Reynolds, Susan, 'Eadric *silvaticus* and the English resistance', *Bulletin of the Institute of Historical Research* 54 (1981).

Reynolds, Susan, *Kingdoms and communities in western Europe, 900–1300* (Oxford, 1984).

Reynolds, Susan, 'What do we mean by "Anglo-Saxon" and "Anglo-Saxons"?' *Journal of British Studies* 24 (1985).

Reynolds, Susan, 'Towns in Domesday Book', *Domesday Studies*, ed. J.C. Holt (Woodbridge, 1987).

Reynolds, Susan, 'Bookland, folkland and fiefs', *ANS* 14 (1992).

Richardson, H.G. and G.O. Sayles, *Law and legislation in England from Æthelberht to Magna Carta* (Edinburgh, 1966).

Ridyard, Susan, '*Condigna veneratio*: post-Conquest attitudes to the English saints', *ANS* 9 (1987).

Rigg, A.G., *A history of Anglo-Latin literature, 1066–1422* (Cambridge, 1992)

Robinson, J. Armitage, *Gilbert Crispin* (Cambridge, 1911).

Roffe, David, 'An introduction to the Huntingdonshire Domesday', *The Huntingdonshire Domesday*, ed. Ann Williams and R.W.H. Erskine (London, 1989)

Roffe, David, 'Domesday Book and northern society: a reassessment', *EHR* 105 (1990).

Roffe, David, 'From thegnage to barony: sake and soke, title and tenants-in-chief', *ANS* 12 (1990).

Roffe, David, 'An introduction to the Derbyshire Domesday', *The Derbyshire Domesday*, ed. Ann Williams and R.W.H. Erskine (London, 1990).

Roffe, David, 'An introduction to the Nottinghamshire Domesday', *The Nottinghamshire Domesday*, ed. Ann Williams and R.W.H. Erskine (London, 1990).

Roffe, David, 'The *Descriptio Terrarum* of Peterborough Abbey', *Historical Research* 65 (1992).

Roffe, David, 'An introduction to the Lincolnshire Domesday', *The Lincolnshire Domesday*, ed. Ann Williams and G.H. Martin (London, 1992).

Roffe, David, 'Hereward "the Wake" and the barony of Bourne: a reassessment of a fenland legend', *Lincolnshire History and Archaeology* 29 (1994), pp. 7–10.

Roffe, David, 'The *Historia Croylandensis*: a plea for re-assessment', *EHR* 110 (1995), pp. 93–108.

Roffe, David, 'Lady Godiva, the Book and Washingborough', forthcoming.

Roffe, David, 'Brought to book: lordship and land in pre-Conquest England', forthcoming.

Rogers, Nicholas, 'The Waltham Abbey relic-list', *England in the eleventh century*, ed. Carola Hicks (Stamford, 1992).

Rollason, *The Mildrith legend: a study in early medieval hagiography in England* (Leicester, 1983).

Rollason, David, *Saints and relics in Anglo-Saxon England* (Oxford, 1989).

Rollason, D.W., 'Simeon of Durham and the community of Durham in the eleventh century', *England in the eleventh century*, ed. Carola Hicks (Stamford, 1992).

Ronay, Gabriel, *The lost king of England* (Woodbridge, 1989).

Room, Adrian, *Dictionary of place-names in the British Isles* (London, 1988).

Rose, R.K., 'Cumbrian society and the Anglo-Norman Church', *SCH* 18 (1982).

Round, J.H., *Geoffrey de Mandeville: a study of the Anarchy* (London, 1892).

Round, J.H., *Feudal England* (London, 1895, reprinted 1964).

Round, J.H., *The Commune of London and other studies* (London, 1899).

Round, J.H., 'Bernard the king's scribe', *EHR* 14 (1899).

Round, J.H., 'The Domesday survey of Hampshire', *Victoria History of the County of Hampshire* volume i (London, 1900).

Round, J.H., 'The Domesday survey of Somerset', *Victoria History of the County of Somerset* volume i (London, 1906).

Rumble, Alexander, *Domesday Book: Cambridgeshire*, ed. John Morris (Chichester, 1981).

Rumble, Alexander, *Domesday Book: Essex*, ed. John Morris (Chichester, 1983).

Rumble, Alexander, *Domesday Book: Suffolk*, 2 vols, ed. John Morris (Chichester, 1985).

Rumble, Alexander, ed, *The reign of Cnut* (Leicester, 1994).

Saunders, I.J., *English baronies: a study of their origin and descent, 1086–1327* (Oxford, 1960).

Sawyer, P.H., '1066–1086: a tenurial revolution?', *Domesday Book: a reassessment*, ed. P.H. Sawyer (London, 1985).

Scott, F., 'Earl Waltheof of Northumbria', *Archaeologia Aeliana* fourth series 30 (1952).

Searle, Eleanor, 'Women and the legitimisation of succession at the Norman Conquest', *ANS* 3 (1981).

Selten, Bo, *The Anglo-Saxon heritage in Middle English personal names: East Anglia, 1100–1399*, Lund Studies in English 43 (Lund, 1972).

Sharpe, Richard, 'The date of St Mildreth's translation from Minster-in-Thanet to Canterbury', *Medieval Studies* 53 (1991).

Sharpe, Richard, 'Eadmer's letter to the monks of Glastonbury concerning St Dunstan's disputed remains', *The archaeology and history of Glastonbury Abbey*, ed. L. Abrams and J. Carley (Woodbridge, 1991).

Sharpe, Richard, 'Peter of Cornwall', *The Dictionary of National Biography, Missing Persons*, ed. C.S. Nicholls (Oxford, 1993).

Sharpe, Richard, 'The prefaces of "Quadripartitus" ', *Law and government in the medieval England and Normandy: essays in honour of Sir James Holt*, ed. George Garnett and John Hudson (Cambridge, 1994).

Short, Ian, 'Patrons and polyglots: French literature in twelfth-century England', *ANS* 14 (1991).

Skene, William, *Celtic Scotland*, 3 vols (Edinburgh, 1886).

Smith, A.H., *The place-names of the East Riding of Yorkshire*, EPNS (Cambridge, 1937).

Smith, Mary Francis, 'Archbishop Stigand and the eye of the needle', *ANS* 16 (1994).

Smyth, Alfred P., *Scandinavian York and Dublin*, 2 vols (Dublin, 1975, 1979).

Smyth, Alfred P., *Warlords and Holy Men: Scotland, AD 80–1000* (London, 1984).

Soulsby, Ian, 'Richard fitzTurold, lord of Penhallam, Cornwall', *Medieval Archaeology* 20 (1976).

Soulsby, Ian, 'An introduction to the Cornish Domesday', *The Cornish Domesday*, ed. Ann Williams and R.W.H. Erskine (London, 1988).

Southern, R.W., 'The English origin of the Miracles of the Virgin', *Medieval and Renaissance Studies* 4 (1958).

Southern, R.W., 'The place of England in the twelfth-century renaissance', *History* 45 (1960); reprinted in R.W. Southern, *Medieval Humanism and other studies* (Oxford, 1970).

Southern, R.W., *St Anselm and his biographer* (Cambridge, 1966).

Southern, R.W., 'The place of the reign of Henry I in English history', *Proceedings of the British Academy* 47 (1962); reprinted as 'King Henry I' in R.W. Southern, *Medieval Humanism and other studies* (Oxford, 1970).

Southern, R.W., 'Ranulf Flambard', *Medieval Humanism and other studies* (Oxford, 1970).

Southern, R.W., 'Aspects of the European tradition of historical writing, 4: the sense of the past', *TRHS* fifth series 23 (1973).

Stafford, Pauline, *Unification and conquest: a political and social history of England in the tenth and eleventh centuries* (London, 1989).

Stenton, D.M., *English Justice from the Norman Conquest to Magna Carta* (London, 1965).

Stenton, F.M., 'St Benet of Holme and the Norman Conquest', *EHR* 33 (1922).

Stenton, F.M., *The first century of English feudalism, 1066–1166* (Oxford, 1932).

Stenton, F.M., 'English families and the Norman Conquest', *TRHS* fourth series 26 (1944); reprinted in *Preparatory to Anglo-Saxon England*, ed. D.M. Stenton (Oxford, 1970).

Stenton, F.M., *Anglo-Saxon England*, 3rd edition (Oxford, 1971).

Stenton, F.M., 'The thriving of the Anglo-Saxon ceorl', *Preparatory to Anglo-Saxon England*, ed. D.M. Stenton (Oxford, 1970).

Stevenson, W.H., 'An Old-English charter of William the Conqueror in favour of St Martin's-le-Grand, London, A.D. 1068', *EHR* 11 (1896).

Strickland, Matthew, 'Slaughter, slavery and ransom: the impact of the Conquest on conduct in warfare', *England in the eleventh century*, ed. Carola Hicks (Stamford, 1992).

Swanton, Michael, *English literature before Chaucer* (London, 1987).

Tanner, Heather, 'The expansion of the power and influence of the counts of Boulogne under Eustace II', ANS 14 (1992).

Tatton-Brown, Tim, 'The towns of Kent', Anglo-Saxon towns in southern England, ed. Jeremy Haslam (Chichester, 1984).

Tatton-Brown, Tim, 'Churches of the Canterbury diocese', Minsters and parish churches: the local church in transition, 950–1200, ed. John Blair (Oxford, 1988).

Taylor, H.M. and J., Anglo-Saxon Architecture, 2 vols (Cambridge, 1965).

Tengvik, G., Old English by-names (Uppsala, 1938).

Thomas, Hugh, 'A Yorkshire thegn and his descendants after the Conquest', Medieval Prosopography 8 (1987).

Thomas, Hugh, 'An alleged confrontation between Bishop Ealdred and William the Conqueror', The Anglo-Norman Anonymous, 8, no. 2, (May 1990).

Thomson, R., William of Malmesbury (Woodbridge, 1987).

Thorn, Caroline and Frank, Domesday Book: Cornwall, ed. John Morris (Chichester, 1979).

Thorn, Caroline and Frank, Domesday Book: Wiltshire, ed. John Morris (Chichester, 1979).

Thorn, Caroline and Frank, Domesday Book: Somerset, ed. John Morris (Chichester, 1980).

Thorn, Caroline and Frank, Domesday Book: Dorset, ed. John Morris (Chichester, 1983).

Thorn, Caroline and Frank, Domesday Book: Devon, ed. John Morris, 2 vols (Chichester, 1985).

Thorn, Frank, 'Hundreds and wapentakes', The Sussex Domesday, ed. Ann Williams and R.W.H. Erskine (London, 1990).

Thorn, Frank, 'Hundreds and wapentakes', The Kent Domesday, ed. Ann Williams and G.H. Martin (London, 1992).

Thorn, Frank and Caroline, Domesday Book: Worcestershire, ed. John Morris (Chichester, 1982).

Thorn, Frank and Caroline, Domesday Book: Herefordshire, ed. John Morris (Chichester, 1983).

Thorn, Frank and Caroline, Domesday Book: Shropshire, ed. John Morris (Chichester, 1986).

Tsurushima, Hirokazu, 'The fraternity of Rochester Cathedral Priory c. 1100', ANS 14 (1992).

Tsurushima, Hirokazu, 'Textus Roffensis: an introduction, chart of gatherings and Calendar of contents', Memoirs of the Faculty of Education, Kumamoto University, 41 (1992) [Japanese, with English summary].

Tsurushima, Hirokazu, 'Bishop Gundulf and Rochester Cathedral Priory as an intermediary between English and Normans in Anglo-Norman local society (State, church and society in medieval England, symposium in the Faculty of Education, Kumamoto University, 1992) The Studies in Western History 31 (Fukuoka, Japan, 1993).

Tsurushima, Hirokazu, 'Feodum in Kent, c. 1066–1215', forthcoming.

Urry, William, Canterbury under the Angevin kings (London, 1967).

Van Caeneghem, R.C., The birth of the English Common Law (Cambridge, 1973).

Vaughan, R., 'The chronicle of John of Wallingford', EHR 73 (1958).

Wallenberg, J.K., The place-names of Kent (Uppsala, 1934).

Warren, W.L., 'The myth of Norman administrative efficiency', *TRHS* fifth series 34 (1984).

Webb, Edgar and John Duncan, *Blitz over Britain* (Tunbridge Wells, 1990).

Whitelock, Dorothy, 'Scandinavian personal names in the *Liber Vitae* of Thorney Abbey', *Saga-Book of the Viking Society for Northern Research* 12 (1949); reprinted in Dorothy Whitelock, *History, law and literature in the tenth and eleventh centuries* (London, 1980).

Whitelock, Dorothy, 'Wulfstan's authorship of Cnut's laws', *EHR* 70 (1955); reprinted in Dorothy Whitelock, *History, law and literature in the tenth and eleventh centuries* (London, 1980).

Whitelock, Dorothy, 'The dealings of the kings of England with Northumbria in the tenth and eleventh centuries', *The Anglo-Saxons; studies . . . presented to Bruce Dickins*, ed. Peter Clemoes (London, 1959); reprinted in Dorothy Whitelock, *History, law and literature in the tenth and eleventh centuries* (London, 1980).

Wilcox, Jonathan, 'The dissemination of Wulfstan's homilies: the Wulfstan tradition in eleventh-century vernacular preaching', *England in the eleventh century*, ed. Carola Hicks (Stamford, 1992).

Williams, Ann, 'The Domesday survey of Dorset and the Dorset Geld Rolls', *Victoria History of the County of Dorset* volume iii, ed. R. B. Pugh (Oxford, 1968).

Williams, Ann, 'Land and power in the eleventh century: the estates of Harold Godwineson', *ANS* 3 (1981).

Williams, Ann, ' "Cockles amongst the wheat": Danes and English in the west midlands in the first half of the eleventh century', *Midland History* 11 (1985).

Williams, Ann, 'The knights of Shaftesbury Abbey', *ANS* 8 (1986).

Williams, Ann, 'An introduction to the Worcestershire Domesday', *The Worcestershire Domesday*, ed Ann Williams and R.W.H. Erskine (London, 1988).

Williams, Ann, 'An introduction to the Gloucestershire Domesday', *The Gloucestershire Domesday*, ed. Ann Williams and R.W.H. Erskine (London, 1989).

Williams, Ann, 'The king's nephew: the family, career and connections of Ralph, earl of Hereford', *Studies in medieval history presented to R. Allen Brown*, ed. Christopher Harper-Bill, Christopher Holdsworth and Janet L. Nelson (Woodbridge, 1989).

Williams, Ann, 'A vicecomital family in pre-Conquest Warwickshire', *ANS* 11 (1989).

Williams, Ann, 'A bell-house and a *burhgeat*: lordly residences in England before Norman Conquest', *Medieval Knighthood* 4 (1992).

Williams, Ann, 'From kingdom to shire: Kent, c.800–1066', forthcoming.

Williams, Ann, 'The spoliation of Worcester', forthcoming.

Williams, Ann, 'A west-country magnate of the eleventh century: the family, estates and patronage of Beorhtric son of Ælfgar', forthcoming.

Williams, John, 'Judhael of Totnes', *ANS* 16 (1994).

Wilson, R.M., *The lost literature of medieval England*, 2nd edn (London, 1970).

Wormald, Patrick, 'Bede, the Bretwaldas and the origin of the *gens Anglorum*', *Ideal and reality in Frankish and Anglo-Saxon society*, ed. Patrick Wormald, Donald Bullough and Roger Collins (Oxford, 1983).

Wormald, Patrick, 'Charters, law and the settlement of disputes in Anglo-Saxon England', *The settlement of disputes in early medieval Europe*, ed. Wendy Davies and Paul Fouracre (Cambridge, 1986).

Wormald, Patrick, 'Domesday lawsuits: a provisional list and preliminary comment', *England in the eleventh century*, ed. Carola Hicks (Stamford, 1992).

Wormald, Patrick, 'Quadripartitus', *Law and government in medieval England and Normandy: essays in honour of Sir James Holt*, ed. George Garnett and John Hudson (Cambridge, 1994).

Wormald, Patrick, '*Laga Eadwardi*: the *Textus Roffensis* and its context', ANS 17 (1995).

Wormald, Patrick, 'The Oswaldslow immunity: a proposition with discussion', forthcoming.

Wright, C.E., *The cultivation of saga in Anglo-Saxon England* (London, 1939).

Zarnecki, George, Richard Gem and Christopher Brooke, *English Romanesque Art 1066–1200* (London, 1984).

INDEX

Holderness 31, 38–8, 57, 58n
Hubald, bishop of Odense 70
Hugh d'Avranches, earl of Chester 7n,
  53, 66n, 121, 122
Hugh de Bolbec 54n
Hugh de Grandmesnil 10, 27n
Hugh d'Ivry 114
Hugh de Montfort 10, 16, 82, 83,
  91n
Hugh de Port 82
Hugh fitzBaldric, sheriff of York, and
  Aldwine 66, 151; befriends Benedict
  the monk 43; houses 202; land
  161; lordship 40
Hugh fitzGrip, sheriff of Dorset 78
Humphrey de Bohun 105
Humphrey de Thaon 216
Humphrey de Tilleul 10, 18, 27n
Humphrey the chamberlain 79, 80n,
  114, 115n
Hunning 89, 90
Huntingdon 26, 34, 47n, 179
Huscarl of Swaffham 86

Ingelrann 92n
Ingereda, wife of Godric the steward
  108
Ingulf, abbot of Crowland 131 and n,
  147
Ipswich 36
Isabel de Neville 200
Ivarr, sacristan of Peterborough 48

Jarrow, church of 39, 66, 182; manor
  of 151
John, king of England 107
John de Villula, bishop of Wells 126,
  136
John fitzAlan 117
John Marshal 201
John of Salisbury 127n
John of Worcester, early promise 171;
  on Harold I and Swein 180; opinions
  and feelings 176; and Orderic 175;
  views on Harold II 169; William of
  Malmesbury and 171, 172n; St
  Wulfstan and 169; see also Florence
  of Worcester
  works: Chronicon ex Chronicis 149,
  165; sources 168–9
Jordan of Trecharl 123, 124
Judhael of Totnes 21, 35n, 210

Judith, wife of Earl Tostig 42, 51 and n,
  55n
Judith, wife of Earl Waltheof 58, 183

Karli son of Thorbrand, and house of
  Bamburgh 30; kills Earl Ealdred 30;
  Hunmanby 31; sons of 29, 30, 31,
  40 and see Carl, Gamall, Sumarlithr
  and Thorbrand
Kent, absence of Englishmen as tenants
  81, 111–12; disturbances in 1067 14,
  15; documentation 77–8; during
  Conquest 166; gavelkind 198; land
  tenure 80–85; Norman invasion 80;
  number of major landholders TRE
  72; Odo of Bayeux 111; planned
  re-organization of administrative
  units 18
Ketel 108
Ketilbjorn of Longdon 103n, 104
Ketilbjorn, tainus 112

land, acquisition by marriage 12, 198,
  200; alods 190–2; beneficia 191;
  bookland 73, 191, 192, 209;
  burgesses 203; confiscated 50;
  dispossession of 19; encroachment
  on Church lands 142–4; English
  families holding 40; farming of 79,
  83; fiefs 190–91; held by
  knight-service 142, 192–94;
  hereditary fees 194; knightly and free
  tenures 197–9; land-holding and
  services due from it 191–2; lænland
  76, 141, 142, 191, 194; and
  non-payment of geld 12–13;
  Norman customs of tenure 190–91,
  209; Norman settlement and
  redistribution of 71, 76;
  pre-Conquest tenures 71–3;
  redemption of 9, 19; sokeland 74,
  75–6, 143–4; tenure in
  Cambridgeshire 86–9; tenure in
  Dorset 78–80; tenure in Kent
  80–85; tenure in Shropshire 89–97;
  thegnland 75–6, 141, 142; types of
  tenure 191; Vale of Gloucester 174
Lanfranc, archbishop of Canterbury, and
  abbacy of St Augustine's 134; and
  Abbot Adelelm 133; advises Bishop
  William of Saint-Calais 151–2;
  Æthelwig and 148; appoints prior of